The New Shell Guides

Gloucestershire and Hereford & Worcester

The New Shell Guides

Gloucestershire and Hereford & Worcester

Christopher Catling and Alison Merry

Introduction by John Julius Norwich

Series Editor John Julius Norwich
Photography by Nick Meers

Michael Joseph · London

MICHAEL JOSEPH LTD

Published by the Penguin Group
27 Wrights Lane, London W8 5TZ, England
Viking Penguin Inc., 40 West 23rd Street, New York, New York
10010, USA
Penguin Books Australia Ltd, Ringwood, Victoria, Australia
Penguin Books Canada Ltd, 2801 John Street, Markham, Ontario,
Canada L3R 1B4
Penguin Books (NZ) Ltd, 182–190 Wairau Road, Auckland 10,
New Zealand

Penguin Books, Registered Offices: Harmondsworth,
Middlesex, England

First published in Great Britain in 1990

Typeset in Linotron 10/11pt Plantin by Cambrian Typesetters,
Frimley, Surrey
Colour reproduction by Scantrans, Singapore
Printed and bound by Kyodo-Shing Loong Printing, Singapore

A CIP catalogue record for this book is available from The British
Library

ISBN 0 7181 3174 6

The name Shell and the Shell emblem are registered trademarks

Shell UK Ltd would point out that the contributors' views are not
necessarily those of this company

The information contained in this book is believed to be correct at the time
of printing. While every care has been taken to ensure that the
information is accurate, the publishers and Shell can accept no
responsibility for any errors or omissions or for changes in the details
given.

Title-page photograph:
View from the edge of the Cotswold escarpment at Birdlip Hill,
looking towards Gloucester and, in far middle distance, May Hill

Contents

We would like to thank the owners – the National Trust, English Heritage and private owners – for their permission to photograph and feature their properties in this book. We are particularly grateful to the Dean and Chapter of Hereford Cathedral for permission to photograph the Chained Library (page 158) and to Professor H.D. Edmondson of Huddington Court.

John Julius Norwich was born in 1929. After reading French and Russian at New College, Oxford, he joined the Foreign Office where he served until 1964. Since then he has published two books on the medieval Norman Kingdom in Sicily; two historical travel books, *Mount Athos* (with Reresby Sitwell) and *Sahara*; two volumes on the history of Venice; a book about Glyndebourne; an anthology of travel writing; *The Architecture of Southern England*; and *Byzantium: the Early Centuries*, the first volume of a three-volume history of that city. Since 1970 he has also compiled an annual anthology of poetry and prose, *A Christmas Cracker*. He was general editor of *Great Architecture of the World*, *The Italian World*, and *The Heritage of Britain*; he is now general editor of the *Oxford Illustrated Encyclopedia of Art*.

In addition he writes and presents historical documentaries for television and frequently broadcasts on BBC radio. He is Chairman of the Venice in Peril Fund, Co-Chairman of the World Monuments Fund and a member of the Executive Committee of the National Trust.

Christopher Catling was born in 1955 and educated at Circencester. After reading English at St Catherine's College, Cambridge, he worked as a publicity copywriter, spending several years in Hong Kong and China, before becoming a full-time author. He has written *The Economist Business Traveller's Guides* to China, South-East Asia and the Soviet Union, and a guidebook to Florence. He is currently researching the history of conservation.

Alison Merry is a history and archaeology graduate of Exeter University who later worked in Oxford and the British School in Rome as an archaeological illustrator and research assistant. She first came to her adopted county of Gloucestershire in 1974, to work at the Corinium Museum, Cirencester, and now lives with her husband and their three children in Stroud.

Nick Meers was born in Gloucestershire in 1955. He graduated from Guildford School of Photography in 1978, since when his lenses have captured many aspects of life and landscape in such diverse places as Paris and Puerto Rico, Auckland and Abidjan, Holland and Hawaii and even the National Parks of Canada. In addition to many assignments for the National Trust, he has made the photographs for several of the New Shell Guides and for *The Spirit of the Cotswolds* by Susan Hill.

John Sales, M. Hort. (RHS), F.I.Hort, has been Chief Gardens Adviser for the National Trust for 16 years. With a staff of three Gardens Advisers, he is responsible for advice in all the gardens and historic landscape parks held by the Trust, the largest collection ever owned by one organization. He lectures frequently, writes articles and judges for the Royal Horticultural Society at the Chelsea Flower Show.

Tom Norbury is the youngest son of Christopher Paget Norbury, a noted fruit grower. He was educated at Oundle School and Bristol University, following which he spent 8 years teaching history. In 1981 he returned to help run the family fruit farm near Leigh Sinton and in 1984 he set up Norbury's Cider Company, which produces a variety of ciders, perries and wines.

Wilson Stephens comes of a Shropshire farming family deeply rooted in Severnside and the Welsh Marches. He was Editor of *The Field* for 26 years. He wrote the sport and wildlife sections of the *Encyclopaedia Britannica*, has served on national wildlife organizations and is the author of 6 books and of articles on conservation and the environment in the national press.

James Butterworth was born in 1949. He lived in Worcestershire from 1972 to 1988. Having been ordained in Worcester Cathedral, he served in parish life in Kidderminster and Dudley and was Precentor at Worcester Cathedral for 6 years. He is now Rector of Bridgnorth in Shropshire.

Introduction
JOHN JULIUS NORWICH

The first and most important point to be made in this introduction is that the book which you now hold in your hands covers not two counties but three: it was only the infamous Local Government Act of 1972 that – with a degree of presumption that still, after almost twenty years, leaves the mind boggling – took it upon itself to redraw the thousand-year map of England, abolished some counties altogether, invented several new ones and, among many other similar outrages, flung together the totally disparate Herefordshire and Worcestershire into their present unhappy amalgamation. Thus, whatever the bureaucrats may say, it is with three widely differing entities that we have to deal; and here at least the two latter counties will be given the individual attention and respect that is their due.

Gloucestershire
Gloucestershire suffered from the 1972 Act even worse than its neighbours, losing a whole corner to that monstrous upstart, the new 'county' of Avon; most of it, however, remains Gloucestershire still and divides itself naturally – rather as Lincolnshire and Yorkshire do – into three parts. Admittedly it does not distinguish these regions with official names of their own; nor, in the manner of Yorkshire before 1972 – all right, I won't go on about it any more – does it divide them into Ridings; geographically, however, the differences between the Cotswolds, the Severn Vale and the Forest of Dean are deeper and more immediately noticeable than in either of the other counties.

For most English people and nearly all foreign visitors, our initial introduction to Gloucestershire is the slow climb westwards from Oxford into the Cotswolds, that marvellous range of limestone hills running rather more than fifty miles from north-east to south-west, furnishing their fortunate inhabitants with apparently limitless quantities of building stone as beautiful as any in Europe and enfolding some of the most enchanting small towns and villages – Bibury, Bourton-on-the-Water, Upper and Lower Slaughter, Snowshill – to be met with anywhere. Particularly on the uplands, Cotswold stone tends to be covered with only the thinnest layer of topsoil and lends itself reluctantly to agriculture; it is, however, ideal for the pasturing of sheep and it was this that brought the region its immense prosperity during the great wool boom of the late 14th and 15th centuries. Still today, five hundred years later, the glorious consequences of this prosperity are everywhere visible in the great 'wool churches', many of which are even more sumptuous than their contemporary counterparts in East Anglia, where the boom was of similar proportions but, in the absence of any stone worthy of the name, the church builders had to make do with flint. Nor were the men of the Cotswolds ashamed to reveal the source of their new-found wealth: again and again in their churches – around the doorways, carved into the capitals of the columns of the nave arcades, even incorporated into the decoration of their own tombs – we find the unmistakable symbol of their trade: the sheep shears, open and ready at any

moment, it seems, to spring once again into action and win for their wielder yet another golden fleece.

Grandest of all the wool churches is that of St John the Baptist at Cirencester, one of the most majestic parish churches anywhere in the country. It was originally founded by Henry I in about 1120 and some 12th- and 13th-century work still remains in the chancel; but the great west tower was begun in 1400 or thereabouts and from that time forward work continued, with only brief intermissions, for nearly a century and a half. The tremendous south porch of 1490 looks more like the entrance to a palace than a church and it comes as no surprise to learn that for over two hundred years, from the 17th century until the 1890s, it actually served as the Town Hall. The soaring nave was rebuilt as late as the reign of Henry VIII, whose royal arms can still be seen over the window above the chancel arch.

The Cotswolds rise gently, almost imperceptibly, towards the west: so much so, indeed, that it comes as a considerable surprise to find oneself suddenly poised on the brink of a dramatic escarpment, in some places nearly a thousand feet above sea level, gazing down on the second – and radically different – area of Gloucestershire, the valley of the River Severn. Greener than the hills above, more fertile and more lush, it runs below the Cotswold Edge from Tewkesbury at the far north-eastern end on the Worcestershire border, all the way down to Bristol. About a quarter of the way along lies Gloucester itself. Having to a large extent survived the ravages of the Second World War, it has since been so vandalised by the city planning department that one is mildly surprised to find the Cathedral itself still standing. To enter that Cathedral, however, is to have one's faith in human nature instantaneously restored; for nowhere in the entire Kingdom, with the possible exceptions of Durham and Lincoln, are the miracles of English medieval church architecture so breathtakingly displayed. It was here that the Perpendicular style may well have originated and certainly received the form and character by which we know it today; it is here, too, in the Cathedral's south transept, that we can see the earliest existing window to exemplify the style. It dates from the 1330s; only some twenty years later work began on the east range of the cloister, soon to be crowned with an architectural *tour de force* for whose invention Gloucester was alone responsibile: the fan vault.

Finally, if you still have any lingering doubts as to the Gloucester genius, you have only to look at the way the original Norman crossing was vaulted in the early 15th century. Those astonishingly slender four-centred arches, each crowned with a vertical mullion from which springs the lierne vault above have, once again, no parallel in England. Nowhere else – unless, just possibly, in Bristol – would a master mason have dared such a dazzling piece of technical legerdemain; nowhere else, certainly, would he have brought it off with such brilliant *panache*.

Despite all the glories of Gloucester, however, it must be admitted that the great Abbey of Tewkesbury, its exact contemporary – those two terrific Norman naves were both consecrated in the same year, 1121 – runs it close. In one respect, indeed, the Abbey seems to me even to surpass the Cathedral: its

Fan vaulting in the cloisters of Gloucester Cathedral
(see page 65)

east end. That of Gloucester is dominated by its vast fourteen-light window, another display of virtuosity but in this case one that gives relatively little real aesthetic satisfaction. Although the three outer lights to each side are slightly canted to resist the force of the wind, the general effect is one of a flat glass wall in which the Perpendicular idiom, extended over so immense an area, becomes more than a little monotonous. How much better things are ordered at Tewkesbury: for here we have a polygonal *chevet* on the French pattern, fringed with exquisite 14th-century chapels and set at gallery level with seven fine Decorated windows above which rises a veritable forest of lierne-vaulting, later to be further embellished with a liberal sprinkling of Suns in Splendour – the emblem, during the Wars of the Roses, of the Yorkist cause.

Among the secular buildings of the Severn Vale, the palm must go to Berkeley Castle. Most castles – and almost all those, like Berkeley, of Norman origin – crown high elevations; Berkeley crouches like a great lion, commanding the approaches to the river as it broadens out majestically but unaggressively towards its estuary. Much of its beauty resides in its colour, which is rose-red flecked with grey – 'the colour', wrote Victoria Sackville-West, 'of old brocade'. At sunset on a summer evening it can look positively welcoming: admittedly an undesirable attribute for a castle in former times and to this day a rare one. Inside, the general feeling of friendliness persists more strongly still, even in the charming little room in which, we are told, the luckless Edward II met his untimely and unattractive end. If only they would close up that disagreeable hole in the floor leading to the dungeon beneath it would make, one cannot help feeling, a perfect study.

And so, by way of a multitude of water birds – for nearby Slimbridge is the headquarters of the Severn Wildfowl Trust and the local avian population, at least in winter, overwhelmingly outnumbers the human – we come to the river itself and, beyond it, the third face of Gloucestershire, the Forest of Dean. 'The Queene of Forests all' is how it was described in 1600 by the poet Michael Drayton and although the past four hundred years have inevitably wrought their changes – in Drayton's time the seemingly limitless expanses of oak woods had not been invaded by the sad conifers of the Forestry Commission – we can still see what he meant. Even today, the Forest seems fraught with mystery and magic. Hidden deep within it are the ancient mines of both iron and coal, one or two of which were worked within living memory; but all lie abandoned and their romantically overgrown remains add a further dimension to the enchantment.

Architecturally, one would expect little of so remote and sylvan a region; it is all the more astonishing when suddenly, in the village of Newland, one comes upon the Church of All Saints, proudly described in the guide books as 'the Cathedral of the Forest'. It is in fact not a cathedral at all, or anything like one; its dimensions are no more than those of a medium-sized parish church. But it has a lovely situation on the brow of a hill, perfect proportions and an unusually fine tower and the charming 17th- and 18th-century houses that surround the churchyard undeniably give the effect of a tiny cathedral close. There is also a remarkable collection of monuments, including the famous brass plate depicting in relief – a rarity in itself – a medieval miner of the region, complete with hod and pick and carrying a candlestick in his mouth. The Forest ends on

The Saxon church of St Michael at Duntisbourne Rouse (see page 58)

a note of high drama: the river Wye, normally so serene and gentle in its lower reaches but growing suddenly turbulent again as it snakes its way through the dark ravine of Symonds Yat.

Few counties of England provide a grander architectural panorama than Gloucestershire, dating back even to Roman times, when Cirencester was second in size only to London itself. It possesses the remains of several fine Roman villas, including that of Chedworth (now the property of the National Trust) where several of the original mosaic floors have been preserved. The Saxons, too, settled in considerable numbers both in the Wolds and in the Vale where, at Deerhurst, they left behind one of the two most magnificent Saxon churches remaining anywhere in England. Altogether, Gloucestershire can boast about a dozen churches of Saxon origin; the Normans, however, left more than a hundred, a total that few other counties can match. Best of all for me – leaving Gloucester and Tewkesbury out of the reckoning – is St John's, Elkstone, with its two tremendous tower arches and stone-vaulted chancel. Here, if you ignore the Perpendicular west tower and one or two of the windows – is everything a 12th-century English village church should be.

Of the later architectural styles, the Early English exists only on the high Cotswolds; the 13th century saw a good deal of trouble with the Welsh and to have undertaken any serious church-building any nearer the border would have been folly. The little church of St Laurence at Wyck Rissington, tentatively feeling its way to the concept of tracery, is the most touching of them all. For the Decorated style, you need look no further than the extraordinary south transept at Minchinhampton where, incidentally, there is an additional bonus in the shape of a chancel by the ever-enjoyable William Burges. Finally we

Owlpen Manor and the Church of the Holy Cross (see page 115)

come to the Perpendicular, and the wool churches. Cirencester towers over them all; but there are several others: Chipping Campden, Northleach, Fairford with its unforgettable stained glass which it is worth crossing England, or even the Atlantic, to see.

As for the great houses, Berkeley Castle is only the beginning: any list of great houses would have to include the glorious, golden Stanway, Cirencester Park with its enormous yew hedge, Barnsley, Daylesford and the Nabob's Delight of Sezincote, through to the Victorian culmination of Westonbirt. But for me the most lasting joy of Gloucestershire is to be found less in its stately homes than in the innumerable smaller manor houses, many of which are still lived in, often by the same families who built them several centuries ago. Of those I have visited, Owlpen and Daneway are perhaps the most remote and romantic, Chavenage the most unspoilt, Nether Lypiatt the most classically beautiful; but there are countless others that I have never seen. It would take a lifetime to get to know them all.

Herefordshire
Despite all that I have said above, however, I never enter Herefordshire from Gloucestershire without an appreciable lifting of the heart. No county is more beautiful; few, if any, are more unspoilt. The landscape is quintessential England: that is to say that it is exactly what we all like to think the English landscape ought to be, but what in fact it relatively seldom is – gently rolling hills of an almost unbelievable green; brooks and streams by the thousand, most

Opposite: Suspension bridge over the River Wye at
Sellack near Ross-on-Wye

of them feeding that formerly most strife-torn, now most peaceable of rivers, the lovely, looping Wye; forests of oak and beech – the elms are gone, alas – and, always and everywhere, the apple-orchards, for the cider that is still the Herefordshire industry *par excellence*.

Architecturally, the fascination of Herefordshire lies in its wonderful wealth of building materials and styles. One of the first impressions on crossing the border is of the extraordinary redness of the soil – redder than that of any other county except Devon; it comes as no surprise to learn that the predominant stone is the Devonian Old Red Sandstone. This in fact varies considerably in colour: sometimes, one feels, it is almost *too* red, but more often – as in the Cathedral – it is softened to a warm greyish-pink which, though it never conjures up quite the magic of the honey-coloured Cotswold limestone, is none the less full of character and makes a perfect contrast with the surrounding green. For most of us, however, Herefordshire probably means black-and-white. This local style of timber-framing, almost universal in towns like Pembridge or Weobley, is noticeably different from that, for example, of East Anglia. There is none of the vertical emphasis and still less of the diagonal; the spaces between the timbers are nearly always square. This may occasionally produce something of a grid-iron effect, but it gives the houses a most satisfying broad-shoulderedness and solidity.

The church at Abbey Dore

And then there are the castles. Herefordshire – the fact must never be forgotten – was and is border country and throughout the Middle Ages there was a continual threat from the unruly Welsh. One or two of its castles, notably Croft (which now belongs to the National Trust), have been converted into country houses; most, however, are now in ruins, though several have become even more picturesque in consequence. Best of them all is Goodrich, today little more than a shell but still standing majestic on its cliff above the Wye. Nor are the castles the only testimony to the dangers the county had to face from its neighbours across the border: the city of Hereford still retains part of its medieval walls, while at Ewyas Harold, where the once-proud castle has almost disappeared, the walls of the Early English church tower are well over seven feet thick.

Ewyas Harold, however, is an exception. As in the Severn Vale and the Forest of Dean, the continual border wars during the 13th century provided little incentive for church building and most Herefordshire churches are rather later in date. A few of them, however, are earlier; and of these the one that no visitor to the county should be allowed to miss is the church of St Mary and St David in the tiny village of Kilpeck. Dr Pevsner describes it as one of the most perfect Norman churches in England, which indeed it is; but what makes it unique is its astonishing collection of carvings, both inside and out. Those around the south door – all dragons and scrolls and tendrils and little men wearing curious conical hats – have more than a touch of the Viking about them; but there are others in a remarkably different style around the chancel arch, while the whole building is surrounded by the most enjoyable corbel table I know anywhere – which includes, among many other motifs, a *sheila-na-gig* (or ancient fertility figure) of quite glorious obscenity.

Equally compelling – though for very different reasons – is the church of St Mary at Abbey Dore, some five miles away to the west. It too is Norman, having been first established in 1147 by Cistercian monks from Morimond. Like all Cistercian foundations it stands in marvellous country, on the bank of the Dore river; despite the damage it suffered during the long period of abandonment and decay that followed the Dissolution of the Monasteries – the nave has long since gone, leaving us effectively with only the chancel and the two transepts – the building still casts a strange and powerful spell. All that remains of it today we owe to the first Lord Scudamore, for four years Charles I's ambassador to France. Under the influence of his friend Archbishop Laud, he restored the ruins in the 1630s, closed the west end and added the existing tower; the work was done with care and sensitivity and the 17th-century additions harmonize quite beautifully with the medieval fabric.

The third and last country church that deserves special mention here is that of Shobdon. Its Norman predecessor was demolished and its principal carvings incorporated into an eye-catcher a little to the north, now known as Shobdon Arches. They were, in their time, every bit as remarkable as those of Kilpeck; but wind and weather have done their worst and they can no longer give us any real pleasure. What can, and does – and what makes Shobdon so triumphantly worth visiting today – is the rebuilt church of the 1750s: a riot of blue and white Strawberry Hill Gothick that may have precious little of the religious spirit about it but is none the less enchanting for that.

And so to the Cathedral. We can hardly pretend that it is one of England's greatest. Standing low and having lost both its spire and one of its towers, it makes little impact from a distance; and it further suffers from the absence of any proper close. The west front, by John Oldrid Scott, is an uninspired work dating from early in the present century; from the outside, only the crossing tower and the north transept repay any close study. Inside, however, even though much of the nave is by James Wyatt, the south transept is Norman through and through – and very fine Norman at that – while the Early English Lady Chapel is a model of its kind and the slightly later north transept nothing short of a *tour de force*.

Of the Herefordshire country houses, Hellens at Much Marcle must have been part of a large Tudor (or at the least Jacobean) house of superb quality; Berrington Hall (now the property of the National Trust) is a distinguished work by Henry Holland with a park by Capability Brown; while Moccas Court is another Georgian gem, based on designs by Robert Adam, where Brown was joined by Humphry Repton in planning the grounds. Grandest of them all, however, is Holme Lacy, built almost certainly by Hugh May in the last quarter of the 17th century. It has had an unfortunate recent history: after many years' service as a mental hospital it is empty at the time of writing and its future is, to say the least, uncertain. But although it has lost all its original furniture, its plasterwork is still the finest of its date in England. It was built by the second Lord Scudamore, grandson of the saviour of Abbey Dore. To both him and his grandfather – who, incidentally, also developed the Herefordshire redstreak apple – our debt is great; we can only echo the words carved over the pretty strapwork doorway of the former Rectory in the village of Hempsted in Gloucestershire:

> Whoe'er doth dwell within this door
> Thank God for Vicount Scudamore.

Worcestershire

Whereas Herefordshire has survived the ravages of late 20th-century industry comparatively unscathed, neighbouring Worcestershire has been a good deal less lucky. In the extreme north-east, Birmingham has burst through the Clent Hills as far as Hagley and beyond, with its baleful influence creeping as far south as Redditch; while Worcester itself committed aesthetic suicide in the 1960s, when the most hamfisted planners in England – and that is saying a good deal – tore the heart out of the lovely old medieval city with a brutality that even those of Gloucester could not match. To see the best of Worcestershire you must go further south, where villages like Abbots Morton, Overbury and Bredon still stand as examples of what might have been throughout, or to the extreme south-east, where Broadway – undeniably beautiful, if a little too aware of the fact – is really an extension of the Cotswolds and is thought by most people to be in Gloucestershire anyway; or to the south-west, where Herefordshire overflows across the border with its rolling green hills which,

The Malvern Hills: looking towards British Camp from Worcestershire Beacon

around Malvern, suddenly get ideas above their station and turn into a range of mountains in miniature.

Where Worcestershire wins hands down, not just over Herefordshire but over almost every other county in England, is in its Norman architecture. It gets off to a magnificent start with the crypt of the Cathedral, scarcely touched since the 1080s; continues with the nave of Malvern Priory, which is worthy to be mentioned in the same breath as Gloucester or Tewkesbury; and reaches its apogee in the south transept of Pershore Abbey. And this is not even to mention the innumerable parish churches, though few of them have survived intact. After 1200 or so the building boom seems to have lost impetus, with a parallel falling-off of quality control: the Early English period has left us with relatively little to remember and the Decorated with not very much more, at least where parish churches are concerned – though there is some splendid 14th-century work in the nave of Worcester Cathedral and the east range of its cloister and Dr Pevsner assures us that the lierne vault of the chancel at Pershore may be, with those of St Stephen's Chapel in the Palace of Westminster and the chancel of Bristol Cathedral, the earliest in the country. Then, with the arrival of the Perpendicular, Worcestershire comes into its own again, especially at Evesham where the church of St Lawrence has a simply magnificent fan-vaulted chapel of 1520. (For another memorable bit of vaulting, look at Prince Arthur's chantry in the Cathedral; it was built to house the tomb of Henry VIII's elder brother, who died in 1502.)

Worcestershire is also, even more than Herefordshire, the timber county *par excellence*. The church at Besford is completely timber-framed, as is Besford

Evening light in Broadway, with Fish Hill behind
(see page 131)

Court adjoining and several other churches have timber towers. Where secular buildings are concerned, the 15th-century Booth Hall at Evesham is among the most impressive and Lower Brockhampton with its tiny gatehouse (National Trust) perhaps the most endearing. But there are plenty of other good manor houses too, of which Huddington Court is among the finest. Mere Hall at Hanbury is only very slightly later, but can one call it beautiful? Not, certainly, compared with Hanbury Hall next door (National Trust again) which is probably by William Talman and as distinguished a late William and Mary house as you could ever wish to see.

But there is nothing vernacular about Hanbury Hall; it is one of the county's most elegant houses. Among the others, Croome Court is, alas, no longer what it was; but Westwood Park still looks everything that a great 17th-century house ought to be and Hagley, where Sanderson Miller tried his hand at the Palladian idiom instead of his more usual Gothick, still keeps its superb rococo plasterwork, skilfully restored after a disastrous fire in 1925. (The Temple of Theseus in the grounds, the work of 'Athenian' Stuart, is the earliest example of Greek revival architecture in the world.) Among Victorian houses, moated Madresfield was the model for Evelyn Waugh's Brideshead and Hewell Grange at Tardebigge, by Bodley and Garner and now a Borstal institution, is an admirable essay in the Jacobean.

One last word of advice: when in Droitwich, stay at the Château Impey hotel. It is one of the few places you can't see the town from.

Note on using the Gazetteers

Entries in the two county Gazetteers are arranged alphabetically. 'The', if part of the name, follows the main element: **Malverns, The** (alphabetized under M).

Entry headings consist of the name of the place or feature in **bold** type, followed by a map reference in parenthesis: **Cheltenham** (4/2C). The figure 4 is the map number; 2C is the grid reference, with 2 indicating the across and C the down reference.

If a name mentioned within the text of an entry is printed in capital letters – i.e. HOARWITHY – this indicates that it has its own entry in its county Gazetteer.

Bold type is used for certain places, buildings or other features of interest and importance referred to within Gazetteer entries; most of these also have map references.

The abbreviated forms Glos. (Gloucestershire) and H. & W. (Hereford & Worcester) are used in cross references.

Every effort has been made to ensure that information about the opening to the public of buildings, estates, gardens, reserves, museums, galleries, etc., and details of walks, footpaths and trails, was as accurate and up to date as possible at the time of going to press. Such particulars are, of course, subject to alteration and it may be prudent to check them locally, or with the appropriate organizations or authorities.

Gloucestershire Gazetteer

Ablington (4/4E)

Although it is less than a mile north-west of much-visited BIBURY, few travellers stop to enjoy the quieter pleasures of this hamlet in the Coln valley. The Manor House behind its high wall was built by John Coxwell in 1590. Here J. Arthur Gibbs wrote *A Cotswold Village* (1898), in which he describes with equal pleasure the joys of hunting and the beauty of the local wildlife. Gibbs was writing during an agricultural depression, hard times that he did his best to alleviate locally.

The two noble barns opposite the Manor House are 15th century, or perhaps earlier: monuments to more prosperous times. The 1727 date stone here must refer to the extension rather than the main structures.

Also behind a high wall is Ablington House, converted from a 17th-century farmhouse in the 1920s. The gateposts are embellished by two 19th-century stone lions, brought here from the Houses of Parliament.

Upstream, **Winson** (4/3E), has 17th- and 18th-century cottages, some of them thatched. St Michael's is a simple early Norman church: just a nave, surmounted by a bellcote, a 13th-century porch, and a chancel decorated with 19th-century vine and honeysuckle wall paintings. Near by, the handsome Manor House of *c*.1740 exemplifies the work of James Gibbs. The ground-floor doors and windows have characteristic Gibbs surrounds.

Winson Farm was the home of the novelist Robert Henriques (1905–67), who also wrote lovingly about the area in *The Cotswolds* (1950) and *Through the Valley* (1950).

Adlestrop (4/5C)

The village is about 3 miles east of STOW-ON-THE-WOLD, just north of the A36. The railway came to Adlestrop in 1853. The station is not in the village itself, however, but a mile away downhill in the flat Evenlode valley.

Edward Thomas (1878–1917) made this humble station famous with the poem ('Yes, I

The Cotswold village of Guiting Power seen from Naunton Downs

remember Adlestrop') that countless British schoolchildren once learned by heart.

Trains still thunder through from Paddington to Worcester, but the station is closed and the platform sign now fills the village bus shelter.

Jane Austen used to visit the village. Adlestrop House, formerly the Rectory, was the home of her uncle, the Reverend Thomas Leigh. Her mother's family had owned Adlestrop Park since the Reformation; its 18th-century Gothick façade may have been the model for her descriptions of *Northanger Abbey*.

The park grounds, just visible from the churchyard, were landscaped by Humphry Repton. Various members of the Leigh family are commemorated in the church of St Mary Magdalene, which has been rebuilt more than once – in the 18th century (see the 'Gothick' window in the south transept); and in the 19th (see the king-post roof over the nave).

Adlestrop is only about a mile from **Daylesford** (4/5C), the estate of Warren Hastings (1732–1818), the man who became Governor-General of India in 1773, and was later impeached for alleged cruelty and corruption. He was finally acquitted in 1795. Hastings bought back Daylesford Manor, which had belonged to the Hastings family since the Norman Conquest but had been sold at the end of the 17th century. He employed Samuel Pepys Cockerell, architect to the East India Company (he went on to design SEZINCOTE), to build a splendid new house in the classical manner. (The house is not open to the public.)

Hastings is buried beneath a Greek Revival monument in the graveyard of St Peter's church, whose restoration he had paid for. A tablet in the north nave wall, designed by Sir John Soane, records the history of the church up to the beginning of the 19th century. In 1860, however, it was largely rebuilt in Early French Gothic style.

Alderley (3/4F)

The village is just over a mile south of WOTTON-UNDER-EDGE, on a spur between two narrow wooded valleys. Numerous cloth mills once lined the valley bottoms; one continues to prosper as a trout farm. There are several fine houses in the village, built or enlarged on the profits of the textile industry.

Alderley Grange was built in 1608 and given its handsome porch in the mid-18th century. It was the probable birthplace of Sir Matthew Hale. Known as the 'Upright Judge' for his administration of the law during the Common-wealth and Restoration periods, he was created Lord Chief Justice by Charles II in 1671.

The walled gardens of Alderley Grange were planted by Alvilde Lees-Milne (see 'Gloucester-shire Gardens' p. 77). The garden (but not the house) is open in June under the National Gardens Scheme.

The little church of St Kenelm was rebuilt c.1802 and the interior is a pleasing early example of Georgian Gothick. It now serves as the chapel to next door Rose Hill School, built in 1860 by Lewis Vulliamy (see WESTONBIRT). The churchyard contains the grave of Marianne North (1830–90), the traveller and botanical artist.

Alderley lies on the COTSWOLD WAY, and there are fine walks through the woods of Wortley Hill, or along the stream to Ozleworth Bottom. A narrow, shaded road threads through the same secluded valley before turning abruptly north to Ozleworth.

Here, the church of St Nicholas is surrounded by a circular drystone wall which, according to the landscape historian Finsberg, marks the boundary of a 6th- or 7th-century Celtic burial ground. The beautiful Norman central tower is hexagonal, a rare survival whose only parallel in England is at Swindon (see BISHOP'S CLEEVE). The tower may originally have served as the nave, with an apse to the east and a vestibule to the west, similar to Romanesque churches of this period elsewhere in Europe.

The village of Ozleworth has disappeared. The isolation of the church is shared only by Ozleworth Park, an 18th-century house with Regency additions, and bow windows to make the most of the views.

Just to the west, on the edge of the Cotswold scarp, is Newark Park, owned by the National Trust. Newark was built as a hunting lodge by Sir Nicholas Poyntz, using stones and timber from Kingswood Abbey near WOTTON-UNDER-EDGE, which was demolished around 1540; a typical example of the gentry deriving prompt benefit from the Dissolution of the Monasteries.

The original 16th-century east front has a handsome central bay window above a classical porch, which survived when James Wyatt re-modelled the house in 1790. Wyatt added battlements and a Gothick south porch, and designed the striking apsidal-ended hall.

Alderton *see* Dumbleton

Aldsworth (4/4D)

The village, about 3 miles north-east of BIBURY, consists of stone-built houses and an inn dating from Georgian times. Situated on the Cotswolds uplands, Aldsworth has a series of well-preserved Iron Age fields, probably a continuation of those of the EASTLEACHES. Each field is a third to half an acre in size, bounded by stony banks, probably the remains of collapsed walls.

Aldsworth, along with Bibury, was a 'peculiar' of the Abbey of Osney in Oxfordshire, which meant that, from the Reformation period until the present century, there was no resident priest. Instead, a vicar would drive the 30 miles from Oxford to Aldsworth by gig every Sunday to St Bartholomew's with its pretty octagonal spire.

The arms of Osney Abbey are carved over a window of the north aisle of the church, rebuilt c.1500, and there are other exceptionally fine carvings, including a group of large grotesques.

The churchyard contains several headstones marking the graves of members of the Garne family of Kilkenny Farm. Robert Garne founded the Cotswold Sheep Society in 1892 and pio-neered the conservation of the large-limbed, heavy-fleeced 'Cotswold Lion'. This was the sheep on which the medieval prosperity of the Cotswolds was based and for many years Alds-worth had the sole surviving pedigree flock.

Will Garne continued to farm using traditional methods, maintaining the Cotswold Lions (and a famous herd of pedigree Shorthorn cattle) until his death in 1967.

Alstone *see* Dumbleton

Amberley *see* Minchinhampton

Ampneys, The (4/3E)

The three Ampneys (the 'p' is silent) were once close neighbours along the meandering Ampney Brook, about 2 miles east of CIRENCESTER. Then, in 1348, the population of little **Ampney St Mary** was struck by plague, the village abandoned and a new settlement of small cottages and farms created half a mile north on the Ashbrook. St Mary's church is all that survives of the original village, and was formerly neglected and overgrown. Even now, the walls of the 12th-century nave and 13th-century chancel bulge alarmingly.

The church is worth visiting for the strange Norman carving, apparently depicting the triumph of Good (the lion) over Evil (two fat-faced, coiled, wormlike creatures).

Inside the simple nave with its possibly Saxon window are wall paintings of St Christopher, St George and the Dragon and an unusual 14th-century depiction of the wounds inflicted on Christ by those who violate the Sabbath by their labour.

Ampney Crucis (4/3E) is the largest of the three villages. Holy Rood church forms a pretty group with Upper Mill (1804) and the Jacobean rectory. The north doorway points to a Saxon date for the original church, which has been embellished several times in successive centuries. Restoration in 1870 revealed 14th-century wall paintings, including the arms of Fitzhamon of TEWKESBURY Abbey, which owned the manor.

Another Tewkesbury abbot, Giraldus, is said to be depicted on one of the faces of the fine 15th-century cross in the churchyard; others have said it is St Lawrence. The cross was

found walled up in the entrance to the rood loft in the 19th century. On its other three faces it shows the Crucifixion, the Virgin and a soldier in armour.

Ampney St Peter (4/3E) has an immaculate cul-de-sac of gentrified houses. The nave and low tower of St Peter's church are thought to be late Saxon because of the use of through stones forming a wall only 2 ft thick between the tower and nave. Sir George Gilbert Scott made additions in 1878, but Victorianization spared the licentious carving on the nave north wall.

The countryside around the Ampneys is crossed with footpaths; one skirts the Iron Age enclosure of Ranbury Ring before turning towards **Poulton** (4/4E) to the east. In the centre of the village, where the A417 road makes a right-angled turn, is the handsome Manor House of 1680, whose gardens are occasionally open under the National Gardens Scheme. The side road north to Ready Token leads to a crossroads known as Betty's Grave, believed to be the burial place of Elizabeth Batsoe. The precise circumstances of her death in 1786 are unknown: a local legend suggests she was a witch, though suicides and murderers were also commonly buried at crossroads.

Ampney St Peter

Andoversford *see* Dowdeswell

Apperley *see* Deerhurst

Arlingham (3/4D)
Situated in a 9-mile loop of the Severn, the now remote village was the site of an important prehistoric river crossing to NEWNHAM a mile away on the west bank and thence to the iron mines of the FOREST OF DEAN. It was superseded around AD 49 when the Romans established a new crossing at Kingsholm, now a suburb of GLOUCESTER, but continued to be used by Welsh cattle drovers until recent times. The lonely pub on the riverside west of the village once served ferry passengers but is now more likely to be patronized by birdwatchers.

St Mary's is a large 14th-century church, surrounded by orchards. It shares with DEER-HURST the oldest stained glass in Gloucestershire, dated to about 1340. Other pieces depict St Catherine holding her wheel and St Margaret crushing a dragon. St James and St Philip in the chancel are all that remain from a separate 15th-century series depicting the Apostles.

In **Fretherne**, just north of the village, Wick Court is a stunning survival of a 13th-century manor, given a new brick face in 1574 when Elizabeth I visited the owner, the Earl of Leicester. Restoration work is due for completion in the early 1990s.

South of the elongated village is St Mary's church, which will delight *aficionados* of High Victorian architecture and was built by Francis Niblett in 1847. A tower and crocketed spire with flying buttresses surmount the north porch. There are sculpted angels in the south chapels, added in 1857–9 by J. W. Hugall. Inside, through wrought-iron gates, the painted roof is lit by dormers and everything that could be, including the organ case, has been brightly coloured and gilded.

Less exalted, but representing a considerable engineering achievement, the decaying remains of the Stroudwater Canal are traceable at several points near by (*see also* Upper Framilode).

Ashchurch *see* Tewkesbury

Ashleworth (3/5C)
The main part of the village lies on rising ground 1 mile west of the Severn, 5 or so miles north of GLOUCESTER. A winding lane leads down to the harmonious riverside group of church, Ashleworth Court and tithe barn. The church of St Andrew and St Bartholomew has a 14th-century buttressed tower of noble proportions and topped by a spire. Inside, between the south aisle and the south chapel is a rare 15th-century painted wooden screen, with the cipher 'ER' – for Elizabeth I, or perhaps even Edward VI?

Ashleworth Court dates from around 1460 and has survived largely untouched. The tithe barn, like Ashleworth Court of stone, was built some time between 1481 and 1515 by Abbot Newland of Bristol Abbey, to which the Manor of Ashleworth belonged from 1154. The barn is owned by the National Trust and open to the public, but still very much part of a working farm.

Beyond the church the lane continues to Ashleworth Quay where fishermen gather in the spring to catch migrating elver, many of which are exported to the Continent for growing into mature eels. Footpaths lead for miles beside the Severn in either direction.

From the village a narrow road leads south-east to Hasfield (*see* Forthampton), past 'The Duckeries', a wildfowl reserve run by the Gloucestershire Trust for Nature Conservation, and Ashleworth Manor, a striking black and white timber-framed house of 1460, built as the summer residence of the Abbots of Bristol.

To the west is the widely dispersed village of **Hartpury** (3/4C). The core of the village is on the busy A417, but the most interesting buildings are well away from traffic in the lovely Leadon Valley.

Here again are a church and tithe barn, once possessions of St Peter's Abbey, Gloucester. St Mary's church is notable for some early 14th-century 'butterfly' tracery. The 14th-century barn rivals the church in dignity: buttresses bear the weight of massive collar beams, and the gable ends have finials carved as heraldic beasts. Half a mile south, the Gloucestershire College of Agriculture and Horticulture occupies the late Georgian Hartpury House. Its gardens are occasionally open in summer.

Ashley *see* Tetbury

Aston Blank (Cold Aston) *see* Notgrove

Aston Subedge (4/4A)
The village is 1½ miles north-west of CHIPPING CAMPDEN below the escarpment, and almost in the Vale of Evesham (*see* H & W). It combines the building traditions of both the Cotswold uplands and the Severn Valley: cottages of brick as well as timber frame and stone mix indiscriminately. Some houses are a mixture of all

three. The 1797 church of St Andrew, consisting simply of a nave and apse, has a complete set of Georgian furnishings.

The handsome Manor House is largely 17th century, and was the home of the unfortunate Endymion Porter (1587–1649), poet and ambassador to Spain, a loyal supporter of Charles I who ended his days abroad in poverty.

The village adjoins the Burnt Norton estate, so named because it stands on the site of a house that burned down in the 17th century. T. S. Eliot had a romantic liaison here in the summer of 1934 and set the first of his *Four Quartets* in the wooded garden (occasionally open to the public under the National Gardens Scheme).

Weston-sub-Edge (4/4B) lies 1 mile south-west along the A46, where little but the gargoyled west tower and a 1590 brass survived the improving hands of Victorian restorers.

Willersey (4/4B) The church of St Peter here was more fortunate. It was improved in the 14th and 15th centuries when the fine Perpendicular tower was added. Stone-built houses line the

Brass monument to William Hodges (1590) in the church at Weston-sub-Edge

wide main street. The late 17th-century Pool House is the prettiest, with velvet lawns and eye-catching gateposts overlooking the village duck pond. Higher up the hill, Willersey House has attractive gardens, occasionally open under the National Gardens Scheme.

Saintbury (4/4B) benefits from being higher up the scarp than its three neighbours; residents enjoy wide views of the orchard-filled Vale of Evesham. The church of St Nicholas is higher still and its 14th-century broach spire is a prominent landmark for miles around. The church is also delightful for its myriad details of all periods, from a Saxon sundial and the zigzag carving of the early Norman doorways to the crocketed and pinnacled ogee arch of the 14th-century piscina. The 17th- and 18th-century furnishings include a fine font cover and Jacobean altar rails.

Avening (4/1F)

The village is some 2½ miles south-east of NAILSWORTH, on the B4014. Ancient tracks and narrow lanes converge on Avening, a network that invites exploration on foot. Several cottages have long and colourful front gardens leading to homely porches.

The fine cruciform church of the Holy Cross that sits so handsomely on a platform on the steep valleyside is Saxon in origin and belonged to the Abbess of Holy Trinity, Caen, at the time of the Norman rebuilding. (The pig's head served at the banquet to celebrate its consecration may be the origin of the costumed 'Pig Feast' that takes place in the village every September. One of the other explanations, however, is that the Pig Feast commemorates the killing of a wild boar in the 18th century that had long terrorized the neighbourhood.)

Romanesque details survive: on one of the capitals by the north door a beast with one head and two bodies peers from the foliage, and, just inside, crude figure carvings under an arcade may have come from a 12th-century font. The north aisle, tower and chancel arches have later Norman work, as does the vaulted first bay of the chancel, handsomely extended in the 14th century.

A monument to Henry Brydges (d.1615) portrays him kneeling at prayer, with no hint that he was, until he married a clothier's daughter and settled in Avening, a notorious pirate, smuggler and highwayman. The south transept has a series of locally carved 17th-century monuments to the Driver family.

Avening lies in an area rich in prehistoric barrows and is on the site of a large Saxon cemetery.

One mile east of Avening is the tiny village of **Cherington** (4/2F). St Nicholas's church has an unaltered 13th-century chancel. The nave was lowered in the 15th century when the timber roof was put in: hence the odd roof line. Above the north door is a Norman tympanum carved with animals. The south door tympanum, with serpent, lion and griffin, was moved to Cherington Park in 1816. The village has several distinguished Georgian stone houses around its green, notably the handsome Yew Tree.

Awre (3/4E)

The A48 GLOUCESTER to Chepstow road passes well to the west of the village, which consists of a scattering of ancient farms reached via narrow, high-sided lanes. This was the birthplace of John Hopkins (d.1570), who with Thomas Sternhold (d.1594) of nearby BLAKENEY, produced a metrical version of the Psalms in 1563. The big church of St Andrew, in which this pioneering psalter was first used, is an unspoiled example of 13th-century Early English style, except for the Perpendicular west tower.

An ancient mortuary chest, said to be as old as the church and dug from a single tree, was used to lay out victims of the nearby Severn. When the tide is out and the river shrinks to a fifth of its normal width, it looks deceptively easy to cross – but there were many who failed.

Aylburton *see* Lydney

Badgeworth (4/2D)

Isolated in the hinterland between CHELTENHAM and GLOUCESTER, between pylons, motorway junctions and trunk roads, Badgeworth has staked out its own claim to fame as the home of *Ranunculus ophioglossifolius*, the 'Badgeworth Buttercup'. This endangered marsh species is protected on a 375 sq. yd official conservation site. In June and July you can see the plant in flower from a nearby gate: there is no public access.

The richly decorated north chapel of Holy Trinity church, dedicated in July 1315, was built by Gilbert de Clare, 10th Earl of Gloucester, who acquired the manor in 1314. The surrounds to the windows and doors, inside and out, are profusely covered with a ballflower motif: a decoration confined to the first quarter of the 14th century.

Up Hatherley (4/2C), 1 mile north-east, is rapidly being swallowed up by Cheltenham, but the chancel of the church of St Philip and St James, built in 1885, as a private chapel, is worth visiting for wall paintings of the Annunciation and the Apostles by J. Eadie Reid, a student of the Pre-Raphaelites.

Bagendon (4/3E)

In about AD 10 the Dobunni, a Belgic tribe, made a settlement here, which became their capital. By AD 60 the site had been abandoned, the people absorbed into the new town of Corinium (CIRENCESTER), 3 miles south. The system of banks and ditches that enclosed the 200-acre Belgic *oppidum* can still be traced, notably along the road from Perrott's Brook to Woodmancote east of the church, where beeches and horse chestnuts top the high bank. The full story of the site is told in the Corinium Museum, Cirencester.

The modest Norman west tower of the church has a priest's chamber complete with sink and drain spout up on the first floor. The original chancel arch, whose footings survive, was narrow, perhaps Saxon. The chancel floor was raised in medieval times to protect it from flooding by the nearby Perrott Brook. The chancel arch and chancel were renewed c.1460–70 when the prosperous Weavers' Guild of Cirencester acquired the manor.

Barnsley (4/3E)

This showpiece village, 4 miles north-east of CIRENCESTER on the A433 to Burford, is the home of Rosemary Verey, writer and creator of the famous garden at Barnsley House (open daily).

The house itself was built in 1697 and served as the village Rectory between 1762 and 1932. Mrs Verey began transforming the 4 acres around the house in 1960, along with her late husband David Verey (1913–84), architect and author of the Gloucestershire volumes of *The Buildings of England*. The result is now a mature and fascinating garden, full of surprises and original ideas (*see also* 'Gloucestershire Gardens', p. 77). A simple memorial here to David Verey is inscribed with the words of John Evelyn:

As no man be very miserable that is master of a garden here; so no man will ever be happy who is not sure of a Garden hereafter . . . where the first Adam fell, the second rose.

It is a short step from the garden to St Mary's

Cottages at Little Barrington

church, originally 12th-century with a surviving corbel table, the corbels carved in the form of beasts and grotesques. The 13th-century chancel arch rests on stout Norman piers.

Part of Barnsley's charm can be attributed to the absence of disfiguring telephone wires and overhead cables. These were placed underground in the 1950s. Television aerials now sprout from many chimneypots but, even so, the main street offers an uninterrupted view of honey-coloured cottages fronted by low drystone walls, cascading with mauve aubrietia in spring.

At the BIBURY end of the village, the road turns sharp right to skirt Barnsley Park, a private house unfortunately not visible from the road. It is a fine Baroque mansion of 1720–31. In 1979 excavations of a Roman villa in the grounds ended after 19 years' work. The associated field systems have been plotted and it has been suggested that many drystone walls in the Barnsley area (and probably elsewhere in the Cotswolds) could be Roman in origin.

Barnwood *see* Gloucester

Barringtons, The (4/5D; 4/4D)
Great and Little Barrington are on opposite banks of the Windrush 6 miles east of NORTH-LEACH. Together with neighbouring Taynton, just over the Oxfordshire border, their quarries provided the stone for a long list of notable buildings: the original St Paul's; the crypt and corridors of Sir Christopher Wren's Cathedral, and numerous other churches in the City of London rebuilt after the Great Fire of 1666; and many of the Oxford colleges. The inferior oolite is close to the surface here and easily quarried. It is uniquely plastic: soft enough to carve when fresh from the ground, then hardening and weathering to a warm honey colour.

There is a former quarry right in the heart of **Little Barrington** (4/4D), but a charming one whose bumpy hollows now form the village green. Around the rim stand 16th and 17th-century houses, demonstrating all varieties of Cotswold vernacular building.

St Peter's church stands apart to the east. A Norman tympanum of Christ in Majesty with angels overhead is now in the north aisle. This may have been the nave of the original church, for the west tower is aligned on the aisle, not on the 14th-century nave.

North of the church a public footpath crosses the Windrush via two footbridges, past Barring-ton Mill and up the hill to **Great Barrington** (4/5D), a compact estate village of 17th-, 18th-and 19th-century stone houses.

Again, St Mary's church is slightly removed, in the grounds of Barrington Park. Apart from its deeply incised chevron-moulded chancel arch of the late 12th century, it is notable for some moving 17th and 18th-century memorials.

Barrington Park is a richly decorated Palladian mansion, built 1736–8, possibly by William Kent – the imposing domed pigeon house and Doric temple in the landscaped gardens may also

Autumnal colours at Batsford Arboretum

be his. This private house is best seen from the footpath linking WINDRUSH and Little Barrington on the opposite side of the valley.

From Barrington Park the road descends beneath a high garden wall to the mill stream and on to Strong's Causeway. This road and its bridge are named after Thomas Strong, who answered the call for craftsmen to help in the rebuilding of London after the Great Fire. Wren, impressed by his knowledge of the characteristics of building stone, appointed him chief mason at St Paul's. In his will, Thomas left money to 'make a way between the two Barrington bridges . . . to carry a corpse in safety'. The road was sufficiently repaired for his own funeral cortège to pass along it in 1681.

Batsford (4/4B)

The arboretum at Batsford Park, 1½ miles north-west of MORETON-IN-MARSH, was planted by Lord Redesdale, who came to live here in 1886 (*see* 'Gloucestershire Gardens', p. 77). The E-shaped neo-Elizabethan house was also his creation. The church near the northern entrance to Batsford Park was extensively rebuilt in 1861 in neo-Norman style, with zigzag carving inside and out to make the point. The elaborate Redesdale family pew and their many memorials speak of continuing influence.

Baunton *see* Cirencester

Beachley (3/2F)

The village occupies a broad peninsula where the River Wye flows into the Severn. The Severn Bridge passes directly overhead; until this graceful structure, with its 3240 ft main span, was opened in 1966, Beachley was the site of an important river crossing. Because of its strategic significance the district was fiercely fought over during the Civil War. In 1644 Colonel Massey defeated Royalist cavalry led by Colonel Winter, who is said to have escaped capture by riding up the Wye and hurling himself into the river from the cliffs known as Wintour's Leap, 3 miles north at Lancaut.

Beachley is home to the Army Apprentices College. Its neatly marshalled buildings contrast strikingly with the tumultuous Severn, whose waters rush dramatically over the half-submerged Hen and Chicken rocks when the tide goes out.

The southernmost stretch of OFFA'S DYKE can be seen in the village of **Sedbury** (3/2F), 1½ miles north. Here it is hemmed in by a housing estate and a sewage plant, except for the very final stretch where the bank rises dramatically to meet the wild Sedbury Cliffs.

Sedbury is now continuous with **Tutshill** (3/2F), fashionable in the 19th century for its views of the Wye. A mile north-west, the great Norman tower of St Mary's church at **Tidenham** stands high enough to have been a useful beacon for vessels navigating this difficult stretch of the river. Inside the church is one of Gloucestershire's five late 12th-century lead fonts cast from the same mould, depicting three enthroned figures and three with their hands raised in benediction. The others are at FRAMPTON ON SEVERN, GLOUCESTER Cathedral, Oxenhall and Sandhurst.

Tidenham (3/2F) is the starting point for several interesting walks. One path leads east to Pillhouse Rocks on the Severn, where fish have been netted in vast quantities over the centuries. Another leads west to the dramatic viewpoint at Wintour's Leap (see above) and along the banks of the Wye to **Lancaut**, in a strikingly beautiful setting in an area beloved of rock climbers. Here, in an almost circular river meander, surrounded by oak and beech woods, is the ruin of the small Norman church of St James. The Tidenham Chase Forest Trail offers a 6-mile walk to ST BRIAVELS.

Belas Knap *see* Sevenhampton

Berkeley (3/3F)

The Vale of Berkeley on the eastern side of the Severn estuary is characterized by individual farms and occasional small hamlets, a quite different settlement pattern from the compact Cotswold villages. The Berkeley estate is Anglo-Saxon in origin and, until the 19th century, controlled vast tracts of rich pasture. As a symbol of his wealth and power, Thomas, 8th Lord Berkeley, reconstructed the mid-12th-century castle between 1340 and 1350. It has survived as one of Britain's most imposing feudal strongholds (open daily).

It is entered through a 14th-century gatehouse brought here from Yate (now in Avon). This stands on a former bastion of FitzOsbern's original 1067 keep. The Great Hall is magnificent, with a high double-pitched roof. The windows and the south-west doorway have the distinctive 'Berkeley arch' with four straight sides enclosing a cusped inner arch.

Steps lead from the Great Hall to the state apartments and to the chilling cell in which Edward II was brutally tortured by his gaolers and murdered in 1327.

Berkeley's church of St Mary is an imposing building, on high ground that formed part of the 12th-century castle defences. The tower is rather curiously placed to the north. It was rebuilt in Gothic style in 1750–3.

Inside, the large but somewhat time-ravaged church gives the impression of having no walls, because of the sunlight that floods the nave and,

Hounds at exercise in front of Berkeley Castle

too, the slenderness of the shafts, ornamented with stiff-leaf capitals of *c*.1225–5, which form the nave arcade.

The medieval features of the church – including 13th-century wall paintings – were sensitively restored in Victorian times, notably by Gilbert Scott.

The chancel is entered through a richly carved 15th-century stone screen. The Berkeley chapel is filled with fine family monuments, including those of Thomas, 8th Lord Berkeley (d.1361).

The town was formerly an important local market centre, with its own wharf on the Berkeley Pill. Berkeley High Street, lined by Georgian buildings, leads westwards from the castle. The intrusive silhouette of the nuclear power station 1½ miles away beside the Severn has been successfully screened by trees and will eventually disappear, as Britain's oldest nuclear power station is now being dismantled. The Jenner Museum in The Chantry commemorates the pioneering work on smallpox vaccine carried out by Edward Jenner (1749–1823) during the 1790s.

Beverston (4/1F)

The architect Lewis Vulliamy (1791–1871) designed extravagantly at nearby WESTONBIRT but was here employed to produce the humble estate workers' cottages that line the A4135 about 2 miles west of TETBURY. (Beverston became part of the Westonbirt estate in 1842.) Several pre-estate 17th-century cottages survive, one with steep multiple gables, but most have Vulliamy's bargeboards and Gothick porches.

Tucked away off the road is the church of St Mary, with a weatherworn Saxon sculpture of the Risen Christ on the south face of the Norman tower, a fine 13th-century nave and a restored 15th-century oak screen rescued from the vicarage garden, where it had been used for a rose arbour. Next to the church are the substantial remains of Beverston Castle, and a 17th-century house whose gardens are open on occasion in summer. Parts of the west range of the first castle, built *c*.1225, have survived along with part of a gatehouse added in the 14th century.

Chavenage House (open in summer) is 1 mile north. The hall of this beautiful E-shaped Elizabethan house, which was rebuilt in 1576 and has remained unspoiled, is lit by two splendid Perpendicular mullioned and transomed windows containing medieval glass from Horsley church (*see* Nailsworth).

Bibury (4/4E)

The best time to visit Bibury, 7 miles north-east of CIRENCESTER, is early in the morning, before coaches bear down on the village that William Morris called the most beautiful in England.

The tourists come to see the River Coln with its pretty 17th and 18th-century bridges, and to feed the ducks. They take in the view across Rack Isle, a watermeadow now a nature reserve, to Arlington Row, a group of 17th-century weavers' cottages owned by the National Trust, which stand attractively in the shelter of a beech hanger.

Not so many of them penetrate the village proper to find the rewarding church, which stands next to the village school and in the lee of the many-gabled Bibury Court Hotel, built in 1633 by Sir Thomas Sackville.

At first sight, St Mary's church appears to be 13th and 14th century, but closer inspection reveals substantial remains of Saxon fabric, notably the tall square jambs of the chancel arch. These have been dated to around AD 1000 and the remarkable foliage decoration of the capitals resembles motifs found in Anglo-Saxon illuminated manuscripts of the same era. In the south

Crickley Hill seen from the Peak viewpoint near Birdlip Hill

aisle there are casts from early 11th-century Ringerike-style grave slabs (the originals are now in the British Museum).

The churchyard has several fine table tombs of the 17th and 18th centuries, ornamented with cherubs.

At the opposite end of the village, the 17th-century Arlington Mill was restored as a museum by David Verey in 1966 and, besides working machinery, houses an important collection of Arts and Crafts furniture (*see* Sapperton).

From Arlington Row, a track goes up Awkward Hill to a signposted footpath which leads to Coln St Aldwyns (*see* Colns, The). From the crest of the hill there are splendid views of the village. Equally dramatic is the view back to Bibury Court from the Bibury to Coln St Aldwyns road.

Birdlip (4/2D)

The bypass that opened in 1988 has relieved Birdlip, 6 miles south-east of GLOUCESTER, of the heavy traffic that used to thunder through the village along the course of the Roman Ermine Way. It is now a quiet cul-de-sac with some characterful buildings at its western end,

including the ornate 19th-century Royal George Hotel and the former coaching inn called Black Horse Ridge. This sits literally on the edge of the Cotswold escarpment and the 17th-century coach road to Gloucester plunges down steeply through attractive beech woods from here into the vale. The layby, ½ mile north of the village, is the best place to take in the sweeping views over the Vale of Gloucester to the Malverns. The escarpment here, known as Barrow Wake, was the site of an important Iron Age cemetery, revealed by quarrying in 1879. The rich grave goods, including one of the finest examples of Celtic art found in Britain, a delicately engraved bronze mirror ornamented with red enamel, are in Gloucester Museum.

At the Air Balloon Inn, the A417 almost doubles back on itself as it negotiates the scarp to skirt **Crickley Hill**. This dramatic promontory was much loved by the Gloucester poet, Ivor Gurney, who in his much-loved poem *Crickley Hill* wrote:

The orchis, trefoil, harebells nod all day
High above Gloucester and the Severn Plain,
Few come there, where the curlew ever and
    again
Cries faintly, and no traveller makes stay,
Since steep the road is,
And the villages
Hidden by hedges wonderful in May.

The hill is now a Country Park managed jointly by the County Council and the National Trust, with an information centre, special interest trails and guided walks. Excavation of the massive hillfort on the summit revealed that Neolithic farmers lived on the hill as early as 3500 BC, but the substantial surviving ramparts were built in the Iron Age, between 500 and 400 BC.

Bishop's Cleeve (4/2C)

Hi-tech industry has transformed this town, a little way north on the A435, into a fast-growing satellite of CHELTENHAM. Once it was under the patronage of the Bishops of Worcester (hence the name), one of whom built the splendid H-shaped Old Rectory around 1250. The Venetian windows of the cross wings were added when the house was refronted in 1667. The 15th-century barn opposite was sadly truncated to half its original length when it was converted into a community centre.

The west end of the church of St Michael and All Angels has turrets enriched with arcading used to balance the gable, a rare surviving example of a late Romanesque feature from the end of the 12th century. The upper chamber of the porch preserves a section of the Norman corbel table and some wall paintings executed by the schoolmaster, in 1818, when the porch served as the village school.

The nave is essentially Norman, but the long chancel was rebuilt in the 14th century. The Norman transept has a remarkable staircase of stone which then gives way to a 15th-century one of wood, still used to climb to the belfry.

Several other notable churches, all of which are well worth visiting, adjoin the parish of Bishop's Cleeve. **Southam** (4/2C) lies south-east under the scarp, where the Church of the Ascension forms a photogenic group with the heavily restored 15th-century timber-framed tithe barn (used in July and November for exhibitions by the Gloucestershire Guild of Craftsmen) and the 14th or 15th-century Pigeon House. The small church was restored in elaborate neo-Norman style in 1862 as a private chapel.

Wooden staircase in the church at Bishop's Cleeve

The church of St Lawrence at **Swindon** (4/2C), 2 miles west of Southam, has a rare Norman hexagonal tower, but was otherwise drastically altered by T. Fulljames in 1845. He was roundly – and rightly – condemned by his own architectural contemporaries for the destruction of original Norman features.

Elmstone Hardwicke (4/2C) lies just east of the M5. Its church of St Mary Magdalene now stands almost alone without a village. It belonged to the priory at DEERHURST: the carved Saxon stone (possibly a cross base) has similar ornamentation to that on Deerhurst's font. The tower is Perpendicular, of similar date to the 15th-century pulpit, font and screen. The wildly disproportionate stone reredos of 1886 is carved with almost life-sized figures of saints.

Stoke Orchard's (4/2C) tiny church is dedicated to St James and contains wall paintings of national importance, the earliest scheme dating from c.1190–1220. They illustrate the life of the Apostle. His shrine at Compostela, northern Spain, was such a popular goal of medieval pilgrims that many similar cycles must once have existed, but this is the only one to have survived complete in England.

During restoration in 1953–5, E. Clive Rouse made drawings which are useful in deciphering the fragmentary remains of the paintings, which run around the nave.

Tredington's church of St John the Baptist, 1 mile to the north-west, is notable for the 9 ft-long fossil ichthyosaurus preserved in the floor of the porch, but now scarcely distinguishable. This fishlike reptile lived around 150 million years ago. The Norman nave has an Elizabethan plaster ceiling decorated with rosettes and heads, and in the 14th-century chancel there is a fine fragment of glass showing the head of a king.

Bisley (4/2E)

The inaccessibility of Bisley, about 4 miles east of STROUD, only adds to its charm. Approached by narrow, steep roads, often impassable in winter, the village centre is a huddle of cottages threaded by paths that lead between the dry-stone walls of terraced gardens, smothered with aubrietia and rock plants in early summer.

Bisley's charm is reflected in its property values; nearly every available barn has been converted – including the fine Rectory Farm Barn on the eastern hilltop, with its unusual bull's-eye windows in the gabled porches.

Even so, the village retains its rural ambience, with a smallholding in its centre, and ducks floating in the stone troughs of Bisley Wells, great tanks placed to catch the water that runs off the hillside. Thomas Keble (1793–1875), brother of John Keble, the divine and poet (see Fairford), was vicar here from 1827 until his death. He added the gabled waterspouts in 1863 and instituted the well-dressing ceremony held every Ascension Day.

The church is approached up a path, past the 16th-century Wesley House where the founder of Methodism sometimes stayed, and through a lychgate. The carved stone in the churchyard is a mystery. It is most commonly interpreted as a chantry where candles were lit for the souls of the poor. If so, its position outdoors makes it unique in England.

The church of All Saints was restored early in the 19th century. However, a good deal of earlier work survives, notably the 15th-century carvings (removed from the nave roof) of musicians playing bagpipes and recorder.

It was on Thomas Keble's initiative that the over-large parish of Bisley was carved up into smaller units in the 19th century, which explains the proliferation of Victorian churches in the glorious wooded valleys round about. They include Oakridge (see Sapperton) the French Gothic church of St John the Baptist at **France Lynch**), built by George Frederick Bodley in 1855–7; and St Michael's church, Bussage, built in 1846 using funds donated by undergraduate followers of John Keble's Oxford Movement.

There are Roman altars from the vicinity in Stroud District Museum and part of a Saxon cross stands beside the road to that town.

Of the many fine 17th- and 18th-century houses around Bisley, one of the loveliest is Nether Lypiatt Manor (1702–5), visible through its wrought-iron gates from the lane due west of the house (gardens open under the National Gardens Scheme). There are many footpaths between Nether Lypiatt and Bisley following the beautiful Toadsmoor valley.

Blaisdon see Huntley

Blakeney (3/3E)

Situated on the A48 GLOUCESTER to Chepstow road, this 'gateway' to the FOREST OF DEAN consists of a scattering of largely 19th-century cottages and smallholdings established by colliers who worked the Forest drift mines. Fruit growing was also of local importance: the Blakeney Red Pear is one of the best-known varieties of perry pear in the Three Counties. It was also used during the First World War as a source of khaki dye for British Army uniforms.

Just south of Blakeney is **Gatcombe** – not to be confused with Gatcombe Park (see Minchinhampton). The beauty of this riverside hamlet is somewhat spoiled by the GLOUCESTER to Cardiff railway line which runs between the houses and the shore.

Purton (3/3E) is 1 mile further downstream. Both hamlets were once busy ports at the highest point of the river navigable by deep-draught ships. Cargo was unloaded here and transferred to shallow-draught Severn trows, which could sail upstream as far north as Shrewsbury. Several old trows are still beached at the other Purton (see Sharpness) on the opposite bank.

North of Blakeney, the Forestry Commission has laid out several trails with picnic facilities, accessible from the B4431 road to Parkend (see Coleford). The 3-mile Wenchford Trail follows Blackpool Brook and the course of a 19th-century tramway used to bring coal, iron and timber out of the Forest. The fine stretch of paved road at Blackpool Bridge, long held to be Roman, was excavated in 1986 – and carbon-14 dating showed it to be 17th century. Even so, it is known to follow the route of a Roman road from Highfield, near LYDNEY, to Weston-under-Penyard (the Roman Ariconium) and used for exploiting the iron ores of the Forest (details in the Dean Heritage Centre: *see* Cinderford).

Interesting walks further west are the Mallards Pike Lakeside Trail, and the New Fancy Walk, named after the New Fancy colliery, where the tip has been landscaped and provides fine views.

Bledington (4/5C)

This village lies south-east of STOW-ON-THE-WOLD, on the B4450. Here in the 19th century on May Day and late into the long summer evenings, the Bledington Morris once danced to fiddle accompaniment on the village green. A maypole still stands on the wide and lovely green, bounded by a stream with ducks and a village street that curves south to the church of St Leonard.

This Norman building was altered in the 15th century when the living belonged to the wealthy WINCHCOMBE Abbey. Master masons were employed to heighten the nave and put in a clerestory. Several windows were given image niches with ogee-arched canopies. John Pruddle of Westminster was probably the glazier, and the result, before the later destruction of the statues and much of the glass, must have been magnificent.

Fortunately, some of the glass has survived and other fragments are thought to have been rescued from the nearby church of ODDINGTON during the Civil War.

Several of the gardens in the village are opened to the public once a year in summer. To the west, at nearby **Icomb** (4/5C), the woodland and streamside garden of Icomb Place is open in the autumn. The house itself dates from about 1420. The church is mainly 13th century, with typical Early English features.

Blockley (4/4B)

This large and very attractive village, between the wool-market towns of CHIPPING CAMPDEN and MORETON-IN-MARSH, is built on a terrace above the deeply cleft valley of the Knee Brook. Early prosperity was based on sheep, whose needs were often given priority: around 1384 the bishops of Worcester cleared the village of Upton, 1 mile west of Blockley, to create further grazing for their vast flocks. The bumps in the pasture on the hillside opposite Blockley are all that remains of Upton.

The sheep were herded into Blockley every spring for shearing, and much of the wool was processed locally in the numerous mills that lined the spring-fed valley. In the late 17th century, several of these were converted to more profitable silk production to supply the ribbon weavers of Coventry.

Prosperous mill owners monopolized the level hilltop, building themselves splendid houses along the High Street in the 17th and 18th centuries. This left little enough space for the homes of the mill workers, which tumble in a cascade of mellow stone down the steep valley side, squeezed on to the narrowest of terraces. Even so, many of their owners manage to find space for vividly coloured cottage plants in gardens scarcely large enough to sit in.

In 1887 one of the old mills was used to generate electricity – and Blockley claims to be the first English village so lit.

Blockley's large church, dedicated to Saints Peter and Paul, is late Norman. Shafts and capitals in the chancel show that elaborate vaulting was intended but never completed. Nearby Northwick Park is a splendid mansion, begun in 1686; some of the ancillary buildings have recently been converted into apartments. The hilly road from Blockley which runs along the west side of the park provides one of the best views of neighbouring Chipping Campden.

Bourton-on-the-Hill *see* Moreton-in-Marsh

Bourton-on-the-Water (4/4C)

This is a village that draws crowds of visitors. First among its attractions is the one-ninth scale model of the village, opened in 1937, faithful in every detail to the original and delightful enough to enchant even reluctant viewers.

Birdland was created by the late Len Hill in the gardens of Chardwar Manor and filled with over 600 species. As visitors flocked, so the attractions proliferated: now a perfumery, pottery, trout farm, model railway, Village Life Museum and Motor Museum (specializing in caravan memorabilia) provide interest and information to fill a whole day.

Through it all the Windrush flows undisturbed (except on August Bank Holiday Monday, when local teams play football along its course) under a series of elegant 18th-century bridges. Bourton Bridge, west of the village on the Foss Way (A429), has a plaque bearing the emblem of the Roman XXth legion, which built the first bridge here in the 1st century AD.

River Windrush in Bourton-on-the-Water

There are many fine houses around the village green, most notably the Palladian-style Harrington House, built around 1740. The Manor House to the west of the green was rebuilt in 1919; it has a 16th-century circular dovecot.

St Lawrence's church has been rebuilt on several occasions, each age adding something of interest. The tower, topped by a lead-covered cupola, belongs to the 1784 rebuilding. The nave, with its fine king-post roof, was completed in 1891. The chancel is 13th century, but with a gorgeously painted ceiling, oak screens, rood and reredos of 1928, by F. E. Howard.

About 2 miles south is **Clapton-on-the-Hill** (4/4D), high up and overlooking the Windrush valley. Its tiny Norman church of St James (45 ft long, 13 ft wide) has an indulgence carved in Latin on its diminutive chancel arch.

Boxwell (3/5F)

The 13th-century church of St Mary, surmounted by a massive octagonal bellcote, and the 15th-century Boxwell Court (refronted this century) stand alone at the head of a valley, surrounded by woods which, true to name, contain a quantity of ancient box trees.

The house and park are private but the church is accessible by way of a metalled road from the A46, about 5 miles south of NAILSWORTH.

Opposite this turn-off, a road leads south-east from the A46 past a 270 ft-long, tree-covered Neolithic long barrow to **Leighterton**, (3/5F), a tightly packed farming village with two large 18th-century barns, and chest and tea-caddy tombs of the same date in the churchyard.

Newington Bagpath lies remote on the steep slope of Ozleworth valley to the north. The church of St Bartholomew, redundant and padlocked, has a simple Norman nave and a 14th-century porch, but 19th-century tower and chancel. From the south-east corner of the overgrown churchyard it is possible to see the substantial and impressive remains of the Norman motte and bailey in the next-door (private) field. It is said that the last two Englishmen hanged for highway robbery were buried here.

A short walk is the best way to get from Newington to **Lasborough**, ½ mile south, where the church of St Mary stands in a beautiful valley. The church was ruinous in the mid-19th century and all its monuments were moved to Shipton Moyne (*see* Tetbury). Lewis Vulliamy rebuilt the church in 1861–2, immediately before beginning work on nearby WESTONBIRT House.

Brimpsfield (4/2D)

This village high on the wolds just west of the Ermine Way (A417, between CIRENCESTER and

GLOUCESTER) has a fine church and the ruins of a castle side by side, standing remote from the rest of the village and only accessible by footpath across fields. The castle, described in the early 14th century as having four proud towers, was demolished in 1332 when its owner, John Gifford, was executed for treason. Now tangled undergrowth fills the moat and trees grow over the castle mound, which can just be seen in the field to the right of St Michael's church.

The unusual internal arrangement of the church itself is due to the addition of a central tower in the 15th century, carried on buttresses which close in the approach to the chancel. The carved oak pulpit is dated 1658, so must have been installed during the Commonwealth period – which is unusual. The stone marked with four consecration crosses is probably the original Norman altar; it survived use as a stile post in a nearby field before being returned to the church in 1937. Just north of the church stood a Norman priory which, along with Brimpsfield Castle, was used as a quarry for stone for many of the older houses here.

A mile south, the road plunges into the Frome valley at Caudle Green. The road back up the other side of this valley leads back to **Syde** (4/2D). A cottage here with 14th-century windows and doors is probably the chantry chapel founded in 1344 by Thomas Berkeley.

Syde's little church of St Mary is a gem, secluded by trees, with a diminutive 14th-century saddleback tower and a Norman nave. The 15th-century king-post roof crowns an atmospheric interior, still gaslit and furnished with rustic 17th-century box pews. Two noteworthy 15th-century details are the heart-shaped closing ring of the north door, and the stained glass roundel depicting St James of Compostela.

Next to the church is a 14th-century tithe barn – almost all roof, with low walls – with traceried windows that may indicate its part use as a priest's house.

A little south of Syde, **Winstone's** (4/2E) views are blighted by a forest of radio masts, but it should not be passed by since the simple Saxon and Norman church of St Bartholomew is in the characteristically rugged style prevailing just before the Norman Conquest. The north door is in the Saxon tradition; the lintel and tympanum of the south door show the first signs of Norman influence.

Broadwell *see* Stow-on-the-Wold

Brockhampton *see* Sevenhampton

Brockweir (3/2E)

At the mouth of a steep-sided valley, this delightful place has the heights of the ST BRIAVELS and Hewelsfield Commons to the north and magnificent overhanging woods to the south. A pretty iron bridge and genteel tea gardens now attract visitors to what was formerly a busy trans-shipment port and boatyard on the Wye. Goods were unloaded here from seagoing vessels on to barges that were hauled upriver to Monmouth, originally by teams of men, later by horses. After the Wye Valley Railway opened in 1870 (*see* Lydney) the barge trade declined. The only relics are the screw and drive shaft from the steamship *Belle Marie* in front of the Quay House, and the Moravian Chapel (open to the public), founded here in 1832 as a mission to the heavy-drinking sailors and bargees.

The parish church is high up at **Hewelsfield** (3/2E), 2 miles away, where it commands wide views of the FOREST OF DEAN. The circular churchyard surrounds a Norman church with a squat central tower and a steep-pitched roof that sweeps down over nave and aisle to within a few feet of the ground.

Brockworth (4/1D)

This parish, to the east of GLOUCESTER, is now a suburb of that city, but the fine group of St George's church, 16th-century Brockworth Court and an 18th-century barn stands at the northern edge of the former village, far enough from the housing estates to retain its unspoiled charm. The tower of the Norman church survives, supported on splendidly chevroned tower arches; the rest of the church was rebuilt in Decorated style in the 14th century. The earliest surviving wing of Brockworth Court was built in 1534–9 for Richard Hart, the last prior of Lanthony in Monmouthshire.

Cooper's Hill can be reached from the car park at Fiddler's Elbow, off the A46 just south of Brockworth. Several colour-coded nature trails, with information on the local archaeology and wildlife, have been laid out through the beech and birch woodlands.

One trail leads to a steep slope where a maypole marks the start of the annual Whit Monday cheese-rolling contest. This may have begun as a ceremony performed by local people to stake out their rights of common grazing. Brave-hearted contestants chase a specially encased 7lb Double Gloucester cheese down the near-vertical grassy slope. The first to catch the cheese takes it home.

The Belvedere in Chalford

Just east of the M5 is **Upton St Leonards** (4/1D). Nearly every Victorian architect working in Gloucestershire at the time contributed to the rebuilding of the church of St Leonard. The best work is the chancel, with its gold reredos and choir stalls by Woodyer, the least prolific and least conventional architect of the group.

Brookthorpe *see* Gloucester

Buckland *see* Stanton

Bulley *see* Highnam

Cam *see* Dursley

Chaceley *see* Forthampton

Chalford (4/1E)

The Frome valley, from Chalford down to STROUD 4 miles to the north-west, has long been heavily industrialized, but the modern factories totally lack style, whereas their 18th- and 19th-century forebears have handsome proportions and Classical detailing. A few of the latter have survived, converted to other uses, but they need seeking out. The best way to see them is to park at the head of the valley, where the steep back road to Chalford village joins the A419 to Stroud, and walk.

On the steep north side of the valley some of the houses of former mill owners had to be built on terraces cut into the hillside. The front doors, entered from the lane, are sometimes two or even three storeys higher than the garden entrances.

The mills in the valley bottom straddle the Frome, while the **Thames and Severn Canal** (*see also* Sapperton) and the railway (the old Great Western) run parallel. The canal towpath is convenient for exploring, being well away from the busy road. The first stretch of the canal emerges from a culvert, not far from a lengthman's roundhouse at the former Chalford wharf. Here are the first of several fine mills with Classical pediments and Venetian windows, and the 15th-century Company's Arms Inn.

A little further on, the towpath passes close to Christ Church, built in 1724, worth visiting for its Arts and Crafts furnishings. These include a font cover and panelling by Norman Jewson and a lectern by Peter Waals, whose factory was housed in one of the nearby mills in the 1920s. Around the church are several typical 18th- and 19th-century mill workers' cottages.

From here the towpath enters a comparatively rural stretch. Of the several mills along this reach, Iles Mill is particularly fine.

The towpath continues to Stroud (where the District Museum features local industrial history in its collections), but the best stretch ends at Brimscombe, once a busy port on the canal, with warehouses and its own merchant bank.

Charlton Abbots *see* Sevenhampton

Charlton Kings *see* Leckhampton

Music in the Three Counties

JAMES BUTTERWORTH

The very air round the vales of Severn and Wye breathes a sense of well-being. The sight of distant hills and rolling meadows is an inspiration to the artist. Housman delighted in Bredon, Elgar worked his beloved Severn and Worcester into a Suite for Brass Band, and thousands of painters and photographers have made images of the Cotswold churches, Hereford orchards and Worcester villages. It is a restful landscape; and although time has brought many changes yet, as Elgar found, there is music in the reeds.

It is not just the sophisticated and highly educated who have left their mark. In the same area that produced the Hereford Missal and the Worcester Antiphoner, we know of carols and folk songs that have just a simple line and basic rhythm.

As the Middle Ages reached their high point, the church became the main source of musical creativity. At the time when Henry III's masons were building Westminster Abbey, the monks of Worcester (or perhaps their organist) were composing the anthems that we know as the Worcester Fragments. These act as a bridge between the earlier unison singing of Gregorian chant and the polyphonic or harmonic creations that were beginning to emerge. The Fragments are a series of vellum manuscripts which were stitched into other books as strengthening. The music in them is full of rhythm and cheerfulness. *Alleluya psallat*, for instance, is a joyful dance which says that it is good to live together in community, and to praise God together. There are echoes here of the Troubadours' music; perhaps, too, there is the influence of the Grey Friars of St Francis, because we know that they reached Worcester in Henry III's reign.

There are other, gentler pieces in the collection in praise of the Virgin, such as the lullaby notes of *Beata viscera*, or the triumphant *Salve sancta parens*. Their importance, of course, lies in their use of polyphony and in the sheer genius of their composition.

It is possible that there were bands or orchestras around at this time. Sculpture in many churches and abbeys shows us angels playing all manner of instruments. Do they represent the sort of group that might have stood at a street corner, or even come into the church to accompany the service? Records do not suggest an answer, although we know that by the 16th century Prior William Moore of Worcester kept a troupe of actors and musicians.

All three cathedrals certainly employed musicians. Hereford developed a tradition of worship all its own. The Hereford Missal, which can still be seen, sets out the order both for movement and music within the service. Not only did the cathedrals have their musicians, but the abbeys, priories and convents had theirs too. Their records and service books were the casualties of the Reformation and few, if any, survive. Those that do survive present us with a picture of immense competence in the art of plainsong.

As the Reformation gained hold on England, spreading to the Three Counties, Evesham, Hailes, Malvern, Tewkesbury, Abbey Dore, Wigmore and dozens of other monasteries were closed, apparently without much sadness from the local people. In 1549, Thomas Cranmer's new English prayer book was published. From Worcester Cathedral's library comes the following record:

> On 23rd April this year was mass, matins, evensong and all other services in English. All books of divine service were brought to the Bishop and were burned.

One service book, however, did survive. It is thought that this was because it was being mended by a local bookbinder at the time. The bookbinder's family held on to their precious treasure, until in the 18th century, they returned it to the Cathedral. It is still there, and the Worcester Antiphoner is an unparallelled source of information about English monastic music. Some of it was written in the 14th century but most is from the 13th, and in three different hands. From it come chants, hymns, psalms and liturgical instructions: a precious relic of a long-departed tradition.

The church, however, was not the only source of music, even if what survives of folk music is largely religious in content. Gloucester, Hereford and Worcester are particularly fertile sources for the gatherers of carols. The great Cecil Sharp, who spent his life collecting folk songs, found many of our finest carols in the Three Counties. Admittedly, some had been collected and published in popular 18th-century broadsides or broadsheets, which provided a link with bygone days, but Sharp's work in the Three Counties provides us with many that are familiar. 'The Holly and the Ivy' was written down, both tune and words, at Chipping Campden. We can only guess as to its origin, but it does sound very much like a 'teaching aid' carol, from the days when the symbols of the Incarnation and Passion of Jesus were an important part of church teaching – blood, purity, pain and everlasting life, of which the evergreen was an obvious symbol.

> The rising of the sun and the running of the
>   deer
> The playing of the merry organ, sweet singing
>   in the choir

From the borders of Hereford and Worcester comes 'King Herod and the Cock'. It tells of the Three Kings coming to Herod and of the king's exclamation –

> 'If this be true', King Herod said, 'as thou
>   hast told to me,
> This roasted cock that lies in the dish shall
>   crow full fences three.'

Of course, the cock does so.

The Hereford Carol, which comes from Dilwyn and was one of the 18th-century broadsheet carols, probably has ancient origins. It echoes the medieval carols found in manuscripts and books of hours. The Cherry Tree Carol, which is found all over the country, is specially associated with Gloucestershire.

There are so many of these carols; two special favourites, to this day, are the beautiful Advent carol 'The Truth from above', which originates from King's Pyon in Herefordshire, and the 'Gloucestershire Wassail', which was written down at Buckland and at Little Sodbury (now in Avon). 'The Truth from above' combines the elegance of plainsong with the romance of a love song and its words, which remind us both of the Fall and Redemption of mankind, are powerful in the extreme. The 'Gloucestershire Wassail' is completely secular. (Wassail comes from Old English words meaning 'be whole' 'be in good health'.) We are told that at Over near Gloucester, in the early 19th century the wassailers would go round with their bowls, singing for their supper, and telling their listeners all about their horses and cows which they had dressed up with ribbons in honour of Christmas. The carol gives the animals' names. It is all very quaint and innocent, but it is a very close relative musically of the songs or anthems in the Worcester Fragments,

composed back in the 13th and 14th centuries.

All this music, glorious child of departed parents, gives us a clue about the kind that ordinary people performed. It survived, probably because the Three Counties, and especially Herefordshire, were so remote from the mainstream.

The Reformation brought its sadnesses, and a great deal was undoubtedly lost that would have told us much about our musical past. But the Church of England as established represented a moderate reform, and the liturgy was retained. Thomas Tallis, for instance, seems not to have had too much trouble in turning his attention from the music of The Lamentations of Jeremiah for pre-Reformation *Tenebrae* at Waltham Abbey, in Essex, to the setting of Cranmer's first prayer book.

We know that John Bull was the organist at Hereford in Elizabeth I's reign, a man whose madrigals and anthems are still sometimes performed. Bull's great contribution to music, however, was as a keyboard composer. At the same time, across the Malverns at Worcester, Nathaniel Patrick and Nathaniel Giles were writing settings of the new services that are still sung and are more than competent. It was a great period of church music, but it was a great period of secular music, too. Madrigals, glees and solo songs were being published ever more frequently. We can picture evenings spent making music in those handsome half-timbered houses of Hereford and Worcester; and perhaps around the cathedrals, then as now, sounds would come through the windows of the organist practising his choir boys and singing men in both church and secular music.

Dancing had become increasingly popular during the 16th century, and there are galliards and jigs in most of the collections of suites for keyboard and other instruments. From Worcester comes 'Worster Braules'. The English 'braule' is apparently from French *branle*, a dance that was popular throughout France and came to England in Elizabeth's reign. The music for the Worcester braule, however, was the work of no less a composer than Thomas Tomkins.

Tomkins came from a musical family. He became organist at Worcester in the early years of the 17th century. He was also one of the organists of the Chapel Royal, while retaining his position at Worcester. His compositions were collected together in volumes called *Musica Deo Sacra*, and the first printed editions are found in the cathedral library at Worcester. Tomkins also wrote instrumental music and wonderful madrigals, and was a keen amateur astronomer. It was Tomkins' tragedy to be caught up in the Civil

War; and when music in church was abolished by Parliament, he was ousted and died in 1656, having held the position of organist for 50 years. He was a great innovator and experimenter and his ideas are most prophetic, for although his early music is clearly linked to William Byrd and Orlando Gibbons, latterly he was expressing himself in concepts that were to be developed by Henry Purcell at the end of the century. He was buried somewhere in the churchyard at Martin Hussingtree, outside Worcester.

Tomkins' two brothers, John and Giles, were successively organists of King's College, Cambridge, and it must have been some satisfaction to him that his son Nathanael was appointed one of the prebendaries of Worcester. Like his father, Nathanael was ejected from his position, but returned after the Restoration and died still a prebendary, in 1681.

The 16th and 17th centuries were also the age of the Worcestershire bagpipes. We do not know how they sounded, but they probably had the gentle sound of the Northumbrian pipes rather than the Scottish skirl. There is, in fact, a carving in Worcester Cathedral of an angel with bagpipes, fitted with a mouthpiece, and two pipes, in addition to the chanter.

With the 18th century came a growth of interest in using musical gatherings to raise money for children and others in need. Charles II had already built hospitals for the pensioners of his army and navy (at the behest of Nell Gwyn, his Hereford-born mistress) and this burgeoning charitable activity is reflected in such organizations as the Corporation for the Sons of the Clergy (still going strong) and the Foundling Hospital, caring for waifs and strays. In about 1715 someone – probably one of the Gloucester canons – realized that the widows and orphans of the clergy were in need and suggested that a meeting of choirs should be held for the three cathedrals of Gloucester, Hereford and Worcester. Thus was born the oldest musical festival in the world. The meeting has continued to take place ever since, save during the two world wars, and to it we owe some of our most interesting choral music.

Dr Watkins Shaw, in *The Three Choirs Festival: A History*, tells us that a meeting was held as early as 1713 at Worcester to celebrate the Peace of Utrecht; and there is a record of a sermon, preached by Dr Bisse of Hereford in 1720, referring to previous meetings, but 1715 is usually set as the starting date. The money was to be spent on rehabilitating the widows and orphans as might seem most appropriate.

As the 18th century progressed, most of the festival programmes were given over to the numerous works of Handel and the *Messiah* became staple fare almost from the beginning. It was, in fact, sung at the end of almost every festival until about 1960. The festival attracted interest both because the musicmaking was such a rare treat and also because such an active social life buzzed around it. There were concerts in the cathedrals and assembly room, and a festival ball, while the county families provided entertainment for their friends in their town houses. A festival service (usually mattins) was held, at which one of Handel's *Te Deums* would be sung. The sermon, preached by one of the diocesan clergy, would emphasize both the beauty of the music and the needs of the charity.

Contemporary diaries and press cuttings give us the occasional glimpse of the festival. One such comes from the diary of Katherine Plymley, who attended the 1795 festival at Hereford to hear a sermon preached by her brother, Archdeacon of Salop in Hereford.

> The pulpit in the Cathedral being moveable, it was placed in front of the orchestra . . . To the credit of the performers, I remarked that their behaviour was highly decent and attentive. The band was a very good one, Lamer led it, which I thought very fortunate, as I had never heard him. I had too an opportunity of hearing three better singers than I had ever heard before . . . Miss Parke, Mr. Harrison and Mr. Barthelemon. We attended the Music Room at night and were highly entertained by a concert of ancient music.

We know that, had they remained throughout the week, Miss Plymley and her brother would also have heard the *Messiah*, Handel's Overture to *Esther*, *Blessed is he*, by William Boyce (who, incidentally, wrote one of his symphonies for Worcester and came to the festival on several occasions to direct his music), and a 'Grand Miscellaneous Concert'.

As the 19th century began, the influence of the Continent became apparent at the Festival and we find that Haydn, Beethoven and Mozart are all included in the programme. Later, Mendelssohn also became popular; his oratorio *Elijah* has had regular airings ever since. The direction of the festival then was in the hands of men nowadays unknown outside the Three Counties, but their part in keeping the festival alive should be noted: at Gloucester Clarke-Whitfield, at Worcester William Done and at Hereford George Townshend Smith. All these contributed works of their own, both to the services and to the concerts.

Where the 19th century was concerned, however, the last 30 years were the best. Samuel

Performance given in Worcester Cathedral during the Three Choirs Festival

Sebastian Wesley was organist of Gloucester in the early 1870s (having been briefly at Hereford in the 1830s) and brought his influence to bear on the Festival. At his first Gloucester Festival he included Beethoven's *Mount of Olives*, Handel's *Messiah*, Mozart's *Requiem* and Mendelssohn's *Elijah* in the Cathedral and, at the secular concerts, Beethoven's 8th Symphony, Mendelssohn's 1st Piano Concerto and selections from *The Magic Flute*.

In the same period, from 1870 to the end of the century, Purcell, Rossini, Sullivan, Stanford, Stainer and, in 1877, Bach were included. It was, in fact, due to Wesley's successor, C. H. Lloyd, that Bach's *St Matthew Passion* was given its first Three Choirs performance, and the B Minor Mass and *St John Passion* were soon to follow.

In 1878 the programme at Worcester tells us that Mr E. W. Elgar was playing among the second violins, and he appeared again in 1881, and in the great festival of 1884, when Dvořák came to conduct his *Requiem* and 6th Symphony in the Cathedral.

With the turn of the century, the situation became much more exciting. Herbert Brewer was now at Gloucester, George Robertson Sinclair was at Hereford and Elgar's great friend Ivor Atkins was at Worcester. Between them these three, and later Herbert Sumsion and Percy Hull, gave the Three Choirs immense prestige, and attracted some fine music to the festivals of the early 20th century. Herbert Brewer was a fine teacher, and was the mentor of his successor Herbert Sumsion, and of Herbert Howells and Ivor Gurney.

Sir Hubert Parry, a Gloucestershire man who lived at Highnam Court, was often seen at the festival of the late 19th and early 20th centuries. To Parry we owe many important works, now mostly forgotten, but his tune to 'Jerusalem' and his short choral work *Blest Pair of Sirens* show his quality as a composer. He appeared as conductor at many festivals, for the last time on the podium at 1912 in Hereford, by which time, the baton had passed to Elgar (*see below*).

The character of the Three Choirs has changed over the years, and although many works are given their first (and only) performances at the festival, many are heard again and again. Vaughan Williams, who was born in Down Ampney in Gloucestershire, the son of the parson, brought many of his pieces to the festival and conducted them. His *Tallis Fantasia* was first performed at Gloucester in 1910, for example. The very success of his work, albeit now somewhat in eclipse, must partly be due to the immense encouragement the festival conductors gave him.

Ivor Atkins at Worcester encouraged the performance of Bach, and his great scholarship enabled audiences to hear fine editions of the *St Matthew Passion* and B Minor Mass. Atkins was also an excellent editor of early music. He produced editions of Orlando de Lassus and Palestrina that are still admired.

Dr Sumsion, who organized the Gloucester Festivals from 1928 until 1965, was responsible for the encouragement of contemporary European composers, notably the Hungarian Zoltán Kodály.

In our own times, the festival recognizes that it needs to bring itself into the mainstream of British musicmaking, and the commissioning of new work has been significant. In the last 20 or so years, audiences have heard challenging new pieces by Richard Rodney Bennett, Howard Blake, Paul Patterson, Gordon Crosse and John McCabe, and have listened to concerts conducted by the most illustrious of our contemporary conductors, as well as to the Cathedral organists themselves. These all stand in a great tradition and the present festival seems healthy enough, as long as the generous sponsorship of industry and commerce continues.

Edward Elgar

'I am still, at heart, the dreamy child who used to be found in the reeds by Severnside with a sheet of paper, trying to fix the sounds.'

So Edward Elgar once wrote to a friend and the rivers he knew and loved were a great influence throughout his life. On another occasion he instructed an orchestra rehearsing his first symphony to 'play it like something you hear down by the river'; and as he lay dying, in his Worcester house overlooking the cathedral he said, 'I lie here hour after hour, thinking of our beloved Teme, surely the most beautiful river that ever was.' Nor were his feelings only for the rivers. While in exile from Worcestershire, he instructed his friend Atkins to go out on to the terrace by the Cathedral, 'and bless my beloved country for me'.

It is impossible – and ultimately foolish – to try to analyse the reasons for Elgar's ability to compass the character of the Three Counties in his work. Suffice it to say that the character is there, perhaps above all in the slow movement of the 1st Symphony or the reflective sections of the *Serenade for Strings*; and his creative spark was never brighter than when he went cycling down the lanes of Worcestershire and Herefordshire, breathing in the spirit of countryside. The inspiration for *The Apostles* seems to have come to him at Longdon Marsh, and the friends from his days in Worcester are portrayed musically in *The Enigma Variations*.

Edward William Elgar was born in 1857 at Lower Broadheath, in the cottage that is now his museum. He was the son of Roman Catholic parents, his father being the organist of St George's Catholic church in Worcester. The family kept a music shop in Worcester High Street. He had no formal musical education, marvelling in later life to his friend W. R. Reed, 'I say, Billy, they tell me I've written double counterpoint.'

In the later years of the 19th century Elgar earned his living teaching the unwilling daughters of the gentlefolk of Malvern and Worcester to play the fiddle or the piano; and he was director of the band of the county asylum at Powick, for which he wrote a number of pieces.

Elgar married Caroline Alice Roberts, the daughter of a major-general. Her parents totally disapproved of her marriage 'into trade' and, worse still, to a Roman Catholic, and more or less

Edward Elgar's desk at Lower Broadheath (see page 175) where the great English composer was born

ostracized her. She, however, believed in her husband implicitly, inspiring him and encouraging him throughout his life.

By 1899, inspiration had really come to him and it was over the next 20 years that he composed his greatest works: *Enigma Variations*, *Dream of Gerontius*, *The Kingdom* and *The Apostles*, the two symphonies, the *Introduction and Allegro and Serenade for Strings*, the concertos for violin and cello and the chamber works. With these

Mordiford Bridge, which was said to inspire Elgar, and the manuscript of the opening of The Music Makers

went the *Pomp and Circumstance Marches* Nos 1 to 5 and many other smaller pieces.

His beloved Alice died in 1919 and he said, 'I have gone out'. Indeed, he never wrote anything of significance again.

As he lay dying in 1934, he supervised the recording of his works, 'by the ingenious device of a telephone'; and from these and many recordings which he conducted himself we can gauge the interpretative genius of a man whose composition was of such significance in this country and in Europe as a whole.

Yet the mystery remains. How was it that he could capture the feel, the character, the atmosphere of his 'beloved country' so eloquently? Perhaps the answer is in the gentleness of some passages, or in the spiritual struggle of moments like the slow movement of the cello concerto, wrestling with the confusion of living and dying, and the uncertainty of all things around us. Perhaps it is best that it should remain a mystery. Of his conducting his godson, Wulstan Atkins, says: 'It was as though he somehow hypnotized you . . . you sang better than you knew you could sing.'

Neville Cardus, typically, summarized it in 1924: 'The very walls of Worcester cry out to us from the same romantic past that has bred his music . . .' Perhaps part of the solution lies there.

One more question remains to be asked. Why should it be that some of the most significant of England's composers in the last hundred years or so should have come from the Three Counties? Parry, Elgar, Vaughan Williams, Holst, Howells, Julius Harrison, Herbert Sumsion, Ivor Gurney – the list is impressive indeed.

Worcester also gave birth to another great artist and natural musician – Vesta Tilley. She delighted the audiences of Victorian and Edwardian music halls with 'Burlington Bertie' and 'Following in Father's Footsteps'. A natural in every particular, she was graced with the gift of perfect pitch. It is good that the New Concert Hall in Worcester's Lowesmoor in now called The Vesta Tilley Centre, for here was one of her earliest triumphs.

There are festivals galore in Hereford and Worcester and in Gloucestershire. The Cheltenham International Festival began in the early 1950s as a festival of contemporary music and literature and now provides orchestral, chamber and operatic music. At different times of year, you may find enterprising activity in festivals at Bromsgrove, Stroud, Harvington, Madley and many another town or village. In addition almost every town has either a concert club or choral society and the success of both regular music-making and festivals is experienced in places like Malvern every year.

Perhaps it must remain a mystery that in this small section of England so much music is either in the air or the soil. Whatever it is, the very sense of well-being that a sunny day around the Malverns or in the lanes of a Cotswold village can produce seems also to stimulate music, and has done since time immemorial; and certainly there is no reason why it should not continue to do so.

Chedworth (4/3D)

The evidence of the fine Roman villa just north of Chedworth village suggests that the Cotswolds found favour with the prosperous as early as the mid-2nd century AD. This was just one of the many substantial villas belonging to estate owners in the region. Indeed, from the lanes around this village just west of the Foss Way (A429) and 5 miles north of CIRENCESTER, it is sometimes possible to see the legacy of other villas in crop marks, or as bumps in the pasture along the valley of the infant Coln.

This villa lies in a sheltered combe with excellent views. It was a grand house, with all the luxuries: a garden colonnade, mosaic-floored baths and dining rooms with underfloor heating.

In the north-west corner of the site is a *nymphaeum* whose octagonal tank, capable of holding over 1000 gallons of spring water, supplied the villa. A chi-rho symbol now in the villa museum was found on the rim of the tank, suggesting that the villa's 5th-century owners may have been Christian converts. Excavations continuing on the site are concentrating on the later history of the villa, the domestic out-buildings and the estate workers' accommodation. The villa, museum and interpretation centre, which belong to the National Trust, are open most of the year.

It is possible to walk from the villa to the village through Chedworth Woods, along the course of a former railway. St Andrew's church is a fine example of a simple Norman structure enriched with wool money in the 15th century. Arabic numerals included in dates carved in the nave walls illustrate the international scope of the Cotswold wool trade: Roman numerals were still the norm in 15th-century England.

There is a portrait of Elizabeth of York among the corbel heads that support the Perpendicular nave roof and, in the village, the name of Queen Street is a reminder of her visit, which may have been in 1491. Another 15th-century treasure is the beautiful stone carved pulpit, very similar to that at nearby NORTH CERNEY.

At Denfurlong Farm, between the village and the A429, a farm trail, open all year round, enables visitors to see a modern dairy and arable farm at work from close quarters.

Further north-east along the A429 is the entrance to Stowell Park. The 'Strictly Private' notice refers to the house, not the church. (The Stowell Park gardens open from time to time under the National Gardens Scheme.) The cruciform Norman church of St Leonard is well worth visiting since the wall paintings are among the most important in the country.

It takes time for the eye to adjust to the low light, but with patience much of the detail of the late 12th-century Doom painting on the north nave wall can be discerned.

There is no village at Stowell any more, and **Yanworth** (4/3D) to the north-west consists of little but estate cottages. At its western end, sheltered by handsome farm buildings, is the late 12th-century church of St Michael; inside is a 16th-century wall painting of Time, depicted as a skeleton wielding a scythe.

Cheltenham (4/2C)

In many towns, pigeons are considered a pest for the damage they cause to buildings, but in Cheltenham they are honoured on the town's coat of arms. For, in the summer of 1716, a flock of pigeons seen pecking at salt grains in a meadow outside the town (where Cheltenham Ladies College now stands) led to the discovery of the mineral waters that were to make Cheltenham a prosperous spa.

Despite the enterprise of Henry Skillicorne, son-in-law of the meadow's owner, it took several decades to establish the spa's reputation; in 1779, Cheltenham was still only a small market town with a single street lined by brick houses. Not until George III's visit in 1788 did high society adopt Cheltenham as a summer resort and speculative investment begin.

Over the following three decades, the population multiplied sevenfold, the commons were enclosed to provide building land and £5 million was invested in new developments.

Joseph Pitt, Rector and MP, laid out the suburb of Pittville with its fine Pump Room (built 1825–30), modelled on the temple of Ilissus at Athens. The waters can still be taken there. It now houses a museum with a Gallery of Fashion and is used for concerts during the Cheltenham Festival. The early Victorian Pittville Park is a good example of a town park (*see* 'Gloucestershire Gardens', p. 77).

Despite the number of architects and builders involved, Cheltenham's architecture has a remarkable unity. This has much to do with the speed with which the place was developed, so that many of the public buildings and terraces of town houses were put up during the short period when neo-Grecian architecture was fashionable.

Opposite: The Pittville Pump Room in Cheltenham, modelled on the Greek temple of Ilissus

Stone from the LECKHAMPTON quarries was used to dress the fronts of houses, but brick was preferred for the sides and backs as being faster to lay. To decorate the plain façades, cast-iron verandas and balconies (cheaper than wrought iron) were chosen from standard pattern books.

Despite this emphasis on speed and economy the result was, and remains, a fine town in which elegant houses line broad, tree-lined avenues. It quickly became popular with retired army officers and colonial civil servants, of whom William Cobbett was typically contemptuous. 'Cheltenham,' he wrote, 'is a place to which East India plunderers, West India floggers, English tax gorgers together with gluttons, drunkards and debauchees [resort in the hope of] getting rid of the bodily consequences of their manifold sins and iniquities.'

That may have been true of some of the inhabitants; but there was a reaction and Cheltenham became a stronghold of Evangelicalism, whose enduring legacy was to be several schools, for example Cheltenham College, Dean Close School, and Cheltenham Ladies College, and numerous churches, like All Saints, Pittville (by John Henry Middleton, 1868), a sumptuous Gothic expression of the Victorian religious revival.

The parish church of St Mary, hidden peacefully between two of Cheltenham's busiest shopping streets, is one of the few surviving pre-Regency buildings. It is essentially a 14th-century rebuilding of a Norman cruciform church, with a fine rose window.

The Museum and Art Gallery has sections devoted to local archaeology, and the Arts and Crafts movement.

For the horse-racing fraternity, Cheltenham is synonymous with the Gold Cup and Champion Hurdle, the premier events of the National Hunt calendar held in March (*see* Prestbury). Then, hundreds of horse owners, trainers, jockeys, tipsters, turf accountants and punters fill the hotels, lending the town a unique and festive atmosphere.

Cheltenham, with its style and elegance, makes an ideal setting for the literary, music and, indeed, cricket festivals held there every year.

For the rest of the year, Cheltenham's mixture of smart shops and couturier's establishments, antique and second-hand bookshops and good restaurants are an important part of the town's appeal. To the traditional shopping malls of Montpellier and the Promenade, a new attraction has been added, the extravagant Regency Arcade, notable for Kit William's entrancing clock: visit on the hour to watch the duck that lays a golden egg and the giant fish that lazily blows bubbles over the heads of onlookers.

Cherington *see* Avening

Chipping Campden (4/4B)

Approaching from the north-west, along the B4035, the visitor first sees the dramatic ruins of Sir Baptist Hicks' Campden Manor, begun around 1613 and deliberately burned at the end of the Civil War to prevent it falling into the hands of the Parliamentarians. All that remain are the gatehouses, with two garden pavilions and the almonry: illustrations of Jacobean architectural inventiveness at the edge of a town that otherwise displays Cotswolds vernacular at its best. Hicks was one of several wealthy merchants whose gifts did so much to mould the character of this most splendid of Cotswold market towns.

In the 12th century Campden was already a brisk and busy town on the ancient White Way, linking CIRENCESTER and Stratford-upon-Avon. By 1247 it was recorded as having a weekly market ('Chipping' comes from an Old English word meaning market), and was a centre where England's then chief export, wool, was collected and dispatched, much of it destined for the Flemish weaving industry. Despite high taxation, middlemen like William Grevel, described on his brass in the church as 'the flower of the wool merchants of all England', were able to amass comfortable fortunes. He built Grevel House in the High Street around 1380, choosing the new Perpendicular style for his two-storeyed and traceried bay window, but retaining Gothic pointed arches for the doors.

Work began on the church of St James around 1450. It then took 50 years to complete, but the very consistency makes it difficult to tell precisely where work stopped and started again, since the masons (who may also have been responsible for the church at NORTHLEACH) remained true to the original conception.

As a result, the church is strikingly harmonious. Slender columns support the lofty roof, leaving ample space to be filled with light from the large clerestory windows.

Contemporary with the church is the collection of richly embroidered altar frontals and vestments preserved behind glass. The churchyard path leads directly to the remains of Hicks' manor.

The almshouses near the manor gateway exemplify the traditional architectural style of the Cotswolds. They form an 'I' in plan, honouring James I, and were built in 1612 by Hicks. He also donated the fine Market Hall in the High Street in 1627.

The houses that line Chipping Campden's High Street exhibit virtually every variation on the theme of Cotswolds vernacular from the 14th century to the revival of the 19th and 20th centuries. There are triangular gables; mullioned and transomed windows, shielded by drip moulds; and here and there a Regency building in Classical style breaks the pattern – but all is unified by the golden-coloured stone.

The well-preserved state of Chipping Campden owes much to the Campden Trust, established by architects and craftsmen, including Norman Jewson and F. L. Griggs, in 1929. The trust has restored numerous properties.

Before the formation of the Trust, Campden was already established as a centre for the applied arts, following C. R. Ashbee's decision to move his Guild of Handicrafts here from London in 1902. Ashbee was a socialist in the William Morris mould, abhoring work that made men and women mere adjuncts to machines. Workshops were set up in the old silk mill in Sheep Street; descendants of George Hart, the silversmith, still produce hand-crafted silverware here.

The Ashbees themselves lived for a while at Norman Chapel House, Broad Campden (gardens occasionally open under the National Gardens Scheme). This was, when Ashbee found it, a partly ruined chapel with a 12th-century nave.

Dover's Hill, a mile east of the town, is the setting for the 'Cotswold Olympicks', so called by the eccentric Robert Dover (1582–1652) who founded them in 1612. The games, whose events include a shin-kicking contest, continued uninterrupted, except during the Civil War, and were patronized by royalty until 1852, when the rowdy behaviour of 'armed bands of beer-swilling Birmingham yahoos' got them prohibited. They were started again in 1951 and are played every Whitsun Bank Holiday, followed by a torchlight procession into town and by the Scuttlebrook Wake Fair the following day.

For the rest of the year this spectacular amphitheatre on the Cotswold scarp is worth visiting for its splendid panorama of the Vale of Evesham. The hill now belongs to the National Trust, thanks to the efforts of local people and F. L. Griggs of the Campden Trust, who in the 1920s successfully fought plans for a private hotel development.

The inhabitants of **Ebrington** (4/4A), 2 miles north-east of Chipping Campden, were said to be so envious of their neighbours' church tower that they manured their own in an attempt to make it grow as tall and fine:

> Master Kyte, a man of great power,
> Lent 'em a cart to muck the tower
> And when the muck began to sink
> They swore the tower had grown an inch.

The real subject of this satirical rhyme is not known, but several Kytes are buried in the Norman church of St Eadburga and one of them, Sir William (d. 1632), left money to set up a 'Cow Charity': 'Ten Good Milch Kine' (milk cows) were to be distributed annually to the parish poor. The church's most lavish monument is that to Sir John Fortescue (d. 1476), Lord Chief Justice. The less conspicuous monument to Charles Edward Hornby (d. 1918) has lettering by Eric Gill.

Churcham see Highnam

Churchdown (4/1D)

Lying just to the north-east of GLOUCESTER, by the A40, Churchdown has been somewhat swallowed up by that city. However, the ancient village church of St Bartholomew stands high up on Chosen Hill, a Cotswold outlier, aloof from the suburban sprawl. Until recently the only way up there was by a steep footpath, along which coffins were hauled by sled in winter. The earliest parts of the church are Norman and the

Priest's Room in St Bartholomew's, Churchdown

external walls are dotted with fragments of carved stone, perhaps from the original chancel arch. The three-storey 13th-century porch has pre-Reformation graffiti and a room with a fireplace on the first floor, used by priests who served the parish from St Oswald's Priory, Gloucester.

Cinderford (3/3D)

So named because of the local abundance of iron and coal slag, this town on the A4151 was long the centre of the FOREST OF DEAN's coal-mining industry which, at its peak in the late 19th century, produced over 1 million tons a year. A tramway was opened in 1809 to carry coal to Bullo (*see* Newnham) on the Severn, much of it to be barged up the Stroudwater and **Thames and Severn Canals**, and so to the River Thames and beyond. This, and much else to do with the life and industry of the Forest, is explained at the Dean Heritage Centre at **Soudley**, 2 miles south of Cinderfold. This splendid museum is housed in the restored 19th-century Camp Mill and the complex includes a reconstructed Forester's cottage and drift mine, a working smallholding, and displays on the history and management of the surrounding woodlands. Throughout summer there are demonstrations of forest crafts and charcoal making.

Cirencester (4/3E)

The Romans laid out a new capital here in the second half of the 1st century AD from which to administer the wealthy territory of their Belgic allies, the Dobunni (*see* Bagendon), and called it Corinium Dobunnorum.

The Romans were over-ambitious and the town never filled the 240 acres allotted to it, which they enclosed with an earth rampart. Stretches of the stone wall that succeeded the rampart can be seen in the Abbey Grounds, and another well-preserved relic of Roman occupation is the 2nd-century amphitheatre and quarry off Cotswold Avenue.

These are the scant visible remains of the second largest city in Roman Britain; however, the excellent Corinium Museum in Park Street fills in the rest of the picture. The museum shows that Corinium was an important centre of mosaic production, with inventive local craftsmen as accomplished at representing classical subjects and exotic lions and tigers (see the Orpheus mosaic) as they were at depicting local wildlife (the Hare mosaic).

Cirencester was an important town in the 6th century, for the Anglo-Saxon Chronicle names it as one of the places captured by the West Saxons after the battle of Dyrham in AD 577. Half a century later, however, it fell to the Anglian kingdom of Mercia. Churches from the Anglo-Saxon period survive in some numbers around Cirencester (for example at BIBURY, Coln Rogers (*see* Colns, The), and the AMPNEYS).

Cirencester's own large Saxon church did not long survive the Norman Conquest. It was demolished to make way for a new abbey, begun in 1117. At the same time, a new parish church was begun on the site of the present one, so that 12th-century Cirencester had two splendid Romanesque churches side by side.

The Abbey was in turn largely destroyed in 1539 with the Dissolution of the Monasteries. The little that can today be seen of the Abbey consists of the nave of the 12th-century chapel of the Hospital of St John, Spitalgate Lane, and the Spital Gate (*c.*1180), Grove Lane. The Abbey Grounds are now an attractive public park with a lake and an ancient mulberry tree. A fine barn and dovecot at Barton, on the western outskirts of Cirencester, remain from one of the Abbey's farms.

Little has survived of the 12th-century parish church, though in its place we have one of the Cotswolds' finest, and certainly the largest, 'wool churches'. There is a fine view of it from the small churchyard to the east, entered by a little-used alley that runs from the porch and behind the Market Place shops. From here it is possible to see how the church of St John the Baptist grew to its present size by the accretion of the several large chapels clustered around the Tudor nave, all crowned by the richly embellished 15th-century tower.

This tower was built with funds from certain property of the Earls of Kent and Salisbury, which Henry IV granted the townspeople in gratitude for their help – they had in fact executed the rebel noblemen.

Once the tower was completed, chapels were added, beginning with the Garstang chantry. Then came the Trinity chapel and the beautiful St Catharine's chapel, begun in 1460; the stone fan vault, one of the treasures of the church, was added later, in 1508. The gracious fan-vaulted south porch, so large that it almost obscures the nave from view, was added in 1490. Finally, the 13th-century nave was demolished and the new nave built between 1516 and 1530. The church is satisfying not only for its wealth of fine architecture, but also for its numerous monu-

Market day in Cirencester

ments, the precious 1535 Anne Boleyn cup, the lovely wine-glass pulpit, the vestments and the stained glass.

To get a view of Cirencester Park the 132 ft church tower has to be climbed. It has truly been said of the builder of the house, Allen, first Earl Bathurst, that his interests were more horticultural than architectural. Certainly the house, built in 1714–18, is very plain: its glory is the 30,000-acre park (open to the public throughout the year). Bathurst planned the landscaping himself with the help of his friend Alexander Pope (*see* 'Gloucestershire Gardens', p. 77).

From May to September there is a programme of polo matches at the Park.

Cirencester Park was previously a manorial estate, which effectively blocked the western spread of the medieval town. The best of the surviving buildings are squeezed in between it and the Abbey: Dollar Street, Thomas Street, Coxwell Street and Cecily Hill are all well worth exploring for their predominantly 17th- and 18th-century wool merchants' houses.

The Market Place has a mixture of Georgian façades fronting older buildings, painted in pastel blues, pinks and greens, and Victorian replacements. Some, like the Corn Hall (1862), are more pleasing than others.

Cirencester is an excellent, and interesting, town for shopping: a former England Test cricketer runs a first-class fish and game shop at the corner of the Market Place and, in nearby Black Jack Street, the butcher is worth a visit for the art nouveau tiles there. Friday is the main market day, with stallholders selling all manner of produce and wares. The Women's Institute sells its home-made cakes and preserves in its own market hall in Dyer Street. Off Cricklade Street, the former brewery has been converted into the Cirencester Workshops, where craftsmen both work and sell their products.

Siddington (4/3F) lies west of the River Churn. It is already virtually joined to Cirencester by a 1950s housing estate. St Peter's church has an outstanding south door, decorated with Norman beak heads and comparable to the one at ELKSTONE. The tympanum is carved with Christ in Majesty, and the chancel arch hood moulds terminate in dragon heads. The Langley Chapel once held the stained glass now in Cirencester parish church.

Alongside the church is a dignified barn, thought to have been built by the Knights Hospitallers who owned the manor, and so probably of the 13th century. It has so far survived several applications to demolish it.

Baunton (4/3E) lies 1½ miles north along the Churn valley. Immediately on entering the church of St Mary Magdalene, visitors are faced by a huge 14th-century wall painting of St Christopher. Sadly, it has deteriorated in recent years, but the detail is still remarkably vivid.

Fabulous fish swim at the saint's feet, a ship rides at anchor in the lower right-hand corner, while on one bank is a fisherman and on the other a hermit with a lantern by a church. Running across the top is a landscape of windmills and towers.

The west of Cirencester has, so far, largely escaped development, and on this side of the town, open farmland reaches to within less than a mile of the Market Place. Just off the A419 STROUD road is the renowned Royal Agricultural College, founded in 1845 and the first ever institution devoted to the teaching of the agricultural sciences. The splendid neo-Tudor buildings (not open to the public) were begun in 1846. Built around a quadrangle, they have all the atmosphere of an Oxford or Cambridge college. Recent extensions, built in Cotswolds vernacular style and out of specially quarried stone and roof tiles, have been widely praised by, among others, Prince Charles.

Clapton-on-the-Hill see Bourton-on-the-Water

Clearwell see Coleford

Cleeve Hill (4/2C)

Just to the east of CHELTENHAM the Cotswolds reach their highest point at West Down, above Cleeve Hill parish, 1083 ft above sea level. Around the summit are several deep troughs: one particularly striking group can be seen on the spur above Postlip. They have been variously explained as ancient earthworks and (by pre-Darwinian geologists) as erosion caused by sea waves dashing against the Cotswold scarp in the time of Noah's Flood. In fact they are caused by the slippage of the scarp face as the underlying oolitic limestone is undermined by water percolating through joints and fissures in the rock. Cleeve Common is a Site of Special Scientific Interest, noted for its undisturbed limestone habitat which supports numerous lime-loving plants, such as harebells, gorse and rarer musk, frog and bee orchids.

The area, which offers rock climbs as well as splendid views, is crossed by the Cotswold Way and is also of archaeological interest, with an Iron Age hillfort at Cleeve Cloud.

Postlip is north-east of Cleeve Hill and best approached from the golf course on the common for the best views of the Jacobean Postlip Hall and 15th-century cruck-built tithe barn, sheltering together in the valley of the young River Isbourne. The grounds of the Hall, and the well-preserved tithe barn, are occasionally open to the public. Near by there is a tiny Norman chapel now used as a Catholic church.

Coates (4/2E)

Those who enjoy walking can approach the village along a footpath (not signposted) that begins about 1½ miles to the east in the grounds of the Royal Agricultural College, CIRENCESTER. This turns into a green lane near the village. The delightful Norman church of St Matthew is set a little apart from the village, to the west, where it forms a charming group with the handsome 17th-century former manor house and Church Farm. The church acquired its fine Perpendicular tower in the mid-14th century. The carved date on the west buttress, 1733, refers to the later restoration. High up on the south-west angle is an anthropophagus, a mythical cannibal, in the process of swallowing a victim.

A footpath from the church leads to the eastern portal of the **Thames and Severn Canal** tunnel and the Tunnel House Inn. Built originally for the navvies working on the tunnel, the Inn later served the 'leggers' who propelled barges through the tunnel by lying on their backs and 'walking' along the tunnel roof.

Entrance to the Thames and Severn Canal tunnel

From here it is possible to follow the towpath for 1½ miles to the point where the canal passes within yards of the source of the River Thames, at **Thames Head**. This spot was marked by a fine statue of Neptune, but because of frequent vandalism it was moved in recent years to a less isolated spot near LECHLADE. Perhaps in 1992, when the newly designated Thames Long Distance Footpath officially opens, the birthplace of England's great and historic river will once again be marked by an appropriate monument.

Tarlton (4/2F) is a small farming hamlet on the downs south-west of Coates, in which several solid barns stand close to the Norman church, rebuilt in 1875. More good barns line the road to **Rodmarton** (4/2F). Here the 13th- and 14th-century church of St Peter contains a small brass to John Edward (d.1461), portrayed in his lawyer's cap and gown.

The gardens of Rodmarton Manor are occasionally open under the National Gardens Scheme, but, regrettably, not the house itself. This was built by the Arts and Crafts architect Ernest Barnsley (*see* Sapperton) between 1909 and 1926, for the Hon. Claud Biddulph. It has been hailed as England's last great country house and was built in the Cotswold vernacular tradition and furnished by local craftsmen. Mrs Biddulph was responsible for the lovely garden (*see* 'Gloucestershire Gardens', p. 77), which affords glimpses of the house.

Coberley (4/2D)

A couple of miles south of CHELTENHAM, by the side of the A436 and close to its intersection with the A435, Seven Springs marks the source of the River Churn, the longest tributary of the Thames. Local people unsuccessfully petitioned Parliament in 1937 for this to be recognized as the true source of the Thames in preference to Thames Head (*see* Coates). Regardless of the merits of the argument, the Churn valley is undoubtedly prettier than the upper reaches of the Thames, and contributes greatly to the charm of the village of Coberley.

The church of St Giles is approached through the arched gateway and private gardens of a farmhouse. A heart buried in the sanctuary is presumed to be that of Sir Giles de Berkeley (d.1295). His son, Sir Thomas, is credited with rebuilding the church around 1340. When he died his young widow, Joan, married Sir William Whittington (of Pauntley: *see* Redmarley D'Abitot) and bore a famous son – Dick Whittington.

The Churn flows on due south to **Cowley** (4/2D), where it has been dammed to create an adventure playground for local schoolchildren who camp in summer beside the County Council-owned Manor. From the Manor itself, rebuilt in 1855 in the Italian style, a series of stone terraces with ballustrades, tanks and cascades descends the hillside to a small lake teeming with ornamental fish.

The house was bought and enlarged in 1858 by Sir James Horlick, co-inventor, with his brother, of the famous beverage. St Mary's church in the Manor grounds is of *c*.1200 with a 14th-century wagon roof and 15th-century porch.

The fact that Lewis Carroll enjoyed walking along the banks of the Churn while staying with Alice Liddell's uncle (who was rector of Cowley) has led to speculation that the local scenery inspired passages in *Alice in Wonderland*. Certainly the narrow lane behind **Colesbourne** (4/2D) resembles a leafy tunnel in summer when the towering trees on top of the high banks meet overhead. There is an abundance of wood anemones and wild strawberries here in season.

The church of St James, tucked away down a lane off the A435, has a fine Perpendicular tower but its greatest treasure is the 15th-century stone wine-glass pulpit on a fluted stem. The church overlooks lakes and plantations full of rare trees. These were planted by Henry John Elwes (1846–1922), the traveller and botanist.

Cold Aston *see* Notgrove (Aston Blank)

Coleford (3/2D)

This market town in the FOREST OF DEAN has an industrial history of national distinction. Its name means 'charcoal ford', and the fuel was indeed produced here in great quantity. It was used for smelting iron ore from the Iron Age to the end of the 18th century, when coke-fuelled blast furnaces were invented. Commercial production of charcoal continued on a smaller scale until 1947, and the Christchurch Forest Trail, north of Coleford, passes by several charred platforms where charcoal burners once lit their fires (there are demonstrations of charcoal production during the summer months at the Dean Heritage Centre, CINDERFORD).

Coleford itself is plain and businesslike. The fiercely independent Free Miners were Nonconformist in denomination, if religious at all, and the town's most prominent buildings are all chapels, notably the Baptist Chapel (1858) with its neo-Romanesque façade. Anglicanism is represented by the 1880 church of St John, and the tower of the former parish church built in 1821 by Henry Poole. The octagonal nave of this church was demolished in 1882, but a visit to Poole's 1822 church of St Paul at **Parkend** (3/3E), 3 miles to the south-east, will show what it looked like. This Regency church is cruciform with its four arms meeting in an octagonal nave. Pretty cast-iron handrail and balusters decorate galleries in the transepts and west end.

Back in Coleford, Forest House, on Cinder Hill, was the home of the pioneering metallurgist David Mushet (1772–1847) and his son Robert Forrester Mushet (1811–91). Robert made critical improvements to Henry Bessemer's method of producing steel. Coleford is ringed by the relics of furnaces. One of the earliest surviving examples is the Whitecliff Furnace, a ½ mile south-west of the town and recently restored.

Just north of Whitecliff is a hamlet called Scowles – the local name for surface mines and quarries. The settlement is one of the oldest in the Forest of Dean, and the deep passageways and crevices in the adjoining wood may be pre-Roman in origin. Another extensive area of scowles has been opened to the public at Puzzle Wood, **Milkwall** (3/2E), on the B4228 south of Coleford. Here, in dense woods, paths wind in and out of old mine workings between fern-covered rocks and bare tree roots.

From Milkwall it is less than a mile to the cave system and underground mines at **Clearwell** (3/2E) Caves (open March to October). Prehistoric miners found a ready source of iron ore here. More recently the caves have been used to get at rich lodes below the ground and the system was extended to cover some 600 acres.

The church of St Peter in Clearwell, built in 1866, uses local blue lias and red sandstone, combined with white Bath stone, to create an exuberant polychromatic nave; the sanctuary is even more colourful in its blend of marbles and serpentine. Clearwell Castle, currently under restoration, was built around 1727 in the Gothick style, of which it is thus a very early example – albeit damaged and rebuilt.

Staunton (3/2D) lies 2 miles north-west of Coleford. The Norman and Early English church of All Saints is one of the oldest in the Forest; a noteworthy feature is the pulpit of around 1500, projecting from the belfry stair turret. One of the two fonts is early Norman, cubical, and thought to have been carved from a Roman altar.

A path opposite the church leads to the Buck Stone. This huge lump of conglomerate once stood on a natural pedestal and would rock gently in the wind. Vandals pushed it off its slender support in 1855 and so, following restoration with concrete and metal pins, the rock sways no more. Inevitably the stone has attracted tales of magic powers and Druidic ritual, as have several other nearby megaliths.

Colesbourne *see* Coberley

Colns, The (4/3 D&E)

The Coln valley is one of the most rewarding corners of the Cotswolds, only properly appreciated by those who walk from village to village along the banks of the unpolluted river. All possible pleasures are to be found along the route: abundant flora and birdlife; hills and woodland that look as if they were designed by an artist of supreme talent, expressly to give pleasure; ancient churches nestling in their own wooded hollows; and the varied architecture of humble cottages and grander mansions.

The first of the villages (they are taken in order downstream) that derive their name from the gentle, clear-flowing River Coln is reached by turning east off the A429 at Fossebridge, about 8 miles north-east of CIRENCESTER. **Coln St Dennis** (4/3D) is named after the church in Paris to whom the land was granted in 1060 by Edward the Confessor. The simple Norman church of St James, consisting of nave, central tower and chancel, lying low in a watermeadow, survives intact but for an unwise 15th-century addition to the tower, which has caused the buttressed walls to bulge.

Coln Rogers (4/3E), originally Coln St Andrew, was renamed in the 12th century after Roger de Gloucester who, grievously wounded in battle, gave the living to GLOUCESTER Abbey 'for the good of his soul'. Although less grand, the church of St Andrew ranks with BIBURY and DEERHURST as one of Gloucestershire's best-preserved Saxon buildings. Long-and-short work in the quoins, tiny round-headed windows, and the round-headed chancel arch are all typical of Saxon church architecture on the eve of the Norman Conquest.

Coln St Aldwyns (4/4E) is separated by some 4 miles from Coln Rogers. In between lie Winson and Ablington (for both *see* Ablington) and Bibury.

Coln St Aldwyns, named after St Ealdwine, is unmistakably an estate village. Sir Michael Hicks Beach (1837–1916) restored the 16th-century Manor House, with its barn and dovecot,

Barbara de Mauley's tomb in Hatherop church

in 1896 when he was Chancellor of the Exchequer. It stands next to the church of St John the Baptist, which retains a few Norman features. John Keble was vicar here from 1782 to 1835, and his more famous son was curate from 1825 to 1835, serving the parish from their home at FAIRFORD.

Williamstrip Park, to the east, was a considerably larger estate than that of Hicks Beach, covering most of the land between Coln St Aldwyns and **Hatherop** (4/4E). At the centre of the estate the Jacobean-style Hatherop Castle (now a girls' school) and the church of St Nicholas were built in the 1850s by Henry Clutton, with William Burges, for Lord de Mauley. The church, in French Gothic style, has some fine, vigorous carving. The mortuary chapel is especially rich, with a frieze of castles, leaves, flowers, and repeated B's for Barbara, Lady de Mauley.

Quenington (4/4E) lies south of Coln St Aldwyns on the Fairford road. The manor was given to the Knights Hospitallers of the Order of St John around 1193 to help fund their crusades. Quenington Court now stands on the site of their commandery, remains of which include a 13th-century gatehouse.

The presence of the Knights may well explain the richness of the carving in the 12th-century church of St Swithin, next to the Court. The tympanum of the north doorway illustrates the Harrowing of Hell.

The south doorway has beak heads that include homely portraits of an ox and of a horse. The tympanum represents the Coronation of the Virgin, with Christ seated by her side, with the emblems of the Evangelists and seraphim, close to a domed temple that might represent the Heavenly Mansions.

Compton Abdale *see* Withington

Condicote *see* Longborough

Cooper's Hill *see* Brockworth

Corse *see* Redmarley D'Abitot

Cotswold Park Farm *see* Guitings, The

Cotswold Way, The
Conceived in the 1950s, but not realized until 1970 as one of Britain's initiatives for European Conservation Year, the Cotswold Way runs for 100 miles from Bath to CHIPPING CAMPDEN. For much of its route it follows the high and unbroken edge of the Cotswold scarp, with westward views of the Vales of Severn, Gloucester, and Evesham.

Many prefer to walk the route from south to north, keeping the prevailing wind behind them. The Way is marked (footpaths for walkers with yellow arrows, bridleways with blue), and maintained by the Cotswold Voluntary Warden Service and the Ramblers' Association. Guides to the Cotswold Way are available at most bookshops, and all the important sites are described in this gazetteer. Allow 10 days to walk the route from end to end, although the historical and environmental landmarks are so numerous that it is tempting to linger a lot longer.

Cowley *see* Coberley

Cranham (4/1D)

In BIRDLIP the road makes a sharp left turn to follow the scarp south-west then west to Cranham. Below the hamlet beech woods, glorious in autumn, hides the source of the River Frome, which once drove the many mills of the STROUD valley. Above is the common and the church of St James: 15th-century, with a battlemented tower sporting a pair of sheep shears carved into the buttresses.

Many visitors come to the common here for the views, and for the Cranham Feast in August. This began as a deer and ox roast and has grown into a big event, with village sports and an attendant fair.

Gustav Holst (1874–1934) used to come here from CHELTENHAM to walk. When he wrote his haunting melody to Christina Rossetti's words, 'In the Bleak Midwinter', he dedicated the carol to Cranham.

Further down the scarp, on the opposite side of the A46, is **Prinknash Abbey** (pronounced Prinnage), founded by Catholic Benedictine monks in 1928. They took over a 16th-century country house that had once belonged to the abbots of GLOUCESTER and laid the foundation stone of a new abbey in 1939. The Second World War interrupted the work and when peace returned the original plan was abandoned in favour of one less ambitious and costly.

The revised design, by F. G. Broadbent, was rejected by the local authority on the extraordinary grounds that abbeys should be Gothic, not modern in style. The monks were given the go-ahead only after an appeal to the appropriate minister. They paid for the work, and continue to support themselves, by making the famous Prinknash black, lustre-glazed pottery and by farming. The public may visit the pottery, as

well as the bird garden and deer park, and attend services in the chapel, where many of the fittings were designed by the monks themselves.

Being away from through roads, in its own secluded valley, **Sheepscombe** (4/1D) has kept something of the pastoral atmosphere of former times. The church of St John, built around 1820, has a diminutive tower and stands on one side of the valley, separated by steep pastures from the main part of the little village, with its Cotswold stone cottages, on the opposite slope.

Crickley Hill *see* Birdlip

Daglingworth *see* Duntisbournes, The

Daylesford *see* Adlestrop

Dean Heritage Centre *see* Cinderford

Deerhurst (4/1C)

England does not have very many surviving pre-Norman churches, so a visit to Deerhurst, some 3 miles south-west of TEWKESBURY, will quicken the pulse of any student of the Anglo-Saxon period, for it has two. Not only is the priory church of St Mary substantially complete, and outstanding for its wealth of sculpture, but archaeological evidence suggests it is considerably earlier than the 10th-century date once assigned to it.

It is known that a monastery already existed in AD 804, when Æthelric bequeathed it 30,000 acres, stipulating that he should be buried here. It was previously thought that the earliest church was destroyed during the later 9th-century Viking attacks. The revised view suggests that the tall, narrow nave with its triangular windows is the original late 8th- or early 9th-century monastic church. The round-headed doors and dragon-head stops, the now-ruined polygonal apse, the chancel arch and the side chapels all belong to the early 10th-century restoration.

Of the sculpture, the Virgin and Child in the porch is possibly 8th century, the angel in the east wall 10th century and the font somewhere between the two. This splendid piece is ornamented with double spirals and was found in use as a washtub in a nearby farmhouse in 1884. The base was found in the garden of Apperley Court (*see right*).

Odda's Chapel stands just south-west of the priory church and was identified, encapsulated within a timber-framed farmhouse, during building work in 1885. It is named after Odda

Double-headed window at the Saxon church, Deerhurst

because an inscribed stone (now in the Ashmolean Museum, Oxford) was found near by in 1672. This gives the date of the chapel's dedication, 12 April 1056, and records that Earl Odda built it in memory of his brother Ælfric. Even more remarkably, the original altar stone, inscribed with a dedication to the Trinity, was later discovered, having been used as a window lintel.

The extraordinary survival of this priory church and chapel was due to the early decline of the monastery, overshadowed even before the Norman Conquest by GLOUCESTER, WINCH-COMBE, by Tewkesbury, about 2½ miles north-east, and Evesham (*see* H&W). It thus escaped rebuilding in later centuries and the priory became the parish church of this village by the Severn at the Dissolution of the Monasteries. The other monastic buildings were, however, demolished and some of the stone used to build Wightfield Manor, home of the Casseys, at **Apperley** (4/1C), 1 mile south.

Here, the pert and pink neo-Romanesque church was built in 1856 by the young Francis Cranmer Penrose (1817–1903), who was surveyor of St Paul's Cathedral at the time. He returned in 1890, at the age of 73, and spoiled the effect

by adding an apse with incongruous pointed windows and a campanile.

Didbrook *see* Hailes

Didmarton (3/5G)

This neat village on the doorstep of Badminton Park (now in Avon), and 6 miles south-west of TETBURY, has several 18th- and 19th-century houses that were once coaching inns on the Bath to CIRENCESTER road (now the A433). The small medieval church of St Lawrence was abandoned in 1872 in favour of the new church of St Michael, and so retained its 18th-century box pews (some painted) and three-decker pulpit, as well as much of the atmosphere of a Georgian country church. It is maintained by the Redundant Churches Fund. Also redundant, but more dilapidated, is its neighbour, St Arild, at Oldbury on the Hill, ¼ mile north up an unmarked track through farmyards. It, too, retains its Georgian country pulpit and pews.

Donnington *see* Stow-on-the-Wold

Dowdeswell (4/3D)

This village lies east of CHELTENHAM, just south of the A40. In the 1790s there was a dispute between the vicar and the squire over the payment of tithes to the church. In the course of a personal altercation in 1793 the former knocked the latter's hat off – and was successfully sued. This is said to explain why the gallery at the west end of St Michael's church belonging to the manor, and that in the transept, belonging to the rectory, were built out of sight of each other and entered by separate outside doors.

The cruciform church was largely rebuilt in the late 16th century, its stumpy spire raised in 1577 according to the inscription on an inside window. The Tree of Life tympanum from the original Norman church has been reset in an outside wall.

Beside the church is Dowdeswell Court, built in about 1834 and now a nursing home, and the 16th- and 17th-century Home Farm.

The Old Rectory, with its 18th-century façade, commands fine views – for this village is on the steep slopes of the Chelt valley.

At Upper Dowdeswell there is a late 16th-century manor.

A mile south on Pegglesworth Hill, and visible from a public path, is St Paul's Epistle round barrow, said to be so called because the Epistles were read from its summit during the

annual beating of the parish bounds. Further west the Woodland Trust maintains the 110 acres of Lineover Woods.

At **Andoversford** (4/3D) to the east of Dowdeswell there is a 17th-century manor house, with some modern work sensitively carried out. The Royal Oak Inn is small and faced with ashlars. About a mile south-east of Andoversford are the twin villages of **Shipton Oliffe** and **Shipton Solers** (4/3D). They were united into one parish in 1776, but kept their two medieval churches. St Oswald's at Oliffe is the older, with a Norman doorway and massive Norman chancel arch piers, but a rare 13th-century double bellcote. St Mary's at Solers is 13th century, with a Jacobean pulpit with an hour-glass stand for timing sermons.

Down Ampney (4/4F)

Less pretty, but far more famous, than the three AMPNEYS further up the brook, Down Ampney, about 5 miles south-east of CIRENCESTER, was the birthplace of Ralph Vaughan Williams (1872–1958). He edited *The English Hymnal* (1906) and contributed to it the well-loved hymn tune 'Down Ampney' to the words 'Come Down O Love Divine'. He was born in the Old Vicarage, which, despite its name, was newly built in 1865, seven years before the composer's birth. There is a display of Vaughan Williams' memorabilia in the church, which is filled with lavish 19th-century neo-Gothic woodwork.

Cotswold Horse Fair at Andoversford, the auction being conducted from inside a horse box

Members of the St John's Ambulance Brigade, modern-day successors of the Knights Hospitallers of the Order of St John of Jerusalem, hold an annual service here close to the medieval effigy of the crusader knight, Sir John de Valers (d.1300); as do Second World War pilots who flew from the nearby airfield and whose war dead are commemorated in the stained glass windows.

At **Driffield** (4/3F) St Mary's church belonged to Cirencester Abbey until the Dissolution of the Monasteries, when the last abbot was pensioned off to spend his final years here on a comfortable £200 a year. The church he knew was rebuilt in 1734. Of interest are the memorials to the Coleraine family. Of the father, his epitaph simply says: 'Here lieth, in expectation of the last day, Gabriel Hanger, Lord Coleraine; what manner of man he was, That day will disclose.'

In the little hamlet of **Harnhill** (4/3E), ½ mile north-west, St Michael's church has a Norman tympanum of the Archangel and Satan as a dragon being driven from Heaven; another fine dragon forms the 18th-century weather vane. The church stands by the manor house, dated 1584, and a good group of barns, dovecot and farm buildings.

Drybrook *see* Ruardean

Dumbleton (4/3B)

The village, about 5 miles north of WINCH-COMBE, shelters in the lee of Dumbleton Hill, a Cotswold outlier isolated by eastward erosion of the scarp. Typically the villages round about mix the building traditions of the hills and the vale. In Dumbleton, timber-frame construction predominates, but warm golden limestone was used for St Peter's church and the interesting group of headstones in the churchyard carved with scenes of the Resurrection. Norman features include sections of a corbel table and a tympanum carved with a three-tongued feline head. The plain whitewashed interior has good oak furnishings carved with fruits (1905).

From Dumbleton a footpath leads east across the shallow Isbourne valley to the farming village of **Wormington** (4/3B). Inside the church of St Catherine is a Crucifixion, probably late Saxon and perhaps from Winchcombe Abbey, as well as stained glass and drapes from the factory of William Morris. There is also an unusual brass depicting Anne Savage (d.1605) with her infant lying in a four-poster bed; perhaps she died in childbirth.

South-west of Dumbleton are the villages of **Alderton** (4/2B), with several good timber-framed cottages and the 14th-century church of St Margaret; and, south of the A438, **Alstone** (4/2B), where the church has a surviving late Norman south doorway and 17th-century pulpit and bench ends.

Duntisbournes, The (4/2E)

Pronounced 'Dunsbourne', these four villages north-west of CIRENCESTER and west of the A417 are all named after the Dunt brook, which makes numerous fords as it flows over the narrow lanes linking each parish. Signs warn that several lanes are unsuitable for motor vehicles – and it would be a great pity to destroy the peaceful atmosphere by attempting to drive along them. Far better walk and discover the rich flora of the high-banked lanes. One meticulous botanist has estimated that of the 2369 species native to the British Isles, 1039 of them grow in this region.

The Dunt rises in **Duntisbourne Abbots** (4/2E), the largest of the four villages, named after St Peter's Abbey, GLOUCESTER. It is an attractive cluster of ancient stone cottages built on terraces cut into the hillside. St Peter's church stands high on its own platform. The lower stage of the tower is Norman, the higher Perpendicular, but not the grandiose affair of larger 'wool' churches; this one is saddle-backed with bell openings and in proportion to the nave. Nothing special lies within (the church was restored in 1872), but note the early ironwork and 15th-century closing ring of the south door.

The Dunt does not merely cross the lower of the two lanes linking Duntisbourne Abbots to **Duntisbourne Leer** (4/2E), it actually flows

The ford at Duntisbourne Leer

along it for some 30 yds. The brook is too deep for most vehicles to negotiate safely, but pedestrians can use a raised, stone-flagged path. The brook was deliberately diverted here to create a water lane, to wash the clay off the wheels of carts and fetlocks of horses returning from the fields.

Duntisbourne Leer belonged to the abbey of Lire in Normandy, although no church survives here, nor at neighbouring **Middle Duntisbourne** (4/2E). Instead both hamlets consist of groups of farm buildings around pretty fords where ducks paddle.

Duntisbourne Rouse (4/2E). The church of St Michael at Rouse (pronounced to rhyme with mouse) stands all alone above the Dunt. The village has long since disappeared, but the church is all the more romantic for its isolation, a little wayside chapel inviting the traveller to stop and contemplate. The bank on which the church stands falls away so steeply to the east, that builders were able to insert a small crypt below the chancel. Was it ever used, perhaps, to house saintly relics, or just for some more mundane purpose?

Daglingworth (4/2E) is the southernmost village of this pretty valley, and the only one not to be named after the Dunt. Its church, Holy Rood, is considerably grander than the little church at Rouse, although of the same early date. Despite over-restoration in the 1840s, it retains long-and-short work quoins, laid proud of the wall face and cut back in part.

The south doorway with wheat-ear ornamentation on the imposts is Saxon, as is the sundial above (the door itself is 15th century).

Important Saxon sculptures were discovered and reset during the 1845–50 restoration. Outside on the east wall of the chancel, high up (bring binoculars) is a Crucifixion; inside is another one showing a soldier bearing a spear and scourge, and another offering the vinegar-soaked sponge to the figure of Christ. Two more sculptures show Christ enthroned, and St Peter with his key.

The church stands on a hill above the village beside 19th-century Daglingworth House. A separate group of buildings clusters around the Manor at Lower End; the circular medieval dovecot in the gardens, with its revolving ladder, may be viewed by appointment.

Dursley (3/4F)

The town lies just east of the M5 and about 8 miles south-west of STROUD. It is industrial in character, as befits one of the former main textile production centres of the region. The coincidence of natural resources here gave Dursley an advantage from the 15th to the 18th centuries: clear streams for washing the wool, fast-flowing water to drive mill wheels, and a humid valley microclimate that made working the wool fibres easier. Fuller's earth deposits are plentiful near by; teasels for raising the nap on cloth grew well in the valley clays; and woad for blue dye was once abundant here. In time, however, steam replaced water as a source of power; labour was cheaper further north; and high taxes on wool combined with consumer preference for lighter cotton textiles to drive Dursley's mills out of business.

Dursley also flourished briefly as a butter market, hence the elegant Queen Anne market house and town hall. But this business, too, was halted with the arrival of the railway in the mid-19th century. Salvation from economic decline came through the development of the R. A. Lister concern. Originally metalsmiths, the firm is now a manufacturer of widely exported diesel engines of types that are particularly valuable in the Third World.

Dursley's mainly 15th-century church of St James is a product of the wool age, built in the local limestone called Dursley tufa, with a vaulted porch and the Tanner chapel, named after its merchant patron.

From the church it is a small step to the Market Place and Long Street, in which the finest of Dursley's 18th-century houses are to be found. Note the Old Bell Hotel with its Venetian windows, and no. 56 Long Street, with a shell hood over the doorway.

The older parts of the Lister factory are built in a style that owes something to Art Nouveau. The newer extensions spread so far northwards that there is now little countryside between Dursley and the large former village of **Cam** (3/4F). The church of St James in the upper part of the town was rebuilt about 1340 by Thomas, Lord Berkeley, in atonement for the murder of Edward II (*see* Berkeley). The Victorian church at **Lower Cam** (3/4E), which has a good hammer-beam roof, was designed in 1844.

Stinchcombe (3/4F) lies a mile west, sandwiched between the M5 motorway and the golf course on Stinchcombe Hill, which gives good views of Berkeley and its castle. The tower of St Cyr's church and the fine vaulted porch are Perpendicular.

Several country houses were built around

Stinchcombe, away from Dursley's industry, to take advantage of the vale views: 17th-century Melksham Court has a good barn and Italianate water gardens; 18th-century Piers Court was Evelyn Waugh's home from 1937 to 1956. Both are private, but the garden at Stancombe Park is now open occasionally under the National Gardens Scheme (*see* 'Gloucestershire Gardens', p. 77).

Just west of the motorway, at Blanchworth, the Cider Mill Gallery makes cider using a traditional horse-powered apple mill in October and November (open Tuesday to Saturday).

Dymock (3/3B)

This village on the B4216 in the north-west corner of Gloucestershire is remarkably beautiful: rich red soils contrast with green fields that are filled with wild daffodils in the spring. For decades, those in the know have been coming to see this pleasing sight. Many more are likely to come now with the opening of the Daffodil Way. This circular 8-mile walk also takes in KEMPLEY and is waymarked (guides available locally). The daffodils, now much diminished, once bloomed so profusely that they were picked and sold commercially, as John Masefield recorded in one of his poems.

Masefield was not alone in celebrating the local scenery. In the halcyon days before the

Wild daffodils near Dymock

First World War, a group of poets chose Dymock as a place in which to live, work and provide mutual inspiration. Their themes were pastoral, celebrating English country life; Lascelles Abercrombie wrote most about his idyllic surroundings, including these lines in which he revels in the sound of English place names:

From Marcle Way,
From Dymock, Kempley, Newent, Bromsberrow,
Redmarley, all the meadowland daffodils seem
Running in golden tides to Ryton Firs.

The church of St Mary, approached through a lychgate by the side of an ancient yew, has an exhibition devoted to the Dymock poets in the west end. The walls incorporate Saxon herringbone masonry, but much is early Norman. There is a slightly later Norman south doorway with a Tree of Life tympanum. There is sufficient similarity between this and the carving at Kempley and other churches in the area to suggest that an accomplished school of masons was at work here in the 12th century.

Three miles north-west of Dymock along the B4215, which follows the course of a Roman road, is the church of **Preston** (3/3B) and the splendid Preston Court. The six-bay house, with overhanging gabled upper storey, is not spoiled by any additions later than 1608. Alongside, the Norman church of St John the Baptist has a 14th-century timber-framed porch sheltering a Lamb of God tympanum.

Eastington *see* Leonard Stanley

Eastleaches, The (4/4E&5E)

The broad meandering valley of the River Leach exemplifies what geologists call a misfit, so called because the river now is tiny in proportion to the width of the valley. This was carved out at the end of the Ice Age when the river was swelled by glacial meltwater. By 500 BC, the river must have been back to a mere trickle, for the banks were under cultivation; there is a well-preserved and prominent group of Iron Age strip lynchets, caused by ploughing, close to the point upstream from the Eastleaches where Akeman Street crosses the river. During dry spells the river often disappears completely, although by the time it reaches the villages that bear its name, it is very much alive. An ancient clapper bridge links the two churches on opposite banks of the river. For these are twin villages sharing a river crossing, about 4 miles north of LECHLADE, and each with its own medieval church.

The crossing is known as Keble's Bridge, for the Keble family had held the manor at **Eastleach Turville** (4/4E) since the 16th century. John Keble (1792–1866) was non-resident curate (he lived at FAIRFORD) of both churches and served them energetically, preaching two sermons every Sunday.

Now, only the church of St Andrew at Turville is used for services. It has an early 14th-century saddle-backed tower and a Norman tympanum of Christ in Majesty. The chancel was elegantly enriched in the 13th century by the addition of the shafted triple lancet. In 1959 the red and gold carpet was given by an Oxford embroidery group to commemorate Keble.

The church of St Michael and St Martin at **Eastleach Martin** (4/5E) is redundant now but as pretty as its neighbour, with a pleasing hip-roofed tower framed by the nearby woods. The whole church seems wonderfully rustic in atmosphere with its ancient furnishings and oil lamps and the absence of restoration work.

Most of the village lies on the Turville side; some cottages date to the 18th century, but many were built as estate houses in the 19th century.

Southrop (4/4E), 1 mile downstream, was, like Quenington (*see* Colns, The), a possession of the Knights Hospitallers, though St Peter's church and the important font pre-date their ownership. Built around 1100, the north and south walls of the nave retain extensive stretches of herringbone masonry, a Roman building technique revived by the Normans and aesthetically a most pleasing sight. Just as exciting is the font, unmatched in England for interest and accomplishment. It shows a group of armoured figures representing the Virtues trampling and stabbing beasts that represent their antipodal Vices. The names of the Virtues are carved around the trefoil-headed arches above; the names of the Vices are scratched in the blanks below, in mirror writing to stress their perversity. Another allegorical scene depicts Ecclesia (the Christian Church) turning her back on the blinded figure of Synagogue (Judaism) by the side of Moses holding the Commandment stones. Above this rich iconography, a series of Romanesque-style towers represent, perhaps, the Heavenly Mansions.

In the village there are several fine houses, best seen when their gardens are open under the National Gardens Scheme. They include the Manor House, built on Norman foundations, with a fine stew pond that may date from its ownership by the Knights. Also open for its garden, Fyfield Manor is a pretty Queen Anne house. Not open is the old Vicarage where John Keble began the discussions that led to the formation of the Oxford Movement.

Ebrington *see* Chipping Campden

Edgeworth *see* Miserden

Elkstone (4/2D)

In this village about 6 miles south of CHELTEN-HAM, the 12th-century church of St John is remarkable for its Norman decoration. Of the smaller parish churches of the region, it has the best and most complete examples of such work. The beak-head ornamentation of the south doorway includes a human head among the beasts and one mischievous inverted figure that grasps the snouts of its neighbours. The corbel table that runs around the eaves is decorated with animals, birds and signs of the zodiac. The splendid tympanum over the south door shows Christ in Majesty, with symbols of the Evangelists beneath the disembodied hand of God.

These features are characteristic of Romanesque architecture and spread from churches in northern Spain via south-west France to Normandy, and on to England – roughly along the pilgrim routes to the shrine of St James at Compostela in north-west Spain.

The bold character of this 12th-century work continues inside the church; here the two arches of the tower crossing (the tower itself collapsed in the 13th century) create a sequence that leads to the richly enchevroned east window. The chancel's side windows are filled with 20th-century glass whose golden tones lend a candle-lit hue, even on the gloomiest day. The west arch hood moulds terminate in dragon-head stops, another Romanesque feature.

Above the chancel, reached via a stairway by the pulpit, is a pigeon loft (unusual in a church, although monasteries commonly had dovecots). The nave roof of oak is beautiful 15th-century work. This is contemporary with the Perpendicular west tower.

There is a 14th-century priest's house in the south-eastern corner of the churchyard. To the north is the 18th-century Rectory.

Gertrude Jekyll laid out the gardens at Combend Manor, 1 mile south-east of Elkstone. They are being restored and are occasionally open under the National Gardens Scheme.

Elmore (3/4D)
GLOUCESTER'S sprawl stops abruptly along the line of the Gloucester and Sharpness Canal. Westward, around Elmore, the tempo and landscape change dramatically. This is orchard country, with grazing cattle and views across watermeadows to the riverside where crowds gather in spring and autumn to watch the SEVERN BORE.

Elmore's church of St John the Baptist has good Early English features, and 18th-century table tombs in the churchyard. One shows Time standing on the wheel of Fortune. Alongside, Death as a skeleton bestrides the globe.

Time has taken its toll of the mausoleum of the Guise family, the church's patron, which stands near by, an ivy-covered ruin. The family home, Elmore Court, has fared better and the gardens are open under the National Gardens Scheme. It was given a Georgian front in the 18th century, but the best visible feature is the sumptuous wrought-iron entrance gate, surmounted by the Guise swan and coronet.

The twisting lane from Elmore, lined with timber-framed farmhouses, eventually reaches **Longney** (3/4D), a couple of miles to the south-

west. The best parts of the church of St Laurence are the porches: both 15th century, one of stone with arcading, the other of ornamented timber.

Elmstone Hardwick *see* Bishop's Cleeve

English Bicknor (3/2D)
This village stands in beautiful country above the Wye, with views across the FOREST OF DEAN. St Mary's church stands within the outer bailey of a motte-and-bailey castle, possibly one of those thrown up in the first half of the 12th century during the civil war between Stephen and Matilda – although finds of masonry suggest that an earlier, more substantial castle stood here in what is border country; a Welsh Bicknor across the Wye emphasizes this fact.

The soft, easily eroded sandstone of the church has had to be restored, so that the external appearance does not reflect the building's true age. Inside are Norman piers with scalloped capitals; one arch has beak-head ornamentation, suggesting that it was formerly the south door.

OFFA'S DYKE, another reminder of the ancient frontier, runs to the north and west where, on the forest trail south of Symond's Yat (*see* H&W), it passes round a large Iron Age hillfort.

Evenlode *see* Stow-on-the-Wold

Ewen *see* Kemble

Fairford (4/4E)
The town lies 8 miles east of CIRENCESTER on the A417. Its name means 'clear ford', a reference to the waters of the Coln, a tributary of the Thames. Fairford was granted its market in the 13th century. John Leland, however, visiting in the mid-16th century, gave his opinion that 'Faireford never flourished afore ye Tames came to it'; and, ever since, the Tames, father and son, wool merchants, have been credited with establishing the town's fortunes.

Their most visible contribution is St Mary's church. This magnificent Perpendicular structure has one of England's finest sequences of stained glass, illustrating the Bible story from Creation to the Crucifixion.

It has been suggested that the probable source for much of the iconography at Fairford was a so-called *Biblia Pauperum* (Poor Man's Bible); first published in the 1460s, these were illustrated with woodcuts. Besides the beauty of their

Tombstone of Tiddles in Fairford's churchyard

stained glass, the Fairford windows offer an insight into popular religious belief on the eve of the Reformation.

When John Tame decided to fund the rebuilding of the church, which began in 1490, he employed only the best masons, possibly the same ones that rebuilt St Mary the Virgin, Oxford. After John's death in 1500, his son Edmund Tame continued the work and seems to have been equally selective in his choice of glaziers. The style suggests that the glass was produced in the workshops of Barnard Flower, master glass painter to Henry VII (his work included the windows of the Lady Chapel, Westminster Abbey).

Flower was known as the 'Alleman' (German) and he employed Continental as well as English glaziers in his workshop. Some of the scenes show distinctly Dutch architecture, and the Continental fashion for elaborate female headdress; others are set in a purely English environment.

The choir screen is another treasure of great interest, a rare survival of the Protestant objection to separation between priest and congregation, and delicately carved. The pomegranate emblem of Katharine of Aragon puts it in the period between 1501, the date of her marriage to Prince Arthur, eldest brother of Henry VIII, and 1527 when Henry, who married his brother's widow, began suing for divorce. The choir stalls are of similar date; the misericords depict scenes from fables and popular sermons.

In the churchyard is the tomb of the master mason Valentine Strong of BARRINGTON, who came to the town in 1661 to build the new mansion at Fairford Park. Valentine died the following year while the old house was still being demolished.

The house, which was completed by Valentine's son, Thomas Strong, was demolished in turn in the 1950s and a school now stands on its site. The public can visit the grounds, landscaped in the naturalistic manner of Capability Brown.

The artificially widened river which flows through the Park divides Fairford into two; west is the Milton (Mill Town) End; east lies the old town dominated by 18th-century former coaching inns, a reflection of its position on an important route. There are pleasant walks beside the river.

Along the London Road is Keble House, birthplace of John Keble (1792–1866). His father was vicar of Coln St Aldwyns (*see* Colns, The) and, following his ordination in 1815, John was curate at EASTLEACH, Southrop and later Coln St Aldwyns, while continuing to live at Fairford. He became Professor of Poetry at Oxford in 1831. In 1833 he preached the famous sermon on national apostasy that marked the start of the Oxford Movement, and led to liturgical renewal, and to the building of many fine churches in the region (around BISLEY, for example).

Farmcote *see* Hailes

Farmington *see* Sherborne

Forest of Dean
The Forest occupies the wedge-shaped area between the Wye on the west and the Severn on the east and south. It consists of an upland trough of old red sandstone. Over this lies a deposit of carboniferous limestone, much used as a substitute for marble in the Middle Ages and now as a durable paving material. Overlying this is the millstone grit containing iron ores, and the coal measures, running in three parallel north–south ridges.

This is one of England's largest ancient forests, with abundant wild life and wild flowers in a variety of habitats. These can be explored via footpaths and the forest trails that have been laid out by the Forestry Commission (*see* Blakeney).

The Forest has been exploited since prehistory as a source of iron. There was a little coal mining even in Roman times; and Free Miners' rights go back a long way. But coal mining on a commercial scale is relatively recent. Charcoal

The Giant Chair, part of the sculpture trail in the Forest of Dean near the Speech House Hotel

was the principal fuel for the forges, consumed in such quantity that the felling of trees threatened the Forest's vital role as a source of naval timber. Irresponsible asset stripping did not help matters. The Crown leased the Forest and its contents to Sir John Winter in 1640. He felled drastically, as did Parliament under the Commonwealth, and when Winter was forced to relinquish his rights in 1668 there were said to be only 200 trees left.

In 1668 the Dean Forest (Reafforestation) Act was passed, and the modern administration of the Forest dates from this time. Enclosures for replanting were set at 11,000 acres, divided into six areas (walks), each with a keeper. A courtroom was added to Speech House, 3 miles east of COLEFORD, in 1680. This was to house the newly revived Verderers' Court, responsible for resolving Forest disputes. Speech House is now a hotel, although still used occasionally for Court meetings. The surrounding arboretum and sculpture trail, open daily, includes ancient holly trees said to date from the massive replanting of the late 17th and early 18th centuries.

From this time on ironworking was discouraged, as too great a consumer of timber, in favour of coal mining, which became the predominant industry. Even so, the affairs of the Forest did not run smoothly; by 1735 the keepers were reporting that squatters were felling trees and burning the undergrowth. However, many of these so-called squatters were Free Miners with established rights, already ancient, confirmed in 1300 by Edward I.

These long-established Foresters had, through marrying within their own community, retained distinct physical characteristics. Many lived in disused mine caves and huts built in forest clearings, freely availing themselves of timber for fuel, housing and pit props.

There are now around 30 Free Miners still working drift mines in the Forest, more than two decades after the last big commercial colliery closed in 1965. Anyone born of a Free Miner, within the Hundred (a subdivision of the county) of ST BRIAVELS and who has worked a year and one day in one of the mines, still has the right to open up a new seam in the Forest.

Today the Forest continues to be an important source of timber, but with increasing emphasis on ecology and mixed woodland. At Ladywood Park (1 mile north of Staunton: *see* Coleford) 90 acres have been set aside to monitor the behaviour of natural woodland in the absence of planting and felling. Unsightly industrial relics, such as the New Fancy Tip, a colliery slag heap, have been landscaped.

The fascinating history of the Forest is now the subject of several attractions, including the splendid Dean Heritage Centre, CINDERFORD, which both provides information and a starting point; Clearwell Caves, COLEFORD; and the Dean Forest Railway, LYDNEY.

Forthampton (4/1B)
The village lies just south of the A438 a couple of

miles west of TEWKESBURY. Sadly only fragments remain of St Mary's history before its 19th-century rebuilding: the south door has damaged dragon-head stops and a grotesque head keystone; the altar stone is of about 1300; and some 16th-century pews with linenfold carving survive. West of the church is a whipping post and stocks, with chains and manacles.

The village itself has the half-timbering characteristic of this orchard country.

Footpaths thread the watermeadows south of Forthampton, providing a choice of routes to **Chaceley** (4/1B), a village that has frequently been flooded, but thrives on the business from pleasure craft using the River Severn. The church of St John the Baptist was largely rebuilt in the 14th century, and has a series of portrait corbel heads and a 14th-century stained-glass Crucifixion.

Tirley (4/1C), 1½ miles south-west, is even closer to the river and a plaque on the chancel arch of St Michael's church marks the water level reached in the great flood of 1947. The church walls are built of the local muddy blue lias, so soft that concrete render has been applied to prevent further erosion. The river terraces of silt and pebbles, resulting from the rise and fall of the water level at the end of the Ice Age, are particularly noticeable hereabouts.

The road to **Hasfield** (3/5C) is built on the edge of such a terrace. The church of St Peter here is 14th century. Hasfield Court is early Tudor, but now hidden behind a 19th-century neo-Renaissance façade.

Frampton Mansell *see* Sapperton

Frampton on Severn (3/4E)

This village lies about 8 miles south-west of GLOUCESTER, just west of the A38. When, around 1731, Richard Clutterbuck drained a large expanse of land beside the Severn to create the site for his house, Frampton Court, he also provided the village with one of the largest and finest greens in England. It has since acquired the name 'Rosamund's Green': the 15th-century half-timbered Manor Farmhouse on its eastern side is said to have been the birthplace of Henry II's celebrated mistress, 'Fair Rosamund' Clifford.

Clutterbuck's architect, probably John Strahan, borrowed freely from Stourhead in Wiltshire – to the extent that John Wood of Bath called Frampton Court 'piratical'. The upper part of the Orangery in the garden is just visible from the village green. Built in the Gothick style in 1743, it stands at the end of the garden's ornamental canal.

Recently a group of 300 watercolour illustrations of the local wild flowers was discovered in the attics of the Court and published as the *Frampton Flora*. They were the work of the granddaughters and nieces of Nathaniel Winchcombe, a distant relation of the noble de Cliffords, who bought the Court at the beginning of the 19th century. The house and grounds can be visited only by written appointment.

St Mary's church stands at the opposite end of the village, past a number of interesting cruck-built and timber-framed farmhouses, cottages and barns. The furnishings include a very fine 12th-century lead font with seated figures, one of five such in Gloucestershire – *see* Tidenham (under Beachley) – and a good 18th-century chandelier.

Just outside, the Gloucester and SHARPNESS Canal passes between high embankments. Huge barges sometimes loom by, gliding through meadows. Near by, at Splatt Bridge, is an early 19th-century lock-keeper's cottage in neo-Grecian style.

France Lynch *see* Bisley

Fretherne *see* Arlingham

Frocester (3/4E)

Coaley Peak and Frocester Hill, some 5 miles south-west of STROUD, are typical examples of unenclosed Gloucestershire upland, where Cotswold sheep still graze the rough grass in summer. Walks have been laid out with information boards, and a topograph on Frocester Hill points to the landmarks visible from this high point, 778 ft above sea level. Near to it is the Neolithic Nympsfield long barrow, 90 ft long, originally covered with a mound but now, following excavation in 1937, consisting of three stone chambers open to the sky. The dramatic fall of the land and the rising air currents make this spot popular with hang-gliding enthusiasts.

Frocester lies down in the vale to the north, on the prehistoric and Roman route that can still be clearly traced on the map from Easton Grey, Wiltshire, to the river crossing at ARLINGHAM. The church of St Andrew was originally the chapel to Frocester Court. It was removed to its present position in the 17th century (the date 1637 is carved on a rood beam). One mile to the west are the remains of the original parish church of St Peter – 14th-century porch, 19th-century tower and broach spire. The rest was pulled down in 1952, and the remains of a substantial Roman villa were discovered beneath it. This shows that the site has been farmed from prehistoric times to the present.

Another Roman villa is currently being excavated in the grounds of Frocester Court. There is fascinating evidence of a Roman formal garden with flowerbeds. The estate itself belonged to the abbey at GLOUCESTER as early as AD 823. The mainly 14th-century house has 16th-century additions and a pretty timber-framed gatehouse. The great barn (ask at the Court for permission to visit) is one of the oldest and best preserved in the country. Records show that it was largely built by about 1300.

Gatcombe *see* Blakeney

Gloucester (3/5D)

This city on the Severn has featured prominently in history. It was the site of one of the earliest Roman forts, established shortly after their invasion of AD 43. William the Conqueror held court here in 1085 and ordered the survey known by the English as the Domesday Book. Monarchs were crowned and buried in its magnificent cathedral. From the 16th century onwards it became one of the country's busiest ports.

Visually, the city has not always reflected this distinguished past, so that H. J. Massingham could write: 'No royal or ancient town in England has murdered its past more thoroughly . . . and is meaner, shabbier and more sordidly pretentious in its present' (*Shepherd's Country*, 1938). Much effort is, however, now being channelled into redressing the insensitivity of the past. The development of a museum complex in the restored warehouses of the splendid Gloucester Docks area indicates a better appreciation of the city's heritage (*see below*).

The rich alluvium of the Vale of Gloucester supported numerous prehistoric communities; one of the classic sites of British archaeology is at **Barnwood**, now an eastern suburb of the city, where finds indicate continuous occupation from the end of the Ice Age.

Around AD 49, the Romans established a temporary encampment for the XXth legion at Kingsholm, north of the modern city centre. In AD 75 the XXth legion moved to permanent quarters at Caerleon. Kingsholm then became a *colonia*, a settlement for retired army veterans, with a substantial Romano-British community on its doorstep. Finds from the excavations here can be seen in the City Museum.

Although less important initially than CIRENCESTER, Gloucester emerges as a prosperous town in Anglo-Saxon times with a mint and a monastery, established in about 681. The town was important enough by the 11th century for Edward the Confessor to hold court here. Even so, when the new Norman Abbot Serlo took over the monastery in 1072, it had dwindled to a mere two monks. The reforming Serlo began the magnificent new abbey church in 1089, starting with the crypt and proceeding westwards.

Work was sufficiently advanced for a consecration ceremony to be held in 1100; another in 1121 perhaps marked the completion of the nave. The following year fire interrupted work – intense heat has turned several of the nave pillars a rosy pink. Even so, only the roof was seriously affected and much of this solid, dignified Norman structure has survived to afford pleasure to modern visitors.

The other great building period began in the 14th century after Edward II, murdered at BERKELEY in 1327, was buried in the Abbey. The combined income from pilgrims to the late king's tomb, and money given by successive monarchs in expiation of the crime, enabled Abbot Thoky to embark on large-scale schemes.

He began in 1331 with the south transept. This is sometimes hailed as the place where the Perpendicular style began, for the windows are among the first to have the characteristic vertical mullions from sill to arch. It is also argued, however, that Gloucester's masons took windows in the Chapter House of Old St Paul's and of St Stephen's Chapel, Westminster, as their model.

The cusped ogee arch did make an early appearance in the abbey (see Edward II's tomb), and the ceiling of the east range of the cloister was ornamented in about 1351 with a fan vault, that splendid Perpendicular feature created by Gloucester masons. The fan vault became a popular motif throughout the Cotswolds for the next 150 years (notably at Cirencester).

At Gloucester the entire the choir was next remodelled in the new style and given the soaring, slightly bowed window that fills the whole of the east wall of the nave. It is filled with 14th-century glass illustrating the Coronation of the Virgin. The choir stalls and misericords are contemporary with the window; carvings include an early representation of the game of football.

The abbey became a cathedral after the

Dissolution of the Monasteries under Henry VIII. With Hereford and Worcester Cathedrals, Gloucester is one of the centres for the Three Choirs Festival (see page 38).

Many of Gloucester's finest early buildings lie in and around the Close, called College Green, where good Regency houses stand on the site of former monastic buildings.

In the passageway off the green, called College Court, there is a small Beatrix Potter Museum in the house of the Tailor of Gloucester. Beatrix Potter heard the tailor's story while staying at HARESCOMBE and although this little house by the cathedral close was not the tailor's true home, she thought it the perfect model for the illustrations for her famous book.

The children's rhyme 'Doctor Foster' is also set in Gloucester. It is said to derive from Edward I's visit to the city when he and his horse sank ignobly into the mud of a dirty Gloucester street, and he vowed never to go there again. The city of Gloucester lies south-east of the cathedral. It retains a street pattern based on the underlying Roman grid system, and its two principal streets meet at The Cross. Here a medieval cross stood until 1751. Near by stands the surviving tower of St Michael's church, now the Tourist Information Centre.

Notable buildings in the centre include Bishop Hooper's Lodging in Westgate Street, a timber-framed building of c.1500 with jettied upper storeys. The house is now the Folk Museum with excellent collections relating to industry, crafts and trades.

In Northgate Street, the New Inn is a rare survival of a courtyard inn, almost completely enclosed and surrounded by tiers of open galleries, built in about 1457 to accommodate pilgrims to Edward II's tomb; it was often used for theatrical performances.

In Southgate Street, an amusing clock of 1904 above a watchmaker's shop has figures of Father Time, John Bull, a kilted Scot and women in Irish and Welsh costume who strike a melodic chime upon the hour.

In 1988, Gloucester Docks were opened after restoration as a Heritage Centre. The status of port was granted to the city by Elizabeth I in 1580, and it prospered despite the vagaries and dangers of the Severn tides. The work of Robert Mylne and Thomas Telford meant that by 1827

Opposite: Cathedral Yard, Gloucester. The stone-mason in the foreground is working on curved coping for the cathedral's west end

there was a safer and swifter route to the docks in the form of the Gloucester and SHARPNESS Canal, so that by the mid-19th century Gloucester ranked in importance with Bristol as a grain port.

The whole area has now been rejuvenated to feature historic ships, a working ship maintenance yard, the Robert Opie Collection (a museum of advertising and packaging), the National Waterways Museum and the Gloucesters' Regimental Museum. The *Gloucester Packet* is used to take visitors on trips around the docks and along the canal.

About a mile further south-west is the village of **Hempsted** (3/5D) with its church of St Swithin that was rebuilt in 1467 by Henry Dene later Archbishop of Canterbury. It is notable for several memorials, including one to Samuel Lysons the antiquary, whose *Reliquiae Britannico-Romanae* (1801–17) was one of the earliest attempts to interpret Britain's archaeological heritage.

The Gloucester suburbs almost encircle **Robins Wood Hill**, a Cotswold outlier, which has now been saved from further quarrying by designation as a Country Park. Good views of Gloucester Cathedral and the docks can be had from the topograph on the 651-ft summit, and a network of nature trails has been laid out around the wooded lower slopes (information from the Park Centre, by the car park off the A38).

The fossil-rich former Tuffley quarry is now protected as a Site of Special Scientific Interest. The quarry was opened primarily for the thick bands of blue-grey lower lias clay that underlies the limestone and was used for brickmaking. Higher up, the quarry face is orange in colour, indicating the iron-bearing strata. The cliff top is stepped back to expose a 15-ft buff-coloured bed of marlstone, which sparkles from its mica content.

The hill was named after the Robins family, who leased it from 1526 until 1759 for sheep grazing. The hill's older name was Mattes Knowle, after the de Matteson family who owned the manor following the Norman Conquest. The suburb of Matson, east of the hill, preserves their name.

South of Robins Wood Hill on the A4173 is **Brookthorpe** (4/1D). Royalist troops were garrisoned in the timber-framed Brookthorpe Court, so it was perhaps with some satisfaction that a local Cromwellian carved a covert reference to the execution of Charles I in the cornice of the south porch of St Swithin's church next door.

Eric Gill carved the name of Detmar Blow

(d.1939) into the splay of a window in the nave. Blow's works included a number of extremely good country houses. One of the best is Hilles House, which he built for himself high on the scarp due west of here and which can be seen from a distance, although it is not open to the public. It is also one of the purest expressions of Arts and Crafts principles in the country.

Great Barrington *see* Barringtons, The

Great Rissington *see* Rissingtons, The

Great Witcombe (4/2D)
At BIRDLIP, 6 or 7 miles south-east of GLOUCESTER, a narrow road drops precipitously over the scarp. This coach road, made in the 17th century, originally led to the Hicks family home at Witcombe Park, set in a combe with the whole of the Vale of Gloucester spread out to view. A fine gazebo of 1697, but not the original house, still stands in the splendid parklike gardens (open occasionally under the National Gardens Scheme).

Panelling from the Hicks' 17th-century house was used to make the pulpit for the Norman parish church that stands further down the hill.

The remains of the Roman villa at Witcombe can be reached by following a signposted track (off the A417 at BROCKWORTH) for 1½ miles back up the hillside. Beautiful as the situation is, it caused problems for the villa owners; it had to be rebuilt and buttressed constantly because of the instability of the subsoil caused by underground springs. The exposed remains, including the well-preserved baths, date to the later 3rd- and 4th-century phases of its history. A large coulter discovered here during excavations shows that the Romans used very substantial ploughs on the heavy Cotswold lias clays.

Gretton *see* Winchcombe

Guitings, The (4/3C)
The beautiful, wooded countryside of the Windrush valley about 7 miles west of STOW-ON-THE-WOLD remains unspoiled, despite being an important source of roofing tile and building stone. Now that the source of the Windrush has been tapped as a water supply it is harder to imagine the torrent that once drove the heavy hammers of the fulling mills of **Temple Guiting** (4/3C) – pronounced 'guyting'. Mills existed here as early as the 12th century when the Knights Templar owned the manor.

The ruins of Hailes Abbey (National Trust)

St Mary's church was restored in the 18th century and given a fine inlaid oak pulpit and a new set of windows. These included, unusually, one Venetian window of domestic style. Near by stands Manor Farm, a perfect early 16th-century mansion built as a summer residence for the Bishops of Oxford, commanding views of the beech trees of Guiting Wood, splendidly gold in autumn.

Downstream by 3 miles, the village of **Guiting Power** (4/3C) stands around a green, its cottages well maintained by a trust established in 1958 for their upkeep. St Michael's church has a 15th-century nave roof supported on corbel heads, to which the portraits of Edward VII and Queen Alexandra were added in 1903.

Between the two villages, on rolling downs, is Bemborough Farm – better known as **Cotswold Park Farm** and headquarters of the Rare Breeds Survival Trust. When Joe Henson first opened the farm in 1970, neighbouring farmers thought this concern for endangered farm breeds an eccentricity. Now this form of conservation is recognized to be vitally important in maintaining a gene pool from which new breeds can be developed.

Changing consumer tastes are once again creating a demand for the meat of old pig varieties, such as the Gloucester Old Spot; and the Old Gloucester cow is enjoying renewed popularity with farmers and cheesemakers. These breeds, and rare goats, wild boars, sheep, oxen and fowl, can all be seen on the farm when it is open during the summer.

Hailes (4/3B)

The ruins of Hailes Abbey stand east of the A46 about 2 miles north-east of WINCHCOMBE. The Abbey (owned by the National Trust and administered by English Heritage) was founded in 1246 by the crusading Richard, Earl of Cornwall (son of King John), in gratitude for having escaped shipwreck. He endowed it handsomely. His son, Edmund, did better, bringing to Hailes a relic of the Holy Blood authenticated by Pope Urban IV. This guaranteed Hailes' prosperity: pilgrims were, like modern tourists, a valued source of income.

At the Dissolution of the Monasteries under Henry VIII the relic was declared a fake, the Abbey suppressed and the buildings plundered for materials so that little remains but for the foundations, the east range of the cloister and the chapter house. Even in its ruinous state, however, the Abbey is well worth visiting for its romantic setting and well-tended grounds. The finds from excavations indicate the Abbey's former splendour and are now housed in the Abbey museum.

The parish church, which was founded before the Abbey, has many fine 13th-century encaustic tiles and some interesting wall paintings of about 1300. One shows the heraldic eagle of the Abbey's founder, Richard, who was elected King of the Romans and ruler of the German Empire in 1257. There are also some imaginatively painted demons, the figures of St Margaret and St Catherine, and a recently discovered scene depicting a huntsman and greyhounds in pursuit of a hare.

From the Abbey, a waymarked track leads between Hayles Fruit Farm and Hailes Wood. At the far end of the wood a path forks left and ascends a hillside with numerous strip lynchets caused by medieval, or earlier, ploughing, to reach the Iron Age Beckbury Camp and Cromwell's Seat. This monument marks the spot from which Thomas Cromwell, Henry VIII's Vicar General, is said to have watched the destruction of Hailes Abbey.

Alternatively, the main track can be followed south to the remote hamlet of **Farmcote** (4/3C) with its medieval barns and farm buildings, formerly a grange to the Abbey. The small Norman chapel of St Faith has largely escaped the hands of improvers and consists simply of a nave with bellcote – the chancel has disappeared. Inside are 16th-century benches, 17th-century pulpit and communion rails and a table supporting a much earlier stone altar.

In the opposite direction, 1 mile north of Hailes, is **Didbrook** (4/3B), a village with a cruck cottage. The 1475 church of St George is all of a piece, its Perpendicular fabric untouched by later hands, although sections remain of Georgian wood panelling that once encased the nave. There are good oak benches, a pulpit, communion rail and family pew of the 17th century.

Hampnett *see* Northleach

Harescombe (4/1D)

The village is about 5 miles south of GLOUCESTER, just west of the A4173. Beatrix Potter first heard the true story of the Tailor of Gloucester while staying with her cousins at Harescombe Grange. She used the son of the coachman there as her model for portraits of the tailor – in real life one John Prichard who, having cut out the parts of a waistcoat intended for the Mayor of Gloucester, returned to find the garment complete and attributed the work to fairies. Here, too, Beatrix Potter rescued the mice that she used in illustrations to *The Tale of Two Bad Mice*.

Harescombe Grange is high up on the hillside where it commands spectacular views. The village lies lower down at the junction between the wolds and the vale. The simple 13th-century church of St John the Baptist is topped by an elaborate spired bellcote and surrounded by handsome table tombs. Inside is a delightful new west window by the local artist E. R. Payne, installed in 1986.

The Tailor of Gloucester, John Prichard, moved to the next-door village of **Haresfield** (3/5D) later in life when he gave up tailoring to become a schoolmaster. Several of the buildings in the village were designed by locally born Francis Niblett (1814–83), who produced several spirited churches in his lifetime, including Fretherne (*see* Arlingham). He was still a student when his own parish church of St Peter was restored in 1841. Like PAINSWICK it has two chancels and several good table tombs.

A steep road climbs from the village to a car park close to the summit of Haresfield Beacon, one of the very best lookout points in Gloucestershire. It juts out of the Cotswold scarp, thrusting into the Vale of Berkeley which lies below, a patchwork of dairy farms and orchards. To the west the River Severn runs through the middle distance, in a vast loop around Arlingham; further off, the red sandstone cliffs of the eastern edge of the FOREST OF DEAN are just visible. To the north-east the Cotswold scarp runs in an almost unbroken line for around 30 miles before finally merging into the Northamptonshire uplands.

In December 1327 the body of the murdered king Edward II stopped overnight in St Nicholas's church at **Standish** on its journey from Berkeley Castle for burial in the abbey church at Gloucester. The church had only recently been rebuilt and remains unaltered from that time, an outstanding example of early 14th-century architecture. The narrow tower and graceful spire are magnificent, the wide chancel arch drawing attention to the east wall, which is entirely filled with the beautiful tracery of a huge Decorated window.

A single splash of colour in the nave comes from the monument to Sir Henry Winston. This was repainted and regilded in 1965 in honour of Sir Winston Churchill, who died that year and was Sir Henry's descendant. The churchyard has an especially rich collection of 17th- and 18th-century table tombs. Near by is the 14th-century gatehouse to Standish Court, built as a residence for the Abbots of Gloucester.

Moreton Valence (3/4E) lies 2 miles west between the M5 and the Gloucester and SHARPNESS canal. The timber-framed north porch of the church shelters a Norman tympanum carved with the Archangel Michael fighting a dragon. The Perpendicular nave arcade has concave octagonal piers. Around the church are the scant remains of the castle built by Aymer de Valencia, who died in France in 1260, leaving only his name, which has stuck to the village.

Olive Lloyd-Baker, who was born in 1920 and inherited **Hardwicke Court** (3/4D), 2 miles north, early in life encouraged her tenants to continue with old-fashioned methods of farming. She built up the comprehensive collection of agricultural equipment and tools that now forms the core of the Cotswold Countryside Collection at NORTHLEACH.

She is commemorated in a stained-glass window in the church of St Nicholas at Hardwicke village – a simple monument compared to the 17th-century Baroque tomb chests there.

Hardwicke Court (open in summer) was rebuilt in 1818, but a late 17th-century formal garden survives and is being restored.

Harnhill *see* Down Ampney

Hartpury *see* Ashleworth

Hasfield *see* Forthampton

Hatherop *see* Colns, The

Hawling *see* Sevenhampton

Hazleton *see* Notgrove

Hempsted *see* Gloucester

Hewelsfield *see* Brockweir

Hidcote Manor *see* Mickleton

Highnam (3/4D)

The A40 west of GLOUCESTER passes by a forest of pylons as well as Telford's bridge across the Severn at Over. From here the spire of Highnam church is already visible, although still 1½ miles away. The church dedicated to the Holy Innocents stands high on a promontory in the grounds of Highnam Court, and is a masterpiece of Gothic Revivalism to rival any in the country. Built in 1849–51, it is the combined work of the architect Henry Woodyer and his client, Thomas Gambier-Parry, who was responsible for the masterly wall paintings that cover every surface, including the splendid Christ in Majesty of the chancel arch.

The stained glass and the fittings are representative of the best workshops of the period; there is some glass designed by Pugin in the south aisle. There is also a memorial to Parry's second son, Sir Hubert Parry (1848–1918), who lived at Highnam Court a generation later and set Blake's poem 'Jerusalem' to music.

Highnam Court itself was built during the Commonwealth (around 1658) but is now encased in a 19th-century shell. The park and churchyard retain traces of the earthworks thrown up by the Welsh Royalist army of Prince Rupert in 1643.

Highnam village is now encircled by housing estates which spread north, almost reaching the tiny hamlet of Lassington. Here, by the side of Lassington Court, now a farmhouse, is a late

Saxon tower, once attached to the church of St Oswald. The ruinous church was restored in 1875 but demolished in 1974, leaving only the rugged tower with its hipped roof.

Rudford lies 2 miles further north, up the B4215. The parish consists of little more than a church, mill and farmhouse, reached via a humpbacked bridge that crosses the filled-in Gloucester and Hereford Canal, and the dismantled railway that runs parallel. The little Norman church of St Mary contains a 16th-century altar frontal.

West of Highnam, either side of the busy A40, are the hamlets of **Bulley** and **Churcham** (3/4D). Bulley's church of St Michael is Norman with a chancel rebuilt in the same style by Sidney Gambier-Parry (son of Thomas, *see above*), using alternate bands of blue lias and red sandstone to good effect. The pyramidal spire of St Andrew's at Churcham is a copy of the Saxon spire at Sompting, West Sussex, and was added in 1878, although much of the rest of the church is Norman. Above the north doorway is a Romano-British sculpture of a figure in a hooded tunic – perhaps 3rd century and one of the *genii cucullati* (hooded spirits) revered by the native community.

The village of **Tibberton** (3/4C), 1½ miles east of Rudford, is surrounded by acres of orchards and market gardens. Areas of herring-bone masonry in the nave walls, and long-and-short work quoins, suggest a late Saxon or early Norman date for Holy Trinity church. This stands next to the intriguing Tibberton Court, a handsome Georgian house extended in 1853 by the architect James Medland, who added the bell tower.

Horsley *see* Nailsworth

Huntley (3/4D)
Huntley is on the A40 about 8 miles west of GLOUCESTER, where orchard country ends and the FOREST OF DEAN begins. The church of St John the Baptist, built 1861, is a fine Victorian structure, with effective use made of alternate bands of red and white stone for the walls, arcade voussoirs and chancel arch, contrasted with the bold verticals of the roof rafters. The lectern, pulpit and reredos were shown at the Great Exhibition a few years earlier before being installed here. Huntley Manor, also by the architect T. E. Teulon, was completed at the same time as the church, in French château style.

St Michael's church at **Blaisdon** (3/4D), 2 miles south-west, was built by F. R. Kempson in 1867. It lacks Huntley's theatricality, but has some fine naturalistic carving to the capitals, with birds, flowers and animals. It stands in a pretty village and in spring it is half-hidden by flowering plum trees. Every summer there is a Plum Festival.

Icomb *see* Bledington

Kemble (4/2F)
The village, on the A429 south-west of CIREN-CESTER, has a busy railway station of 1872 serving commuters on the former Great Western Railway ('God's Wonderful Railway' to admirers of Brunel's achievement). From the platform it is possible to see the entrance to the 415 yd tunnel that exists for no other reason than that Robert Gordon, the local squire, insisted on it, along with £7500 in compensation when the railway was built close to his land.

The gardens of Gordon's home, Kemble House, are occasionally open under the National Gardens Scheme, as are those at Ewen Manor, a solid Georgian house with hipped roof in the hamlet of **Ewen** (4/3F), 1 mile to the east.

The church at Ewen was demolished in the 19th century, and the best of its masonry incorporated into All Saints church at Kemble, which was rebuilt in 1872–8. The outstanding south chapel, for example, with its Early English tomb recess, sedilia and piscina originally came from Ewen. The spire was added during the restoration of 1872–8 and is topped with a red warning light for aircraft flying in and out of the RAF base near by.

North of Kemble, on the A429 at Smerill Farm, there is a very fine barn. These great churchlike structures are an outstanding and neglected part of Europe's architectural heritage. This barn is one of many excellent examples in the area that have survived since the 14th century.

Kempley (3/3C)
The village lies a couple of miles west of the M50, on the newly designated Daffodil Way (*see* Dymock), and demands plenty of time for the full appreciation of both of its rewarding churches. The earlier of the two, St Mary, has the most complete, and some of the earliest, fresco paintings in the country. They cover the whole of the chancel vault and walls, depicting Christ in Majesty seated on a rainbow and

St Mary's church, Kempsford

around him the sun, moon and stars, the Virgin, Evangelists and seraphim. The Apostles are seated beneath arcades around the walls. The scheme dates to between 1130 and 1140.

The work was discovered in 1871 and covered with varnish to conserve the bright colours. Only in 1955 was it discovered that this covering, which has since been removed, was unnecessary, for the paintings are true frescos, applied to wet plaster so that the colour is absorbed into the surface. Later wall painters, like those who executed the 14th-century Wheel of Fortune and scenes from the Ten Ages of Man in the nave, lost the technique and painted on a dry surface, using a fixative.

The colours used in the scheme are red and ochre, derived from iron oxide, and white from lime. Even with such a restricted palette, the artists achieved great range and diversity by the skilful mixing of colours and effective use of contrast.

Except for the paintings, the church is relatively humble, its only other adornment being the south doorway, surrounding a Tree of Life tympanum similar to that at Dymock, perhaps by the same school of masons. The church

stands alone by the Kempley brook. The rest of the village, apart from Kempley Court (dated 1689), has moved to higher ground at Kempley Green, 1½ miles south-east.

Here, the church of Edward the Confessor was begun in 1903, designed by Randell Wells with bravado: he was only 25 at the time. All the materials came from the area and local craftsmen provided most of the furnishings; the ironwork was from the village blacksmith, and the carpenter made the figure of Christ over the north door. Those that were not made near by, including the pews, lectern and candlesticks, came from the SAPPERTON workshops of Gimson and the Barnsley brothers. The church beautifully exemplifies the principles and practice of that branch of the Arts and Crafts movement that briefly flourished in the Cotswolds in the early 20th century.

Queen's Wood to the south has marked forest trails.

Kempsford (4/4F)

The village is about 3 miles south of FAIRFORD, close to the US Air Force base, known for its International Air Tattoo and an annual steam traction rally. The church and Manor Farmhouse stand on the Gloucestershire bank of the Thames looking over to the watery flatlands of Wiltshire. St Mary's church is surprisingly grand for the size of the village, but the owners of the manor were the Lancasters, one of England's noblest families. In 1361 the Lancaster estates passed to John of Gaunt, son of Edward III.

Gaunt is credited with building the tower of Kempsford church between 1385 and 1399, by which time he was in semi-retirement. It is a stately work, with an elaborate vault decorated with armorial shields and the red rose of Lancaster, all painted in 1862.

The Norman nave, with intact decorated north and south doorways, was heightened in the mid-15th century by the addition of a clerestory and a magnificent timber roof.

G. E. Street, who carried out restorations between 1858 and 1862, sympathetically and faithfully copied what he found, picking up details from existing work for his extensions. He also designed the splendid choir stalls.

The Manor Farmhouse was rebuilt in 1846 but stands on the site of a 12th-century castle, itself erected on pre-Norman earthworks, constructed to defend the strategically important river ford. A barn, with mullioned windows and

Tudor doorways, survives and other parts of the 17th-century mansion that was on the site stand in the gardens of the Vicarage.

The course of the old **Thames and Severn Canal** runs parallel with the River Thames between the church and the village. On its brink is a former canal warehouse, built in 1789 – the two side wings were used for storage while the central bay, beneath a triangular pediment pierced by an oval window, served as the wharf manager's home.

Kiftsgate *see* Mickleton

King's Stanley *see* Leonard Stanley

Kingswood *see* Wotton-under-Edge

Lancaut *see* Beachley

Lasborough *see* Boxwell

Lassington *see* Highnam

Lechlade (4/5F)
Two roads, the A417 and the A361, cross at Lechlade and three rivers, the Coln, the Cole and the Leach, join the Thames here, swelling its flow and making it navigable on down to its estuary. Most of the boats using this upper

Lock on the River Thames at Lechlade

stretch of the river today are pleasure craft, mooring where barges once loaded up with stone for Oxford and London.

There is no better way to approach Lechlade than along the river. From the footpath on the north bank there is a splendid view of Church House, 18th century with a hipped roof, and the elegant church and spire, rising above the surrounding watermeadows. The path begins at St John's Bridge, rebuilt in the mid-19th century but on the site of one of the earliest stone bridges across the Thames outside London, existing since the 13th century.

The Trout Inn, close by, stands on the site of the Augustinian Hospital of St John, which was suppressed in 1473 and its revenue diverted to the rebuilding of the parish church.

Shortly after the bridge comes the lock and the statue of Neptune that once stood at the source of the Thames (*see* Coates). This friendly reclining figure (known affectionately as Old Father Thames) was sculpted by the Italian Rafaelle Monti around 1855 and came to Gloucestershire, from the Crystal Palace, in 1958.

The final destination of the footpath is Lechlade's handsome parish church. Originally dedicated to St John, it was re-dedicated to the Spanish St Lawrence in deference to Henry VIII's first wife, Katherine of Aragon, who owned the manor. It overlooks the market place of a Cotswold town with much good Georgian architecture. The nave was heightened in the early 16th century and given the clerestory, which contributes to the spacious, airy feeling of the church; the north porch with its star-shaped lierne vault was added at the same time.

Over the chancel, angels carved into the roof bosses carry the instruments of Christ's Passion but one boss is entirely different from the rest, depicting a pair of collar wrestlers.

In the churchyard there is the tomb of Sarah, wife of the GLOUCESTER printer Robert Raikes whose school (opened in 1780) was the progenitor of the Sunday School movement.

The poet Shelley so liked the peaceful atmosphere here that he sat down to write a sonnet, 'A Summer Evening Churchyard', in eulogy of the town. He visited in 1815, having rowed up the Thames from Windsor.

Many travellers have stopped to break their fast at the New Inn, in the Market Place, for Lechlade stands where two coach roads cross. The Inn, along with nearby Morley House, is early 18th century but, unusually, built of red brick, still expensive enough then to be thought a fashionable alternative to stone.

Lechlade, now, is ringed by gravel quarries. As new ones are opened up, archaeologists struggle to keep one step ahead of the diggers, and with spectacular results: scores of sites have been discovered, from Iron Age villages to Saxon cemeteries so rich in grave goods that the local newspaper dubbed one grave occupant 'Mrs Getty', on account of her copious jewellery. (The finds are now in the Ashmolean Museum, Oxford.) Those gravel pits that have already been exhausted have been landscaped and converted into a popular water park for anglers, yachtsmen, water skiers and windsurfers.

It is only a short distance over Halfpenny Bridge, with its early 19th-century tollhouse, to the lonely meadows south of the town where the flat landscape of the Wiltshire border is crisscrossed with water channels fringed with willows.

Here, just north of Inglesham, is the 18th-century round house, warehouse and bridge that marks the junctions of the Rivers Coln and Thames and the **Thames and Severn Canal** (*see* Sapperton). It is a humble terminus for the canal hailed by *The Times* on its opening in 1781 as 'the grandest object ever obtained by inland navigation'. Some of the canal's original backers had ambitious plans to extend the navigation to Abingdon, but lack of capital forced the building of a temporary junction here that was to prove permanent.

Leckhampton (4/2D)

Stone from the quarries on Leckhampton Hill just south of CHELTENHAM was used to face many a fine terrace in the town, and a tramway was constructed in the 19th century to supply the insatiable demand for building stone and lime. So many of the townspeople used the tramway (unofficially) as an easy way up the scarp to enjoy the views that the Hill came to be regarded in time as common property.

Consequently, the late 19th-century owner's attempt to re-open the quarries led to a riot, and prominent citizens, including Miss Beale, the founder of Cheltenham Ladies College, campaigned against the Hill's enclosure. Finally, in 1929, Cheltenham Town Council purchased the Hill for public enjoyment and the 400 acres of grassland have since been declared a Site of Special Scientific Interest. The Cotswold Way passes through the area, there are traces of an Iron Age hillfort – and the views over Cheltenham are splendid.

Before the Second World War, Leckhampton Hill was promoted as a weekend attraction by the Great Western Railway; contemporary photographs show foolhardy visitors standing on top of the Devil's Chimney, a prominent pillar of stone deliberately carved out by 19th-century quarrymen on the sheer cliff edge. Climbing is now strictly prohibited – not only because it is dangerous but also because of the threat to this popular landmark from erosion.

Even before Cheltenham's boom, Leckhampton Hill supplied stone for local buildings, including the church of St Peter at Leckhampton. Apart from the delicate spire and vaulted chancel, both early 14th century, the church is best known for its monuments. That of Sir John Giffard (d.1327) and his fine-featured wife is one of the best in Gloucestershire.

Ex-colonial civil servants and soldiers are commemorated here and a churchyard cross records the death of Dr Edward Wilson, one of the explorers who reached the South Pole with Scott in 1912 and died with him on the return journey.

Opposite the church is the moated Leckhampton Court (now a Sue Ryder home), which encapsulates the Giffards' original 14th-century manor, just visible through the entrance gates.

Charlton Kings (4/2C) was a village until the 1840s, when it became a fashionable suburb of Cheltenham. The church of St Mary has a 15th-century tower, surviving from village days, but the rest of the church was largely rebuilt in 1877–8 to accommodate a much enlarged congregation. A second church, Holy Apostles, was built in 1871 at the junction of the CIRENCESTER and Andoversford roads. Its spire was dismantled after lightning struck in the 1970s, leaving a truncated stump. The Cotswold Way passes high up along Charlton Kings Common.

Shurdington (4/2D) lies 2 miles south-west of Leckhampton on the A46, the former turnpike road that links Cheltenham and Bath. The church of St Paul has a graceful 14th-century octagonal spire, 109 ft tall and very like that at Leckhampton. According to local legend the builder of Leckhampton's spire killed himself for failing, in his estimation, to match the beauty of Shurdington's.

At the opposite end of the village, a track called the Green Way leads straight up the Cotswold scarp past the 18th-century Greenway Hotel and the Crippetts, the 19th-century mock-Tudor former home of the Antarctic explorer, Edward Wilson. The Green Way was a sheep-walk linking the high summer pastures with the more sheltered winter grazing in the vale. The upper ½ mile of this Saxon trackway is now part of the Cotswold Way.

Leigh, The (4/1C)

The village lies west of the A38 to the north of GLOUCESTER. It consists of a circle of brick, timber and thatched cottages with the church of St Catherine a little distance away, close to a partly moated farmhouse. The church was a chapel to the priory at DEERHURST and has pleasing features, including its Perpendicular tower with St Catherine headless in an image niche.

North of the village is an early 19th-century canal, only 2½ miles long. The land here floods so often that a waterway across the flat fields was thought more practical than a causeway. From the River Severn, the canal heads for Coombe Hill and the neglected brick wharf where cargo, principally coal, was unloaded on to carts for the final 5-mile road journey to CHELTENHAM. After the failure of schemes to convert the canal into a marina, it has now been taken in hand by the Gloucestershire Trust for Nature Conservancy as part of a wetland nature reserve.

Wainlode Hill overlooks the Severn with its riverside walks, about a mile to the west of The Leigh, and there are camping and caravan sites.

Leighterton *see* Boxwell

Leonard Stanley (3/4E)

The village lies south of the River Frome and the A419, about 3 miles west of STROUD. The former Augustinian priory of St Leonard and its associated buildings are of great interest but difficult to appreciate fully, since several of them stand within a private farmyard. The priory was founded by Roger Berkeley between 1121 and 1129, and its church (now the parish church) was exclusively for the monks to worship in. Parishioners used the chapel of St Swithin, south-west of the priory church, which is late Saxon in origin and much obscured by farm buildings – it is itself used as a barn.

In the 15th century a rood was inserted half way down the nave of the priory church. This suggests that the church was then split in two, with the parish using the nave, the monks the area from the tower crossing to the sanctuary.

Since the Dissolution of the Monasteries the parish has had full use of the church and all subdivisions have been removed. The very fine capitals in the chancel are exceptional, even for a region rich in good Norman carving. They depict the Nativity and Mary Magdalene washing the feet of Christ with her hair.

The monastic buildings lay to the south of the church; a 14th-century barn and fishpond are all that remain. The farmhouse dates to the mid-18th century, a solid, dignified building with a central pediment carved with the arms of the Sandford family.

Close to the church is a group of 16th- and 17th-century buildings, but much of the village dates from the later industrialization of the Frome valley. It merges with **King's Stanley** (3/5E) where the magnificent Stanley Mill straddles the river, still producing high-quality cloth and woollen felt, and somewhat obscured by later buildings.

The mill, completed around 1815, was intended to be fireproof. Wood was totally excluded and the flagstone floors are carried on huge iron plates supported by iron columns and trusses.

The church of St George at King's Stanley is part Norman, part 15th century, restored in 1876. It has painted ceilings. Several headstones in the churchyard have copper plaques in place of carved inscriptions.

From King's Stanley the A419 heads west to

the M5. Industrial Stonehouse (3/5E) lies to the north of this road while the Stroudwater Canal (*see* Arlingham) runs parallel to the south, crossed by a series of 18th-century bridges. One of these carries the lane to **Eastington** (3/4E), with its church of St Michael, alongside the Frome.

The south aisle has elaborate tracery and is filled with memorials that illustrate the changing fashions in funerary style: the brasses and stone effigies of the 16th and 17th centuries, the marble urns and statuary of the 18th, the neo-Gothic of the 19th.

Little Barrington *see* Barringtons, The

Littledean (3/3D)
This village on the A4151 east of CINDERFORD is not quite in the FOREST OF DEAN, as officially defined, but is definitely part of it, for the church of St Ethelbert in this mining community has a large collection of Forest-type headstones. The regional speciality here is a flat stone of hard grey 'Forest marble' (carboniferous limestone), carved in relief with allegorical figures, cherubs or symbols representing the trades of the deceased.

These early headstones contain many a biography in miniature; and there is material here to fill a novel. We read of a policeman murdered by poachers, of infant mortality, and of young colliers cut off in their prime by the collapse of a colliery ceiling.

The church itself has a stump of a tower, all that was left after a gale in 1894. Most of the nave and chancel are Perpendicular.

Littledean Police Station was built as a gaol in 1791 by the prison reformer Sir George Onesiphorus Paul. Although stark and forbidding, his prisons were a considerable improvement on the standards of earlier lock-ups (*see also* Northleach).

The road from Littledean to NEWNHAM passes the newly opened historic mansion, Littledean Hall. The owners make much of its haunted history and lay great claims for the antiquity of the house, much of which is 16th and 17th century with some fine oak panelling. Excavations in the grounds have uncovered Roman remains, with what may have been a 4th-century Christian church. A walk through the grounds crosses a hilltop, with fine views eastward over the River Severn, and leads to a tree-covered Norman motte.

Little Rissington *see* Rissingtons, The

Site of the Norman motte at Littledean Hall

Gloucestershire Gardens

JOHN SALES

In the 12th century Alexander Neckham, Abbot of Cirencester Abbey, wrote 'there [in the garden] you should have parsley, alecost, fennel, southernwood, coriander, smallage, lettuce and garden cress . . . nor are there wanting if the occasion further thee, pottage herbs, beets, orach, sorrel, mallows, anise, mustard, wormwood . . .' There were extensive vineyards at Gloucester Abbey, where the cloistered courts also contained medicinal and other herbs, and probably some vegetables and flowers.

The tradition of gardening is strong in Gloucestershire. It is exceptionally rich in historic gardens, with 51 listed by English Heritage in the *Register of Parks and Gardens of Special Historic Interest in England*. Almost every style and influence affecting gardens over the past 300 years can be seen, together with traces of even earlier layouts, such as at the Roman villa at Chedworth and the 16th-century courtyard at Thornbury Castle.

Today this tradition is stronger than ever, with a wide range of gardens open regularly through the season, and more than 90 gardens or village groups of gardens receiving visitors from time to time under the National Gardens Scheme. The county has been enriched by the works of some of the best-known and most talented garden writers of recent years, such as Alvilde Lees-Milne and Rosemary Verey, as well as by eminent postwar gardeners like Mary Biddulph of Rodmarton Manor, Diana Binney of Kiftsgate Court, Lady Kleinwort of Sezincote and Penny Pollit of Yew Tree Cottage, Ampney St Mary. The first half of the 20th century had already made Gloucestershire a world trendsetter in garden design and plantsmanship through Lawrence Johnston's Hidcote and through the influence of other important gardens of the period, such as Mark Fenwick's Abbotswood, Heather Muir's Kiftsgate and Charles Wade's Snowshill Manor.

The deep and widespread interest in plants is exemplified by a thriving Gloucestershire branch of the National Council for the Conservation of Plants and Gardens, whose members save and cultivate worthwhile plants of the past. Hosts of good garden plants have been raised or introduced by distinguished plantsmen and discriminating collectors who have lived in Gloucestershire. One of the earliest was John Banister, who collected plants in Virginia after 1678 and introduced,

among other things, the scarlet oak (*Quercus coccinea*), box elder (*Acer negundo*) and the dainty *Gillenia trifoliata*. Possibly the greatest Gloucestershire plant collector was Henry Elwes (1846–1922) of Colesbourne, author of a monograph on *Lilium* and after whom many bulbs and corms are named. An interest in trees led to his planting the Colesbourne Arboretum and his co-authorship with Dr Augustine Henry of *Trees of Great Britain and Ireland*. Between the First and Second World Wars, Helen Milford of Chedworth introduced many South African plants, including the popular daisy *Dimorphotheca (osteospermum) barberiae compacta* and the silver *Helichrysum alveolatum* (*H. splendidum*). The large early snowdrop *Galanthus* 'Atkinsii' gets its name from James Atkins, a nurseryman who retired to Painswick in 1871.

Many plants are named after Hidcote and Lawrence Johnston. These include some of the most popular in horticulture, such as *Lavandula angustifolia* 'Hidcote' and the scarlet *Verbena* 'Lawrence Johnston'. His friend Mark Fenwick's garden gave its name to the white *Potentilla* 'Abbotswood' and *Lychnis coronaria* 'Abbotswood Rose'; and the name Kiftsgate has become widely known through that magnificent climbing rose *R. filipes* 'Kiftsgate'.

E. B. Anderson, who died in 1971, wrote several books, always quoting from personal experience largely gained in his own garden at Lower Slaughter. A past president of the Alpine Garden Society, he is associated with a number of dwarf bulbs and alpines including a golden thyme, *Thymus* 'E. B. Anderson' and *Oxalis* 'Beatrice Anderson'; also several valuable shrubs, such as *Buddleia* 'Lochinch' and *Ceanothus* 'Italian Skies'. Another alpine specialist, Joe Elliott, ran a successful nursery at Broadwell from 1946 and wrote *Alpines in Sinks and Troughs*. He had a wonderful eye for a good plant. Several of his introductions are widely grown, for example *Sedum* 'Vera Jameson' and *Campanula glomerata* 'Joan Elliott'.

If we take the historic boundary rather than the present-day Gloucestershire, then 19th-century Bitton, near Bristol, provided the country's most famous gardening author. Following a series of articles about his garden at Bitton Rectory in the *Manchester Guardian*, Canon Henry Ellacombe published his modest but influential book in

Westbury Court (National Trust)

1895. At a time when massed bedding-out using flamboyant tender plants was the fashion, Canon Ellacombe's discriminating interest in hardy plants, and his descriptions of the qualities and values of each in the garden, came as a refreshing change. His acute and accurate observations were expressed simply but elegantly to make *In a Gloucestershire Garden* one of the great gardening classics.

In the late 17th and early 18th century Mary Somerset, Duchess of Beaufort, became an expert horticulturist at Badminton (no longer in Gloucestershire); the tender Australian shrub genus Beaufortia is named after her. From her time onward the influence of women on gardening in Gloucestershire has never waned; and since the Second World War they have outshone their male counterparts in artistry, commitment and expertise.

Why is it that so many gardens of such high quality have been made in Gloucestershire? And why have so many survived to be further elaborated and enriched over the years? The Gloucestershire soils vary according to the underlying geology and the sedimentary deposits laid down over millions of years. The Cotswolds are derived from oolitic limestone and soils are therefore mainly calcareous, often deep and heavy in the valleys, but on the hillsides usually thin and stony, covering broken limestone brash. Given plenty of manure or other organic material, and hard work, they can be very fertile – but hardly easy. Being formed from limestone they cannot grow rhododendrons and many other interesting plants that are lime-haters. The Severn Valley soils overlie clay. They vary from sandy alluvial deposits to sticky soils derived from the parent material. Although rich when drained, few notable gardens have been made on such soils. The Forest of Dean provides the only part of the county with ideal conditions for rhododendrons. But again the area has not spawned many important gardens. It is the Cotswolds that have inspired most of the great gardens of the county, at any rate in the last 100 years or so, in response to the great beauty of the landscape.

Despite a sharp climate – colder than the surrounding counties, with winter temperatures as low as Norfolk in the east – and a short growing season, people garden the Cotswolds more intensively and more successfully than almost any comparable area of the British Isles.

Gardens are made according to the fashion of the day and in response to site and climate. But the origin of great gardens is almost always in the ideals of their creators. Gloucestershire has had the good fortune to produce, and often to attract, some of the most imaginative gardeners, and the most creative designers in horticultural history. The result is a series of gardens hardly equalled in artistry, variety and interest anywhere in the world.

The formal late 17th-century gardens of the county were faithfully recorded, in all their detail, in engravings by Johannes Kip (after Leonard Knyff) for *The Ancient and Present State of Gloucestershire*, published by Robert Atkyns in 1712. The site of Atkyns' own house and garden, Sapperton Manor, which was illustrated, can still be distinguished near Sapperton church, with its terraces intact. It was destroyed by Allen, the first Earl Bathurst, after he bought the estate. Of the many gardens in the fascinating bird's-eye views engraved by Kip, few survive in anything like their original form. Traces can be seen at Bradley Court, Flaxley Abbey and Misarden Park.

Westbury Court, set 9 miles south-west of Gloucester, is an exception; here the formal water garden has been almost miraculously preserved while the original house and its two successors were destroyed. Now the house site is occupied by an old people's home. Since 1967 the garden has been restored from dereliction and continually improved by the National Trust, as far as possible according to Kip's engraving and using the meticulous account books kept by Maynard Colchester, who made the garden after he inherited the estate in 1694. Enclosed by high walls, with its elegant pavilion, its canals and its emphasis on horticulture, Westbury Court is a rare survival of the formal style developed in 17th-century Holland from Renaissance origins. Here is a garden for the architect and the historian as well as for the plantsman with a wide range of Carolean plants and fruits, climbers and herbs, trees and topiary.

Of medieval origin, Owlpen Manor was re-modelled in the 16th and 17th centuries and again in the early 18th, from which time its oldest terraces and topiary – its most famous feature – are thought to date. Overlooking a lovely valley near Uley, Owlpen is the quintessence of the 'old English' style. It was one of the Cotswold craftsmen, Norman Jewson, who restored the house in 1926.

The place that boasts perhaps the longest pedigree among Gloucestershire gardens is Stanway House between Winchcombe and Broadway. With a medieval deer park, developed as a formal landscape in the late 17th and 18th centuries, a magnificent gatehouse of about 1630, traces of the late 17th-century garden shown in engravings by Kip and Knyff, the remains of a canal and cascade dating from a grand scheme of 1730, together with a pyramid of 1750, it is the stuff of garden historians – as well as being a serene and beautiful place.

The most important formal 18th-century garden in Gloucestershire is Painswick House. In 1748 Thomas Robins painted a bird's-eye view of the newly completed garden, recording precisely

Snowdrops in the Rococo Garden at Painswick House

its terraces near the house, the 'Red House' pavilion at the north-east corner, the Doric Seat, the Gothic Alcove and the Eagle House, all set in a geometrical layout of hedges, orchards, pools and vegetable garden.

Alone among the many charming examples, in pictures Robins painted, Painswick survived as a garden, sleeping under a blanket of vegetation. Having made this astonishing discovery, Lord and Lady Dickinson set about an ambitious restoration; its progress makes return visits all the more rewarding.

At Frampton Court the geometrical canal that leads to William Halfpenny's 'Strawberry Hill' Gothic orangery is an interesting late example of 18th-century formal design. All around are fine old trees, including holm oaks, Scots and Austria, pines and a splendid weeping ash, and near by is a charming octagonal dovecot. Beyond the house an Italianate Victorian terrace with beds of colourful roses overlooks an 18th-century land-scape park. The view to the lake through the towering lime trees and willows is stunningly beautiful.

The typical English landscape park of 'Capability' Brown and Humphry Repton is comparatively rare in the present Gloucestershire. Barnsley Park, north-east of Cirencester, stands in mature parkland, the exquisite house flanked by a classical orangery, fully stocked with oranges and tender conservatory plants. Inside the sunken fence, or ha-ha, the layout is a formal goosefoot of avenues framed by hedges and adorned by flower borders, roses and statuary. Repton is said to have advised at Sezincote, and he certainly laid out Adlestrop Park at the end of the century. But in Cirencester Park we can enjoy the very cradle of the English landscape style, one of the very greatest contributions of this nation to European art and culture. At the hand of the 1st Earl Bathurst, and with the help of Alexander Pope, the geometrical formality of the Baroque style began to break down.

With its Queen Anne's Monument, Pope's Seat, Alfred's Hall and a variety of other eye-catchers, Cirencester Park seems regular and geometrical to the modern viewer, especially along the avenue of horse chestnuts, which was extended towards the parish church in the 19th century. But it was here that Bathurst took the first steps towards asymmetry within the traditional formal structure of avenues. The park was first opened in 1714 – since then it has been the best free treat in Gloucestershire.

The rapid development of Cheltenham as a spa in Regency times gave rise to its magnificent town parks. These mostly began as privately owned places where clients of the spa would indulge in gentle exercise. This culminated in Pittville Park, a well-preserved early Victorian town park next to John Forbes' splendid classical Pump Room. With its lake, twin bridges, arboretum, shrubberies and flower beds, its style is what John Loudon, the leading horticultural writer of the time, would have termed the 'gardenesque', a style between formal and informal that aimed to display every plant to best advantage.

Stancombe Park, at Stinchcombe (near Stroud) is set in a mature early Victorian landscape park, with lovely views to Wotton-under-Edge. It has a charming garden near the house developed by the owners in the post-war country-house style, with soft colours and bold foliage, silver predominating. It is a fine collection of plants and trees sensitively arranged, including magnificent double borders and a pretty gazebo. But the real excitement of Stancombe is the 'secret garden' concealed by woodland in a valley a little way from the house. Created by the Reverend David Edwards around 1850, it is a fascinating miniature landscape arranged around a small lake. The walk leads past a trickling spring and through mysterious tunnels to give a succession of well-staged surprises and melodramatic changes of mood. This is a place to discover.

The 19th century was when plant hunting developed from a simple interest in adorning English gardens with beautiful exotica from the colonies into a passion for novelty, and a competi-tive urge to collect and display as much as possible of what was outlandish and rare. Professional plant hunters – Archibald Menzies, David Douglas, the Lobb brothers and others – were dispatched far and wide on behalf of prosperous landowners who planted the stream of novelties with ever-increasing enthusiasm.

Robert Holford, who began work in 1829, was in the forefront of the development of English arboreta and Westonbirt, near Tetbury, remains among the finest in the world, thanks to continuous care and renewal. He planted the great groups of North American conifers – Wellington-ias, Douglas firs, redwoods – and aligned the main avenues on the monumental Westonbirt House (now a well-known school for girls). The garden, which is open occasionally, is similarly impressive, with spacious terraces, and massive stonework. A superb semicircular Italian garden is entered through domed pavilions with intricate carvings, and what is then revealed is a sym-metrical pattern of stone-edged beds arranged around urns. A conservatory is set in the north wall and an exuberantly sculptured fountain and lily pool are on the opposite side.

The Holford family (in competition with Lord Ducie at Tortworth Court, where there remains a fine arboretum) continued to develop the Westonbirt Arboretum, through Robert's son Sir George Holford and, in this century, the Earl of Morley. Since 1956 the Forestry Commission has kept up the good work at Westonbirt. Open, and beautiful, throughout the year, the arboretum is especially lovely in spring for its blossom, wild flowers and rhododendrons; and of course in autumn, when its famous glades of Japanese maples are spectacular.

Of comparable quality but later date is Batsford Park, near Moreton-in-Marsh, a rich and varied arboretum incorporating a Japanese garden. It was planted by Algernon Bertram Freeman-Mitford, 1st Baron Redesdale, who had been on diplomatic service in the Far East, and moved here in 1886. Author of *The Bamboo Garden* (1896), he also espoused the 'wild garden' ideas of William Robinson. We can now enjoy the outcome in its full maturity, an informal layout that takes full advantage of its varied contours, natural water and fine prospects over the Evenlode valley. Although the outstanding collection of bamboos for which it was famous in Edwardian times is now depleted, this is amply compensated by the remarkable range of interesting trees, including many planted for autumn colour, added since 1956 by Lord Dulverton. When the cherry trees are in blossom is also a good time to visit the arboretum, which is open daily, April–October.

Medieval Sudeley Castle at Winchcombe has a

garden first laid out by Emma Dent, who also restored the castle in the mid-19th century. The arrangement of clipped yew hedges and topiary enclosing intriguing pathways remains intact; and her slightly sunken Queen's Garden now has a foursquare pattern of lavender and box to complement the colourful bedding plants. The surrounding terrace walk also gives fine views over the park to the Cotswolds beyond. There are several shrub borders and magnificent climbers on the castle walls; also noble trees and masses of naturalized bulbs.

Romantic Berkeley Castle, also medieval, was first given its famous terraced garden by Lady Georgina Fitzhardinge in the 1880s. Then it was developed by Major Robert Berkeley. Ellen Willmott of Warley Place, Essex, was his aunt, and both Gertrude Jekyll and Vita Sackville-West (of Sissinghurst) were approving visitors; so he was caught up in the reaction against lavish Victorian bedding out. Furnishing three terraces that fall away below the castle to the south, the borders show all the abundant luxuriance and the plantsmanship of the time. Exotic plants and climbers bask in the reflected warmth of the ancient walls with the emphasis, Jekyll-style, on strong architectural foliage: *Acanthus mollis*, *Magnolia dalavayi* and *Magnolia grandiflora*, *Vitis coignetiae*, large-leaved ivies and yuccas. This is a plantsman's garden of great distinction.

Gertrude Jekyll's influence on Gloucestershire gardens has been profound. Developed largely in conjunction with the architectural layouts of Sir Edwin Lutyens, her principles of colour, texture, arrangement and form in planting have been freely adapted and developed in Gloucestershire as the dominant theme of the 20th century. But there was another great gardening genius at work in the first half of the century. At Hidcote Manor, in Hidcote Bartrim, near Mickleton, Lawrence Johnston was making his own intensely personal paradise in a style never seen before. Here was the full flowering of the Jekyll style of planting encapsulated in an imaginative architectural layout. But it escaped the house and the Lutyens-style dominance of the architect and the builder. Responding to an exposed site Johnston, like all great artists, made a virtue of necessity and gardened within a framework of hedges and topiary of every kind and variety, creating garden 'rooms' linked by bold vistas like the corridors of a house. By contrasting intricate planting with plain lawns, intimate enclosure with open views, light with shade, formality with informality; and by manipulating colour and texture, paving, water and a vast variety of plants in an imaginative way, he produced the most exciting and original garden of the century, possibly the most influ-

The Bathing Pool at Hidcote Manor (National Trust)

ential in the world. A garden made for perhaps 100 visitors a year now receives 100,000; the sum of the enjoyment it gives and the ideas it stimulates must be vast.

Nearby Kiftsgate was made by Heather Muir, a friend of Lawrence Johnston, after the First World War. She developed the paved garden and a series of colour-related borders below the house. Thanks to her daughter, Diana Binney, these retain their beauty and the free and unforced arrangement that is a mark of the style. Throughout this second generation Kiftsgate has been further developed, especially with planting on the steep banks, and also in the sunken White Garden. Cotswold gardens tend to come to their peak in midsummer. The garden of old roses, with the gigantic 'Kiftsgate' rose alongside, ensures that this rule is proved here too.

Mark Fenwick was another friendly rival of Lawrence Johnston and his garden at Abbotswood was second only to Hidcote in its influence at the time. Like Jekyll, and unlike Johnston, Fenwick employed an architect – Sir Edwin Lutyens – not only to rebuild the house but also to lay out the main structure of the garden. Broad terraces fall away to the south with a summerhouse and a glorious view over the park. To the west is an enclosed rectangular lily pool linked to the house by Lutyens' characteristic concave fountain. As well as a flower garden there is an expertly arranged rock garden of water-worn Westmorland limestone, with a stream and masses of naturalized dwarf bulbs. The arboretum contains a vast range of choice trees and shrubs, now in their maturity, showing us the genius of a great gardener.

The Long Garden at Rodmarton Manor

The influence of the Arts and Crafts movement was felt in gardens as well as in houses, and there was a fashion for the 'old English' style – simple formal layouts of yew hedges, grass and topiary, incorporating local materials and seemingly unsophisticated masses of hardy plants. The Cotswold craftsmen favoured this style and it was one of them, Ernest Barnsley, who built Rodmarton Manor in the 1920s. With William Scrubey, the first head gardener, he also laid out the garden. Their design is still apparent, especially in the Long Garden with its profuse double borders leading to Barnsley's charming summerhouse. Mary Biddulph has restored and redeveloped the garden since 1954 and its interesting and beautiful plants include an astonishing collection of snowdrops.

A farmyard until 1919, the garden at the Tudor Snowshill Manor about 6 miles north-east of Winchcombe was first laid out by architect M. H. Baillie Scott at the invitation of Charles Wade, the new owner. But almost immediately Wade altered, developed and extended the stiff Italianate scheme, according to his own individual, even eccentric, ideas. He created a jewel among smaller Cotswold gardens, full of fascinating diversity and cunning changes of mood, yet disarmingly simple in its planting. Like Hidcote it consists of a series of enclosures, but here on different levels, first concealing and then revealing a new pleasure at every turn.

Like Abbotswood, Misarden Park, north-west of Cirencester, shows the hand of Lutyens, who rebuilt the east wing in 1920 after a fire. A loggia and a succession of small terraces were made as part of this scheme, now furnished with lavenders, Mexican orange and a splendid magnolia. Double herbaceous borders lead up to the main lawn via delightful grass steps with Cotswold stone risers.

The outline of this fascinating garden was laid down in the 17th century when the walled garden was made west of the house. Here are sumptuous herbaceous borders and a central walk bounded by yew hedges of unusual design. Elsewhere there are fine trees, a variety of shrubs, masses of naturalized bulbs and glorious views over the Golden Valley.

A visit to early 19th-century Sezincote, just south of Bourton-on-the-Hill, is worth the journey for a sight of the orange-brown house with its onion-shaped copper dome and Mogul Indian decoration; also the curving Orangery elaborately carved in a paler stone. The influence of India on the architect Samuel Pepys Cockerell and his collaborator, the painter Thomas Daniell, both of whom had served there, also shows in the garden. The drive crosses a stream by Daniell's bridge, decorated with cast-iron Brahmin bulls. This stream with its shallow valley forms the spine of the informal garden, beginning at the round Temple Pool with its Indian shrine. Thence the stream descends through a series of pools and a wonderful variety of trees, shrubs and plants, beautifully arranged, to a lake at the bottom. Humphry Repton was consulted about the park, which provides the serene foreground to glorious views across the lake and over the Evenlode valley.

Lydney Park, situated in the western corner of the county, has that rarity in Gloucestershire, a full-blown rhododendron garden. With ideal lime-free soil in a moist, sheltered valley, lent mildness by the Severn Estuary close by, this is an ideal place for rhododendrons, and for the many choice trees, shrubs and plants that prefer semi-woodland and abhor limestone. Mountains of the old rhododendron 'Cynthia' grow at the top of the valley. Further down the selection is wide, embracing old cultivars, species and modern hybrids and Pieris, magnolias, snowdrop tree and many more riches: a feast of colour in May.

The work of gardener and author Alvilde Lees-Milne at Alderley Grange, south of Wotton-under-Edge, has been faithfully perserved and, of course, developed (for gardens cannot remain static) by the present owners. Within its climber-covered walls the garden progresses, like Hidcote, from one brilliant and original colour scheme to the next. Each enclosure is set in a carefully contrived structure of pleached limes, hedges, walls and shrubs.

Rosemary Verey has become Gloucestershire's most famous and distinguished gardener and writer, not only here but also in the United States, whence comes a stream of pilgrims to visit Barnsley House. A comparative late-comer to gardening who started only in the 1960s,

Rosemary, and her husband David, soon created an intriguing layout, using a classical temple from Fairford Park, a sundial, statuary and a fountain by Simon Verity as focal points; all cleverly combined with the existing features of this beautiful Cotswold house and garden. As at Alderley Grange, the influence of Hidcote can be seen in the subtle colour schemes and the use of contrast and form. But original features and touches are everywhere, not least in the ornamental vegetable garden, or potager, the pretty pattern of the herb garden and the immaculate knot garden – all ideas from Rosemary Verey's collection of old gardening books and herbals. This is a garden that is beautiful at all seasons.

With so many to choose from, omission of a number of worthy gardens is inevitable in anything shorter than a large work of reference. Such richness and variety, open to the public at one time or another, makes garden visiting in Gloucestershire rewarding for a surprisingly long period of the year. Do not miss the many small cottage gardens, often open in village groups. Yew Tree Cottage at Ampney St Mary, Bank Cottage at Eastington, Bliss's Cottage at Chedworth, 38 Cecily Hill, Cirencester, and many more, are little jewels, cherished with loving care by their owners. As much as the grander gardens they play their part in continuing the rich tradition of Gloucestershire gardening.

The Vegetable Garden at Barnsley House

Longborough (4/4C)

This village is just east of the A424 about 3 miles north of STOW-ON-THE-WOLD. It is all of stone, its thick-walled houses affording the inhabitants protection against the weather, for the winds can blow fiercely across the hilltop here. One of the principal houses – called Windyridge – was built in 1949 and exemplifies the revival of the Cotswold vernacular; many hardy plants grow in the shelter of its rugged walls (gardens open under the National Gardens Scheme).

The church of St James has noteworthy transepts. That to the south has generous and beautiful tracery in its early 14th-century windows, best appreciated from the outside. Was the patron, perhaps, the unknown knight who lies within? The rich decoration of his tomb chest resembles that of the beautiful font, suggesting that the same mason worked both.

The north transept was built as a private chapel for the Cockerell family of SEZINCOTE after the church there was destroyed in the Civil War. It is filled with family memorials and an early 19th-century pew, lavish as an opera box, with velvet curtains and elbow rests.

Two miles south-west, up a steep hill, is the ancient hamlet of **Condicote** (4/4C), site of the only known Neolithic henge monument in the county. The road passes through the middle of the henge, which consists of a circular ditch and bank enclosing 4 acres. Eubery Camp, on the hillside east of the village, was previously interpreted as an Iron Age enclosure, but its discontinuous banks may in fact be the result of quarrying and natural outcrops of hard rock.

Condicote itself is a neat hamlet of 17th- and 18th-century farmhouses grouped around the village green. The little Norman church of St Nicholas was rebuilt in 1888, but the south doorway, with its chevron moulding and diapered tympanum, gives a flavour of the original work.

Long Newton *see* Tetbury

Longney *see* Elmore

Lower Cam *see* Dursley

Lower Lemington *see* Moreton-in-Marsh

Lower Slaughter *see* Slaughters, The

Lower Swell *see* Stow-on-the-Wold

Lydney (3/3E)

This is a small industrial town on the A48 GLOUCESTER to Chepstow road. Its industries have included shipbuilding and cargo handling, tin-plate, metal and paper manufacture. The result is not a pretty town by any means, but one full of interest to industrial archaeologists.

The church, dedicated to St Mary, stands on the southern edge of the town. It is large and mostly Early English in style, with many a fine

A corner of Condicote, with St Nicholas's church

tombstone in the churchyard. Opposite the church, and close to the school that now bears its name, is the site of Whitecross. This was the house that Colonel John Winter (of Wintour's Leap: *see* Beachley) pulled down rather than let it fall into Parliamentary hands towards the end of the Civil War.

Also of Elizabethan date is Naas House, right on the bank of the Severn, built around 1580 and scarcely touched since. It can be seen from the towpath that leads to Lydney Harbour. This consists of a short canal that begins south of the church and has now been made into a marina. It was used from 1813 to the present century to carry iron and coal to the riverside.

The same purpose was served by the Dean Forest Railway. This connected Lydney to Lydbrook and opened in 1809, originally as a tramway using horse-drawn trucks. The society that is working to preserve the Lydney to Parkend section has provided a museum of memorabilia and rolling stock at the Norchard Steam Centre, 1 mile north of the town. Passenger trains run, in summer, along the short stretch of track that has been re-opened.

South-west of the town, on a wooded spur above Lydney Park with views over the Severn, there is an Iron Age site. The Romans mined for iron here; one of their shafts cuts through the earlier earthworks.

Around AD 367 the character of the site changed completely. A temple was built on the hilltop with a guesthouse and a bath suite for visitors. It was dedicated to the Celtic deity Nodens, associated with healing, water and the sun. Finds from Sir Mortimer Wheeler's excavations are on display in the house at Lydney Park and indicate that Roman souvenir sellers did a flourishing trade.

Other attractions at Lydney Park include the New Zealand museum containing the memorabilia of Charles Bathurst, 1st Viscount Bledisloe (1867–1958), Governor-General of New Zealand, 1930–5. The 2nd Viscount laid out the park which is stocked with fallow deer and has extensive woodland. The rhododendron and azalea garden is a splendid sight.

The church of St Mary at **Aylburton** (3/3E) was moved to its present site in 1856, but all the 14th- and 15th-century masonry was retained, including the richly decorated south door.

A treat lies in store for garden lovers at Prior's Mesne, 4 miles west of Lydney, best reached via the minor road from Aylburton. Here is the little-known 19th-century woodland garden that featured in the 1984 film *The Assam Garden* (open under the National Gardens Scheme).

Maisemore (3/5C)

This village is just north-west of GLOUCESTER on the A417. The Gloucester-born poet and composer Ivor Gurney wrote homesick verse from the trenches of the First World War in praise of the watery landscape around Maisemore. He particularly liked the view to Gloucester in those days, his 'sober and glorious City of the Plain'. Gurney's grave is in the churchyard of the Victorian church of St Matthew at nearby Twigworth.

Of these villages north of Gloucester, **Sandhurst** (3/5C) retains something of its agricultural past. The church of St Lawrence, rebuilt in 1858, has one of the county's five identical lead fonts (*see* Beachley: Tidenham).

Further east across the A38, **Down Hatherley** (4/1C) is being absorbed by the spread of Gloucester and the industrial estates around Staverton Airport. The church of St Mary has an interesting late Tudor lead font decorated with roses and foliage.

Meysey Hampton (4/4F)

This pretty village is about 3 miles west of FAIRFORD on the A417. The very fine cruciform church of St Mary stands on raised ground surrounded by watermeadows. It was probably built by the Knights Templar, which explains why this small village possesses such an ambitious church. The best of the beautiful architecture, however, dates not from the original consecration of 1269 but from the alterations of the 14th century, when the chancel was rebuilt and given its outstanding tomb recess and sedilia.

Mickleton (4/4A)

This north Gloucestershire village on the A46 is about 3 miles north of CHIPPING CAMPDEN. It has a number of thatched cottages, and the Norman church of St Lawrence has a 12th-century crucifix that may be from the old churchyard rood. Neither, however, is the reason so many visitors from home and abroad journey to this part of Gloucestershire; it is to admire the two outstanding gardens that stand opposite each other in the hills to the east, one at Kiftsgate Court, the other at Hidcote Manor.

Hidcote Manor (National Trust) in the hamlet of Hidcote Bartrim. It is an encouragement to every gardener to realize that this magnificent achievement has been created from nothing in such a short time (*see* 'Gloucestershire Gardens', p. 77). While Major Lawrence Johnston was busy carving his garden out of the bare hillside Kiftsgate's garden was created by Heather Muir, just after the Second World War.

Kiftsgate (open April–September) is of course renowned for its vigorous climbing rose, a variety of the Himalayan species *Rosa filipes* 'Kiftsgate'. It is a relatively informal garden, and has a swimming-pool terrace with fine views over the Vale of Evesham (*see* 'Gloucestershire Gardens', p. 77).

Middle Duntisbourne *see* Duntisbournes, The

Milkwall *see* Coleford

Minchinhampton (4/1E)

This prosperous small town is sometimes called the 'horsicultural' capital of the Cotswolds. It lies south of the Frome, about 4 miles south-east of STROUD. Nearby Gatcombe Park is the home of the Princess Royal, and hosts the British Open Horse Trials every August. Racehorse breeders and amateur horsemen alike exercise on Minchinhampton Common, owned by the National Trust, west of the town. They share the use of the common with golfers, kite fliers and model aircraft enthusiasts.

Picnickers shelter in the lee of the many banks that divide up the flat surface of the plateau. The most prominent of these, called the Bulwarks, are thought to be Iron Age in origin, thrown up hastily as part of the Belgic resistance to the westward marching Romans. Less prominent ditches north of the town enclosed a medieval deer park.

One very prominent mound, called Whitfield's Tump, is a reminder of the sermon given by the Gloucester-born Nonconformist preacher George Whitefield before a crowd of 20,000 in 1743.

Until the Stroud to CIRENCESTER turnpike road was opened in the early 19th century, Minchinhampton was the busy meeting place of several routes, an important market town and the prosperous centre of the local cloth trade. Now it is considerably quieter, still with an air of modest affluence. Narrow streets lead to the Market Place, where the pillared Market Hall of 1698 is surrounded by 17th- and 18th-century town houses and hotels.

Holy Trinity church has an eye-catching spire, reduced in height in 1543 when in danger of collapse, with a coronet that gives it the appearance of a giant chess piece. Considerable rebuilding of the church in the 19th century spared the glorious early 14th-century south transept, with its rose window.

The need for the slim buttresses is revealed inside. The ceiling is formed of massive and weighty stone slabs, sculpted with ribs and supported by scissor bracing – a technique common enough in timber but rare in stone.

In the valley south of Minchinhampton, Longford's Mill, established by 1705, still produces cloth. It is one of the main manufacturers of Melton cloth, which is used to cover tennis balls – including all those used at Wimbledon.

Amberley (4/1E) lies on the western edge of Minchinhampton Common, where steep pack-horse roads plunge down the scarp. The novelist Dinah Mulock (Mrs Craik) stayed at Rose Cottage here while she was writing *John Halifax, Gentleman* (1857), and set much of the action in the rambling 19th-century Amberley Court, the model for her Beechwood.

Minsterworth (3/4D)

This village some 5 miles west of GLOUCESTER is set among orchards and meadows, between the A48 and the Severn. The church of St Peter stands right on the bank of the river. Its predecessor was regularly battered by the elements and entered by flood waters. After a catastrophic deluge in 1852 and a lightning strike in 1869, it 'reached a state which precluded all repair'. It was therefore rebuilt by Henry Woodyer in 1870 with the floor raised by a prudent 4 ft. Smaller and simpler than Woodyer's church in nearby HIGHNAM, it is, even so, a considerably finer building than many of its era. There are lovely details in the carving of the nave corbels, including a vignette of three Severn salmon caught in a net.

Minsterworth was the childhood home of the poet F. W. Harvey who, like his friend Ivor Gurney (*see* Maisemore), celebrated the local landscape.

Miserden (4/2E)

The hamlet is on the lovely wooded slopes of the upper Frome valley, about 7 miles north-west of CIRENCESTER. St Andrew's church is Saxon and more of the original fabric survived the 1866 rebuilding than at first appears, for the nave has long-and-short-work quoins and the remains of

Opposite: Aerial view of Amberley and Minchinhampton Common

two crudely fashioned doorheads. Inside, heraldic imagery is transformed into a charmingly naturalistic carving of a goat, contentedly chewing at a cabbage leaf, at the foot of William Kingstone (d.1614).

Misarden Park Manor (so spelled) on its spectacular hillside site was built by the Sandys. It is open April–September. The original Elizabethan house has a two-storeyed porch and multiple gables. The east wing is the work of Sir Edwin Lutyens and links with the garden design (*see* 'Gloucestershire Gardens', p. 77).

A woodland trail passes a Norman motte and bailey to the east of Miserden.

Nearby is **Whiteway**, very much a private community, with mainly simple single-storey timber houses built by the founders of the settlement. They came here in 1898 and were early pioneers of self-sufficiency.

Edgeworth (4/2E) lies 2 miles south of Miserden overlooking the same beautiful valley. The welcoming church stands beside the manor, which was built around 1700 and refronted in 1889. Dedicated to St Mary, it was restored in the 19th century with scant respect for the Saxon fabric, but a blocked north doorway survives.

Mitcheldean (3/3D)

This town is on the A4136 in the north of the FOREST OF DEAN and within reach of a Countryside Trail, woodlands, and Plump Hill with its fine views. The church of St Michael itself justifies a visit. The 15th-century masons created a building of remarkable height and width, using the plentiful timber from the Forest to create a series of splendid roofs. The nave roof

15th-century painting in Mitcheldean church

alone has 133 bosses, with many more in the two wide aisles. The chancel, rebuilt in 1853, is continuous with the nave. Instead of a chancel arch there is a 15th-century painting of great rarity in oil on wood, depicting Christ in Majesty seated on a rainbow.

The town's considerable growth began in the late 18th century with the opening of the Monmouth turnpike road. More recently, it has become a centre of high-tech industry, with much new building.

At **Longhope** (3/3D), north-west of Mitcheldean, the much-restored church of All Saints contains a 13th-century effigy of a priest in vestments. There are several attractive timber-framed houses in this valley village.

One mile south of Mitcheldean is the tiny hamlet of Abenhall. Its pretty red sand-stone church contains a 15th-century octagonal font that clearly demonstrates that the Free Miners and ironsmiths of the Forest regarded their birthright as every bit as honourable as any nobleman's. Their shields, incised with pick and shovel, horseshoes and tongs, are carved there alongside the arms of the leading families of the region, and on an exterior wall.

Two miles further south-east is the Abbey of Flaxley, founded around 1151 as a Cistercian house by Roger, Earl of Hereford.

There are substantial remains of the abbey, but they are incorporated into the 18th-century Adam-style house that now stands on the site and invisible from the road. The ornate church of St Mary was rebuilt in 1856 by Sir George Gilbert Scott. The setting, in a broad, wooded valley, is very beautiful. True to the Old English meaning of its name, Welshbury ('foreign fortified place') Wood has an Iron Age hillfort.

May Hill. This 969-ft hill about 3 miles north-east of Mitcheldean stands proud of delightful wooded and undulating countryside. The summit is crowned by a distinctive tree clump associated with Queen Victoria's 1887 Jubilee, surrounded by heath and grassland, open to the winds but affording exhilerating views.

Two miles east of May Hill is the hamlet of **Taynton** (3/4C) with its church of St Lawrence. Unusually, the church was built during the Commonwealth and is oriented north-south instead of west-east. It replaced the original church, looted and burned in 1643, and was intended simply as a meeting hall; for the Puritans the altar was no longer the focal point of the church. The Victorians added a chancel but left the original furnishings.

Moreton-in-Marsh (4/5B)

This busy town was laid out in the 13th century where the Roman Foss Way (A429) crosses the later Worcester to Oxford road (A44). Essentially still a market town, it has its fair share of the passing trade of travellers, and the High Street is lined with coaching inns still enjoying a brisk trade. They include the Manor House Hotel, dated 1658, with its broad carriageway, the White Hart Hotel, dated 1782 but probably older behind the façade, and the 18th-century Redesdale Arms.

Away from the busy road junction, the character of Moreton undergoes a sudden change. Towards the southern end of the High Street is a cluster of good local shops: butchers that specialize in pies and game; hardware stores that have that old-fashioned smell of wax and paraffin, and sell everything from garden spades to gas mantles; and bakers offering rich lardy cake made to a local recipe.

The oldest building in the town is the 16th-century Curfew Tower, an unusual survival. Curfew continued to be rung in the town until 1860, originally as a warning to householders to cover their fires for safety reasons. By happy coincidence Moreton today has the Fire Services Training College on its outskirts. The Tower stands on an island in the middle of the A44, next to the Mann Institute built in 1891 as an adult education centre. Opposite is the Redesdale Hall of 1887, topped by a pretty timber and lead cupola, the focus of the town's Tuesday market.

Both these buildings date from the period of the town's rapid expansion after the arrival of the railway had provided the whole district with a swift means of getting produce to London. At the same time, the church underwent substantial alteration and enlargement. Its most attractive feature is the golden ashlar tower surmounted by battlements, pinnacles and a pretty octagonal spire pierced by gabled openings.

The Four Shires Stone stands 1½ miles east of Moreton, just north of the A44. The names of Gloucestershire, Worcestershire, Warwickshire and Oxfordshire are carved on the four faces; a reminder of when Evenlode, just to the south, was a Worcestershire enclave.

From here the road can be followed to **Todenham** (4/5B), north-east of Moreton. This attractive village has a church, of St Thomas of Canterbury, with a beautiful octagonal spire, which may have been the model for Moreton's. It is 14th century, the same date as the outstanding chancel tracery.

A road back into Moreton passes near **Lower Lemington** (4/5B), with its tiny Norman church of St Leonard, its old barn and farm buildings. The rest of the once populous village was cleared in the Middle Ages for sheep grazing. Sufficient of the parish survives to keep the pleasingly simple church in good order.

Two miles due west of Moreton is the village of **Bourton-on-the-Hill** (4/4B). Its undoubted beauty is somewhat marred by the main road that passes steeply through, complete with labouring heavy lorries.

It is possible to park below the church, off the road, and walk up to St Lawrence's church by a path that passes between the stone walls of the neat cottage gardens. The church is handsomely Perpendicular, with splendid gargoyles, but inside the fat piers of the nave arcade are characteristically Norman. From the churchyard the lovingly planted garden and pretty 17th-century gazebo of next-door Porch House can be glimpsed. On the other hand the gardens of Bourton House, with its gabled barn dated 1570, and the Manor House are open occasionally under the National Gardens Scheme.

Moreton Valence *see* Harescombe

Nailsworth (4/1F)

This mill town south of STROUD is split by the A46 Bath road. East of the road the valley side rises steeply to MINCHINHAMPTON Common, threaded with steep packhorse roads. Squeezed between the road and the scarp are several mills dating to the 17th and 18th centuries, excellent examples of industrial architecture. Some are still working, although converted to other industrial uses; some are gradually being adapted to community use or to enterprise workshops.

On this side of the road, too, is the suburb of Watledge and the cottage, called Glendower, that was the last home of W. H. Davies. He described his wanderings in Britain and America in the *Autobiography of a Super-tramp* (1908) and gave to the world that oft quoted couplet:

> What is this life if, full of care,
> We have no time to stand and stare?

West of the A46 is the town itself. A clock tower, erected in 1951, marks the centre of the town. Market Street has some good buildings, beginning with the late 18th-century Clothiers Arms and, opposite, a group of mill workers' cottages, with many gables and much charm. Chestnut Hill has the splendid Stokes Croft, a

17th-century house with oval windows in each gable. Further up, in an attractive courtyard, is the Quaker Meeting House of 1689, built in Cotswold vernacular style with all its original fittings.

As so often in these mill towns, Nonconformist churches seem to have attracted bigger congregations than the less egalitarian Established Church. There was no Anglican church here until All Saints was built in the suburb of Shortwood. This was followed by the church of St George in 1898, Early English in style and its tower never completed. The church is now enlivened by a colourful mural painted by the local artist Oliver Heywood in 1985, depicting local life, scenery and flora.

South of Nailsworth the B4058 climbs the hill to **Horsley** (4/1F), past fish-breeding ponds and an old turnpike tollhouse. The huge church of St Martin stands on the site of an Augustinian priory and was entirely rebuilt in 1838–9 by Thomas Rickman, who in 1817 had published a series of lectures classifying the main styles of English church architecture. A curiosity is the Twelve O'Clock Stone, positioned on the churchyard path in such a way that the church tower acts as a huge sundial; its shadow falls across the stone at noon precisely.

Naunton (4/4C)

This handsome village, 6 miles west of STOW-ON-THE-WOLD, shelters in a deep and narrow valley of the Upper Windrush. The river itself runs through the back gardens of the cottages and farmhouses that line the south side of the winding, mile-long main street.

Naunton's builders did not have to look far for their materials. Quarries to the north-east of the village are still worked for roadstone, although not, any longer, for the roofing slates the village was once famous for. One of the oldest houses in Naunton, the late-16th-century Cromwell House, is built of small blocks of rubble, suggesting that the quarries were not yet open at that date; but most of the later buildings to the east end of the village are of good quality ashlar. Even the 19th-century cottages are of this material, and have mellowed to a satisfying creamy yellow, with lichens colouring their walls and roofing slates. Some cottages are set back from the street, approached through colourfully planted front gardens; others have ammonites displayed on their windowsills, chiselled out of the fossil-rich local stone.

In the centre of the village is the Manor House, surrounded by old farm buildings, including a handsome 17th-century dovecot, one of the finest examples of a type peculiar to this part of the Cotswolds, with four tall gables crowned by a central lantern.

At the west end, the street climbs past the village school and the Baptist Chapel, with its overgrown churchyard, before dropping to the oldest part of Naunton. Here the clear River Windrush emerges to flow between willow-fringed banks and beneath a bridge built by the rector, John Hurd, around 1819.

Fine-looking houses, including the 17th-century Old Rectory and 18th-century Church House, surround St Andrew's church, which has a small Saxon cross reset in the north nave wall and a Norman corbel table. The solid Perpendicular tower has an especially good set of gargoyles, but the chief treasure of the church is its delicate and richly decorated stone pulpit of around 1400.

Newent (3/4C)

This small town some 9 miles north-west of GLOUCESTER is the unofficial capital of the lovely rural and undulating north-west corner of the county, more like Hereford and Worcester in its charming mix of brick-fronted and timber-framed houses. The Market House stands at the junction of the principal streets, a pretty timber structure of about 1600, supported on twelve wooden posts.

Newent's carpenters were as skilled in their craft as their stonemason counterparts of the Cotswolds. Edward Taylor, who worked for Christopher Wren in the rebuilding of London after the Great Fire, created the fine nave of Newent's parish church in 1675–9, following the collapse of the original building. Charles II donated 60 tons of oak from his royal forests for the work; using this, Taylor was able to create an exceptionally broad roof span without the need for supporting pillars. The body of the church is thus unusually spacious.

Following the practice established under the Commonwealth, the galleries and pews were oriented north to face the pulpit rather than east. Sadly, this arrangement was changed in 1865, the high-backed pews lowered, the east gallery removed and everything brought to face the chancel, resulting in an awkward compromise of what once must have been an impressive church.

Several tourist attractions have been established in or near the town. A fine barn in Culver Street is the home of the long-established Cowdy

Glass works, continuing an industry introduced by Huguenot refugees. Visitors can watch crafts-men at work from a viewing platform. The Shambles, an 18th-century building in Church Street, has been furnished as a late Victorian tradesman's house.

South of the town is the Falconry Centre, where birds of prey are bred and trained, and where demonstrations are given. North of the town is the tropical butterfly house of the Newent Butterfly Centre and, near by, the Three Choirs Vineyard (which can be viewed by arrangement).

Just on the north-western outskirts of Newent is the church of St Anne at Oxenhall, rebuilt in 1865 by John Middleton in polychromatic stone and full of lush carving. The font is one of the six lead Norman bowls, decorated with enthroned figures, that came from the same mould, five of which are in Gloucestershire churches (*see* Beachley).

About 2½ miles north-east of Newent is the parish of **Upleadon** (3/4C), so called because it lies on a shallow hill above the valley of the River Leadon. The church of St Mary lies further east, only yards from the river. It was built on an artificial clay mound, probably as a precaution against flooding, but settlement of the soil has created its own problems, necessitating frequent repairs to the church. The beautiful Tudor timber-framed tower is a masterpiece of con-struction. It is built of close-set studs, filled with brick nogging, which run through four storeys

The church of St Mary the Virgin, Upleadon

from floor to pyramidal roof. This is sophisticated work, with bold continuous vertical lines to enhance the appearance of height. To counteract any latent instability without spoiling the exter-nal lines of the tower, the carpenters placed all the massive cross bracing inside. The king-post nave roof is another fine example of the car-penter's art. All this is later work to an essentially Norman church, of which the north door with its tympanum has survived.

Newland (3/2E)

High on the steep valley side, this village on the B4231 a mile east of the Wye presents the fairest face of any in the FOREST OF DEAN. The Old Grammar School of 1639, the almshouses founded by William Jones in 1615, the Georgian houses and the church form a group as lovely and as intimate as a cathedral close; indeed, the church has been called the 'Cathedral of the Forest' because of its size. The well-maintained state of the surrounding buildings is due to the charity (now administered by the Haberdashers' Company) established by William Jones, who went to London to make his fortune but never forgot his native village.

It is hard to believe that the magnificent church of All Saints was described as almost ruinous in 1861 when William White began restorations. Admirably, he did the least possible to bring it back into sound condition, and the

The 'Miner's Brass' in All Saints, Newland

elevated and airy church, with its very wide aisles, is substantially 13th century.

Among the splendid monuments are several reminders of the life of the Forest. An effigy of Wyrall, Forester of Fee, dated 1457, depicts him in hunting costume with horn, knife and sword. And there is the famous 'Miner's Brass', unique in its depiction of a medieval miner in belted tunic and boots, a pick in one hand, a candle-holder clenched between his teeth and a coal hod on his back.

Newnham (3/3D)

Quiet and residential now, this town on the A48 was until the 19th century a bustling port with a ferry across the Severn to ARLINGHAM, and the main focus of traffic between the FOREST OF DEAN and the GLOUCESTER Vale. Old Newnham was built close to the river bank and precipitous Severn Street was the ancient ropewalk to the quayside. Several converted warehouses still stand, built in part from black blocks of dross from a glass factory that stood near by until the 18th century. The present High Street climbs to the town's hilltop church; running up the middle is a narrow green, planted with trees, where medieval houses once stood back to back.

Newnham was unlucky with its churches. Successive buildings near the river were abandoned because of flooding and subsidence. In 1380 a new church was built higher up in the town on its present site, but this was blown up during a Civil War siege in 1644. The rebuilt church was destroyed by fire in 1881. The church that now stands reuses fragments of Norman masonry rescued from earlier buildings, notably the excellent font depicting the Apostles.

Bullo, about 1½ miles south of Newnham, is a little hamlet of whitewashed houses, built around a tidal inlet. It has come down in the world even more than Newnham, for it was once an important coal dock and the terminus, in the early 1800s, of an industrial tramway, now dismantled. Its course can be followed up to the blocked entrance, near the Haie, of what is claimed to be the world's first railway tunnel.

North Cerney (4/3E)

From CIRENCESTER, the winding A435 to Cheltenham passes through the lush watermeadows of the Churn valley. The road and the river meet at North Cerney, where the Churn flows through the garden of the pleasant Bathurst Arms public house. On the opposite side of the road, All Saints church stands on a high bank forming an attractive group with the 17th-century Rectory and 15th-century Old Church House. Visitors often stop for a fleeting visit, attracted by the look of the church, and end up staying an hour or more, so rich is it in architectural interest and accumulated treasures.

The tower is 12th-century Norman with original window and pilaster buttresses, with a bell stage added c.1200. When it was restored in the 15th century, following a fire, a buttress was added on to which a mason later doodled a heraldic leopard. Another doodle, of a legendary manticore, is beneath the south window of the south transept. A 16th-century date has been suggested because the graffiti resemble illustrations in bestiaries of that period.

Inside, the eye is at once drawn to the beautiful rood: the figure of Christ is Italian, of about 1600. Thanks to various benefactors it is possible to see what many a parish church would have looked like before the Reformation and the removal of roods, or before improvers in the 19th century cleared away those few that had survived.

From the rood the eye moves naturally upwards to the 15th-century roof, carried on the north wall by portrait corbels. Outstanding, too,

is the pulpit of about 1480, cut from a single block of Cotswold stone.

The delights of this beautiful part of the Cotswolds do not end here. It is a short drive north to the next parish of **Rendcomb** (4/3E): better still is the mile-long walk along the winding River Churn. After the bridge, the road climbs steeply to the church which stands just inside the grounds of Rendcomb College.

Sir Edmund Tame, son of John Tame who built FAIRFORD church, bought Rendcomb Manor in 1503 and paid for the rebuilding of St Peter's church which is, in several respects, the handsome offspring of the former. The date inscribed in the lockplate of the church door is taken to be 1517, suggesting that work at Rendcomb began very shortly after the completion of Fairford. The fine wooden screen is probably the work of the same carver who made the screen at Fairford.

Comparisons aside, Rendcomb has some fine treasures of its own: a 16th-century Crucifixion sculpture in the east wall gable, a rare Angelus bell of *c*.1450 and an intriguing Norman tub font, which originally came from ELMORE. Its 11 Apostles stand under arcades, between pillars; the space for Judas is left blank.

Rendcomb College was designed in Italianate style as a country house for Sir F. H. Goldsmid in 1863 by Philip Hardwick. It appears to be built of seamless ashlar: no joint was allowed to be thicker than the width of a penny.

St Peter and St Paul, Northleach

Northleach (4/4D)

The town lies about 11 miles up the Foss Way (A429) from CIRENCESTER, near its intersection with the A40. It was founded in about 1230 by the Abbot of GLOUCESTER as a market town. It succeeded in fulfilling this function so well that by the 15th century it was an important international market for the buying and export of raw wool to the Continent. As at Cirencester, CHIPPING CAMPDEN and FAIRFORD, the wool merchants who benefited materially from this trade counted for their spiritual salvation on the money they left to rebuild the church.

It is the 15th-century clerestory, including the glorious window filling the whole east gable of the nave, that first strikes visitors approaching the church of St Peter and St Paul from the Market Place. Rising above the nave is the graceful 100 ft tower, covered with ogee-headed blank arcading. The south porch has the same ogee heads above image niches with sculpture that has survived iconoclasm but not the weather; enough survives, however, to indicate how refined the originals must have been. The inside of the porch has more image niches with bracket corbels; one shows a cat playing the fiddle to an audience of rats.

The nave is radiantly light and spacious, and the four-centred arches of the arcade, the clerestory and the timber ceilings are all typical of the Perpendicular style. The nave piers, however, are unusual and daringly original; here they are concave and octagonal, slender and so deeply cut as to be star-shaped in section. Two of the masons left their names on the base of one of the columns: Henri Winchcombe, perhaps the master mason, and one Edmunde, whose name is carved above the words 'God grant His Grace'.

The church abounds with other fine examples of the mason's skill, notably the sumptous font and pulpit and the corbel heads in the Lady Chapel, depicting Henry VII and his wife, Elizabeth of York.

The church has a quite remarkable collection of memorial brasses. Best of all is the Fortey brass of 1450, depicting Agnes Fortey between her first husband, William Scors, and her second, Thomas Fortey, merchant and generous patron of the church. Close inspection of the inscription around the margin reveals a series of little pictures punctuating the words: a snail, a hedgehog, a crab, a pig, oak leaves, rose and hunting dogs. Note too that the inscription gives the year of Thomas' death as MCCCC47: the '47' here represents one of the earliest uses of arabic numerals in England, indicating that even Spanish merchants came here to buy wool in the 15th century (*see also* Chedworth).

The inscription describes John Fortey as a mender of roads as well as patron of the church. It seems that the roads around Northleach always had a bad reputation. The 18th-century traveller Arthur Young described the Northleach to Witney road as 'the worst turnpike I have ever travelled in'. Even so, the roads proved to be the salvation of the town in the 17th century when the centre of the wool trade shifted to STROUD. By the 18th century scores of coaches were passing through Northleach every week, since the town was on the crossroads of the Foss Way and the Oxford road.

Until very recently, when the bypass was completed, the town continued to be heavily congested. Now it is pleasantly quiet but, as a legacy of the past, there are a number of former coaching inns in the town. Walton House was once the King's Head and the Antelope was converted into cottages in the 19th century. The half-timbered Red Lion still functions as an inn. Also in the High Street, Oak House contains Keith Harding's entertaining collection of musical boxes, pianolas, barrel organs and automata (open daily).

At the crossroads west of the town is the former Northleach House of Correction, one of several late 18th-century prisons in the county built to the specifications of the penal reformer Sir George Onesiphorus Paul (*see also* Littledean and Tetbury). It now houses the Cotswold Countryside Collection, a museum that illuminates three aspects of social history.

The museum has a large and diverse collection of agricultural equipment and machinery – including superb examples of the cartwright's craft – the use of which is explained through contemporary photographs and tape recordings of Cotswold farmworkers discussing their tasks. Further displays show the woman's role in agricultural communities, with reconstructions of the kitchens in which many wives and daughters worked as domestic servants. Finally, in the cells of the former gaol, is a full explanation of prison conditions in the 18th century and of Paul's attempts to help prisoners learn skills that would enable them to avoid a life of crime.

Just north-west of the museum is the lovely hamlet of **Hampnett**, with a small green where the River Leach springs from the ground, attractive farm buildings and the church of St George. This has a very fine Norman vaulted chancel (comparable to the one at ELKSTONE), entirely covered by pseudo-medieval painting by the Rector, the Reverend W. Wiggin, around 1871; the work will delight some visitors and appal others.

North Nibley (3/4F)

This southern Cotswold village, on the B4060 about 2 miles north of WOTTON-UNDER-EDGE, is where the Victorians believed that William Tynedale was born in 1484; they honoured his memory in 1866 by building an 111-ft high tower on top of the hill above the village, called Nibley Knoll. Scholars now think that they got the wrong Tynedale, and that the man who translated the New Testament, the Pentateuch and the Book of Jonah into English was actually born in the Welsh Marches. There is no doubt where this great Reformation figure died, however, for in 1536 he was strangled and burned at the stake in Vilvoorde, north of Brussels, accused of heresy. His translation, which enabled his fellow countrymen to read the Bible in their own language, and his insistence on the authority of scripture in the Church, threatened to undermine the position of the clergy and so he was condemned.

Avenue leading to St Bartholomew, Notgrove

Tynedale's tower may be climbed after obtaining the key from the house at the bottom of Wood Lane, which descends from the monument through noble beech woods to North Nibley village. This lies on a plateau below the scarp around Nibley Green, site of the last private battle fought in England in 1470 – between the Berkeleys and Lord Lisle over the ownership of Berkeley Castle.

The Cotswold Way passes through the area, round the Iron Age hillfort of Brackenbury Ditches, south of the village.

The church of St Martin stands away from the village west of the green. The lofty nave has a 15th-century king-post roof with portrait corbels, and a chancel rebuilt in 1861, richly painted and with a splendid 1874 gold mosaic reredos.

Notgrove (4/4C)

The village is south of the A436, about 4 miles west of BOURTON-ON-THE-WATER. This and its neighbouring parishes stand on the high wolds which can be chillingly stark in winter. Notgrove is pleasing with its solidly built farms and estate cottages, immaculate cricket ground and Norman church (built on the supposed site of a Roman cemetery) with a Saxon carving: all the ingredients of a trim Cotswold village are here.

The windowless east wall of the church has been put to good use. It is now hung with a colourful needlework tapestry completed in 1954. The lower section shows the 14th-century reredos as it might have appeared before being smashed by 17th-century iconoclasts. In other panels the village is glimpsed through a border of hazel branches – a pun on the name of this and the neighbouring village of Hazleton. One image in the church survived the iconoclasts: the lovely stained glass fragment of the Virgin and Child in the vestry.

The excavated gallery and chambers of a 160 ft Neolithic long barrow lie north-west of the village. North-east, near the A436, is Folly Farm (open daily), which specializes in rare breeds of farmyard and waterfowl.

A mile east of Notgrove is the parish of **Aston Blank** (4/4D), sometimes also known and signposted by its alternative name, Cold Aston. Both names indicate the bleakness of the surrounding upland terrain. The church of St Andrew, like Notgrove's church, has a windowless east wall. In this case, however, the elaborate 14th-century reredos has survived in a good state of preservation.

From Aston Blank a bridleway following an ancient track across the wolds offers an attractive alternative route to the road which leads to **Turkdean** (4/4D), just over a mile south-west. The bridleway descends into the hamlet, passing several woods and avenues of chestnut and beech planted in the 19th century as windbreaks. Ancient stone houses and farms stand around Turkdean's church of All Saints. This is essentially Norman, but with two interesting additions of this century. One is the stained glass memorial window portraying Dame Julia Bolton (d.1924) and her bereaved husband, in Oxford bags. The oak chancel screen was carved in 1949 and is vividly painted with butterflies.

The next-door parish of **Hazleton** (4/3D) to the west once belonged to WINCHCOMBE Abbey; the present patchwork of arable and pasture, crossed by hedges and drystone walls, was once open wold grazed by the Abbey's great flocks. Hazleton's church of St Andrew is Norman, simple and pleasing, although the 12th-century masons planned a grander building; shafts in the chancel show where the work stopped before the intended vaulting could be completed.

A road drives north past long barrows and tumuli before turning east to **Salperton** (4/3C). The church of All Saints is away from the village, close to Salperton park. The setting is beautiful with snowdrops and aconites in spring; and entry is through a pretty porch. Inside, besides some fine 19th-century stained glass by C. E. Kempe and W. Tower, there is a 15th-century wall painting of a skeleton with a spear and wheel.

Nympsfield *see* Uley

Oakridge *see* Sapperton

Oddington (4/5C)
This village is on the A436, about 3 miles east of STOW-ON-THE-WOLD. The original parish church of St Nicholas was more or less abandoned in 1852 when a new church was built in the village. It remained open to the elements until the Reverend T. Hodson, appointed rector in 1912, began the restoration work that saved this lovely church from terminal decay. It stands isolated along a wooded track, scarcely altered since the 13th century when the Archbishop of York made substantial alterations.

The Archbishop had a residence here and was often visited by Henry III, so he needed a church fit for royal patronage. He built a new nave and chancel north of the original Norman nave, which now forms the south aisle, to give the church its impressive proportions. The stone-flagged interior has great atmosphere. Just discernible is a suitably grim, but sophisticated, 14th-century Doom (Last Judgment) painting.

Oddington village, formerly two settlements of Lower and Upper Oddington, has many charming houses built on the hillside that climbs gently to Stow-on-the-Wold. Oddington House and its neighbour, the Old Rectory, are much older than their 19th-century classical façades indicate. The unspoiled barns and outbuildings of Rectory Farmhouse date from the 17th century; the Post Office from 1728. Beyond Holy Ascension church, in Upper Oddington, the Old Stone House is a characteristically deceptive work of the Arts and Crafts architect Sir Guy Dawber: converted around 1900 from three 16th-century cottages, it looks mellow, timeless and rooted in the best traditions of the Cotswolds vernacular style.

Offa's Dyke Path
According to the Anglo-Saxon Chronicle, Penda, king of Mercia, captured the area roughly corresponding to modern Gloucestershire in the early 7th century AD. The Celtic tribes that lived west of the county were considerably more warlike and difficult to defeat. Another century passed before the great Mercian king Offa (757-96) negotiated a treaty with the South Welsh, who had put up brave resistance to every invader from the Romans onwards.

Mercia, the Midland kingdom, was extended westward as a result, taking in what is now Herefordshire. Offa's Dyke was built to mark the political boundary – and may sometimes have had a military function as well. It was constructed quickly, perhaps in less than a year, but has lasted well over a thousand years. In places it still marks the modern boundary between England and Wales.

Offa's Dyke was not built as a continuous earthwork; natural features such as the cliffs of the upper Wye valley or the dense forests of Herefordshire provided a sufficient boundary. Thus, when the Countryside Commission designated the Offa's Dyke Long-Distance Footpath in 1971 – about 170 miles of it – it took in the best-preserved stretches and, in the gaps between, sought out the most scenically attractive countryside. The result is one of the most popular long-distance paths in the country, walked by thousands of visitors who follow the white acorn signs used to waymark the route.

Gloucestershire is fortunate in having some of the most dramatic lengths of the Dyke within its borders: especially the continuous stretch that follows the great gorge of the River Wye in an unbroken line from Redbrook, via the Devil's Pulpit, with dramatic views of Tintern Abbey in Gwent, to Sedbury. (For other stretches *see* Offa's Dyke Path in H&W Gazetteer.)

Owlpen *see* Uley

Oxenton (4/2B)

The village is about 2 miles north of BISHOP'S CLEEVE, to the east of the A435. A hill, a Cotswold outlier with an Iron Age site (The Knolls) on its summit, rises above the village. The church of St John the Baptist lies up the slope at the high end of the village street, unspoiled and full of interesting detail. The local stone was well used in building the Perpendicular tower. Inside, the king-post nave roof is an exact and respectful copy of the 15th-century original. The chancel roof is original, its curving arch braces springing from carved corbels to moulded collar beams. The medieval furnishings – communion table, pulpit, screen and benches – are all good 14th- and 15th-century work.

Painswick (4/1E)

This lovely Cotswold wool town is about 5 miles south of GLOUCESTER, on the A46. The town has become one of the most popular in the Cotswolds, the base for numerous traders in antiques, a centre for the arts with a popular annual exhibition of work by members of the Gloucestershire Guild of Craftsmen, and a place for taking late afternoon tea after a walk in the beautiful surrounding hills and valleys.

South and east of the church, narrow lanes plunge into the valley of the Painswick Brook, which makes a good starting point. Straddling the brook are several former fulling mills, many converted recently into apartments. The fields along the brook were once bright with the yellow flowers of woad, grown to produce black and blue dyes for the clothiers of STROUD. The steep approach up to the town from here forces a leisurely pace in which to enjoy the harmony of stone and the details of many fine 17th- and 18th-century houses. Only Friday Street breaks the pattern: one side of it was hit by a stray Luftwaffe bomb in 1941, intended perhaps for Gloucester's aircraft factories.

At the top of the hill, the narrow streets suddenly emerge into the magnificent churchyard. This is a work of inspired artifice, planted in 1792 with avenues of clipped yew trees, interspersed with an outstanding collection of handsome stone table tombs. Although all based on the simple form of a box, no two tombs are alike: square, oblong, pepperpot-shaped, hexagonal, round or triangular, each is individually embellished with buttresses, pie-crust frills, scrolls, shells, swags, putti and foliage.

The brilliance of this work almost eclipses the achievement of the church, for it is a handsome building, with a pencil-thin spire added in 1632, which has all too often had to be repaired after being struck by lightning. Much of the fabric dates from the rebuilding of about 1480, with 18th-century additions.

An annual ceremony of great antiquity is performed by parishioners on 19 September, or the first Sunday following. Called the Clipping Ceremony, from Old English *clyppan* ('surround' or 'embrace'), children wearing circlets of flowers in their hair link hands to surround the church

Painswick

while singing the Clipping Hymn to the accompaniment of a band. Painswick churchyard is an enchanted place.

On the outskirts of the town, the Rococo gardens of Painswick House are open on certain days throughout the summer and the 'Snowdrop Sundays' in February and March, when the wooded glades are carpeted in the large-flowered Atkyn's snowdrop (*see also* 'Gloucestershire Gardens', p. 77).

About 1½ miles north of the town is the popular local beauty spot, Painswick Beacon, site of a large Iron Age hillfort, sadly mutilated by quarrying and a golf course, but still worth climbing for the wonderful views from the summit.

South-west of Painswick is the hillside parish of **Pitchcombe** (4/1E). The church of St John the Baptist was rebuilt in the 19th century, but it too has some good Painswick-style table tombs in the churchyard.

Parkend *see* Coleford

Pool Keynes *see* South Cerney

Poulton *see* Ampneys, The

Prestbury (4/2C)
The parish is now a suburb of CHELTENHAM, much expanded in recent years. The first Cheltenham Gold Cup was run on nearby Cleeve Common in 1819, but in 1830 the grandstand was burned down by Evangelicals whose sensibilities were outraged by the 'degeneracies of the sport'. The racecourse was moved to its present site at Prestbury Park in time for the Gold Cup the following year, and it continues to be held here every March, the premier event of the National Hunt calendar.

Another demonstration took place in Prestbury in 1878. This time, the subject of the protestors' wrath was the vicar, who was forced to resign in 1881, branded as a Papist for his High Church practices. The church of St Mary, consecrated in 1136, was restored in 1864 by G. E. Street and became a focus for supporters of the Oxford Movement founded by John Keble. Street's chancel and the 19th-century furnishings reflect contemporary High Church taste. The 15th-century nave, clerestory and splendid chancel arch all escaped restoration.

Prestbury claims to be England's most-haunted village. One story is of a Cavalier shot as he rode through. His horse, they say, can still be heard.

Preston *see* Cirencester

Preston *see* Dymock

Prinknash Abbey *see* Cranham

Purton (East) *see* Sharpness

Purton (West) *see* Blakeney

Quenington *see* Colns, The

Randwick *see* Stroud

Redmarley D'Abitot (3/4B)
This village about 10 miles north-west of GLOUCESTER, down a high-banked lane just south of the M50, is an example of a community that nearly died. A 15th-century document records that many houses were empty and falling down at that time – presumably as a result of the climatic changes that, together with the Black Death, had led to so many villages being abandoned in the 14th century. Wetter weather would certainly have made it harder to work the heavy red marl that the village name, quite by chance, suggests. (The first part of the name actually means reed-filled mere or lake. D'Abitot, now often omitted, refers to the first Norman lord of the manor.)

In 1644, during the Civil War, Redmarley was the scene of a bloody engagement (*see also* Bromsberrow *below*). With the peace, however, the village soon revived: a number of its pretty red-brick and timber-framed cottages date from the 17th and 18th centuries; Church House, however, is 16th century.

In 1854 the village was able to rebuild St Bartholomew's church. It has interesting memorials to officers and administrators who served in Bengal in the 19th century and later retired here.

Bromsberrow is a scattered hamlet across the M50 from Redmarley D'Abitot. It stands at the southernmost limit of the Malverns. St Mary's church has an eye-catching timber-framed belfry and spire. This was added in 1875; it may have had a predecessor, however, since a supporting beam in the west wall is dated 1502.

The Yate family mortuary chapel, added in 1725, intriguingly contains two Civil War battle standards – one Royalist, one Parliamentarian. The Yates moved here in 1707 and built Bromsberrow Place.

Further south at **Staunton** (3/4C) the mostly 14th-century church of St James has a monument to William Horton (d.1612) and family; they all sport generous noses, except for one small child. The church stands attractively beside Staunton Court, 16th century and timber-framed with a dovecot. A row of houses between the church and the Swan Inn, along with those south of the village at Snig's End, were built by the Chartist leader Feargus O'Connor, who set up a land scheme in 1845. His ambition – to provide industrial workers with a healthier way of life and a plot of land – foundered with his bankruptcy in 1848.

South again at **Corse** there is little remarkable about St Margaret's church except for its setting alongside Corse Court, a medieval cruck-built farmhouse with contemporary dairy, best seen in spring when the surrounding orchards are in blossom.

The current well-maintained state of the church of St John at **Pauntley** is due to help from the Corporation of London. They funded the restoration in honour of London's most famous Mayor, Dick Whittington, who was born at the Manor, the son of Sir William Whittington and Joan, the young widow of Sir Thomas Berkeley (*see* Coberley). The chancel north window has 14th-century heraldic stained glass, which includes the Whittington arms. Otherwise, the chief architectural interest lies in the Norman south door and the big chancel arch with its grotesque heads.

Rendcomb *see* North Cerney

Rissingtons, The (4/C&D)

These three villages lie east and south-east of BOURTON-ON-THE-WATER, high on the sides of valleys, but below the windswept top of the wolds, which is left to the runways and hangars of the former RAF Central Flying School.

Great Rissington (4/4D) is the southernmost of the three villages. The great cruciform church of St John the Baptist was rebuilt in 1873 in the Early English style, but the powerful Norman arches of the central tower crossing remain. A First World War memorial in the church includes photographs of all the local men who perished, among them five brothers.

The church is surrounded by handsome buildings, including the 17th-century Manor, whose gardens are open under the National Gardens Scheme, and the splendid early 18th-century Rectory, embellished with classical architectural motifs. The village street runs up to a triangular green before dividing to encircle a

RAF memorial in Little Rissington church

larger green surrounded by smart houses, many built early this century, but in traditional style, of locally quarried stone.

One road out of the village climbs uphill to the RAF station; another follows the course of the River Dikler, north to **Little Rissington** (4/4D). This pretty village, nestling into the west-facing hillslope, is full of gentle surprises: springs that flow out of the bankside beneath 19th-century stone niches; a cottage converted from a 17th-century four-gabled dovecot; and Manor Cottages, subdivided from a large house, with its sweeping roof and dormer windows, each one crowned by a stone finial.

The church of St Peter stands a little apart from the village on a spur above the river and provides a view of the 18th-century mill half a mile away across the pasture from the beautifully maintained churchyard. This has the graves of several airmen who died during service at RAF Rissington, and a memorial window in the church commemorates their bravery.

The road to **Wyck Rissington** (4/4C) passes by the triangulation point at Wyck Beacon, 820 ft above sea level, and the nearby Bronze Age round barrow. The road drops steeply again to the church of St Laurence, at the entrance to the village. This church is of great interest because of the unusual form of the chancel windows, clearly representing the first hint of the intricacies of window tracery that were to come. What the 13th-century masons actually achieved here was a bizarre but endearing arrangement of concave lozenges piercing the east wall.

The pretty tower has four diminishing stages culminating in a parapet pierced with trefoils. Inside the church is a rare and beautiful 14th-century Crucifixion in stained glass. The organ was played by Gustav Holst: he was appointed organist here in 1892 in his late teens, the composer's first professional engagement.

Rodmarton *see* Coates

Bigsweir Bridge over the Wye near St Briavels

Ruardean (3/3D)

Ruardean is in the north-west corner of the FOREST OF DEAN, on the B4227 and not far from the highest point in the Forest. The ancient church of St John the Baptist enjoys a hilltop position with views over the Wye Valley that alone justify a visit. Close links with the neighbouring county are evident in the tympanum, a work of the Herefordshire school of Norman sculptors (*see* Kilpeck, H&W). It is outstanding, not only for its unusually good state of preservation but also for the liveliness of its subject: St George on a galloping horse, his cloak flying, purposefully thrusting his spear into the mouth of a serpentine dragon.

The small carved stone depicting two fishes set in the wall near the font is the work of the same masons, possibly representing Pisces from a series of zodiac corbels. More fine carvings, this time the work of 18th- and 19th-century masons, are found on the tombstones lined up around the churchyard.

A miner's lamp kept burning in the chancel reminds us that this region, for all its beauty, was once extensively mined, and **Drybrook** (3/3D), to the east is still predominantly industrial in character. Its church of the Holy Trinity was built as late as 1817 and resembles a Nonconformist chapel with its intersecting Gothic tracery; inside is a pleasing gallery supported on classical columns.

Lower Lydbrook on the east bank of the Wye is popular with anglers and canoeists. On the steep road that leads up to the hillside village of Upper Lydbrook there is a striking black-and-white 16th-century house that was once the home of Sarah Siddons (1755–1831).

St Briavels (3/2E)

The village is on the B4228, about 1½ miles east of the River Wye. It is dominated by a castle that now serves as a Youth Hostel and is open to the public on occasion. The church here and the village are named after a Welsh bishop who lived in the 5th century AD, a reminder that this is border country.

According to the 12th-century Welsh historian Giraldus Cambrensis, the original castle was built by Milo (d.1143), the oppressive Sheriff of Gloucester and Constable of the Forest. The magnificent gatehouse dates from a later building of around 1292.

Until 1754, the castle was used for meetings of the Court of Verderers to try those accused of trespass or of illegally taking game or timber from the Royal Forest. Here, too, the Gaveller presided over the miners' court convened to hear disputes or register the claims of Free Miners to open up new coal seams. Both courts were later revived and continue to meet at Speech House (*see* Forest of Dean).

The church is opposite the castle. It is

Norman with interesting snakehead stops in the tower crossing. The parishioners perform an ancient ceremony on Whit Sunday when bread and cheese are distributed to the chant of:

St Briavel's water and Whyral's wheat
Are the best bread and water King John ever eat.

The custom commemorates King John's love of the Forest and frequent visits to St Briavels for hunting. The distribution of the food is said to date back 700 years and to commemorate restoration of the right of local people to gather wood from the Forest.

The village of St Briavels makes a pleasant centre for visiting the wooded beauty of the Wye Valley.

Saintbury *see* Aston Subedge

Salperton *see* Notgrove

Sandhurst *see* Maisemore

Sapperton (4/2E)

Sapperton is some 6 miles west of CIRENCESTER, just north of the A419.

If on arrival you are prepared to abandon the car and walk, you may well end up agreeing with local people past and present that there is no more beautiful place in England than this lovely wooded valley of the River Frome. It repays repeated visits, one of which should be in spring. This is when the wild daffodils at Pinbury Park, 1½ miles north of Sapperton, are at their best and the garden is open to the public under the National Gardens Scheme.

This ancient house is situated on a shoulder above the Frome with fine views of the Gloucester Beeches on the opposite slope of the valley. It is said that the house stands on the site of the royal residence of Penda, the 7th-century king of Mercia. The yew-lined Nuns Walk is a reminder that the manor was given to the Abbess of Caen at the Norman Conquest.

Ernest Barnsley discovered the house in a state of disrepair in the last decade of the 19th century. He moved in with his bachelor brother Sidney and their partner in business, Ernest Gimson, and established the Pinbury Workshop. With help from local craftsmen, they produced extremely fine furniture, admirable in its simplicity.

In 1901 all three moved to Sapperton. Their impact on the village was lasting, for they built

Jacobean figures on the bench ends, Sapperton

several houses and the village hall. Their work is virtually indistinguishable from the older cottages, such was their respect for craftmanship and natural materials. The inspiration for their work lay all around them in the delightful cottages that tumble down the hillside, intersected by paths running between the drystone walls of terraced gardens.

One of these paths leads to the church of St Kenelm where Gimson and the Barnsley brothers lie buried. The Atkyns family rebuilt the church around 1702. The big round-headed windows still have their original green-hued glass that allows light to flood into the handsome nave. This is filled with good Elizabethan and Jacobean woodwork, taken from Sapperton House when it was demolished in 1730, and the magnificent monuments of Henry Poole (d.1616) and the county historian, Sir Robert Atkyns (d.1711).

From the churchyard a path leads down the valley side to the Sapperton entrance of the **Thames and Severn Canal**. Strewn around the canal basin are building materials, the remains of a recent heroic attempt at restoring the tunnel entrance and even of opening a length of the canal.

The canal was completed in 1789 – the year of the French Revolution. It won plaudits from *The Times*, which hailed it as a stupendous achievement. By comparison with the turmoil in France, it was a sign of relative stability in

England that a canal involving a 2-mile long tunnel through solid limestone should have been completed in record time.

It was not long, however, before the cost of maintaining the canal became a serious burden. Water leaked prodigiously through the porous limestone of the tunnel; rock falls were a continuous hazard. The Great Western Railway arrived shortly afterwards and built within feet of the canal, which it bought up in 1876 to prevent any rival rail company building a track along its course.

Since then, the canal has been left to nature. In places it has burst its banks and flooded the valley bottom. It has become the resort of birds and the River Frome flows alongside, adding its music. Flowers carpet the woods in spring; marsh marigold, mint and musk fill the banks in summer; the woods blaze with colour in autumn, fully justifying the name Golden Valley.

Anyone walking the towpath can stop for lunch at the Daneway Inn, built as a place of refreshment for the bargees and leggers who pushed the narrow boats through the tunnel by lying on their backs and walking along the ceiling.

Near by, Daneway House can be visited by advance arrangement. This dates in part to the 13th century – the original medieval hall is basically still there – and little has been added since 1717. Gimson and the Barnsleys used it as their showroom at the beginning of the century. The 17th-century plasterwork so impressed Ernest Gimson that he borrowed its motifs for his own work.

The hamlet of **Frampton Mansell** (4/2E) clings to the valley side and is reached from the canal by a path that crosses the railway by means of a precipitous packhorse bridge. The railway itself is built high up on a viaduct; a steep road passes beneath one of its arches before climbing the opposite valley slope to **Oakridge** (4/2E). Here, the church of St Bartholomew was built for John Keble's brother Thomas (see Bisley) and shows Oxford Movement influence.

Saul see Upper Framilode

Sedbury see Beachley

Selsley (3/5E)
Selsley Common occupies a plateau on the Cotswold scarp, just south-west of STROUD, but high above the industrial conglomeration and offering views, fresh air, and a prehistoric long barrow. Below, in the valley, stands the great Ebley mill, owned by Sir Samuel Marling in the 19th century. Its six-storey tower, surmounted by iron railings and weather vane, was added in about 1862 by G. F. Bodley, who also designed the new church for Selsley, a village on the hillside below the common. Marling had discovered that he shared his name with the village of Marling in the Austrian Tyrol and allegedly insisted that Bodley should build him a church based on the one in Austria. What Bodley gave him was certainly eye-catching and daringly foreign in appearance, but far more French in style than Tyrolean.

While working on the church, Bodley saw the work of a newly formed company – Morris & Co. He liked it and commissioned William Morris and his partners to supply the stained glass and furnishings for Selsley. The church is thus an early example of their collective work. Morris, Philip Webb, Ford Madox Brown, Dante Gabriel Rossetti and Edward Burne-Jones were all involved. The Creation window is rich in colour and strong in design; the Visitation and the Nativity are also depicted.

Sevenhampton (4/3C)
It was fortunate for this village some 5 miles east of CHELTENHAM that John Camber died here in 1497. His will stated that he should be buried wherever he died, and also that the church there must be rebuilt. That is how St Andrew's, which could be Gloucestershire's smallest wool church, came to be greatly enriched. Appropriately, Camber's brass shows him in fine costume with a bulging purse, for the work must have been expensive. Alterations under his will included building a central tower that is carried on flying buttresses inside the church, which gives the nave its unorthodox appearance.

Just north-west of the main part of the village, which is beside the River Coln, stands the Manor House. Its ruinous southern end, partly destroyed by fire in the 1950s, can be seen from the pretty church pathway, lined with flower beds and standard roses. Another footpath leads north ½ mile to the hamlet of **Brockhampton** (4/3C), source of the Coln which flows south to join the Thames through BIBURY and the COLNS. The hill above Brockhampton forms a watershed, for descending the other side to the hamlet of **Charlton Abbots** (4/3C), we find the source of the River Isbourne, which flows north to join the Severn at TEWKESBURY. The church here

Neolithic long barrow of Belas Knap

was rebuilt from ruins around 1887, re-using some 13th-century features. There is also an Elizabethan manor house and steep-roofed barn.

High up on a hilltop with a good view north-east to Sudeley Castle (*see* Winchcombe) is **Belas Knap**, one of the great Neolithic long barrows characteristic of the Cotswolds. Thirty-eight inhumations were found in the stone chambers of the 180-ft long mound, restored in the 1930s and now maintained by English Heritage. A peculiarity of the Cotswold barrows is their false entrance, set between beautifully laid drystone walls, perhaps to frustrate whatever malign spirits might seek to enter.

The farming hamlet of **Hawling** (4/3C), a couple of miles east of Brockhampton, has a simple Georgian church, rebuilt in 1764, an Elizabethan manor and 18th-century barns and farmhouses. The downs above the village are an interesting example of the way in which the Cotswold landscape has changed over the last 2000 years. There are numerous earthworks and barrows around the village, indicating prehistoric settlement. The White Way, later known as the Salt Way, passes just west of the village and seems to be prehistoric in origin. It was used by the Romans, and well into the 18th century, as a Salt Way – a route for transporting Droitwich salt (*see* H&W).

The Ordnance Survey map shows several Roman villa sites in the region and some of the existing fields are Roman in origin. A radical change occurred in the 14th century when Winchcombe Abbey cleared the downs of villages to create uninterrupted sheep grazing; the former village of Roel, 1 mile north of Hawling, is now just a field name. Roel Farm, 1½ miles north-east of Hawling, incorporates the remains of the former parish church.

Then, in 1755, another great change took place: the open downs were enclosed. The land was divided into rectangular fields, bounded by hedges and drystone walls, and planted with lines of trees to act as windbreaks, thus changing the landscape to what we now think of as quintessentially Cotswold, but, in fact, just registering one more phase in the evolution of that landscape.

Even so, life has changed little for the local inhabitants: Hawling is still essentially an agricultural village; the landlords may have changed over the years, and mechanization eased the tasks of the farm labourer, but it can still be bitterly cold rising early in the morning to work the bleak upland fields which Sydney Smith described as 'a region of stone and sorrow'.

Whittington (4/3C) is 1½ miles south-west of Sevenhampton. St Bartholomew's church and the manor are separated from each other by a gap of a mere 3 ft. A head stop in the nave illustrates the fashionable horned headdress of the 15th century and, along with two 14th-century knights and a lady, is the brass of Richard Cotton (d.1556) and his wife. They built the adjoining manor, fronted by the remains of a defensive moat from an earlier house on the site. The church and manor stand near the A40, set apart from the unspoiled village which is little more than one street.

Severn Bore, The

The Bore is a fairly frequent occurrence at high tide, when the rising waters of the Severn Estuary gather speed through the deep Sharpness channel before hitting a sudden rise in the river bed, caused by a step of hard limestone, at

Frampton Sand. The effect of the step is to lift the waters into a tidal wave which increases in height and speed as it continues up the steadily narrowing channel. It can reach a maximum height of around 6 ft between Framilode and Stonebench, travelling at an average of 10 mph; but, equally, it can be little more than a ripple. The weirs south of GLOUCESTER have the effect of breaking the wave, but it has been known to travel on as far as MAISEMORE.

The actual size of the Severn Bore depends on a complex of factors, including atmospheric pressure, the direction of the wind and the gravitational pull of the sun and moon. The dates and times of expected bores, and their forecast sizes, are published annually and are available from local Tourist Information offices. Particularly good points from which to watch the Bore are from the roadside at Framilode, MINSTERWORTH and Stonebench.

Sezincote (4/4B)
Alec Clifton-Taylor honoured it among his *Buildings of Delight*; Talbot Rice called it 'a good joke but a good house too'; and it so amused the Prince Regent when he visited it in 1807 that he scrapped existing plans for the Brighton Pavilion and commissioned new designs to be drawn up 'more like Sezincote'. To every first-time visitor it will come as a surprise, for here, in the Cotswolds, Samuel Pepys Cockerell, inspired by Thomas Daniell's drawings in *Oriental Scenery* of 1808, blended Perpendicular features with Indian colonnades, purdah windows, chattris and chajas, and even a reproduction of Hyder Ali Khan's mausoleum, to produce one of the most curious and delightful country houses ever built in England's countryside.

The client was the architect's brother, Sir Charles Cockerell. Both had served with the East India Company, and it was Samuel's deep practical knowledge of Hindu and Mogul architecture, combined with the eccentric Charles's nostalgia for the East, that resulted in an Indian style being chosen for the house, begun in 1805. Even the barns are a simplified version of Hindu style, though the dominant features of the design, from the central onion window to the peacock's-tail windows, are Mogul and therefore Muslim in origin. Guided tours reveal, however, that the interior is largely classical, elegantly restored and refurnished since the Second World

War by the present owners. (*See also* 'Gloucestershire Gardens', p. 77).

Sharpness (3/3E)
The New Docks here were constructed in 1874; today this is a busy container terminal where cargo is unloaded from sea-going vessels on to lorries, to be carried north and south along the M5. The Old Dock, still entered by the lock that Thomas Telford built in the early 19th century, marks the junction of the Severn and the Gloucester and Sharpness Canal.

This was begun in 1794 so that ships could avoid the difficult waters of the Severn and sail right into GLOUCESTER. Shortage of capital, however, forced the builders to reduce its planned length so that, when it finally opened in 1827, it joined the Severn at Sharpness, not BERKELEY as was originally intended.

The canal is one of the largest in Britain, being 18 ft deep and 70 ft wide, and capable of taking ships of up to 1000 tons. The neo-Grecian lock-keeper's cottages along the canal were probably designed by Robert Mylne, the engineer responsible for the earliest stretch of the canal; Telford continued with the design when he completed the cut.

In the muddy sands of **Purton** (East; 3/3E) can be seen the decaying hulls of several Severn trows, shallow-draught sailing vessels that once carried cargo as far north as Shrewsbury. Also at low tide the stump of a pier that once supported the Severn railway bridge is occasionally visible. This graceful bridge, opened in 1879, linked Gloucester to Chepstow. Too costly to rebuild after it had been damaged by a tanker, it was dismantled in 1968. Between Purton and Sharpness is the entrance to the disused Severn tunnel, completed in 1885, which runs for a mile under the river: another railway relic.

Sheepscombe *see* Cranham

Sherborne (4/4D)
This pretty village is about 4 miles south of BOURTON-ON-THE-WATER, just north of the A40, and on the banks of the Sherborne Brook. The National Trust acquired the village with its little clusters of identical 17th- and 18th-century estate cottages in 1988, together with part of the Sherborne estate, including the magnificent parkland, although not Sherborne House itself. The Trust will also open, in due course, the beautiful classical house called Lodge Park, originally built in the 1640s as a grandstand. In its original form, this consisted simply of two

The Bore at Stonebench

rooms. The upper room was used for banquets and gives on to a balcony where spectators could enjoy a panoramic view of the deer park as well as watch the then popular sport of deer coursing. Restoration plans involve reinstating this room, which was subdivided when the Lodge was converted to a dwelling.

Next to the church of St Mary Magdalene stands Sherborne House, the west elevation of which was completed in 1663 and survives without change.

About 2 miles west of Sherborne is the village of **Farmington** (4/4D). The road through the village also passes through the middle of a large Iron Age enclosure called Norbury Camp. By the quiet village green there is an octagonal pumphouse of 1874, roofed in stone and topped by a small cupola. The church of St Peter is essentially Norman, but with a Perpendicular tower. The unusual clock faces are carved into the stone fabric of the tower.

Shipton Moyne *see* Tetbury

Shipton Oliffe *see* Dowdeswell

Shipton Solers *see* Dowdeswell

Shorncote *see* South Cerney

Shurdington *see* Leckhampton

Siddington *see* Cirencester

Slad (4/1E)
This hillside village 2 miles north-east of STROUD was the childhood home of the poet Laurie Lee (born 1914), and the setting for his autobiographical first novel, *Cider with Rosie* (1959). The novel charts changes in the village during the 1920s, at a watershed in its history. The author chronicles the death of the last squire, who lived at the house called Steanbridge, and the arrival of the first brass-lamped car, symbol of the mechanization that was to change, for ever, a rural way of life that had altered little in any essential respect down the centuries. Now the once quiet village is spoiled by traffic, speeding through between BIRDLIP and Stroud, past Holy Trinity church, built in 1831–4. Only the 'jungly, bird-crammed, insect-hopping woodland', on the opposite side of this deep, beautiful Cotswold valley, has survived unviolated.

Slaughters, The (4/4C)
Once a single village, Upper and Lower Slaugh-

ter had divided into two manors by 1066. They lie just to the north-west of BOURTON-ON-THE-WATER, across the A429. Both are very pretty and attract large numbers of visitors who come to see what are often thought of as typical Cotswold villages. **Lower Slaughter** is especially charming; the River Eye flows round the green and is crossed by several simple stone bridges.

The slough or muddy place once formed by the river accounts for the name of the villages, but the Eye now flows tidily between stone banks and neatly trimmed lawns. A number of the cottages around the green were deliberately 'antiqued' at the beginning of this century to give them older features. The 19th-century mill at the upper end of the village forms the focal point of the view.

St Mary's church was rebuilt in 1867 and given the glass-fibre top to its spire in 1968. Next door the Manor House, with its massive gate piers and large 16th-century dovecot, was built by Valentine Strong and is now an hotel.

Upper Slaughter (4/4C) has much to offer visitors looking for more than a 'chocolate-box' view. The road north from the little village square encircles a Norman castle mound before crossing the river by a ford. Wild flowers grow on the banks and most of the houses were built with stone from local quarries.

One of the Cotswolds' finest-looking Elizabethan manor houses can be seen from the road between the two villages. A row of cottages by the church was remodelled in 1906 by Sir Edwin Lutyens, who came here to work on the house called Copse Hill, a ½ mile east of the village. Another fine house of the same era, Eyford Park, was built in 1910 by Sir Guy Dawber in Queen Anne style; it lies 1 mile north-west of the village. The newly designed garden is open occasionally under the National Gardens Scheme.

St Peter's church has some Norman sculpture which was re-used when the church was rebuilt in the late 19th century. It also has an elaborately ornamented mortuary chapel, housing the tomb chest of the Reverend Francis Edward Witts. Witts was the highly esteemed Rector and village squire who lived at the Manor. Extracts from his diary, kept between 1820 and 1852, were published in 1978 as *The Diary of a Cotswold Parson*, and provide a lively picture of local life.

Slimbridge (3/4E)
The Severn has always been a notoriously shifty

and temperamental river. Early in the 13th century the outgoing tidal waters ripped away the west bank at AWRE and washed the silt up at Slimbridge a couple of miles downstream. For this reason the Slimbridge marshes became a subject of dispute and, to this day, the land concerned is called the New Ground. It was here, between FRAMPTON ON SEVERN and Purton (East) and among the meres and marshes of the estuary, that Peter Scott founded his Wildfowl Trust (now called the Wildfowl and Wetlands Trust) in 1946. The site was ideal, for the area was already well populated with native birds, their numbers swelled annually by over-wintering waterfowl. The Trust provides a haven for species threatened with extinction by large-scale drainage of the wetlands of Europe. The restored 19th-century decoy here was originally used to trap waterfowl which were served up at the tables of BERKELEY Castle. It is now used, more laudably, to lure birds in for purposes of monitoring and research.

The site is open to the public and is a popular place to visit.

The village of Slimbridge is about a mile inland, close to the A38. The church of St John here is an exceptionally complete example of early Gothic architecture, with fine foliated capitals. The lead font of 1664, decorated with cherubs and roses, is a rare object. The church's handsome spire is a landmark, visible for miles around in these flatlands.

Snowshill (4/3B)

Snowshill Manor and village are on minor roads about 6 miles north-east of WINCHCOMBE. Charles Wade, who lived at Snowshill Manor from 1919 until he presented it to the National Trust in 1951, was a collector of eclectic taste who filled the house with an extraordinary range of objects, from *samurai* armour to an early Victorian earth closet. Some of his magpie collection he put to good use, for he restored the handsome 15th- to 18th-century house himself, using period tools to carve the Tudor-style oak panelling. He also cleared unsightly 19th-century buildings from around the house to create a very fine series of terraced gardens (*see* 'Gloucestershire Gardens', p. 77).

The fascination of the house and its contents, and the charm of the garden, with its carefully planned changes of level, attract a prodigious number of visitors; the quieter weekdays are best for visiting.

Beyond the manor, the little village (pronounced 'Snozzle' by local people) consists of a knot of stone-built cottages beneath the steep, sheep-grazed slopes of the wolds, looking over the paddock-like graveyard of St Barnabas's church, rebuilt in 1864.

South-west of the village are barrows that yielded the Bronze Age Snowshill Dagger and other treasures now in the British Museum.

Snowshill village and the Manor (NT)

Somerford Keynes *see* South Cerney

Soudley *see* Cinderford

Southam *see* Bishop's Cleeve

South Cerney (4/3F)

The village is about 3 miles south-east of CIRENCESTER, to the west of the A419. South Cerney is in the Wiltshire Vale but has a distinctly Cotswold character and attractiveness. There is, however, a big RAF base on its northern border; and large-scale gravel extraction has brought water-filled pits, and a pall of yellow dust on all the approach roads.

There is much more gravel still to be dug here, but as exhausted pits close and fill up with water they are being integrated into a scheme that will create over 7000 acres of lakes by the end of the 1990s. These Cotswold Water Park lakes serve a variety of recreational and educational needs. Local schoolchildren learn to sail on their waters; some have been stocked for anglers; others are big enough for waterskiing; still others are for the conservation of wetland flora and fauna. The Somerford Lakes Reserve is a 100-acre private scheme of a similar nature.

The River Churn lends considerable appeal to the village itself, flowing along the edge of the streets in a stone-lined channel bridged, occasionally, by slabs that enable cottagers to reach their front gardens. Church Lane runs past grand 17th- and 18th-century houses to All Hallows church. The much-weathered Norman south door is decorated with beak heads and dragonhead stops, and the niche above contains Christ in Glory and the Harrowing of Hell.

This is mid-12th-century work of great richness, but far surpassed in beauty by the head and foot of Christ displayed in a case in the nave. These are faithful resin copies of the originals, now in the British Museum, which were made of wood and painted gesso. The work has been called the earliest wood carving in the country. Views on its provenance differ. Some say that it is English; others suggest that it was brought from Spain, perhaps by a pilgrim visiting the shrine of St James at Compostela.

The westward exit from South Cerney leads to **Shorncote** (4/3F). All Saints church, at the centre of the tiny farming parish, is redundant now and well worthy of sympathetic maintenance. Behind a pair of 15th-century wooden doors there is a tiny sanctuary with fragments of 12th-century decorative wall painting and a

15th-century Easter sepulchre. The eastern gable supports a fine 14th-century double bellcote and proud bronze cockerel.

One mile south is the village of **Somerford Keynes** (4/3F). In AD 685 the land here was granted to St Aldhelm, who was Abbot of Malmesbury. The doorway surviving in the north wall of All Saints church is of Saxon date.

Much of the rest of the church is Early English, but with a fine 15th-century oak screen and the marble effigy of the stylishly dressed Robert Strange (d.1645). His forebears acquired the attractive 15th-century Manor House west of the church from the Norman de Keynes family.

More gravel works separate this village from its neighbour to the west, **Poole Keynes** (4/3F). Its rather plain church, rebuilt *c.*1770, is dominated inside by a fine brass chandelier of 1740, in which the candle-holding branches issue from the heads of grotesques.

Southrop *see* Eastleaches, The

Standish *see* Harescombe

Stanley Pontlarge *see* Toddington

Stanton (4/3B)

The village lies about 5 miles north-east of WINCHCOMBE. It was fortunate in having an architect as its squire. Sir Philip Stott bought Stanton Court in 1906 and restored many houses that had become dilapidated following several decades of agricultural depression. It is due to him that the gently rising main street is lined with distinguished stone cottages, many of whose gardens are open on weekends in summer under the National Gardens Scheme.

Stott commissioned Sir Ninian Comper to refurbish the late Norman church of St Michael. This he did excellently, incorporating 15th-century stained glass from HAILES Abbey into his own modern design for the east window, signed with his wild strawberry trademark. He also added the west gallery, rood and alabaster reredos.

The village is on the Cotswold Way and a walk up Shenberrow Hill to the south-east leads to an Iron Age hillfort.

Less than 2 miles north-east, the village of **Buckland** (4/3B) lies sheltered beneath the scarp. St Michael's church is exceptionally interesting, with work of every period since its foundation to the present day. The nave was heightened and given a clerestory in the 15th century; also its splendid king-post roof, which has recently been repainted, the colours based on fragments of original paint.

The wooden furnishings are outstanding: some pews are 15th century; the high-backed stalls in the aisles are dated 1615; the handsome west gallery and pulpit are late 17th century. Six early 15th-century stone panels are painted with angels.

William Grafton, Rector here from 1466 to 1510, possibly donated the stained glass in the east window, which William Morris expertly restored in 1883. Grafton may also have built the stone and timber-framed Rectory near by (open occasionally in summer), with its open hall and impressive hammerbeam roof.

Stanway (4/3B)

The village is on the B4077 about 3 miles northeast of WINCHCOMBE. The rich golden colour of ashlar unifies the diverse styles of the buildings that surround Stanway House. One of these is the church of St Peter, with its 15th-century tower decorated with gargoyles. Another is the distinguished Jacobean gatehouse, which follows the earlier practice of having an architecturally exuberant entrance to the courtyard of the main house. Its bell-shaped gables are surmounted by finials sporting scallop shells from the crest of the Tracy family, who acquired the manor from TEWKESBURY Abbey at the Dissolution of the Monasteries. This gatehouse was long thought to be by Inigo Jones, but it is now believed to be the work of Timothy Strong, founder of a whole dynasty of masons (see Barringtons, The).

Stanway House itself (open in summer) seems relatively sober in comparison, enriched only by tall mullioned and transomed windows. The house dates, in parts, to the 16th century, and has been occupied continuously by the same family from then to the present day. The result is an unusually complete collection of furnishings and paintings built up by the family over the centuries (see also 'Gloucestershire Gardens', p. 77). The huge 14th-century tithe barn was restored for use as a theatre in 1925. Its size indicates just how wealthy Tewkesbury Abbey was in its heyday.

One of Stanway's most famous visitors was the playwright James Matthew Barrie. Moonlight flickering across his bedroom wall, reflected off the church weathervane, is said to have been his inspiration for the fairy Tinkerbell in *Peter Pan*. A keen cricketer, Barrie designed the thatched pavilion that stands on staddle stones beside the village pitch.

Staunton see Coleford

Staunton see Redmarley D'Abitot

Stinchcombe see Dursley

Stoke Orchard see Bishop's Cleeve

Stow-on-the-Wold (4/4C)

At 800 ft above sea level, Stow is the highest town in the Cotswolds and has long had to live with the ancient taunt of 'Stow-on-the-Wold, where the wind blows cold'. The hamlet of Maugersbury, south-east of the town, bears a name that pre-dates the creation of Stow, which was founded in the mid-11th century by Evesham Abbey. The mid-19th-century top to the medieval market cross in the square depicts the Abbot receiving Stow's market charter from Henry I in 1107.

Standing where eight roads meet, Stow was well placed to profit from the growth of the wool trade. It needed its big market square for the great flocks brought in for sale. The town was granted two annual fairs in the 15th century; as the Stow Horse Fairs, they persisted to the 1980s.

The town was originally called Edwardstow, probably after the 10th-century English king and martyr. The parish church is dedicated to St Edward, but whether this means the Martyr or the Confessor is not known. The original 12th-century building was enlarged during subsequent centuries as the town grew more prosperous. Thus, it is now almost wholly 15th century in character, with a fine clerestory and angel corbels surviving from the original roofs. It had to be restored in the 1680s, since the Civil War had left it almost in ruins. One of the last, and fiercest, battles of the war was fought here; over 1000 Royalist prisoners were confined in the church, which subsequently suffered much damage.

The north porch of the church was added during the 17th-century restoration and is a curious work: Gothic and flanked by two twisted yews.

The market place with its cross and wooden stocks is now partly turfed. It is dominated by St Edward's Hall, a 19th-century assembly room, and surrounded by 17th- and 18th-century houses, many of them now tearooms and antique shops. Lilian Middleton's Antique Doll Shop in Sheep Street has a small museum and a factory where bisque-head dolls are made.

There are a number of springs, or wells, in and around Stow. The discovery of a mineral spring in 1807 led to the building of the Indian-style Spa Cottages. The town is ringed by some attractive villages. At **Lower** (or Nether) **Swell** (4/4C) the church of St Mary the Virgin has noteworthy Norman carving, carefully conserved when the Reverend David Royce, an energetic archaeologist, supervised the restoration in the late 19th century. The Norman tympanum, carved with a dove and unfinished, is composed not of one monolith as at first appears, but ten stones sandwiched together. The chancel arch is carved with a procession of 26 symbolic creatures.

This village, just west of Stow-on-the-Wold, has one of the last traditional blacksmiths still working in the Cotswolds.

The village of **Upper Swell** (4/4C) is just under a mile further north up the valley of the Dikler. It can be reached via a pretty riverside walk that skirts the Abbotswood estate with its fine house of 1902, built by Sir Edwin Lutyens. Characteristically, he designed the very striking house and its gardens as an integral whole: (*see* 'Gloucestershire Gardens', p. 77). The gardens open occasionally under the National Garden Scheme.

At Upper Swell there is also a 19th-century mill, millpond and 18th-century bridge. The church of St Mary is Norman with a stone-flagged floor, ancient timber roof and beautiful Perpendicular font. The road north follows the River Dikler, source of the water for Donnington Brewery's excellent beers. The brewery build-ings – the three principal ones were mills in the 18th and early 19th centuries – form an attractive group around a lake.

Donnington (4/4C) itself is no more than a hamlet, 2 miles east of the brewery. The parish is served by the church of St Paul in the neighbouring village of **Broadwell** (4/5C). The Norman origins of the church are evident in the tympanum, carved with a Maltese cross, now built into the tower stair. Some older carved stones, possibly Saxon, are in the porch, and the churchyard has a collection of fine early 17th-century table tombs.

Evenlode (4/5C) lies about 1½ miles north-east of Broadwell, close to the river of the same name but separated from it by the Worcester to Paddington railway. The church of St Edward has a distinctive carved oak pulpit, pre-Reformation and therefore a rarity, since surviving pulpits of this date are usually of stone. It is

Aerial view of Stroud and the Golden Valley

beautifully shaped and carved with tracery and three small heads.

Stratton *see* Cirencester

Stroud (4/1E)

The town with its light industry and commerce tends to be cold-shouldered by many visitors to the Cotswolds, but there is much that will appeal, particularly to the industrial archaeol-ogist. The Thames and Severn and the Stroud-water canals join here, and stretches of towpath have been restored. A railway station and viaduct by Isambard Kingdom Brunel survive. Appropriately, perhaps, this is the home town of the Reverend W. H. Awdry, writer of the *Thomas the Tank Engine* stories.

Stroud was the capital of the Cotswold cloth industry in the 18th and 19th centuries. The Stroud District Museum, housed in a richly carved Victorian building, has a miscellany of collections and charts the rise and decline of the industry. At its zenith, over 150 mills operated here in the steep-sided valleys, producing the brilliantly coloured broadcloths worn by the military of the day. Of the great mill buildings that dominate the skyline from the eastern to the western suburbs, only a handful are still working today, turning out the finest of cloths, including baize for billiard tables and tennis balls, scarlet ceremonial uniforms and the white cassocks worn by the Pope.

One of a series of town trails plotted by the local Civic Society takes in the landmarks of this once-flourishing industry. The Stroud District Museum also proudly exhibits the first ever lawnmower, patented by a local man in 1830.

The parish church of St Lawrence, built of local stone in 1866–8, has Byzantine features. All Saints church at Uplands, a suburb on the B4070 road to Slad, is a fine example of Edwardian architecture, built in 1908–10 in Decorated style with a broach spire. Older than either is the octagonal Methodist chapel in Acre Street. Founded by Wesley's followers in 1763, this is the oldest such chapel in the county still in use as a place of worship.

The centre of Stroud is dominated by the Stroud Subscription Room. This was built by public subscription in 1833. It still serves its public purposes, as both an art gallery and a venue for events of the long-running annual Stroud Festival, which involves the region's poets, musicians and artists. Close by is the handsome 1837 Congregational chapel with its domed circular entrance hall.

The hamlet of **Randwick** (4/1E), north-west of Stroud, is one of the town's prettier suburbs.

Clothiers and mill workers once lived here and several are commemorated in the 18th-century tombs of the church of St John. A cheese-rolling ceremony, the Randwick Wap, takes place every first Sunday in May.

There are prehistoric barrows in nearby Standish Woods.

Swindon *see* Bishop's Cleeve

Syde *see* Brimpsfield

Symonds Yat (3/2D)
From 500 ft above the Wye, Symonds Yat Rock overlooks the river as it doubles back on itself in a great 4-mile loop on the county border. Many visitors come to see the wooded, dramatic gorge, to follow the Forestry Commission trails – and in recent years birdwatchers have been attracted here by the peregrine falcons that have begun nesting on the cliffs.

Tarlton *see* Coates

Taynton *see* Mitcheldean

Teddington (4/2B)
The village lies 5 miles east of TEWKESBURY,

Ferry across the River Wye to Symonds Yat

on the northern slope of Oxenton Hill, a Cotswold outlier, amid acres of orchards. HAILES ABBEY was the source of the stone for the splendid tower of St Nicholas's church, built in 1567 but displaying an Early English aspect because 13th-century piers from the apse at Hailes were used in the tower arches.

The nave walls are covered in 16th- and 17th-century wall paintings, including the text of the Creed and the Lord's Prayer, and the large coat of arms of William and Mary dated 1689.

The **Washbournes** (4/2B) stand in a basin ringed by the Oxenton, Dumbleton and Bredon hills – and by the Cotswolds themselves. Here in this enclosed landscape, threaded with brooks, the church of St Mary at Little Washbourne is set among lush pasture and orchards. It retains its basic Norman form, but with a complete set of 18th-century country box pews, pulpit, communion table and railings.

Great Washbourne's church of St Mary stands beside a street of timber-framed houses. It is early Norman with a Maltese cross tympanum and wall paintings consisting of simple geometric patterns that might also be Norman. The font stands in front of the altar where it dominates the little chancel – an awkward and highly unusual arrangement.

Temple Guiting *see* Guitings, The

Tetbury (4/1F)

About 9 miles south-east of STROUD and not far from the Wiltshire border, this is a quiet market town with some elegant 17th- and 18th-century houses. The town suddenly became fashionable when Prince Charles moved to Highgrove House on its south-western outskirts.

Several roads meet at the Market Place in this town where, since the 13th century, wool from the Cotswolds and dairy produce from the Vale of Berkeley and Wiltshire have been traded. The handsome Market House was built in 1655. It rests on three rows of pillars and has a pretty cupola surmounted by a weathervane in the form of a pair of gilded dolphins.

A large livestock market is still held every week below Gumstool Hill. Every Spring Bank Holiday, as part of the Tetbury Festival, contestants in the Woolsack Race run up and down this steep hill, each carrying a 65 lb bale of wool. Women now take part as well as men, but the original contest probably started as a trial of strength between young drovers out to impress the local girls.

Tetbury's church of St Mary was rebuilt in 1781. It is a building of great distinction, in its particular Gothic Revivalism wholly unlike any other Cotswold wool church. Slender columns, wooden with iron cores, rise to a vaulted plaster nave roof. The 18th-century high-backed pews are entered from passages around the outside of the nave. Splendid many-branched chandeliers contribute to the fashionable 18th-century elegance of the nave.

From the church it is just possible to see Highgrove House across the fields. It was built in 1796–8 for the Paul family of Huguenot origin, immigrants who became prosperous clothiers. One of the family, Sir George Onesiphorus Paul (1746–1820), was a prisoner reformer.

Shipton Moyne (4/1F) The village is about 4 miles south of Tetbury, on the Gloucestershire–Wiltshire border. The Foss Way, an important Roman road but now no more than a bridlepath, marks the county boundary.

The church of St John the Baptist was rebuilt in 1864 but has several sophisticated monuments, some of which were moved here from Lasborough (*see* Boxwell) in the 19th century.

Holy Trinity church at nearby **Long Newnton** (4/2F) was rebuilt in Early English style in 1841. It has a pleasing early 19th-century lectern and a tiny brass to John Exton (d.1503), a priest.

Ashley (4/2F) lies 3 miles north-east in flat countryside more Wiltshire than Cotswold in character. The church of St James has a Norman tympanum and steep roofs with fine Cotswold tiles. The Manor House stands to one side (gardens open occasionally under the National Gardens Scheme).

At **Tetbury Upton**, just north of Tetbury, there is an elegant Palladian house, with a garden open occasionally under the National Gardens Scheme.

Tewkesbury (4/1B)

This is a lovely old town in north Gloucestershire, by the confluence of the Severn and the Avon. From the 13th to the 15th centuries, Tewkesbury Abbey was one of England's biggest landowners, with estates stretching across the county as far east as FAIRFORD. At the Dissolution of the Monasteries the magnificent church survived because, in 1539, the townsfolk paid Henry VIII £453 so that they could keep it.

It was William Morris who intervened to stop the drastic restoration proposed by Sir Gilbert Scott in 1875 and, as a direct consequence, he went on to found the Society for the Protection

Tewkesbury

of Ancient Buildings in the hope of influencing architects to adopt principles of conservative repair.

Thus was preserved one of the finest large Norman churches in England, one of the few to retain its Romanesque west front, nave and tower, and rhythmic blank arcading. The lierne vault of the nave dates from about 1340 and is studded with bosses illustrating the life of Christ. Choir, transepts, presbytery and ambulatory all have brightly painted and vaulted ceilings of the 14th century, and contemporary windows filled with heraldic glass.

There is a lifelike effigy of Edward Despencer (d.1375), the knight whom the chronicler Froissart described as 'the most honourable, gallant and valiant knight in all England, much beloved of ladies'. His chantry, and the chapel of Robert FitzHamon (d.1107), second founder of the Abbey, both have later Perpendicular fan vaults of great delicacy. They are surpassed, however, by the extraordinarily rich Beauchamp Chapel with a pendentive vault that represents the medieval mason's art at its most sublime.

Tewkesbury's medieval street plan has survived in good measure. It grew out of the town's situation on the floodplain. Because there was a shortage of suitably dry sites (the land at the confluence of the rivers could not be used at all), Tewkesbury people built their half-timbered structures tall and crammed them in around courtyards and alleyways. The same rivers nevertheless brought prosperity to the town.

The wharfs and warehouses of a thriving inland port were built near the convergence of the Rivers Severn and Avon, and a side stream diverted to the town in the 12th century provided the power for several flour mills. One of these, the 19th-century Borough Mill in Quay Street, still operates.

Today a good deal of recreation is centred around the rivers, with boat trips from the centre, sailing and fishing, and there is a marina.

Tewkesbury is the subject of John Moore's *Portrait of Elmbury* (1945), the amusing story of the town between the two world wars (*see also* Bredon, H&W). The name of this local naturalist and author also lives on in the John Moore Countryside Museum, in Church Street. Associated with this museum is the Mythe Railway Nature Reserve just north of the town. Another building in the row, The Little Museum, has been furnished in the manner of a merchant's house when the terrace was originally built, in the 15th century.

Opposite, an alleyway leads to probably the oldest Baptist chapel in England; its baptismal tank and furnishings were installed in the 17th century when the 15th-century hall house was converted to a place of worship. Gravestones in the burial ground describe members of the early congregation as hosiers and framesmiths: weaving was an important local industry and several of the buildings of the town's back alleys have large upstairs windows, designed to light the stocking frames.

Tewkesbury is also a town of festivals and fairs. Occasionally, the townspeople re-enact the decisive Battle of Tewkesbury, fought in what is still called Bloody Meadow, which brought the Wars of the Roses to a close in 1471. In October the streets close for the annual Mop Fair. Originally a hiring fair when labourers and domestic servants would carry mops or other tools of their trades, it is now a funfair. Tewkesbury claims that this is the largest and most ancient of all such fairs held in the county.

In 1826 Thomas Telford's cast-iron bridge over the Severn, with its single 170-ft span, was opened, greatly stimulating the stagecoach traffic.

Tewkesbury was bypassed by the railways. It thus escaped 19th-century development and hardly any new building went up in the town between the 1850s and the 1930s. Instead, the railway went to **Ashchurch**, 3 miles east, where the church of St Nicholas stands close to the line and is surrounded by industrial buildings and warehouses.

Inside the church, beneath the Tudor roofs of the unusually long and narrow nave, is a very fine and complete 15th-century rood screen.

Thames and Severn Canal *see* Chalford, Coates, Lechlade, Sapperton, Stroud

Thames Head *see* Coates

Tibberton *see* Highnam

Tidenham *see* Beachley

Tirley *see* Forthampton

Toddington (4/3B)
This village is about 3 miles north of WINCH-COMBE, on the north side of the A438. The Toddington estate was passed from one generation of the Tracy family to the next, without interruption, from the Dissolution of the Monasteries onwards. However, the manor and church at Toddingon were both rebuilt in the 19th century; the house first, between 1820 and 1835, to the design of the occupant, Charles Hanbury-Tracy. It was modelled on the Gothic buildings of Oxford, especially Christ Church, from which he freely borrowed details. Even so,

the result has individuality and is regarded as an important example of Gothic Revival. Inside, everything was made as Gothic as possible, from the mirror frames to the plastered and gilded ceilings.

G. E. Street began rebuilding the church in 1873. Not always an inspired architect, Street nevertheless did good work here, capping the big nave with an elaborate hammerbeam roof and building a crisp well-lit chancel in pure Early English style. Near the church, by the River Isbourne, are the remains of the gatehouse to the original post-Dissolution manor.

One mile east of the village, Toddington station is now a museum maintained by the Gloucestershire & Warwickshire Railway Company. The station itself comes from Monmouth and was re-erected on the site of the original building, dismantled when the line closed in 1976. A dozen years later, plans were well in hand to reopen the line between Broadway and CHELTENHAM Racecourse; and already the stretch between Toddington and Winchcombe is open to passengers from March to October.

The line runs at the foot of the Cotswold scarp for much of its length. The next stretch of railway to open will take passengers to Gretton, from where it is a short walk to Stanley Pontlarge. The simple church of this tiny village is late Norman, with a rough-hewn oak roof inserted in the 1920s and a stone-flagged floor. Occasionally the peacefulness of this forgotten place is shattered, for, in the hills near by, Bugatti and other vintage car events are held on the Prescott Hillclimb Course.

Todenham *see* Moreton-in-Marsh

Turkdean *see* Notgrove

Twyning (4/1B)
This village about 2½ miles north of TEWKES-BURY for centuries remained isolated in the 'V' of land between the Severn and Avon. Its name in fact comes from Old English words meaning 'between the rivers'. Other names in the neighbourhood are a humorist's delight – The Twit-tocks, for example. The turnpike, now the A38, came in the 18th century, but still the only way to communicate with the neighbouring parish of Bredon (*see* H&W) was by ferry from the Fleet Inn. Then came the two motorways, the M5 and the M50, slicing across the horizon high on embankments above the surrounding water-meadows, and Twyning, now a commuter

village, began to enlarge. Development so far has left the church end of the village relatively untouched and, despite Victorian restorations, the church of St Mary Magdalene still has a measure of simple Norman grandeur.

Uley (3/4F)

The village lies some 6 miles south-west of STROUD. Peaceful and beautiful as it now is, Uley has known periods of strife. In the early 18th century, handloom weavers formed secret, and illegal, societies, the forerunners of trade unions, to try to improve their pitiful levels of pay. They made some of England's finest broadcloths (the Uley Blues), but were paid by the length of cloth they produced, not by the hours they worked. After strikes and riots, compromise was eventually reached, and the weavers were better paid for their skills. That many of the very substantial classical houses surrounding the green were built at this period shows that the prosperity of the local mill owners and clothiers continued nevertheless. Several have hipped and dormered roofs, a local characteristic.

The church of St Giles is high on the Uley valley side; it was rebuilt in 1857. This was during a period of large-scale church building, stimulated by the Oxford Movement which advocated a return to High Church ceremony, as typified by the furnishings of this church.

Uley itself is an attractive village in its south Cotswold setting of good walking country. In the valley below the Bethesda chapel of 1796 now houses the Prema Project, a thriving arts centre for the region.

Just east of Uley is the village of **Owlpen**, tucked away in a little valley and reached down a narrow road. The church is again largely Victorian but richly coloured from the combined effect of the painted ceilings, mosaics and stained glass.

The Daunt family owned Owlpen Manor for three centuries. Part of the house may already have been standing in 1464 when Marjory Ollepen married John Daunt, and succeeding generations added to it, including the terraced garden, believed to be early 18th-century, with its topiary (*see* 'Gloucestershire Gardens', p. 77).

The house stood empty from 1850 to 1926, when the Arts and Crafts architect Norman Jewson restored it with a proper appreciation for its beauty, antiquity and lovely hillside setting.

The steep road north from Uley passes two important prehistoric monuments. Uley Bury Iron Age hillfort is one of the most spectacular in the Cotswolds, built on a high plateau affording wide views over the surrounding country. Finds (now in the Gloucester City and Art Museum and the Stroud District Museum) include late Iron Age pottery, coinage and querns, as well as 1st- to 4th-century material, indicating that the site was occupied in Roman times.

Immediately north is **Hetty Pegler's Tump**, named after Hester Pegler who owned the land in the 17th century. The tump – the local term for a hillock – is a Neolithic long barrow, built around 3000 BC. Sited conspicuously on a hilltop, it consists of stone burial chambers either side of a central passage. It is entered through a portal recessed between two horns at its widest ends.

The village of **Nympsfield** (3/4E) is 1½ miles north-east of Uley, in a hollow. It has two Victorian churches. The Anglican church of St Bartholomew was rebuilt in 1861–3, the Catholic church of St Joseph in 1878. The gardens of the 17th-century Bell Court, and those of several cottages in the village, are open in summer under the National Gardens Scheme.

Up Hatherley *see* Badgeworth

Upleadon *see* Newent

Upper Framilode (3/4D)

This village, on a loop of the Severn some 7 miles south-west of GLOUCESTER, was of importance as the place where the 8-mile Stroudwater Canal had its junction with the great river. Opened in 1779, this canal was constructed to carry coal and building materials from the FOREST OF DEAN to the STROUD valley mills. At Wallbridge, a suburb of Stroud, it joins the Thames and Severn Canal (*see* Sapperton), which was begun in 1786.

The lock basin at Upper Framilode, controlling the entrance to the Stroudwater Canal from the Severn, is now filled in. However, a short stretch of the canal, lined with boatmen's cottages, passes through the village.

The next stretch is visible at **Saul** (3/4E), less than a mile to the south. Here an ingenious system of locks controls what used to be a busy 'crossroads' where the Stroudwater meets the Gloucester and SHARPNESS Canal. The latter is still a well-used commercial waterway; the former is derelict but beautiful. In early summer forget-me-not, marsh marigold and mint thrive along its banks.

The village, with its mid-19th-century brick and stucco cottages, lies a little to the west of the Stroudwater Canal.

Another quiet stretch of the canal can be followed south of **Whitminster** (3/4E), a village 1½ miles south-east of Saul, as far as the A38. The modern village is close to this trunk road; its mostly Perpendicular church is 1 mile to the north-east, near Whitchurch House – 16th century, with a number of later additions.

Upper Slaughter *see* Slaughters, The

Upper Swell *see* Stow-on-the-Wold

Upton St Leonards *see* Brockworth

Washbournes, The *see* Teddington

Westbury-on-Severn (3/4D)

On the A48 and beside the river, Westbury-on-Severn is about 8 miles west of GLOUCESTER. It was the scene of fierce skirmishing during the Civil War. Parliamentary troops routed Royalists who were holding the church; Westbury remained in Parliament's hands for the rest of the war.

The church of St Peter, St Paul and St Mary has a detached tower. It stands some 50 ft from

The Railway Museum and St Peter's, Winchcombe

the body of the church and was originally built as a garrison or watch tower around 1270, against Welsh raids. The spire was added in the 14th century, soaring to 160 ft, covered with shingles and framed internally with hugh oak beams from the nearby FOREST OF DEAN. The nave and chancel, built of local lias, soft and vulnerable to frost fracture, had to be rebuilt in the 19th century, the time of most of the internal work.

Gardens are much more vulnerable to fashion and neglect than houses. No fewer than 22 of the 58 great houses of Gloucestershire illustrated by the Dutch engraver, Johannes Kip (1653–1722), for Atkyns' great 18th-century county history had water gardens. Many of those houses have survived; of the gardens, only that at Westbury Court remains as a complete example of the fashion for Dutch-style gardens that followed the accession of William of Orange in 1689 (*see* 'Gloucestershire Gardens', p. 77).

Westonbirt (4/1F)

The estate and the village of Westonbirt are about 3 miles south-west of TETBURY. Reclining in the north aisle of St Katherine's church here is the marble effigy of Robert Stayner Holford (1808–92), the wealthy owner of the Westonbirt estate who created the 19th-century village as we see it today; work began in 1856, with the building of new semi-detached cottages around the edge of the estate.

This done, the old village was cleared so as not to interrupt the view from the new Elizabethan-style Westonbirt House, which Lewis Vulliamy had been commissioned to build, over its Italianate terraced gardens. Only the church remained in its original position, where it now serves principally as the chapel to the girls' school that occupies the house.

Earlier, in the 1840s, Holford rebuilt all the farms on the estate. In 1829, at the age of 21, he had begun collecting and planting the trees that form the great Westonbirt Arboretum. This is open all year round (*see* 'Gloucestershire Gardens', p. 77). The Forestry Commission, which now runs the Arboretum, publishes a calendar of what is best at different times of the year and runs an excellently informative reception centre.

Weston-sub-Edge *see* Aston Subedge

Whiteway *see* Miserden

Whitminster *see* Upper Framilode

Willersey *see* Aston Subedge

Winchcombe (4/3C)

The town lies about 7 miles north-east of CHELTENHAM, in a cleft on the Cotswolds' northern edge, cut by the River Isbourne. It was an important Anglo-Saxon town, seat of Mercian royalty and capital of a shire distinct from Gloucestershire until the early 11th century. It was defended by an earthen rampart, still visible to the north and west of the town; there was also a minster, one of whose clerics invented the story – now discredited by historians – of the boy Prince Kenelm, said to have been murdered by his sister in AD 819 (*see also* Clent, H&W). Fact or fiction, the prince was venerated as a martyr, and his shrine in the minster attracted many pilgrims, beginning Winchcombe's rise to prosperity.

Few monastic institutions were more powerful than Winchcombe's Benedictine Abbey, until it was so thoroughly razed in 1539 by Lord Seymour of Sudeley that nothing of it remains. It left its mark on the landscape, however: many of the villages on the wolds south of the town were cleared to make way for sheep. In the 13th

century the increasing demands of Flemish weavers for wool stimulated exports from England. By the 14th century, Winchcombe, its flocks greatly increased in consequence, was one of the top 12 wool-producing abbeys in the country.

The parish church of St Peter exhibits all the flamboyance of the earlier prosperous wool age. It was built in Perpendicular style, but late for a wool church – begun around 1465 – and survived an attempt by the motor magnate Henry Ford to buy it and rebuild it in America. The outside walls have a splendidly grotesque collection of heads and gargoyles. There is also a fine 15th-century oak screen.

The George Hotel in the High Street was built in the 15th century for pilgrims visiting the shrine of St Kenelm, and has a fine courtyard with gallery behind. Hailes Street has several more timber-framed houses of the same date. Among the honey-coloured limestone houses lining the long curving main street are a number that betray the patronage of the great families who benefited most from the Dissolution of the Monasteries. The Chandos almshouses of 1573 were built by Lady Chandos of Sudeley. The Dents, who acquired Sudeley Castle in 1837, contributed the Sudeley almshouses and the school, both designed by Sir Gilbert Scott.

The 19th-century Town Hall has local history and international police uniform collections. There is a railway museum in a private house in Gloucester Street and at Greet, just north of the town, the Winchcombe Pottery can be visited.

John Wyatt designed Christ Church in the village of **Gretton** (4/3B), 2 miles north-west of Winchcombe. It was built in 1868 in Early English style, which at that time was regarded as alarmingly untraditional. Near by stands the tower of the previous 15th-century church, surrounded by thatched and timber-framed cottages.

South-west of Winchcombe at **Sudeley** the church and the pinnacled, large-windowed castle (open in summer) stand in lovely countryside. The present castle dates from the 15th century, and was altered and extended in the 16th. It was slighted by Parliamentary forces in the Civil War, then left in ruins for two centuries. It was restored to habitable condition between 1837 and 1936.

The most famous occupant was Katherine Parr, Henry VIII's widow, who married Lord Admiral Seymour in 1547, but died the following year in childbirth. Since 1837 it has belonged to the Dent family. In the mid-19th century Emma Dent was an indefatigable collector of royal personal effects, furnishings – and portraits, including works by Constable, Turner, Rubens and Van Dyck, which now adorn the regal apartments. She also laid out the fine gardens (*see* 'Gloucestershire Gardens', p. 77).

Other features at Sudeley Castle include a falconry, craft exhibitions, and a very large private collection of toys.

Bastion-like yew hedges divide the gardens from St Mary's church, built around 1460. It was damaged in the Civil War and restored by Sir George Gilbert Scott, 1859–63. Some beautiful 13th-century stained glass has survived but the chief delight is J. B. Philip's white marble effigy (1859) of Katherine Parr. Scott designed the canopy above it. The oak furniture and pews here still bear the names of the houses that originally rented them.

Windrush (4/4D)

Some 6 miles south of BOURTON-ON-THE-WATER and just north of the A40, this village in the lovely valley of the River Windrush is all of golden limestone extracted from local quarries. Norman masons carved not one row of beak heads in this stone but two around the south door of St Peter's church, exulting in their skill.

The churchyard has some very fine early 18th-century table tombs, ornamented with classical

Ram's head on corbel in St Peter's, Windrush

friezes, vases, acanthus leaf and scallops. One has a curious mask, halfway between a beak head and a sheep's head.

There are walks through the valley and across the open country round about. South-west of the village a bridleway skirts an Iron Age site.

Winson *see* Ablington

Winstone *see* Brimpsfield

Withington (4/3D)

This village is about 7 miles south-east of CHELTENHAM, on the River Coln. The parish has been much studied by the pioneering landscape historian H.P.R. Finsberg. He argued, from the evidence at Withington, that many of the modern estates of the Cotswolds, and possibly elsewhere, too, are Roman in origin. Places like Withington, or nearby Colesbourne, or CHEDWORTH, may have Old English names, but these later Anglo-Saxon settlers simply took over Romano-British estates, which then in turn passed to Norman landlords, the abbeys and finally to post-Dissolution owners. Through it all, Finsberg believed, the boundaries have remained virtually unchanged for 2000 years.

At all events, it is worth while trying to envisage what may lie beneath the village as it is seen today.

It consists of a compact group of church, former rectory, and Manor House on the high westward bank of the River Coln. These older buildings stand on the site of a Romano-British settlement and a 7th-century monastery. On the opposite bank of the Coln is the straggling village, founded as a new settlement when the Abbess of Withington acquired the land around AD 744.

The fabric of the church of St Michael is Norman, with a corbel table running round the chancel, and a south doorway enriched with flowers and beast beak head stops. Wealth from wool paid for a splendid clerestory and for the heightening of the central tower, with its ogee-arched bell openings, in the 15th century.

Next door stands the magnificent former rectory, 18th century in external appearance but 15th or 16th century inside, with distinctive circular windows in the gables of the cross wings. Due to serious neglect, it is rapidly falling into ruin. Near by is the Jacobean Manor House and dovecot.

Just to the east is the course of the dismantled Midland and South Western Junction Railway, built at great cost at the end of the 19th century. It is now a haven for wild life and an attractive footpath linking the village to the Roman villa at Chedworth.

The road through the village climbs steeply and then drops to **Compton Abdale** (4/3D). The best part of the church of St Oswald, set on a bank behind trees, is its noble Perpendicular tower, crowned with pinnacles in the form of heraldic beasts rearing on their hindquarters and clasping staves. Corbels, including one of a huntsman and horn, decorate the lower stages. Beside the road south of the village crossroads is a 19th-century water spout in the shape of a crocodile, from whose jaws water from hillside springs spills into a stone trough.

Woodchester (4/1E)

The village is about 2 miles south of STROUD, with 18th- and 19th-century mills in the valley bottom, the houses on the hillsides above. Buried beneath the churchyard of the now ruinous Norman church is one of the largest and most beautiful Roman mosaics ever to be discovered north of the Alps. It is probably the work of the 'Corinium' school of mosaicists (*see* Corinium Museum, Cirencester) and depicts Orpheus with his lyre taming the beasts of the earth. In the past it has occasionally been uncovered for repair, and a full-sized replica, made in the 1970s, is seeking a permanent home in the region. The new church of St Mary, built in 1863, contains monuments moved from the old church.

South of the church is the Dominican Priory of 1845, built for William Leigh who was also responsible for the extraordinary Woodchester Park, begun in 1854 but abandoned, half completed, 14 years later. Since then, this *folie de grandeur* has stood open to the elements in its wide parkland; plans have been announced to rescue and develop the splendid remains.

Woodchester is a typical wool village, with several rows of 18th-century weavers' cottages and a round house called the Teasel Tower, used for drying the flowerheads of teasels, which were mounted on a frame and used to card cloth.

Wormington *see* Dumbleton

Wotton-under-Edge (3/4F)

About 10 miles south-west of STROUD, this market town is on the slopes of the southern Cotswold scarp, bordering on the Vale of Berkeley. The early history of Wotton-under-Edge is tied up with the Berkele[ys] they owned the manor. Early in the [ ] the town was burned down by [ ] mercenaries. A new town was lai[ ] plots, each of one third of an acre, can still be traced in the grid of streets south-west of the church. The church of St Mary the Virgin was rebuilt in 1283 and has a late 14th-century tower, a splendid example of Perpendicular style with blank panelling in its upper stages. The church contains the particularly fine brasses of Thomas, Lord Berkeley (d.1417), who fought at Agincourt, and his wife Margaret, Lady Berkeley, wears a long gown and cloak and has a little dog with a collar of bells at her feet.

The local cloth industry here declined in the 19th century, in part at least because mill owners were turning their backs on it. They invested in land and big houses instead, and they encouraged their sons to enter the gentlemanly professions rather than the cloth trade.

Their houses are dotted around Wotton among others that have interesting associations. In Culverhay is the Bluecoats School, founded in 1715. Isaac Pitman taught at the British School (its present building is dated 1843); it was while in Wotton that he published his *Stenographic Sound-Hand*, setting out his system of shorthand (1837).

At the top of the High Street is a fine Georgian building with Venetian windows. Tolsey House, built in the 17th century as a counting house and courtroom, has a lovely cupola and dragon weathervane. In Church Street the delightful 17th-century almshouses endowed by Hugh Perry stand around a quadrangle.

Several of Wotton's buildings, such as the National School in Green Chipping, have fragments of masonry from the Abbey at **Kingswood** (3/4F), 1 mile to the south of the town. This was one of the very last medieval foundations of England and was barely built before the monasteries were dissolved and the assets sold off. Much of the masonry from Kingswood was used to build Sir Nicholas Poyntz's new hunting lodge at Newark (*see* Alderley), but the gatehouse survived and has recently been restored as a council chamber. It has one exceptionally fine window, whose central mullion is carved in the form of a branching lily, symbol of the Virgin to whom the monastery was dedicated.

Wyck Rissington *see* Rissingtons, The

Yanworth *see* Chedworth

Hereford & Worcester Gazetteer

Abberley *see* Witleys, The

Abbey Dore (1/2E)
This hamlet lies at the southern end of the peaceful Golden Valley, about 10 miles south-west of HEREFORD and close to the Welsh border. St Mary's church – reconstructed from the remains of Dore Abbey – is one of the finest in the county, a delightful combination of Early English architecture and the 17th-century woodwork of the master carpenter, John Abel.

The Cistercian Dore Abbey was founded in 1147, but all traces of the Norman monastic buildings have disappeared, leaving only the 13th-century transepts and chancel of the abbey church. These are unusually elaborate for the generally austere Cistercians. There is a certain restraint, however, for some of the capitals of the ambulatory are Norman, and others a simplified version of stiff-leaf; many of the later embellishments of Early English style are absent. Even so the work is undeniably sumptuous. Behind the altar triple arches rise from complex clusters of shafts and the soaring recessed arches of the tall lancet windows give a sense of airiness and height.

By 1632 the church was in a very poor state of repair and used only as a cattle shed. On inheriting the manor, Lord Scudamore was sufficiently concerned to initiate substantial repairs. He employed John Abel, whose talents as an architect were surpassed only by his great skill as a carpenter, to undertake the work. Abel reroofed the chancel, replacing the ruinous stone vault with a new one of beautiful golden oak, and he carved the noble chancel screen sur-mounted by the arms of Charles I.

The church was re-dedicated in 1634 and little has changed since, except that the lovely patina of the woodwork harmonizes so well with the colour of the bare stone that two quite different and equally assertive styles, the Caroline and the Early English, blend rather than compete for attention.

In recent years an effort has been made to

The church of St Michael at Knighton on Teme (p. 147)

conserve the striking early 18th-century wall paintings at the west end. These include a figure of Father Time, with flowing beard, scythe and hourglass, in the style of William Blake.

Abbey Dore Court Gardens, open throughout the summer, lie opposite the church. The River Dore is an important feature of the garden and varieties of poppy, foxglove and fern flourish in the shady woodland. The pond, rockery and walled garden contain many varieties of hardy plant left to seed freely and create many happy accidental combinations of colour and form.

Bacton (1/2E) lies about 2 miles north of Abbey Dore above one of the many brooks that feed the Dore. In the isolated church of St Faith, far from the court where she spent the best part of her life, is the tomb of Blanche Parry, Maid of Honour to Elizabeth I.

The carving above the tomb chest depicts Blanche kneeling in an attitude almost of adora-tion before the Virgin Queen. Elizabeth looks stout and elderly here, but she is richly clothed and bejewelled.

Behind glass in the nave is a very beautiful, richly coloured altar frontal. Close examination reveals scores of birds, butterflies, caterpillars and fish hidden among the exotic foliage, as well as two figures in a punt, a frog, a snail and a dragon.

The road from Bacton follows a winding course to **St Margarets** (1/2E) to the north-west. Here, among the gentler hills that form a prelude to the Black Mountains, there is an almost complete absence of unnatural sound, a peacefulness that enhances the quietest birdsong.

The interior of the church is dominated by a large early 16th-century rood screen, richly carved and exceptionally well preserved, without any unnecessary coats of varnish. A stone staircase leads steeply to the gallery, where the fine oak roof can be admired from unusually close quarters.

Abbots (or **Ab**) **Lench** *see* Lenches, The

Abbots Morton (2/5D)
This pretty village lies west of the A441 about 7 miles north of EVESHAM. The church of St Peter

stands on rising ground at its west end. The first view is of the chancel with its fanciful early 16th-century window. The low walls and roof convey a sense of humble rusticity which is even more evident inside: the chancel arch is timber-framed, and the roof consists of halved and quartered timbers held in place by huge tapering pegs.

In the fields north-east of the church is a group of mounds and fishponds, all that remains of the Abbot of Evesham's medieval summer residence. The village, one of the most attractive in the county, consists of 17th-century timber-framed houses; once the homes of prosperous yeomen, many of them have been sympathetically restored in recent years.

The postbox set in the wall of the house opposite the church gate has its own miniature thatched roof; at the western end of the nearby village of Radford is a Victorian example that is set in a timber-framed structure like a miniature house.

Aconbury (1/4E)
The main feature here, about 4 miles south of HEREFORD and east of the A49, is the church of St John the Baptist. This was a late 13th-century foundation of the Sisters of the Order of St John of Jerusalem, the female counterpart of the Knights Hospitallers. The south nave wall contains the blocked arches and springers for the vaulting of the cloister range, since demolished. The timber porch is 14th century, carved with angels wearing garlands and holding shields. Inside the simple church little has been altered since it was built: even Sir George Gilbert Scott exercised untypical restraint when he restored it in 1863.

There is an Iron Age hillfort on Aconbury Hill, just under a mile west-south-west of the church. The 17½-acre site has yielded Romano-British and earlier pottery.

Acton Beauchamp (2/1D)
The church of St Giles stands in hilly country some 3 miles south-east of BROMYARD at the end of an unmetalled road. It was rebuilt in a plain, featureless style in 1819, but has an interesting 9th-century Anglo-Saxon cross shaft, re-used as a lintel to the tower door. It has, unfortunately, been cut away to create more headroom, but the surviving portions show interlace and vine scroll inhabited by dragons and birds. It is carved from a block of oolitic limestone, not a local material, and no one knows how such an accomplished piece of sculpture came to be here.

A mile north by footpath, but 2 miles by road, is the church of St James at **Stanford Bishop** (2/1D). Victorian historians confidently asserted that the chair in the chancel was Anglo-Saxon, the one used by St Augustine at the synod of AD 603. Its 7th-century date is, however, questionable. It is extremely primitive, with rough-hewn planks pegged together, which alone is grounds for suspicion, for we know that the Anglo-Saxons were skilled woodworkers.

Alfrick *see* Suckley

Almeley *see* Eardisley

Alvechurch *see* Lickey Hills

Ashperton *see* Fromes, The

Ashton under Hill *see* Bredon

Astley *see* Witleys, The

Aston (1/3A)
St Giles is one of those rare churches that has survived with its Norman fabric intact, largely because of its remoteness. It lies in the hills, now, alas, planted with conifers, east of the A4110 and halfway between WIGMORE and Ludlow (Shropshire).

Above the north door is a superb tympanum composed of Evangelists' symbols, Christ the Lamb and a swirling chain of dragons biting each other's tails. Inside, the 12th-century wall painting consists of red lines imitating masonry and stylized flowers. The Norman font could scarcely be smaller, yet the masons managed to cram more of their favourite dragons all over its surface.

Elton (1/3A) is less than a mile south of Aston. St Mary's church stands on a mound by a brook; the path to the church passes under the sweeping branches of a huge and ancient beech tree. Inside is a very distinguished coat of arms of Elizabeth I carved in oak. Unusually, the lion of England is opposed not by the unicorn but by a crisply detailed dragon.

Elton Hall next door is a straightforward Georgian house of warm red brick – except that the windows have Gothic ogee heads instead of flat lintels.

From Elton it is worth making a detour westwards to **Burrington** (1/3A) to see the eight cast-iron grave slabs outside the church. They date from 1619 to 1754 and commemorate members of the Knight family, owners of ironworks at Bridgnorth (Shropshire). These durable slabs have interesting lettering and heraldry. The churchyard is managed as a hay meadow and supports a wide variety of wild flowers, including the rare yellow rattle.

Aston Ingham *see* Ross-on-Wye

Aston Somerville *see* Childswickham

Atch Lench *see* Lenches, The

Aylton *see* Pixley

Aymestrey (1/3B)
The village is on the A4110, about 7 miles north-west of LEOMINSTER. Its church, dedicated to both St John the Baptist and St Alkmund, gained its most distinguished features in the 16th century when 12th-century masonry, possibly from WIGMORE Abbey, was re-used to build the nave, and the handsome rood and parclose screens were put in. The coved canopy of the rood screen is particularly fine, decorated with lierne vaulting and curving graciously to end in pendant bosses. Slender shafts separate this from the dado, with its linenfold panelling.

The Crown Inn, at the north end of the village, stands beside an 18th-century bridge over the Lugg and is the starting point for a short but dramatic riverside walk. After a few hundred yards the path enters the steep-sided Aymestrey gorge, source for centuries of the stone used to build the local houses. Now it is a wildlife haven where wild flowers and many varieties of fungus flourish. The track climbs to the wooded crest of the gorge and continues for a mile, high above the river, to **Mortimer's Cross** (1/3B).

This hamlet, little more than a pub and a scattering of houses, is close to the site of the battle of Mortimer's Cross, a bloody and decisive engagement in the Wars of the Roses. In the remote fields of the Herefordshire Marches, on 3 February 1461, Yorkists fought Lancastrians. After heavy losses on both sides, 19-year-old Edward Mortimer, eldest son of the Duke of York, emerged the victor. He was crowned in March as Edward IV. The only visible memento of the battle is an inscribed stone, erected by public subscription in 1799, to the south in front of the Monument Inn.

Just east of the crossroads, by a bridge, is an 18th-century watermill maintained by English Heritage (open daily), one of the few of the many mills that once straddled the fast-flowing Lugg to have survived with its machinery intact.

Bacton *see* Abbey Dore

Badsey *see* Bretforton

Bayton *see* Mamble

Beckford *see* Bredon

Belbroughton (2/4B)
This large village some 6 miles east of KIDDERMINSTER has escaped suburbanization despite being so near the heavily built-up areas of the West Midlands. Several fine Georgian houses surround the well-kept green, among them the dignified Old Rectory east of the church.

Holy Trinity church is large and contains Norman, Decorated and Perpendicular features. There is also Victorian work and it contains stained glass designed at the turn of the century by C. E. Kempe, friend of William Morris and Sir Edward Burne-Jones. Kempe is now so highly regarded that a society has been formed for the appreciation and conservation of his work.

The pulpit is an outstanding piece of Jacobean woodwork, carved with dragons and fantastic human figures.
Broome (2/4B) is about 2 miles to the north-west, a pretty, unspoiled village with a large duck pond. The diminutive red-brick church of St Peter contains a touching memorial to Anne Hill (d. 1804), sculpted by the great John Flaxman, of a young woman seated reading.

Beoley *see* Redditch

Berrington Hall *see* Leominster

Berrow *see* Birtsmorton

Besford *see* Pershore

Bewdley (2/2B)
This lovely town on the Severn is about 3 miles west of KIDDERMINSTER. The Georgian builders who gave it its present appearance retained the underlying medieval street pattern, and in many cases simply refronted older buildings. Consequently, instead of the straight lines of terraces

characteristic of much Georgian building, Bewdley is a town of narrow winding streets. Exploring is a great pleasure, for new surprises emerge at every turn and the vistas are continually changing.

The prosperity that made all this handsome building possible came from the port on the banks of the Severn. Bewdley was an important collecting point for goods manufactured in the Midlands to be shipped from here to Bristol and beyond. All this changed overnight when the Staffordshire and Worcestershire canal opened in 1771. This bypassed Bewdley at the townspeople's own insistence; they wanted nothing to do with James Brindley's 'stinking ditch', which went to STOURPORT-ON-SEVERN instead.

Bewdley settled for genteel decline and, with neither the money nor the motive to erect new buildings, the town remained frozen, architecturally, in the late 18th century. Severnside, where the town directly faces the river, is a good place to appreciate Bewdley's special qualities. What is rare is that the world of nature begins where the world of man abruptly stops: Bewdley happily lacks the nondescript modern suburbs that ring so many English towns.

Despite admirable efforts to preserve the townscape, a few of the elegant buildings on the embankment look worryingly in need of attention. River House has lost its shellhood doorcase, but still has its Victorian cast-iron balcony, from where there must be enviable views of Thomas Telford's graceful bridge (built 1795–8).

This bridge stands at the widest end of Load Street, which gradually narrows as it climbs the hill with the island church as its focal point. The buildings to either side are for the most part models of measured elegance. Here and there, however, one breaks into exuberance: No 71, for example, with its Venetian windows and Gothic glazing bars; or the Midland Bank building which, despite its deplorable modern facia, has many carved keystones. An alley runs beside the Town Hall (built 1808) to the Shambles, or Butchers' Market. This now houses the excellent working brass foundry and other displays illuminating the town's crafts and industries.

The body of St Anne's church was completed in 1748; the tower was built some 50 years earlier. Its classical appearance and Venetian windows are in accord with the surrounding houses, making a stylistic unity between church and town. Inside, galleries surround the west end and the ceiling is carried on big Tuscan columns.

Beyond the church is the narrow High Street, now almost exclusively residential, showing how the commercial centre of the town shifted with the growing importance of the river. The houses here are plainer: many still show pre-Georgian timber framing. Only the most important were refronted, such as the Manor, originally built in 1607.

Further on, 15 Lower Park was the birthplace of Bewdley's most famous son, Stanley Baldwin, the 'plain man's Prime Minister' who was created 1st Earl Baldwin of Bewdley on his resignation in 1937.

Wribbenhall (2/2B), on the east bank of the Severn, is the best place to enjoy panoramic views of Bewdley's bridge and river embankment. It has a few good Georgian houses of its own. Every so often, the air is filled with the pleasing sounds of a steam locomotive hauling passengers up the Severn Valley Railway line (see Upper Arley).

Just south of Bewdley is the hamlet of **Ribbesford** (2/2B). As you pass along the unmetalled track to the church, Ribbesford House can just be seen on the left. James Lees-Milne, whose grandfather lived here, tells us that beneath the ugly grey render, applied in the 19th century, there is a fine Tudor house, built by the Herberts.

The Herbert arms appear on a pink sandstone building with oval windows, probably dating from the 17th century, in the farmyard close to the church. It now serves as a barn, but looks too grand to have been built as such.

St Leonard's church is entered through an exuberant timber porch, dated 1633, with turned and painted balusters. It shelters a curious tympanum, carved with an archer taking aim at a reptilian creature with many legs and a big flat tail.

The interior is considerably more spacious than at first appears. The nave has a rare and unusual south arcade of oak, rising from octagonal piers.

The west window was designed by Sir Edward Burne-Jones and is typical of his style. It was commissioned in memory of Hannah MacDonald, Burnes-Jones's mother-in-law and the grandmother of both Stanley Baldwin and Rudyard Kipling, who was married in this church.

East of the church the steep churchyard, carved out of ancient pasture, is being managed as a hay meadow because of its valuable stock of wild flowers.

Birlingham *see* Pershore

Birtsmorton (3/4B)
The village is about 7 miles south of Great Malvern (*see* Malverns, The) and just off the A438. Its church of St Peter and St Paul is flanked by the gateposts of Birtsmorton Court. Of little interest in itself, the church nevertheless contains a flamboyant memorial to William Caldwell (d. 1718), Rear Admiral of the Royal Navy's Baltic fleet.

The beautiful, moated Birtsmorton Court, of timber frame and delicate pink brick, dates from the 14th to the 16th centuries. It forms the centrepiece of a fine garden (open under the National Gardens Scheme), where roses clamber over ancient brick walls, and a magnificent spreading yew tree, planted 500 years ago, still flourishes.

Birtsmorton stands on the edge of an area of ancient gravel workings and of marshes, home to rare amphibians such as the great crested newt, and many species of bird. These can be seen in the wild from any of the region's numerous footpaths, or at close quarters in the wildfowl sanctuary (open all year round) west of the village.

The castle at **Castlemorton** (3/4B), less than a mile to the north-west, is now reduced to an earthen motte and bailey just south of St Gregory's. This church has a big Perpendicular tower and spire, and a Norman Lamb of God tympanum.

The road from Pendock village to Eldersfield, some 3 miles south of Birtsmorton, passes by some curiously shaped hillocks, outcrops of the same hard rock as the Malverns. The hamlet consists of little more than a 17th-century church, farmhouse and dovecot by a pond. The church of St John the Baptist, with its big Perpendicular tower and spire, is a huge building for such a small community to maintain. The furnishings include Elizabethan and Jacobean woodwork and the churchyard has some good, though weathered, table tombs.

Bishop's Frome *see* Fromes, The

Bishopstone (1/3D)
The village is just north of the A438 and some 6 miles north-west of HEREFORD. The church of St Lawrence is a little to the north of the village, and a great delight. The chancel roof is the most bizarre in the country, a riot of 'S' curves filling the spaces between the rafters and tie beams.

It looks typically Jacobean, but it has been suggested that it could well be a convincing Victorian imitation.

Perhaps caution is justified, for much of the woodwork of the chancel is 19th century, with re-used Jacobean pieces.

A little to the south, within sight of the River Wye, is the church of St Andrew at **Bridge Sollers** (1/3D). The south door is a lesser work of the Hereford school of Norman sculptors. The lintel on the left is carved with dragons spewing from a man's mouth and curling back to bite his ears. On the right is a winged dragon. It lacks the boldness of the best Norman work in the county but is a pleasing curiosity.

Just over a mile upstream to the west is **Byford** (1/2D). Just visible from the church is Byford Court, a 16th-century house of stone and half-timbering with mullioned windows. Byford House next door is sombre but handsome.

St John the Baptist has a splendid nave arcade of around 1200, with round pillars and octagonal abaci. The arcade between the chancel and south chapel, added 40 years later, is even finer. The chapel contains 14th-century wall paintings. Many still lie beneath the whitewash waiting to be revealed; already visible is St Margaret, with another female saint holding a book.

The River Wye near Bridge Sollers

Blakemere *see* Moccas

Bockleton *see* Edwyn Ralph

Bodenham *see* Hope under Dinmore

Bosbury (3/3A)

This village about 4 miles north of LEDBURY lies in the hillocky countryside to the west of the Malverns. The wide main street separates the church on one side from the several early timber-framed houses on the other, including the 15th-century hall house with cross wings directly opposite the church.

The approach to Holy Trinity church is dominated by the big detached belltower, fortress-like in its solidity. Its simplicity is in stark contrast to the Perpendicular style of the late 15th-century Morton chapel, containing the only fan vault in the county outside of EVESHAM and the city of HEREFORD. Here it has been squeezed into so tiny a space that the ribs of the northernmost bay come together and hang truncated in mid-air.

The chancel contains two wonderful monuments to John and Richard Harford. One is at first glance a mirror image of the other, but closer inspection reveals that the imitator made some substantial modifications. The monument of John (1573) is the nobler work; Richard Harford's (1578), with its figures of Adam and Eve, is livelier and not without unconscious humour.

Brampton Bryan (1/2A)

This neat village of thatched and timber-framed houses, just off the A4113 about 3 miles south-west of LEINTWARDINE, was almost totally rebuilt after a Civil War siege in 1643, which lasted seven days and resulted in the virtual destruction of all the houses and the castle. Ornate timber work rescued from the castle was used in the rebuilding of St Barnabas's church, which has a soaring triple hammerbeam roof (in the 1880s the third tier was unfortunately panelled in, so that its full beauty has yet to be revealed).

A delightful feature of the churchyard is the undulating yew hedge that snakes along the perimeter wall and runs on to surround, and hide from view, the 18th-century house next door. Its grounds (open under the National

Looking north from Bredon Hill

Gardens Scheme) contain the surviving gatehouse of the 14th-century castle.

Bredon (4/2A)

Bredon Hill is the largest of the outliers that were once part of the Cotswolds but were separated in the Ice Age by meltwater cutting through the soft lias and leaving several of these limestone outcrops stranded. The hill is most dramatic to the north, where it rises steeply to over 1000 ft, a counterpoint to the flat Vale of EVESHAM.

A series of minor roads encircles the hill, linking 14 villages and hamlets whose character, because of the freely available stone, is often unlike that of the rest of the county. It takes the best part of a day to visit them all, including time to enjoy the views from the top of Bredon Hill, but it is time well spent, taking in ancient tithe barns, castles, churches and several notable gardens.

Little Comberton (4/2A), south of the A44 about 4 miles west of Evesham, is a good place to start – for it is a sort of hybrid village, partly still of timber-framed houses in the predominant style of the county, partly of stone. Even the church of St Peter has both: the handsome tower is faced in ashlar, but the chancel has one timber-framed gable whose windows let in the evening light. The unusual Norman tympanum, too, suggests that the maker was not a mason by instinct. What do the eight strange whorls surrounding the flat cross represent?

Next is **Great Comberton** (4/2A), a mile to the south-west, where the path to the church of St Michael passes beneath the spreading branches of a giant oak. Inside, the 16th-century benches are of massive hewn oak. Orchards, pretty in blossom time, surround the village to the north.

South-west of the village, before the road makes a dogleg to Eckington, a track leads uphill to Woollas Hall, built in 1611 and now converted to flats. Energetic visitors can continue up Bredon Hill to St Catherine's Well – a spring said to have healing powers, by the side of a ruined chapel – to the 2nd-century BC hillfort on the summit. Within this enclosure is a low tower, called Parson's Folly after the man who built it in the early 18th century.

Eckington (4/2A) is built at the point where the Bredon foothills meet the Avon flood plain. An attractive walk follows the river bank for 2 miles in a wide meander round the village, starting or finishing at the narrow and ancient Eckington Bridge.

Holy Trinity church has a late Norman nave and 15th-century roof, carved here and there with sea monsters. The Jacobean monument in the chancel shows John Hanford (d. 1616), the builder of Woollas Hall, with his wife and children. Some of the modern glass is pleasing, especially the Ethel Cholmondely memorial window depicting a figure in an English Edwardian garden.

About 1½ miles south of Eckington is Bredon's Norton, an attractive village with a church rebuilt almost from the foundations in 1883.

Bredon (4/1B), to the south of Bredon's Norton, is the biggest village on the circuit. Its church of St Giles is the grandest in the area; its 160 ft-high, needle-thin spire can be seen for miles around. Unusually, the church has retained all three of its original Norman doors; the west door is the best, decorated with chevron moulding and dragon head stops, beneath a gable flanked by towers and pinnacles.

All the main periods of church architecture are exemplified in the interior. The nave is Norman, the tower arches are Transitional, pointed but with chevron mouldings, and the south aisle is Early English, with trefoil-headed lancet windows and detached shafts. The chancel is Decorated and retains some original glass.

In the south aisle is the splendid gold and jewel-encrusted Jacobean tomb of Sir Giles Reed (d. 1611) and his wife. It is an architectural monument of great splendour, with antechambers in which the children kneel at prayer, surmounted by obelisks and putti.

The 14th-century encaustic tiles in the sanctuary depict the arms of nearly all the principal aristocratic families of England. Just as pleasing are the geometric tiles that cover the whole nave.

Bredon's beautiful 13th- or early 14th-century tithe barn (National Trust) is at the opposite end of the village from the church and has been successfully restored following a fire in 1980. This aisled and buttressed building is bigger even than the church, and one of its wagon entrances was later converted to a dwelling with a chimney and external staircase.

John Moore's semi-fictional portrait of country life, *Brensham Village* (1946), is set in Bredon (*see also* Tewkesbury, Glos., and *below*). Beautiful as the village still is, it is no longer quite so tranquil, sandwiched as it is between the M5

The Bredon tithe barn (National Trust)

motorway and the railway. Moore lived in the mill in **Kemerton** (4/2B), the village 1 mile east of Bredon. The villagers remember him with great affection, despite his sometimes less than flattering portraits of them.

St Nicholas's church was largely rebuilt in 1847, but is worth visiting to see the ornate enamelled brass and iron chandelier, now lit only at Christmas, that hangs in the nave.

If you take the road north out of Kemerton, you can drive a considerable way up the southern slope of Bredon Hill: far enough to enjoy views of the Malvern Hills in one direction, and a wide sweep of the Cotswold scarp in the other, views that A. E. Housman loved and wrote of in his *Summertime on Bredon*.

The road passes two gardens that are occasionally open to the public. The Priory specializes in rare and unusual plants – particularly those that like Bredon's alkaline soils – planted in thematic groups according to colour and texture. Bell's Castle has a wild garden around the walls of a folly, built in the early 19th century by Edmund Bell.

Overbury (4/2B) village, a short distance to the east of Kemerton, is built almost entirely of stone and will for that reason be judged by many visitors as the most attractive of the Bredon group. Its charm is enhanced by the surrounding open landscape of Overbury Park, planted with many a majestic specimen tree. It was the creation of John Martin, founder of Martin's Bank.

A brook flows along the southern boundary of the churchyard, which is entered by a lychgate. St Faith is, in external appearance, a Perpendicular church, but there is a complete Norman nave and contemporary font within.

North of the church are the wrought-iron gates that mark the entrance to Overbury Court, an ashlar-fronted house built by John Martin to replace the earlier house, which burned down in 1735. The gardens, laid out partly in the 1920s, are open occasionally under the National Gardens Scheme; so, too, are the gardens of the late 17th-century Conderton Manor in the village just to the east.

Beckford (4/2B), 2 miles south-east of Overbury, is the most southerly village of the Bredon group. Its church of St John the Baptist is completely encircled by grand houses, notably the Jacobean Beckford Hall, with its lovely 17th-century gate piers, and Beckford Silk Mill, formerly the Rectory (open throughout the year).

The church has some unusually crude and

enigmatic Norman carving. On the south tympanum are two animals – one, unlikely as it may seem, looks like a rhinoceros. The north tympanum illustrates the Harrowing of Hell, with Christ leading Adam to Paradise and thrusting his cross purposefully into the mouth of a dragon. The chancel is Early English; the arch is carved with two beak heads and a centaur. It seems that the patron who commissioned the work had in mind some of the grand Romanesque churches of the Continent, but he must have been somewhat disappointed at the local masons' inept interpretation of his brief.

The road from Beckford to Grafton passes by an area with lynchets, soil terraces and ancient gravel pits. Excavation has discovered the site of a late Iron Age (2nd and 1st century BC) village here, perhaps consisting of a dozen farming families – not unlike Grafton today, which is still a small churchless hamlet of working farms.

Ashton under Hill (4/2B), about 2 miles north-east of Beckford, is one of the Worcestershire villages that claims to be the model for Ambridge, the home of *The Archers*, the long-running BBC radio serial (*see also* Inkberrow). There is some justice to the claim, for it was the home of one of the programme's early scriptwriters, and the church was used for the recording of Grace Archer's wedding. Bredon

Hill bears a strong resemblance to the Lakey Hill of the serial. The parallels are only superficial, however; the local pub is called the Star, not the Bull; and the village is considerably larger than most listeners would imagine Ambridge to be, with a large amount of postwar housing.

The church of St Barbara is rather plain. The chancel is dated by an inscription to 1624 – an unusual date for rebuilding – and has fish beautifully, but inexplicably, carved in the spandrels of the east window.

Two local gardens may be visited: Bredon Springs, a plantsman's garden from which all chemicals are banned, is open through much of the summer, while Bredon Pound is open under the National Gardens Scheme.

Elmley Castle (4/2A) lies 2 miles north-west of Ashton under Hill and forms a fitting climax to this tour of Bredon villages. The road from Kersoe enters the village through a narrow gap between two solid stone houses, and suddenly the whole stretch of the wide main street is revealed. Its oldest and best building, with a 14th-century floor, is used as the village hall. Elmsley Castle is a serene village of low cottages

Main street of Elmley Castle, with Bredon Hill behind

with a pub called the Queen, commemorating Elizabeth I's visit in 1575. The castle was long ago demolished, but the mound on which it stood can be seen south of the church, accessible by footpath, on the hillside now used as a deer park.

St Mary's church is very beautiful. It sits handsomely against the hillside, all of mellow weathered stone, with a solid tower and battlements running around all the parapets. By far the finest of the monuments here is the 17th-century alabaster memorial to Sir William Savage, Giles Savage and the latter's wife; she is portrayed holding her infant daughter in her arms while the four sons kneel in prayer at their feet.

Much more grandiose is the late 17th-century memorial to the first Earl of Coventry. It is a very fine work of sculpture, but ludicrously pompous; the recumbent Earl is portrayed pointing to his coronet with inordinate pride.

Bredwardine (1/2D)

This village is on the River Wye about 12 miles west of HEREFORD. Visitors come from all over the world to visit this remote spot in the western reaches of the county because it was the last home and burial place of the Revd. Francis Kilvert (1840–79), whose *Diary* was first published in 1938 (and as *Kilvert's Diary* in 1969), and has remained a bestseller ever since. The *Diary* covers the last eight years of the life of this perceptive and sensitive writer. His final two years were spent at Bredwardine; previously he had been curate of parishes in Wales and Wiltshire.

Even without the Kilvert connection, St Andrew's church is well worth a visit. It stands on the hillside and is approached along a beech avenue. The lintel of the north doorway is a curious piece of Norman work, carved with two creatures, one with a bird's head and the other with a monkey-like face. They have been described, mistakenly, as Oriental deities; in fact, they are figures of a type commoner on the Continent, designed as a warning against the sin of concupiscence (*see also* Kilpeck). Their grotesqueness is appropriate to this function.

Inside, the church is huge and barn-like, with a pronounced change of direction between the nave and the chancel. The extraordinary crookedness of the ground plan means that the altar is hidden from a portion of the congregation.

The excellent church guide includes details of a walk around the gentle, hilly countryside, which Kilvert described so affectionately, taking

in the nearby castle motte, the ancient fishponds, and many of the cottages mentioned in the *Diary*. On the opposite side of the pretty brick and stone bridge, built in 1759, is the delightful riverside garden of Brobury House (open in summer under the National Gardens Scheme).

Bretforton (4/3A)

This attractive village, 4 miles east of EVESHAM along the B4035, is well worth exploring on foot, perhaps after lunch at the 16th-century timber-framed Fleece Inn, owned by the National Trust.

The Inn is on the green opposite St Leonard's church; this has a fine 13th-century arcade with richly carved capitals, and a Perpendicular tower.

A walk westward through the village passes a garden gate made up of medieval masonry fragments and one bat-eared figure, several newly thatched cottages, and, best of all, the lovely Bretforton Hall, built in 1830 in Strawberry Hill Gothick style, with a pretty semicircular porch and wrought-iron balustrade. Near by, Bretforton Manor is open throughout the year and, despite its rather forbidding 19th-century façade, is substantially Tudor and Jacobean.

Just over 1 mile to the west is **Badsey** (4/3A), a village of many recent housing estates with a few earlier gems in between, notably the Manor House, built of stone and herringbone-patterned timber framing; the handsome 17th-century Stone House; and Blakesmere, a Regency house with bow windows by the church. St James's has a big Perpendicular tower carved with demons and a nice 17th-century wall monument to Richard (d. 1617) and Margaret Hoby. The kneeling family below face west, not east, indicating that they were Margaret's children by an earlier marriage.

Bridge Sollers *see* Bishopstone

Bridstow *see* Ross on Wye

Brilley *see* Winforton

Brinsop (1/3D)

There is no village here, just a church, reached down an unmetalled track off the A480, and about 1 mile north-west of Credenhill. The church is dedicated to St George and there are fine images of England's patron saint from every period. The earliest is the stunning Norman

Tympanum depicting St George and the Dragon, Brinsop

tympanum of the Hereford School, reset in the nave wall.

St George appears again, in Crusader armour, in the richly coloured 14th-century glass of the chancel, and, in bronze, flanking the rather ugly 1920s reredos. The canopy above the chancel is gilded and painted with the shield of St George and roses. This was the work of Sir Ninian Comper, as is the gilded figure of Christ crucified, above the rood screen, and much of the stained glass – signed with Comper's customary wild strawberry emblem.

One of these windows is dated 1929, 'in memory of William Wordsworth, poet laureate and frequent sojourner in this parish'. Wordsworth's brother-in-law owned Brinsop Court, a 14th-century mansion surrounded by woods that can just be glimpsed from the minor road that leads from Brinsop. Only three of Wordsworth's – minor – poems refer to the area.

About 2 miles north of Brinsop, past the Court, is the redundant church of St Mary, **Wormsley** (1/3D). It is a plain, barn-like building with a Norman tub font and Jacobean pulpit, but its situation, high up and far from the busy world, is exhilarating.

There are two imposing sarcophagi in the churchyard commemorating the brothers Richard Payne Knight (1750–1824), an antiquarian and architect, and Thomas Andrew Knight (1759-1838), a pioneering horticulturalist.

The hamlet of **Kenchester** (1/3D) lies west of Credenhill and near the 22-acre site of the Roman town of Magnis. Bumps in the fields are all that remain of the Romano-British settlement, which replaced the Iron Age village at Credenhill and was, in turn, replaced by Hereford. Even

so, there must have been enough of a medieval population here to support St Michael's church, Norman in origin with a 13th-century bellcote and a Jacobean chancel roof of two bays filled with decorative and curvaceous woodwork. The font could have been formed from a hollowed-out Roman column.

Immediately south of Kenchester and across the A438 is The Weir, a garden owned by the National Trust and open from March to October. It tumbles down the steep bank of the Wye and is a mass of bulbs in spring.

The A480 road that skirts RAF Hereford leads to **Stretton Sugwas** (1/3D). Here, the church of St Mary Magdalene was pulled down and rebuilt in 1877. Watercolours inside show the church in its former state and reveal that the striking timber-framed tower – which looks respectably medieval – was also a Victorian addition, in which timbers from the old church were re-used. The superb Norman tympanum was also saved and reset inside. It is one of the best surviving works of the Herefordshire school.

Broadheath, Lower *see* Lower Broadheath

Broadwas *see* Cotheridge

Broadway (4/3B)
In character Broadway, about 6 miles south-east of EVESHAM, is wholly a Cotswold village of ancient golden ashlar houses. Its beauty is enhanced by the scarp that rises steeply to the east, so that from almost every point in the broad main street there are views of woods and hillside pasture. Visitors crowd the streets on most weekends; yet, despite the boutiques, art galleries, restaurants, and even a shopping mall, Broadway retains an essential dignity. Unlike, say, Chipping Campden (*see* Glos.), few of the buildings have any special architectural merit; it is the happy compatibility of it all that gives the place its charm, and the careful tending by its people of ancient wisterias, clematis and roses, topiary hedges and container gardens adds colour in season.

The most outstanding building in the High Street is the Lygon Arms Hotel, famous for its cuisine, with its big Renaissance doorway dated 1620. Cordon-trained and ancient fruit trees grow the full height of its three-storey façade. Just off the green, in Church Street, is the oldest house in the town, the 14th-century Abbot's Grange, built by Evesham Abbey, but almost invisible behind its tall yew hedge. The church of St Michael was built in 1839 but has a big decorative Elizabethan pulpit from the older church of St Eadburga.

This lies a mile further south, next door to the Court House, whose ancient bulbous topiary yews spill from its garden into the churchyard. It is a handsome church; much of its external aspect is Perpendicular, but it has a basically Norman nave; the central tower was added later, blocking off the narrow aisles. Flying buttresses were added to support it.

Some of Broadway's most pleasing houses are at the upper end of the village, at the point where the High Street begins to climb Broadway Hill. Nearly all were built as farmhouses or farmworkers' cottages in the 17th and 18th centuries. The most handsome of all, Barn House, was originally just that – a barn – until converted in 1908 and given its transomed and oval windows.

From here the A44 climbs steeply up hairpin bends to the Fish Inn. North of the inn is a car park and picnic site, and from here well-signposted nature trails pass through Broadway Tower Country Park.

The culmination of one of these walks is Broadway Tower (open daily from April to

Broadway Tower

October), a Norman-style folly built in 1800 by the 6th Earl of Coventry and designed by James Wyatt. It is 65 ft tall and, standing atop a 1024-ft hill, provides unparalleled views stretching, on a clear day, to WORCESTER and Warwick. There are several exhibitions in the tower; one is devoted to William Morris, who frequently used it as a holiday retreat; another covers the history of Cotswold wool; a third tells the story of the tower itself.

Brockhampton (1/5E)

This village and its neighbouring parishes lie in the land enclosed by a great meander of the River Wye, some 5 miles north of ROSS-ON-WYE. It is gentle, pastoral country, quite unlike the dramatic wooded Wye gorge which begins further south.

The church of All Saints at Brockhampton is an outstanding work of modern architecture that has inspired a rare affection in the parishioners. It was built in 1901–2, but in the Arts and Crafts tradition by William Lethaby.

It is thatched, which lends it immediate appeal, and parishioners have planted roses, evergreen shrubs and colourful climbers to enhance its beauty.

The architecture is simple but effective; from the low nave walls, a series of stone ribs rises steeply to form a pointed tunnel vault. The beautifully composed chancel contains stalls bearing 48 panels carved with wild flowers (the flower theme continues in the exquisitely embroidered altarcloth, hymn book covers and pew cushions). The reredos carries a 15th-century Italian relief depicting the Virgin and Child with another female saint, perhaps St Anne, and is flanked by two tapestries of angels by Sir Edward Burne-Jones, from cartoons originally drawn in 1875 for a stained glass window intended for Salisbury Cathedral.

Opposite the church is the lodge to the Brockhampton Court Hotel, a very good neo-Jacobean timber-framed house built in the late 19th century with quatrefoil decoration in the framing.

The road to **How Caple** (1/5E) church, 1½ miles south, descends past How Caple Court, whose terraced Edwardian gardens are open in summer. The key to the church of St Andrew and St Mary can be obtained from the Court. It is kept locked because of the rare and valuable early 16th-century South German diptych inside, restored to brilliant colour in 1984 by the Courtauld Institute.

The church of All Saints, Brockhampton

The road west to King's Caple passes **Fawley Chapel** (1/4F), splitting the Elizabethan house of Fawley Court on one side from part of its garden and a large duckpond on the other. The colourful gardens are very occasionally open to the public.

At **King's Caple** (1/4F), the big church of St John the Baptist stands opposite Caple Tump, a 12 ft-high circular motte. The church is notable for its complete set of 17th- and 18th-century furnishings, including a west gallery, box pews and an extremely tall and slim Jacobean pulpit with tester.

Brockhampton, Lower, *see* Bromyard

Bromsgrove (2/4B)

This industrial town lies to the south of the West Midlands conurbation, and about 5 miles north-west of REDDITCH. The prosperous High Street is now pedestrianized; unfortunately the ring road that carries traffic away from the centre also cuts a swathe between the town and its red sandstone church. This towers above the town on a hill – a steep flight of steps climbs to the churchyard – and its magnificent 14th-century spire forms a prominent landmark. Two cast iron tombstones in the church yard have witty epitaphs commemorating local railway engineers.

The somewhat gloomy church of St John the Baptist was restored by Sir George Gilbert Scott in 1858. South of the church, in the Kidderminster Road, is the 18th-century Perry Hall, home, for much of his life, of the poet A. E. Housman (1859–1936). The High Street has several other handsome Georgian houses dotted among the more recent shops, and the Bromsgrove Museum, in Birmingham Road, has displays on subjects that include Housman, the local button- and nail-making industries, and the Bromsgrove Guild.

This guild of local craftsmen contributed the furnishings to the church of the Holy Trinity and St Mary at **Dodford** (2/4B), 2 miles north-west of Bromsgrove. The church is a very fine Gothic Arts and Crafts building of 1907, designed by Arthur Bartlett, himself a member of the Guild. The bold tower is linked to the church in such a way as to create a small courtyard, with an unusual outdoor pulpit built into the tower wall.

Bromyard (2/1D)

This market town on the River Frome is roughly halfway between LEOMINSTER and WORCESTER, on the A44. It sits in a hollow and the townspeople enjoy views of the surrounding hills. Bromyard's best buildings are timber-framed and lie around or close to the little Market Place. By far the most ornate, however, is Tower Hill House of 1630, now rather isolated from the rest of the town beside the bypass.

St Peter's church is mainly 14th century but boasts an exuberantly decorated Norman south doorway. Some of the stained glass is excellent, including a 1924 window, and one window of

1932. These contrast with most of the rest of the glass, which is Victorian and unfortunate.

East of the town, the A44 climbs the heather and gorse-covered Bromyard Downs before entering a leafy tunnel formed by the tall trees of the **Brockhampton** estate. A long attractive turning winds down through the estate for well over a mile until it finally reaches a farmyard. Here stands the enchanting small, timber-framed manor house at **Lower Brockhampton** (2/1D), owned by the National Trust. Photographers have to choose their position carefully when taking pictures of the little two-storey timber-framed gatehouse, for it is less than 20 ft away from the utilitarian buildings of a large modern farm. Once inside the house, however, the centuries roll back, for it consists of a superb open hall, unchanged since it was built between 1380 and 1400.

The ruins of a Norman chapel lie to the west, within the farmyard. It was replaced by the New Chapel, back along the estate road, in about 1798. The style is Gothick, and so is the setting, for sombre dark green yews, cedars and holly trees cluster around its grey stone walls.

Broome *see* Belbroughton

Burghill (1/3D)
If you approach this village by the minor road running north-west from HEREFORD, a distance

Lower Brockhampton manor house and gatehouse (National Trust)

of about 3 miles, it seems at first encounter to consist entirely of barn conversions, for a large farmyard group on the southern edge has gone the way of so many similar buildings in the county. Burghill's church of St Mary has a large and beautiful 15th-century oak screen with a deep canopy supported on Jacobean posts. The church, which includes Norman, 13th- and 14th-century work, has an unusual brass, of 1619, to the traveller, Robert Masters.

Credenhill (1/3D) is 2 miles south-west of Burghill. Most of the village consists of housing for the personnel of RAF Hereford, but the church, like Burghill's dedicated to St Mary, stands apart in the grounds of Credenhill Court, now a rest home. The church is approached through a substantial 15th-century porch with a timber roof ornamented with bosses. The thick wall between nave and chancel is pierced by three arches; the middle one is early 13th century and the two lower side arches, knocked through in the 19th century, look contemporary because their cusped ogee heads are re-used 13th-century surrounds from tomb recesses.

Two stained-glass bishops of *c.* 1310 in the chancel cast a lovely warm light. One of them is Bishop Thomas of Cantelupe, whose noble shrine is in Hereford Cathedral. In the nave is another piece of the same date showing the Virgin with St Anne and a memorial to the Bulmer family, famous cidermakers.

Burrington *see* Aston

Byford *see* Bishopstone

Byton (1/2B)
The countryside of this remote corner of the county, some 9 miles north-west of LEOMINSTER and close to the borders with Shropshire and Powys, is wooded, hilly and unspoiled. Steep lanes cut through gorges of exposed rock, host to numerous ferns, or run between well-laid hedges. Most of the buildings are farmhouses attached to smallholdings. There has been almost no building in the region for at least a hundred years: the population is probably less now than it was in the Middle Ages, for the landscape is littered with earthworks and deserted medieval villages. Byton's church of St Mary is itself surrounded by the grassy platforms of long-abandoned houses, and the path to the porch passes through the outer bailey of a Norman castle.

There is some delightful countryside around the ruins of **Limebrook Priory** (1/2B), about 2 miles north and set in a remote valley. Established around 1189, it supported a small community of Augustinian canonesses until the Dissolution of the Monasteries under Henry VIII. Few visitors now seek it out, under the wary eyes of geese and hens from the nearby farm.

A lovely walk of just under a mile passes up the wooded valley from Limebrook Priory north-west of **Lingen** (1/2B). Walking is indeed the only way to appreciate fully the numerous archaeological features preserved in this hilly landscape. They include a motte and bailey in the field north of the largely 19th-century church of St Michael, and a series of six terraces caused by ancient ploughing in the fields south-west of the church.

Canon Frome *see* Fromes, The

Canon Pyon (1/3D)
The village is off the A4110 some 6 miles north-north-west of HEREFORD. In the extraordinary church of St Lawrence, everything is out of plumb. The nave walls slope outwards at an angle of 15 degrees and the pillars of the nave arcade lean in every direction: even the stout-hearted must wonder whether it is safe to enter.

The church has been this way, however, at least since the 14th or 15th centuries, when big buttresses were inserted to arrest the lean.

The chancel contains a curious set of 14th-century stalls, the bench ends carved with poppyheads and two bishops, back to back, riding on monkeys. The misericords portray a fox running away with a goose, a pelican, dog and angel. All are said to have come from the Augustinian priory at nearby Wormsley (*see* Burghill), demolished at the Dissolution of the Monasteries.

The sister village of **King's Pyon** (1/3C) is a couple of miles to the north-west. St Mary's raised churchyard looks over the big pond of Brook House and its charming timber-framed dovecot, now in need of restorative care.

The church door is disconcertingly hinged in the middle and folds back on itself. The roof is a fine example of the local style, consisting of two tiers of cusped windbraces. There is an unusual double-decker tomb in the churchyard, with a small sarcophagus of 1810 atop a table tomb of 1804.

Castle Frome *see* Fromes, The

Castlemorton *see* Birtsmorton

Chaddesley Corbett *see* Harvington (near Kidderminster)

Childswickham (4/3B)
This village lies a mile or so north-west of BROADWAY, on a minor road. The nearby Cotswolds, rising to the east, supplied the stone for the pretty houses that stand around the green, for the village cross (now surmounted by an 18th-century urn), and for the church of St Mary. This was thoroughly restored in 1870, but some elaborate 13th-century shafting survives in the chancel, clearly intended to have received a rib vault. Childswickham is surrounded by ridge and furrow, left by earlier ploughing. An especially prominent group can be seen to the north of the village, by Old Well Farm, standing 3 ft or more high, complete with headlands.

Some 3 miles further north-west is **Hinton on the Green** (4/3A). St Peter's church has a set of 15th-century gargoyles running round the nave and decorated Norman doorways. The original manor house has long since disappeared, but its interesting Jacobean gateway remains, visible from the churchyard. It consists of two gabled dovecots either side of a perfectly hemispherical double arch.

Sedgebarrow (4/3B), a mile to the south, can be reached by road, or by a footpath that follows the gentle River Isbourne. The view as you approach St Mary's church is nicely constrained by tall yew trees so that nothing is visible except the porch and a glimpse of Cotswold tiled roof. Only when you reach the end of the avenue does the pleasing tower and octagonal spire come into view. The interior, restored by Butterfield in 1866–8, is less aesthetically pleasing. His best contribution was the tall oak chancel screen, his worst the unfortunate tiling in the chancel.

The path along the Isbourne continues to the south-east of the village before branching due east to follow a tributary to **Aston Somerville** (4/3B). The attraction of its church is the woodwork, which includes a fine 15th-century oak screen, profusely carved with roses, the 14th-century tie-beam roof of the chancel and a curious low bench made up of Jacobean pieces showing dragons.

There are many tablets to members of the Somerville family who came to the village as conquering Normans and lasted until 1870 when the last Lord Somerville, premier baron of Scotland, died.

Church Honeybourne *see* Honeybournes, The

Church Lench *see* Lenches, The

Cleeve Prior *see* Littletons, The

Clehonger (1/3E)
The church of All Saints is about 3 miles south-west of **Hereford**, off the B4349, well to the east of the modern village, surrounded by sheep pasture and near a large pond. The church has Norman work, and there is a 14th-century chantry chapel built in 1341 in accordance with the will of Sir Richard Pembrugge, one of the first Knights of the Garter, whose very fine armoured effigy it contains. The smaller, unnamed, effigy near by perhaps represents Lady Pembrugge; her head lies on a cushion carried by two angels, and a large bird resembling a goose tugs at the folds of her cloak.

Clent (2/4B)
The Clent Hills form an oasis of countryside right on the doorstep of the heavily urbanized West Midlands, and some 7 miles north of BROMSGROVE. The gateway to the hills is the village of Clent, whose cottages, and the largely

Victorian church of St Leonard, are surrounded by woods planted with rhododendrons. As you climb Walton Hill to the north-west, this domestic planting suddenly gives way to wild, sheep-grazed moorland, much of it owned by the National Trust. A visitor centre on the summit provides information on trails and local wildlife. The NORTH WORCESTERSHIRE PATH links Clent to three other similar areas.

Just over the brow of the hill to the north-east is the fascinating church of St Kenelm, which now stands alone, for the parish of **Romsley** (2/4B) which it serves has shifted to a more sheltered position 2 miles to the south-east. The diminutive tower is a scaled-down version of the grander Perpendicular structures common in the county. The fierce winds blowing across the hills have eroded the gargoyles into shapes more grotesque and fantastic than the original sculptors ever intended, and it is difficult to distinguish where the work of man stops and that of nature begins.

The beautiful Tudor timber-framed porch shelters a splendid Norman tympanum, carved with beak heads, dragons, interlace and a crude Christ in Majesty.

East of the church the ground falls away steeply to a natural spring called St Kenelm's Well. This is said to have gushed forth spontaneously when the body of the 7 year-old saint, Prince Kenelm, said to have been murdered by his sister in AD 819, was exhumed for reburial at Winchcombe Abbey (*see* Winchcombe, Glos.). The story of the saint was a medieval invention, but for centuries his shrine was a popular pilgrimage resort and the spring here still flows freely.

Clifford (1/1D)
The parish is the westernmost in the county, nearly 20 miles to the west of HEREFORD. It stands on the east bank of the Wye looking into the Welsh county of Powys. The approach from the north is via a wooden tollbridge built in 1802. Its owners enjoy a brisk trade in local honey, cider and garden produce.

Until the Norman Conquest the village was Welsh and went by the name of Llanfair-yn-y-cwm (St Mary in the valley). William the Conqueror gave the land to William FitzOsbern, Earl of Hereford, who built a castle, one of a series forming a defensive chain along the disputed border. In time it passed to Walter FitzPontz, first Baron Clifford, father of Henry II's beautiful young mistress, 'Fair Rosamund'

Clifford (*see also* Frampton on Severn, Glos.).

The castle still stands on a dramatic cliff above the Wye. Although severely damaged in a raid led by Owen Glendower (Owain Glyndwr) in 1402, parts of the 13th-century gatehouse and hall have survived. (Ask at the house by the entrance for permission to visit.)

St Mary's church is well away from the river on a hillside south-east of the village. It was probably built in the 13th century by the Cluniac monks of Clifford Priory, which stood where Priory Farm now is.

Clifton upon Teme *see* Martley

Clodock (1/2F)
This hamlet of stone farmhouses is in the far south-west of the county, near the Welsh border. It lies beneath the ridge of the Black Mountains, just south of the point where three valleys merge and their streams join to swell the River Monnow. The river runs just south-east of the church, where it cuts an attractive course through the rocks and tumbles over a weir, filling the churchyard with the sound of water.

The church is dedicated to Sant Clydawg (Saint Clodock is its Anglicized form), who was buried here on the river bank following his murder, around AD 520.

Inside, the church is a treasure house of woodwork, dated on the pews to 1660, 1668 and 1701. There is a musicians' west gallery with tiers of benches; a very tall three-decker pulpit, which rises a good 10 ft above the stone-flagged floor; a set of stalls in the chancel carved with wyverns; and a pretty communion rail dating from about 1650 that, unusually, runs around three sides of a square. Few churches can have such a complete and handsome set of furnishings.

Longtown (1/2F), one mile north, is a village of simple stone cottages and the starting point for a number of walks (the Mountain Rescue Post in the centre of the village is a reminder that sensible precautions need to be taken before going on to the high hills). The OFFA'S DYKE PATH runs west of the village along the top of the plateau that forms a watershed between the Vale of Ewyas and the Olchan valley. A gentler walk follows the course of the Olchan Brook upstream; the energetic can continue northwards to the summit of the Black Hill. The late 12th- to 13th-century castle at Longtown stands on the site of an earlier Roman fort, and its tall, circular keep and outer bailey walls (maintained by English Heritage) are substantially complete.

Coddington *see* Colwall

Colwall (2/2E)
The original nucleus of Colwall lies well to the west of the MALVERNS. Its church of St James has a beautiful 14th-century collar-beam roof and probably late 13th-century encaustic tiles from the monastic tileworks at Great Malvern.

In the 19th century, the village began to grow rapidly. It now includes the districts of Colwall Green, Colwall Stone and Upper Colwall, and spreads a long way eastwards, up the slope of the Malverns. Malvern water is piped from an underground spring at Wynds Point, a mile to the south-east of Colwall Green and near the British Camp Hotel, to a bottling plant in the village. This was first established at the end of the 19th century. The Cadbury Trust owns the house at Wynds Point that was the last home of the phenomenally popular opera singer Jenny Lind (1820–87), the 'Swedish Nightingale'.

The nearby car park is a popular starting point for the short climb to the summit of the Herefordshire Beacon, also known as the British Camp. Although not the highest hill in the range it is the most dramatic, its peak ringed by deep ditches and high ramparts that follow the contours of a 2nd-century BC Iron Age camp. By tradition, Caractacus, the king of the Ancient Britons, fought a last-ditch battle here against the advancing Romans in AD 55.

The three-decker pulpit in the church at Clodock

A little to the west of Colwall is the parish of **Coddington** (2/2E), itself one of the best places from which to view the British Camp. Although the tower and broach spire are 19th century, All Saints' church has a good 13th- or 14th-century collar-beam roof and is surrounded by black-and-white houses.

Cotheridge *see* Lower Broadheath

Cow Honeybourne *see* Honeybournes, The

Cradley *see* Mathon

Craswall (1/1E)
The late Bruce Chatwin set his novel *On the Black Hill* (1982) in this remote corner of Herefordshire, not far from the border with Wales. In it, he follows the fortunes of several generations of farmers and their patient struggle to earn a small living from the land, compensated, in part, by the wild beauty of their surroundings.

The Black Mountain landscape is by no means as forbidding as the name suggests, although the weather can work sudden and dramatic changes. Fields, trees and hedges climb halfway up the side of the Black Hill above Craswall and abruptly stop, giving way to open heath, bare of anything but bracken and grass. In sunshine the scene is peaceful enough, but sunset throws a black shadow across the valley of the River Monnow, and sometimes dark clouds seem to hang permanently over the distinctive mountain plateau.

Craswall is a village of scattered whitewashed farmhouses, built, mostly, in the valley bottom. The church of St Mary looks like an ancient longhouse itself; only a little bell turret indicates its ecclesiastical function. An external stone bench runs the length of the chancel and round its east end, where, perhaps, villagers met for less godly pursuits: north of the church and hidden by undergrowth is a hollow supposed to have been used as a cockpit.

A footpath from the churchyard follows the contour, skirting a wood, to the ruins of Craswall Priory, about 2 miles to the north-west. Founded in 1222 and abandoned in 1441, it was one of only three houses of the Grandmontine Order to be established in England. Parts of the small church and the entrance to the chapter house are all that remain.

The narrow road from Craswall travels south-east for some 3 miles to the turning for **Llanveynoe** (1/2E), with its Welsh name. From the churchyard of St Peter there is often a clear view of the knife-edge southern ridge of the Black Hill, and of the mountains to the west that form the border between England and Wales. The carved stones of the Saxon period in the nave are the chief reason for visiting the church. One has a crude figure of Christ on the Cross, the other the Greek letters Alpha, Omega, Chi

Croft Castle (National Trust)

and Rho, and a Latin inscription stating that 'Hæsdur made that cross'. The lettering is Northumbrian in style and could date from any time between the westward expansion of the Anglo-Saxons in the 7th century and the Norman Conquest.

Credenhill *see* Burghill

Croft Castle (1/3B)

This 1400-acre estate, about 5 miles north-west of LEOMINSTER, belongs to the National Trust. It includes the high open grassland of Bircher Common and the Iron Age hillfort of Croft Ambrey, situated on the peak of a 1000-ft-high limestone ridge, with sweeping views in every direction. Adjacent to both is Fishpool Valley, a wooded gorge containing a series of pools. These have been designated a Site of Special Scientific Interest because of the richness of the aquatic wildlife.

The Croft family has lived in the castle from the Norman Conquest to the present day, except for the period 1746–1923. It was during that interregnum that most of the reworking was undertaken: the Gothick façade, plasterwork, chimneypieces and staircase were all added in 1750–60, after the house had passed to Richard Knight, son of the wealthy Shropshire ironmaster. The work here is a very early example of the Gothick style: Horace Walpole's Strawberry Hill, which made it fashionable, was still being built when the Blue and Gold Rooms received their delightful decorations.

The castle grounds have been planted with flowers known to have been grown in the 18th century. They spill over into the garden around the little church of St Michael. Box pews and a west gallery contemporary with the castle fill the nave.

The village of **Yarpole** (1/3B) lies a mile or so south-east. A brook runs along its main street, crossed at intervals by flat bridges that lead to the garden gates of attractive timbered cottages. South of the church of St Leonard's is its big, detached, possibly 14th-century belltower, with original door and massive internal cross-bracing.

Croome *see* Pirton

Cropthorne (2/4E)

One side of the River Avon east of PERSHORE is flat, the other is hilly. Cropthorne stands on the hilly bank, about 3 miles from Pershore on the A44. Its church of St Michael is sited on a prominent platform and aspires to grandeur, with a tall nave and clerestory, and a tower that is Norman below, Perpendicular above. The inside gives real pleasure for both Norman arcades have survived, four bays each side of rounded arches on circular pillars, and most unusual square abaci in place of capitals. Even more of a surprise is the cross head in the north aisle, not just the best Anglo-Saxon sculpture in the county but one of the finest in the country. One side is so pristine that the fineness of the carving can be fully appreciated, especially the friendly looking griffin in the lower arm. It has been dated to around AD 800.

Close to it are the two splendid Dingley monuments. Edward Dingley (d. 1646) and his wife are impressively lifelike; but it is the memorial to Francis Dingley (d. 1624) and his wife that shouts out for our attention.

Numerous good houses line the main street of the village. Many were built this century, but in the vernacular tradition with projecting upper storeys. The best is Holland House, a medley of stone and half timber, thatch and Cotswold tile.

The road from Cropthorne to **Fladbury** (2/4E), a mile to the north, crosses the Avon at Jubilee Bridge, erected in 1887 to commemorate Queen Victoria's Jubilee, but rebuilt in 1933. On this flat side of the river the tower of St John the Baptist's church is a prominent landmark, rising above the watermeadows.

Such a handsome building from the outside, it is a little disappointing to find the interior gloomy, its walls stripped of plaster to show rubble that should never have been seen, and with some regrettable Victorian glass.

The village has many attractive Regency and Victorian houses grouped around the green. The 18th-century mill, south of the centre, stands on an island in the Avon between two weirs.

Crowle *see* Huddington

Cwmmau *see* Winforton

Defford *see* Pershore

Dilwyn (1/3C)

In a village of attractive timber-framed houses just off the A4112, 6 miles south-west of LEOMINSTER, St Mary's church is of interest for its curious intermixture of Norman, Decorated and Perpendicular features. What is likely to have been its building history can be read in the west wall of the nave; half of the original tower

arch and the ridge line of an earlier nave roof survive, showing that the Norman nave must have stood where the south arcade is now. In the late 13th century the church was rebuilt much larger, with the new nave further to the north and the oddly positioned west window squeezed into the space between the tower and the north aisle. Later still, the nave was heightened and given its Perpendicular clerestory, above the remains of the Norman one. All this makes the church challenging to interpret, if not aesthetically pleasing.

Equally interesting, for similar reasons, is the small, and now redundant, church of Saints Cosmos and Damian at Stretford, 2 miles to the north-east. It consists of two parallel naves and chancels under one striking roof. This, with its four tiers of windbraces, is held up by massive king-post trusses, supported by an arcade down the middle of the church.

The side posts to the oak screens that separate each chancel from its nave are continuous with the roof structure, showing that they were conceived as part of the same scheme. Although 14th-century in style, all this woodwork was added around 1540.

Dinmore *see* Hope under Dinmore

Dodford *see* Bromsgrove

Dormington (1/4D)
This village is some 4 miles east of HEREFORD. St Peter's church is flanked on the one side by

The church and manor house, Stoke Edith

Dormington Court, now a hotel, and on the other by Dormington House. This is an interesting Regency building with a tall central bay and two wings with steeply pitched roofs that align on the tiny central pediment to produce an almost triangular elevation.

The great treasure of the church is the Norman bronze closing ring that featured in the Hayward Gallery's 'English Romanesque Art' exhibition in 1984. A fine and exact replica hangs on the door (the original is far too valuable to be displayed). It consists of the head of a cat-like creature with almond eyes and fine sabre teeth. It is thought to be late 12th century in date and similar in style to the Hereford School sculptures at KILPECK, although it was probably made at Gloucester, where the Cathedral metalworks are well documented.

Stoke Edith. This estate village, about 1½ miles east of Dormington, is built on the northern slopes of the Woolhope Dome, (*see* Woolhope), around the ruins of Stoke Edith Park, which was described as almost completed in 1698, and gutted by fire in 1927. St Mary's church was rebuilt by the Foleys, owners of the Park, in 1740 and is a plain but dignified building, lit by round-headed windows and fitted with contemporary box pews. The squire's pew differs from the others only in being lined with red baize; the parson's pew forms an integral part of the high three-decker pulpit.

Tarrington (1/5E) is the third of these villages strung along the A438 and shares, with its neighbours to the west, a slightly elevated position overlooking the River Frome. The church of St Philip and St James is Norman with much typical sculpture outside and in, although the horse and man on the capital of the porch door look questionable.

Dormston (2/4D)

This village lies north of the A422, some 8 miles east of WORCESTER. The church of St Nicholas is distinguished for its low but pretty timber-framed tower of c. 1450, supported inside by substantial scissor braces and one odd curving timber that serves, in part, as a ladder to the belfry. The nave is fitted with simple rustic benches of riven oak with holes in the top to take candle sconces.

The Moat Farmhouse, ½ mile south-west of the church, is a highly unusual building, dated 1663, with a substantial tiled dripmould bracketed to the walls above the windows: this type of weather protection was once commoner in the county, but has all but disappeared. A handsome dovecot of the same date stands in the grounds, recently restored by the Avoncroft Museum (STOKE PRIOR). It can be visited during daylight hours.

The tiny church of St James at **Kington** (2/4D), a mile to the south, and south of the A422, has a charming, leaning timber-framed bell tower, scarcely taller than the nave, crowned by a proud-tailed weathercock.

Dorstone (1/2D)

This village of pleasing pink sandstone cottages is on the River Dore at the head of the Golden Valley. The river, here still more like a brook, flows through the village and close to the church of St Faith, largely rebuilt in 1889. Arthur's Stone, high up on the hill north of the village, is an impressive megalithic tomb dating to the late Neolithic (3000 to 2000 BC). The soil mound that originally covered it has gone, leaving only the massive slabs that formed the sides and ceiling of the burial chamber.

One mile south-east of Dorstone, the surviving towers and gateway of **Snodhill Castle** (1/2D), built in the 14th century, with remains of earlier date, stand on a prominent spur above the Golden Valley, surrounded by extensive earthworks. Good views reward those with the energy to climb to the summit here.

Doverdale see Hampton Lovett

Downton on the Rock see Wigmore

Droitwich (2/4C)

The ancient and landlocked sea that once overlay much of Worcestershire eventually dried

Droitwich in festival mood

up, but left substantial salt deposits underground where the town of Droitwich now stands. These were known and exploited perhaps in prehistory, and certainly by the Romans. Stretches of road as far south as Cirencester (*see* Glos.) still bear the name 'Salt Way' or 'Whiteway', not because they came into being specifically for the distribution of Droitwich salt, but because it was the most precious and distinctive commodity to be carried along these routes.

Early on, salt was obtained by panning the waters of natural springs. Later, water was pumped underground to dissolve the salts on such a large scale as to cause subsidence, which left many of the buildings in the High Street leaning at crazy angles. New buildings have been deliberately built in the same higgledy-piggledy fashion, with lopsided windows and walls that lean one way, doors another.

This phenomenon is best appreciated from the junction of Gurney's Lane with the High Street. The remains of a 19th-century steam-driven brine pump, used until 1921, stand close to this corner. From here, too, there are good views of the backs of the shops lining the High Street, which show much medieval carpentry. Many of the fronts, by contrast, have elegant Georgian or early Victorian façades.

The relatively humble Town Hall of 1826 stands at the top of the High Street opposite St Andrew's church. This now lacks its tower, taken down in 1926 because of subsidence. The 13th-century tower arches inside are its most handsome feature.

From here on, up St Andrew's Street to Victoria Square, the prospect is considerably grander, a legacy of the town's development in the early 19th century as a fashionable health resort. This produced a valuable income for the town, and several elegant hotels were built to accommodate visitors, many in neo-Tudor style. The best of these is the Raven, a confection of black-and-white timber framing that incorporates a genuine 16th-century core. Near by is the new Brine Baths complex, opened in 1985 and built on the site of the original baths of about 1836.

A former Methodist Chapel, opposite Victoria Square, has been converted into a Heritage Centre with excellent displays on the town's history and the science of hydrotherapy.

One man who made his fortune from the visitors who flocked to the baths, both for pleasure and for health, was John Corbett (1817–1901), and the mansion he built in 1880 at Dodderhill on the town's eastern outskirts is the epitome of *nouveau riche* flamboyance, clearly visible in all its splendour from the A38. Called Château Impney, it is now a hotel and conference centre.

Equally foreign in effect is the Roman Catholic church of the Sacred Heart off the B4090 WORCESTER Road, south-east of the town centre. This church with its campanile was completed in 1921 and loosely modelled on the 6th-century Sant' Apollinare Nuove at Ravenna. The white marble cushion capitals, altar, font and pulpit are all crisply carved in Byzantine style. Mosaics cover every surface. Although simplistic in detail, the colour is extremely rich, the overall effect magnificent.

Salwarpe (2/3C) is a hidden hamlet just south-west of Droitwich, approached by a road which crosses a stone bridge over James Brindley's Droitwich Canal, opened in 1771. This linked the town to the River Severn at Hawford, north-east of Worcester, and is being restored. Tall cypresses and ancient yews surround the church of St Michael. It contains some good 17th-century monuments to members of the Talbot family. They lived at Salwarpe Court next door to the church, its magnificent late 15th- or early 16th-century timber framing and tall, shaped chimney just visible from the churchyard.

Eardisland (1/3C)

This is billed as one of the most picturesque villages in the county. Eardisland, some 6 miles west of LEOMINSTER, on the A44, benefits from having the Arrow flowing through its centre; the river is dammed here to form a millpond, with many ducks and crossed by ancient bridges. By the side of the smaller bridge is a tall, handsome red-brick dovecot attached to the 17th-century Manor House; another one stands in front of recently completed 'executive' houses built in a sad travesty of true timber framing.

Much better black-and-white houses fringe the river, their gardens colourfully planted with annuals. Some owners in this village, however, clearly do not welcome attention. The best house, Staick House, bears prominent signs saying 'Not open to the public'. Still, with discretion, you can enjoy at least the exterior of this wholly unspoiled timber-framed house, which dates in parts to the 14th century.

St Mary's church lies down a narrow back lane and has a fine timber-framed roof above its 13th-century nave. A mile south of the village is Burton Court (open in summer), refronted around 1912 in neo-Tudor style by Clough

The River Arrow and the village of Eardisland

Williams Ellis, the architect of Portmeirion in Wales. The house in fact contains a remarkable early 14th-century hall, open to the fine roof, now housing a collection of historic costume.

Eardisley (1/2D)

This village, not far from the Welsh border, about 5 miles south of KINGTON, has a core of timber-framed houses that cluster around the church of St Mary Magdalene. This handsome Norman building has a set of fine wrought-iron porch gates, made by a local blacksmith in 1848. Inside, the mid-12th-century font is one of the most spirited examples in the county of the work of the Hereford School of sculptors. It depicts the Harrowing of Hell, a large, bold, and inexplicable lion and two Norman warriors fighting.

Two miles to the north-east is **Almeley** (1/2C), a village that is typical of this part of the Welsh Marches. Its components are a church, a Norman motte, a later manor house and a cluster of timber-framed cottages. The motte stands just south of the church, so small that it may be wondered just how useful it would have been for defence. Perhaps its purpose was mainly symbolic, a reminder to local people that the Normans were now in charge.

The 15th-century Manor House can just be seen from the churchyard, a lovely structure of timber frame with brick infill. St Mary's church has only two bays of its original roof, both painted with Tudor roses, their colours now faded but giving a taste of its original splendour. Carved panels have been re-used in the 19th-century pews. They are Jacobean in date, but almost Norman or Viking in spirit, showing rampant snarling dragons with knotted tails.

Another rewarding church and castle group is found 2 miles south of Almeley at **Kinnersley** (1/2D). The castle rises east of the church, its original walls of sandstone heightened by the addition of stepped gables and clusters of chimneys in warm red Elizabethan brick. The garden wall of the castle also forms the southern boundary of the churchyard and is covered in climbing roses.

St James's church is like an old-fashioned museum, full of interesting but haphazard curiosities. The nave walls are painted with green and terracotta floral patterns, the work of the late 19th century as are the bronze and iron chandeliers. The pulpit, of about 1530, and Flemish, is made up of dancing figures, in flowing robes with plaited hair. Several good monuments add to the richness of the church.

Earl's Croome *see* Pirton

Cider making

TOM NORBURY

Cider has been a popular product of this region for a very long time. Today it boasts some of the country's biggest cider makers. Until comparatively recently cider was a drink made from suitable apples on the farm by traditional methods and consumed in vast quantities by farm workers, particularly during the harvest. There are still a few places where the old-fashioned methods and equipment are used, but most cider now is made by the millions of gallons in large modern factories.

The ancient practice of giving farm workers cider as part of their wages did not really begin to die out until the general improvement of their lot following the 1925 Agricultural Wages Act.

The cider made on the farm was very dry and still. It was wonderfully thirst-quenching, and relatively safe in the days when drinking water was often full of germs and bacteria. Some farms had their own cider mills and presses. The gathered fruit was put into stone troughs and a horse walked round and round, harnessed to a large milling stone that crushed the apples. One farm where these old horse-powered mills are occasionally used is Tarrington Court in Herefordshire. At the Cider Mill Gallery in Blanchworth near Stinchcombe (*see also under Dursley, Glos.*) a horse-driven mill is used in October and November (when the mill is open from Tuesday to Saturday).

Some farms were served by a travelling cider maker who moved his equipment from place to place. In later years a mechanical 'scratter', belt-driven from a tractor or engine, speeded up the milling process.

Once crushed the pulp was placed between layers of cloth and gradually the juice was extracted by slowly turning the screw of the press. Occasionally layers of straw were used instead of cloths, but this was a much trickier operation.

The freshly pressed juice went into wooden barrels and was left to ferment. It was a rather hit-and-miss affair, since certain strains of wild yeast could turn the cider into something resembling vinegar. You can still find places that sell this old-fashioned sort of cider – 'scrumpy' in the original sense of the word.

Careful control of the fermentation process is what distinguishes modern cider makers and their product from their farmhouse predecessors. Most of the cider that you can buy today will have been filtered to give it a bright appearance, although some of the draught varieties are cloudy. Cider produced by the large makers will have a consistent flavour, colour and strength, whereas farmhouse cider varies from barrel to barrel. Through all the modernization, the cider apple itself has remained much the same, although there are fewer varieties. Some of these have romantic names like Brown Snout, Foxwhelp and Tremlett's Bitter. Cider makers try to blend the different types of apple with their varying sugar, acidity and astringency.

Most orchards today are planted in the modern intensive manner – gone are the large standard trees with livestock grazing beneath them. The apples used to be picked up by hand, often being shaken off the trees with long poles, and then piled in big tumps to 'ripen' before being pressed. On the most modern farms today tractors, armed with huge claws, grab the tree trunks and vibrate them massively. The fruit is then blown into the orchard rows in lines and picked up by a mechanical harvester. In the Three Counties there are over 6000 acres of cider apple orchards to supply the large cider makers.

The largest cider maker is H. P. Bulmer Ltd of Hereford, founded in 1887. The firm owns 1800 acres of orchard and produces half of the 66 million gallons which are sold annually in Great Britain.

The founder of the firm, H. P. 'Percy' Bulmer, received no formal education because of ill-health. When he reached manhood, with little prospect of employment, he decided to start up a business of his own. With his brother, E. F. Bulmer, he borrowed a neighbour's cider-mill and made a few casks, which they managed to sell. The real breakthrough came through Percy's innovations. Many of his technological ideas were obtained by visiting French cider makers and by studying methods used in sugar-beet factories in Prussia. Successive generations of the Bulmer family have built up the business to the position it holds today.

The second largest cider maker in Hereford and Worcester is Symonds's Cider at Stoke Lacy, established by William Symonds in 1727. In June 1984 this small family business was taken over by

From apple blossom, near Shelsey Beauchamp, to cider vats, at Weston's Cider Mill in Much Marcle. Note the affectionate naming of the vats.

the brewers Greenall Whitley and a massive investment in new plant and machinery was undertaken, increasing production tenfold. Annual output from this, one of the most modern and efficient cider factories in Europe, is nearly 2 million gallons. They became part of Bulmers in August 1988.

Another old-established firm in the county is H. Weston & Sons Ltd at Much Marcle. It has been run by members of the family since 1878.

Henry Weston, its founder, was a farmer worried by the large quantities of cheap agricultural produce that was coming into the country from the Empire, and saw cider as another possible source of income. Today Weston produces 1 million gallons a year.

There are three other smaller cidermakers in Hereford and Worcester. Dunkerton's of Luntley, near Pembridge, is a firm that tries as far as possible to re-create the traditional taste of farmhouse cider by fermenting each variety of apple separately and then blending them to taste. At Storridge, near Malvern, Keith Knight makes Crumpton Oaks Cider. Not far away, on the A4103 half a mile from Leigh Sinton, just over what used to be the border with Worcestershire, is Norbury's Black Bull Cider, of which the author is managing director. The company started making cider in 1980, partly as a means of diversification. It grows all its own cider fruit and sells about a fifth of production from the farm gate. Being a small cider maker is a challenge, since the only course is to make the best possible product. This is invariably more expensive to make than a mass-produced cider, and so being competitive is difficult.

In Gloucestershire there are two small cider makers. Two are near the Wildfowl Trust at Slimbridge. Tony Cullimore's Genuine Farmhouse Cider at Berkeley Heath Farm, and Summers's Cider at Halmore (both near Berkeley).

Perry

Perry is a specialized product of this region. It is a drink similar to cider but made from the juice of perry pears. These trees in some cases have survived many hundreds of years and have grown to a great size.

Perry has a reputation for its potency. This is partly because the fruit contains more sugar than a cider apple and therefore produces more alcohol. Today Perry is made by Bulmer, Symonds, Weston, Dunkerton and Norbury. Perry pear orchards are declining in number, and there is a danger that this drink will completely disappear as all the old trees are grubbed out and no new ones planted to take their place. To add to the difficulties fireblight, which devastates young perry pear trees, has now reached this area (it does not seem to affect older trees so badly). Perry is said to have been Sir Edward Elgar's favourite drink.

Places to visit

In a former cider works in Pomona Place, off Whitecross Road, Hereford, is the Cider Museum and King Offa Cider Brandy Distillery. This is open 7 days a week between April and October,

and on afternoons only for the rest of the year. Parties can visit at any time by appointment. The museum, now run by an independent charitable trust, contains many interesting old presses and mills and there is also a resident cooper, or barrel maker, to watch. (The Bulmer Railway Centre is well worth visiting, *see* Hereford, H. & W.)

The entrance to H. P. Bulmer Ltd is off Grimmer Row in Hereford. Tours of this cider works can be made from March to Christmas, Mondays to Fridays, by appointment only. The conducted tour here is a memorable experience.

Symonds's Cider is at Stoke Lacy, about 3½ miles from Bromyard on the A465 road. Visitors are welcome Monday to Friday all the year round, but by appointment only.

Weston's Cider at Much Marcle, near Ledbury, also welcomes callers to buy its cider. Tours of the works are conducted on Tuesday and Thursday afternoons, mainly from Easter to Christmas, although the facilities are there all year round. Large parties need to be booked in advance.

Do not forget that at any of these factories you will only see the cider presses working from mid-September to Christmas.

The other cider makers of the Three Counties are always glad to sell you some of their produce at their works – but they do not generally have the facilities for guided tours.

You might like to try your hand at making some of your own cider. You could consult Jo Deal *Making Cider* (Amateur Winemaker publications, 1976) or Ben Turner *Farmhouse Wines and Cider* (Weidenfeld & Nicolson, 1986) to make your own special brew. During October and November you could go along to a smaller cider maker who would probably be willing to sell you a few gallons of juice from his presses. Remember this is likely to be the juice of the special bittersweet or bittersharp varieties so it will make a much fuller cider than if you just use the ordinary eating or cooking apples.

Drinking Cider

Cider houses are pubs that sell only this drink. Of course you can buy cider at many other places, although it will not be what purists might consider 'traditional'. Sales in the past 20 years have increased by 250 per cent, and cider is very popular, especially among young people, who perceive it as a healthy and enjoyable drink.

Cider is seen as a drink for both men and women. It has gradually spread throughout the whole United Kingdom from the areas where it is made, and it is not confined to any particular social class or income group. If anything, cider is more fashionable today than it has ever been.

Eastham (2/1C)

The hamlet is in hop country, some 5 miles east of TENBURY WELLS and on the border with Shropshire, where so many farms have hop kilns. In September, when the crop is harvested, the lanes are filled with tractors and trailers piled high with fragrant lime-green hopflowers. The church is reached by crossing the only bridge across the River Teme for several miles, built of brick in 1793.

St Peter and St Paul is a simple Norman church built of the local tufa, except for the red brick tower of 1825. Above and around the projecting south door is a collection of sculpture. Two pieces are Norman and eroded, reset in the course of 19th-century restoration, like the Agnus Dei inside.

About 2 miles to the north-west **Knighton on Teme**, like many of the 'on Teme' villages, is actually quite a way from the river, high up on a hillside, reached via a gated road and surrounded by open sheep pasture. The 12th-century church of St Michael has a projecting Norman south doorcase, decorated with blank arches and flat pilasters. This is a local stylistic feature, found only on a handful of nearby churches (*see also* Rock), all perhaps the work of the same team of masons. The west wall of the nave is timber-framed and the lovely roof has shield bosses and painted panelling.

Eastnor (3/4B)

This estate village 2 miles east of LEDBURY is almost wholly mid-19th century in date, likely to be a leading contender for any best-kept village award, and was built as an adjunct to the 1812 Eastnor Castle.

The church of St John, largely Sir George Gilbert Scott's work of 1852, but with a 14th-century tower and some Norman features, is chiefly of interest for its numerous monuments and the reredos made up of Sienese sculptural fragments.

Eastnor Castle (open in summer) has been described as neo-Norman, but it is Italianate in parts. The big corner turrets, with their corbelled-out parapets, look distinctly Florentine and the Great Hall has Venetian windows. It was built in 1812 to the designs of Sir Robert Smirke (who built Covent Garden and the British Museum), and has a sumptuous Gothic drawing room by Augustus Pugin and a library by G. E. Fox, decorated with mid-17th-century woodwork from the Accademia at Siena. The castle is filled with tapestries, portraits and

Eastnor Castle from the park

armour, and stands in spacious parkland where there are red deer and fine views of the MALVERNS.

Eckington *see* Bredon

Edvin Loach *see* following entry

Edwyn Ralph (2/1D)

The village, 2½ miles north of BROMYARD, seems not to have settled yet on an agreed spelling for its name: Edwin, Edwyn, Edvin and Edvyn appear interchangeably on signposts, all variants of the same Old English name. It is partnered by Edvin Loach, about a mile to the east; originally these were one parish, but were divided between two families – the Ralfs and the de Loges – at the Norman Conquest.

Inside St Michael's church, under the tower, there are some fine monuments to 13th- and 14th-century knights and ladies: the only identifiable figure is Maude de Edefen (yet another version of the name), who died in 1325.

There is no village at **Edvin Loach** (2/1D), just one and a half churches. First there is the roofless nave of the Saxo-Norman church, now maintained by English Heritage, with substantial sections of herringbone masonry and a monolithic tufa door lintel. Then we have the handsome sandstone building of about 1860 by Sir George Gilbert Scott, with broach spire, nave and polygonal apse. The inside is as plain as could be, except for the dramatic ribbing of the close-set roof rafters and scissor braces.

Thornbury (2/1D) is about 2 miles north-west of Edwyn Ralph. Its church of St Anne has a big, castle-like 13th-century square tower, with a pyramidal roof and proud weathercock. The south aisle has gone, but a line of box bushes has been planted along its foundations, parallel to the now blocked 13th-century arcade. There are clear views from the churchyard of the Iron Age enclosure on Wall Hills.

The roads from here to **Bockleton** to the north-west, pass through some of the loveliest countryside in the county: gently hilly, with wide vistas of woods and fields, and scarcely a building in sight as far as the eye can see. It is one of the least spoiled, least populated areas of the county.

The church of St Michael has two Norman projecting doorways, the best examples in the region of this distinctive local feature. Both are decorated with elaborate blank arcading and chains of chevron, lozenge and billet mouldings. The north chapel contains two outstanding monuments, both of which repay detailed study.

Kyre Park, now a Spastics Society residential home, is just under 3 miles north-east of Bockleton. The house is surrounded by handsome Jacobean brick buildings, including a barn with stepped gables and a medieval circular dovecot. Opposite is a huge walled kitchen garden of several acres, only part of which is now used. From the porch of St Mary's church, the part medieval, part 18th-century house can be seen in its lakeside setting; the landscaping is traditionally ascribed to Capability Brown. The big church serves as a chapel to the house.

Elmbridge (2/4C)

The village lies 3 miles due north of DROITWICH in a stretch of unspoiled countryside, much like the Shire landscape that J. R. R. Tolkien made the setting for *The Hobbit* (1937) and whose rapid engulfment by the West Midlands suburbs he so bitterly resented. St Mary's church has a late Norman doorway, carved with chevron and lozenge mouldings, but little else predating the 1872 restoration, except for a good Jacobean communion rail and table. This was removed to

nearby Purshull Hall for protection in the Civil War and was only returned to the church three centuries later, in 1952.

Some 2 miles to the north-west the church of St Michael at **Rushock** (2/3B), built in 1758 and restored in 1872, stands on a hill with good views of the gentle landscape. Comparatively humble itself, it is surrounded by grander neighbours. Rushock Court Farmhouse is a handsome 17th-century building with a fine barn, and the Old Rectory is early 19th century, painted white so as to stand out against the hillside and visible for many miles.

Elmley Lovett (2/3C) lies about a mile south-west of Rushock. The countryside here has a suburban tinge, but the church, 19th century but for the tower and spire, stands alone on a hillside. The site of a deserted medieval village spreads across the fields below, towards what was a large Second World War Mobilization Unit, and is now an industrial estate.

Elmley Castle *see* Bredon

Elmley Lovett *see* Elmbridge

Elton *see* Aston

Evesham (2/5E)

This market town is famous for the fruits of its surrounding orchards, and for the battle of 1265 in which Simon de Montfort, sometimes referred to as the 'father' of the English Parliament and leader of the rebel barons, died fighting Prince Edward, son of Henry III. Of the huge and powerful Evesham Abbey founded in AD 714 and rebuilt after the Norman Conquest, relatively little remains. Instead, the precinct is now a pleasing park leading down to the river meadows.

One entrance to the park passes beneath the imposing belltower built by Abbot Lichfield and completed in 1539, the very year in which the Abbey was dissolved. Unusually it has survived, while many other medieval campaniles have not. This one towers to 110 ft, its west face and buttresses adorned with beautiful blank arcading: a masterpiece of Perpendicular architecture.

East of it are not one but two parish churches, both within the Abbey walls. A possible explanation for this curious phenomenon is that sick pilgrims used one of them so as not to infect the healthy. St Lawrence is the more southerly of the two, deliciously enriched with Perpendicular blank arcading, trefoils and pierced battlements.

Evesham's belltower and two parish churches

The south chapel, built by Abbot Clement Lichfield and dedicated to his namesake, St Clement, has a rich fan vault whose ribs come together to form a central pendant. The church of All Saints to the north shows what a busy builder the Abbot was, for the Lichfield Chapel is also his work, added in 1513, to serve as his mortuary chapel, a burial place fit for an Abbot. Thirty-three years later, in 1546, he was finally laid to rest here.

The Norman gateway north of All Saints leads from the quiet of the Abbey precinct into Evesham's busy market place. Its only really outstanding building is the late 15th-century Booth Hall, once an inn, now a bank. Its special charm derives from the fact that each successive storey is jettied out to overhang the one below. Thus the floor area in the top storey is considerably greater than at ground level.

Another exceptional building, surrounded by nondescript Regency houses and modern shops, is Dresden House, 51 High Street, now occupied by one of the grandest Chinese restaurants in the country. The structure is of 1692 (dated on the rainwater head) with a richly ornamented cornice, keystones and a delicate porch of wrought iron.

Vine Street consists largely of ancient coaching inns with bay windows and courtyards. It is the least spoiled in the town, although it suffers from heavy traffic despite the recently opened ring road. It leads to the western wall of the Abbey precinct and to the little Almonry Museum containing exhibits on the Abbey and other aspects of local history.

Ewyas Harold (1/2F)

This village some 12 miles south-west of HEREFORD combines Welsh and English in its name. Ewias was the name of the Welsh kingdom that stretched westwards from here; Harold was the English king defeated by William the Conqueror at Hastings. At some time before 1051 a Norman, Osbern Pentecost, built a castle here which historians believe was the first motte and bailey type seen in this country. In 1052 Harold ordered the arrest of Pentecost, as part of a purge of immigrant Normans. Ever since then Harold's name has stuck to the village.

Pentecost's castle was destroyed but later rebuilt by his relation, William FitzOsbern, William the Conqueror's right-hand man, who established a chain of castles along the disputed border with Wales. It stood until the early 15th century, when the defeat of Owen Glendower (Owain Glyndwr) at Grosmont brought relative peace to the area. The earthworks, overgrown now, remain to the north-east of the village, marked 'Private' and surrounded by a new housing estate.

The church of St Michael near by has an imposing 13th-century tower; originally detached from the body of the church it no doubt served as a refuge in times of war. As well as the Jacobean stalls and a pulpit in the chancel, there is a reredos made up of 16th-century Flemish panels of gilded wood.

The road north-west from the church leads into the gentle valley of the Dulas Brook, where there are few buildings and great natural beauty. The remains of a Norman church stand in the grounds of Dulas Court (private).

Just over a mile south-west of Ewyas Harold is the delightful hamlet of **Rowlstone** (1/2F), tucked away in the hills with its little Norman church of St Peter. The tympanum is virtually a contemporary copy of the one at Shobdon which is now extremely eroded. Here, the carving is pristine, except that 17th-century iconoclasts chiselled off Christ's face. He sits in majesty in a vesica borne by angels. Cockerels and foliage spew from the capitals, and the lovely imposts of the chancel arch are carved with more animated birds, angels and saints. It is all very typical work of the Hereford School, for the angels' wings and cloaks are deeply moulded.

Eye *see* Leominster

Eyton *see* Leominster

Far Forest *see* Wyre Forest

Fawley Court *see* Brockhampton

Feckenham (2/5C)

The village lies about 4 miles south-west of Redditch, on either side of the B4090. This was originally a Roman road and one of the Salt Ways used to transport Droitwich salt. It is a large, prosperous village with some fine Regency brick houses with fanlights and pedimented doorcases. The best are around or near the village green, where they completely hide the church of St John the Baptist from view. This has a Norman nave, painted with chevron ornament based on fragments of original colour, and work from later periods, and William Butterfield rebuilt the chancel in 1853.

The village was once surrounded by ancient forest, cut down in the Middle Ages to fuel the Droitwich saltpans. An area of undrained peat marshland, created by the build-up of forest debris over many centuries, has survived south of the village. It is now a major bird reserve, laid out with nature trails and hides, managed by the Worcestershire Conservation Trust.

Fladbury *see* Cropthorne

Fownhope *see* Woolhope

Foy *see* Hoarwithy

Fromes, The

The largest of these villages in the broad Frome valley, south of Bromyard, is **Bishop's Frome** (2/1E). The church of St Mary is more a curiosity than a pleasure, rebuilt in 1847 (chancel) and 1861 (nave and aisle). Two genuine Norman chevron-moulded arches survive – to the south door and the chancel – but the rest is heavy-handed neo-Norman. Relief comes from the many interesting monuments.

The church of St Michael at **Castle Frome** (2/1E), about 2 miles south, contains one of the masterpieces of the Hereford School of Norman sculpture. Its font was one of several outstanding works from the county that in 1984 formed part of the Hayward Gallery's 'English Romanesque Art' exhibition. This bold and accomplished work depicts the baptism of Christ. John the Baptist is portrayed as a priest wearing a stole and passing his hand over the head of Christ, who stands waist deep in water. Fishes nibble at the Saviour's feet and the hand of God the Father and the Dove of the Holy Spirit descend from a band of interlace above His head.

The font at Castle Frome church, a masterpiece of the Hereford School of Norman sculpture

Unusually, the bowl is supported on three crouching figures with male features and lions' bodies – indicating, according to Nikolaus Pevsner, the influence of Italy.

Castle Frome receives a steady stream of visitors, including many Mormons from America. In 1840, John Benbow of nearby Hill Farm joined the Church of Jesus Christ of Latter-Day Saints, eventually emigrating to Salt Lake City with 600 other converts, where he became a prominent member of the Mormon commmunity. It was his practice to baptize new converts in the farm pond. This is still occasionally used for the baptism of the children of American visitors.

At **Canon Frome** (2/1E), 2 miles south-west of Castle Frome, the church of St James stands beside the late 18th-century Canon Frome Court, now converted to apartments. The church tower of 1680 is of homely red brick with a black diaper pattern. G. F. Bodley did the rest in 1860; it is unremarkable except for the Victorian stained glass Christ in Majesty of the rose window.

Stretton Grandison (2/1E) lies west of Canon Frome on the busy A4172, which follows the course of a Roman road. The church of St Lawrence is, however, tucked away and approached through a farmyard where disused agricultural equipment lies mouldering in the grass alongside ancient barns and oasthouses. By contrast, the thatched cottage next to the lych-gate is immaculate.

The church is largely of the Decorated period. Just inside, by the door, is an enigmatic 14th-century wall painting of a lady in red, a saint no doubt but without any identifying symbols.

Ashperton (2/1E). This village lies some 2 miles south-east on the A4172. The church of St Bartholomew is on the western fringe of the village and must have been within the outer bailey of the 13th-century castle built by the Grandison family. The church is largely of the early 14th century.

Garway (3/1C)

Beautifully situated in the far west of the county in the valley of the River Monnow, the church of St Michael has a massive 13th-century tower pierced by narrow lights that looks like a castle and did, indeed, serve as a refuge at least once when the Abbot of Monmouth fled here at the Dissolution of the Monasteries. Local historians say that it was later used as a prison.

The nave was originally circular, having been built by the Knights Templar (who modelled it

Medieval dovecot at Garway

on the Holy Sepulchre in Jerusalem, as was their wont). Part of the original foundations are exposed north of the church. This helps to explain why the tower is at such an odd angle to the present nave, which was rebuilt in the 15th century: a drawing of the original plan inside the church shows that what is now an uncomfortable juxtaposition was once an elegant composition.

The noble Norman chancel arch survived the rebuilding: the outer mouldings are chevroned; the innermost are highly unusual, lobed like Moorish arches or window heads. This appearance is accidental, however: the arch is made up of rib sections, originally intended for a vaulted roof.

The south chapel is a 13th-century addition, separated from the chancel by a beautiful arcade whose piers are composed of a circular inner column surrounded by slender shafts and rings. Massive benches of hewn oak are partnered by much finer Jacobean stalls, panels and communion rail.

When the Knights Templar order was dissolved in 1308 Garway passed to the Knights Hospitallers, but the farm next door continued to serve as a Commandery, providing an income

Goodrich Castle, high above the River Wye

to support the work of the Knights. Here there is a circular dovecot (open during daylight hours) with tiers of nesting holes for 666 birds. It is believed to be even older than the 1326 referred to in a Latin inscription.

At **Welsh Newton** (3/1D), about 4 miles to the south-east, on the A466, the church of St Mary the Virgin was built as an outpost of Garway, and the stone bench in the chancel is traditionally said to be the chair used by the Commander of the Knights Hospitallers of St John. A 13th-century rood screen, decorated with ballflower, separates the nave and chancel. It is doubly rare for being of stone and one of the earliest rood screens to have survived anywhere in the country.

The churchyard, a mass of flowers in spring, contains the grave of the Roman Catholic priest John Kemble, one of the Forty English Martyrs canonized in 1970. He was executed in 1679, aged 80, for alleged complicity in the 'Popish Plot', fabricated by Titus Oates in 1678.

A mile to the north-west is the 13th-century moated **Pembridge Castle**, from which Kemble was taken to be hanged at HEREFORD. It is in a good state of preservation, having been restored in modern times, and still lived in. The grounds are open on Thursdays in summer.

Llanrothal (3/1D) is a mile to the west by footpath; four times as far by a switchback no-through road that passes through the gentle Monnow valley. The little church of St John the Baptist stands in fields and was in a dangerous condition until recent restoration work began. The east end is used for services every mid-summer; it contains a primitive gritstone font and stopper, Jacobean furnishings, chained lectern and monolithic stone altar. The path from the church leads to a medieval weir through fields which, when not under crop, show traces of a deserted medieval village. More weirs are visible at Tregate Bridge, a mile to the south. There are some castle remains in the garden at Tregate Farm, which also has a small informal local history museum.

Goodrich (3/2D)

Close to the A40 and 5 miles south-south-west of ROSS-ON-WYE, the majestic castle at Goodrich (open all year) seems almost to grow out of the sandstone bluff upon which it was built. The Wye views are superb and it seems as if the builders intended the castle to be handsome as well as functional: this would explain those tremendous spurs that rise from the rock-cut moat to join the massive angle towers, when sheer walls would have done just as well.

The castle is the fourth to stand upon the site. The first, built by Godric or Goodric Mappestone, has gone. The second, of the mid-12th century, survives as a small keep within the later court-yard. Parts of the curtain wall of the third castle, built in the early 13th century, are incorporated in the fabric of the present structure. This was built in the late 13th century, and expressed strength and impregnability, but provided all the comforts of a nobleman's home: kitchens, great hall, private apartments and a toilet block of three cubicles projecting over the moat.

The only real test of its strength came in the English Civil War in 1646, when the castle and its Royalist occupants withstood a siege (accounts vary as to its length) and pounding by the 200 lb cannonballs of 'Roaring Meg'. Eventually they surrendered. Cromwell ordered the castle to be slighted and it has stood a ruin ever since, although now well maintained by English Herit-age. The picnic site by the castle entrance is also the starting point for waymarked walks along the Wye or up nearby Coppet Hill.

St Giles's church with its handsome broach spire is surrounded by fields and has some fine 15th-century stained glass angels.

The Wye Valley Open Farm has old stone buildings, a cider press and a variety of farm animals. In the summer months these all provide a delightful place to visit.

The B4229 eastwards from Goodrich passes the remains of the 14th-century Augustinian Flanesford Priory, now maladroitly converted to holiday accommodation. It stands by Kerne Bridge, built in 1828 and best appreciated by looking back from the steep road up Coppet Hill that leads south-east to **Welsh Bicknor**.

Here the 1858 church of St Margaret stands on the river bank, reached only by a path that plummets down the hillside from beside the Youth Hostel. The position makes a visit worth while – but the church, with its richly carved Caen stone nave capitals, font, pulpit and chancel arch, is usually padlocked.

Glen Wye, the dower house to the nearby Courtfield House estate, has Italianate gardens (open under the National Gardens Scheme).

Great Comberton *see* Bredon

Great Malvern *see* Malverns, The

Great Witley *see* Witleys, The

Hagley (2/4A)

The village and surrounding countryside are much prettier than their position at the southern tip of the West Midlands – and just 10 miles from the centre of Birmingham – might suggest. Amid the modern development there are fine Regency buildings, including the Lyttelton Arms and Beacon Hill House, close to Hagley Hall. The Hall (open in summer) was completed

The Main Hall at Hagley Hall

in 1760, and has been hailed as the last of the great Palladian houses of England, completed when Gothick was much more the fashion.

Hagley Hall's great glory is its plasterwork, skilfully restored after a fire in 1925. Flurries of garlands and trophies spill from the ceilings and down the walls in the Dining Room, Gallery and Tapestry Room. Equally interesting are the garden buildings, one a scaled-down copy of the Athenian Temple of Theseus – anticipating by several years the neo-Grecian revival – and another a deliberately ruinous castle-like folly.

Hampton Bishop *see* Mordiford

Hampton Lovett (2/3C)

St Mary's church is at the end of a cul-de-sac of new houses on the northern edge of DROITWICH. The attractive 14th-century tower is unusually placed at the south of the very short nave and has a projecting stair turret.

Inside, the big north chapel, built around 1414 as the Pakington mausoleum, is almost as large as the nave. The best memorial is that of Sir John Pakington (d. 1727), handsomely portrayed, semi-recumbent.

He is cited as the model for Addison's 'Sir Roger de Coverley', the bluff provincial Tory squire of many *Spectator* satires, and his epitaph, which he penned himself, says that he 'spoke his mind in Parliament without reserve, neither fearing nor flattering those in power'.

Another monument commemorates Dean Henry Hammond (d. 1660), chaplain to Charles I. After the King's execution, Hammond spent his remaining years at the home of Sir John Pakington writing the commentaries that have earned him the name 'Father of Biblical Criticism'.

Two miles west of Hampton Lovett is the church of St Mary at **Doverdale** (2/3C). F. Preedy's pretty Alpine spire of timber and lead is the best feature of the church which was virtually rebuilt in 1860. There is no village any more, but the churchyard, surrounded by a ha-ha, overlooks a sunken lane and the grass-covered bumps of the former settlement.

Hanbury (2/4C)

The quadrant south of BROMSGROVE and east of DROITWICH contains an area of unspoiled and little-visited countryside, all of which lies spread out below Hanbury's hilltop church of St Mary. This fine multi-period church, with 18th-century box pews, gallery and lovely brass chandelier, is

The Main Staircase at Hanbury Hall (National Trust)

the burial place of many of the Vernons of Hanbury Hall. Their memorials are gathered together in G. E. Street's 1860 Early English style Vernon Chapel.

The delightful Hanbury Hall (National Trust, open in the summer season) was finished in 1701 by the barrister Thomas Vernon. It is in a style reminiscent of Wren and of so many of the city of London buildings that Vernon worked among. Beautifully composed of warm red brick, it is fronted by a pediment on Corinthian columns and crowned by a pretty clock turret.

The front door opens straight into the grand staircase hall, its walls painted by Sir James Thornhill in 1710.

The rest of the house is used as a showcase for the large Watney porcelain collection, but it includes one or two other treasures such as a hybrid musical instrument that is both organ and harpsichord, and two fine chimneypieces.

The informally landscaped gardens contain a well-preserved icehouse and a delicate Queen Anne orangery.

From just south of Hanbury the B4090 (once a Roman road and a Salt Way) heads westwards towards Droitwich, crossing the leisure marina on the Worcester and Birmingham Canal at Hanbury Wharf.

Hanley Castle *see* Upton upon Severn

Hartlebury (2/3B)

Where the eastern suburbs of STOURPORT-ON-SEVERN stop, the nature reserve of Hartlebury Common begins. It is one of the few surviving areas of sandy heathland in this part of the country, home to many interesting reptiles, insects and birds.

At the eastern edge of the Common is Hartlebury Castle, a gracious moated house of pink sandstone, the residence of the Bishops of Worcester. Much of the present structure results from rebuilding from the late 17th to the late 18th centuries. The Bishop still lives there, but the State Rooms are open on certain days in summer. They include the Great Hall, lined with portraits of previous incumbents, and the Hurd Library with its splendid 18th-century bookcases.

The peaceful gardens are worth a visit in their own right. In spring, wild daffodils fill the meadows surrounding the moat, and all summer long the garden within the walls is fragrant with roses and scented plants of Elizabethan origin.

The Hereford and Worcester County Museum is housed in the north wing of Hartlebury Castle (open March to November). Displays on the history, industry and agriculture of the county are supplemented by some excellent thematic galleries.

There is also a comprehensive account of the BROMSGROVE Guild, formed in 1894 and active up to 1966. Their work shows a distinct preference for ornament and Gothicism – unlike the spare, restrained work of the Gloucestershire Arts and Crafts movement, which has generally proved the more lastingly influential (*see* Sapperton and Chipping Campden, Glos.).

Hartlebury village clusters around the slight promontory on which the church of St James stands, a very handsome 1836 building by Thomas Rickman. It has tall, slender nave columns supporting a graceful vaulted ceiling and Georgian-style side galleries, and there is work from earlier periods.

Just to the north of here is the Stourport suburb of **Wilden** (2/3B) on the banks of the River Stour. The dull brick 1880 church of All Saints comes alive, once entered, with the jewel-like colours of stained glass by Morris and Burne-Jones. The glass is based on cartoons drawn several decades earlier and installed several years after the artists' deaths. The client was the ironmaster Alfred Baldwin, father of the Prime Minister and Burne-Jones's brother-in-law.

Harvington (near Evesham) (2/5E)

This village 3 miles north of EVESHAM is large, suburban and still growing, to judge by the number of 'executive' houses springing up around the church and making an awkward contrast to the old cruck-built cottages near by, St James's church has a sturdy Norman tower. Inside, is a poignant series of photographs of all the young men of the village who perished in the First World War.

A mile south-west, the once-pretty village of **Norton** (2/5E) is now blighted by the A435 Evesham to REDDITCH road; a row of cedars offers a scant barrier between St Egwin's church and the road. The church is mostly of 1844, but still of considerable interest. The remarkable lectern must be one of the few archaeological finds still being used for its original purpose; it was dug up in Evesham in 1813 and brought here because the clerical figure rising from the middle of a thicket of foliage is said to be St Egwin, patron of this church and the 8th-century founder of Evesham Abbey.

Eric Gill carved at least two of the monuments in the churchyard. One, to Hannah Maria Boulter (d. 1909), consists of a naïve Crucifixion. That to Walter Consett Boulter, vicar of Norton 1891–1902 (d. 1912), is carved with a beautifully expressive, elongated figure of Christ crucified. A third monument, to Mary Beatrice Boulter (d. 1902), has similar lettering to the other two on a Celtic cross and might well be Gill's work.

Harvington (near Kidderminster) (2/3B)

This attractive village about 3 miles east of KIDDERMINSTER consists of Regency red brick and older timber-framed houses. Unfortunately the village is split by the busy A450. Harvington Hall (open in summer) makes a pretty picture away from the village, rising above its moat and large duck ponds. Here, throughout the 17th century, recusant Roman Catholic priests found a safe haven; if danger threatened, they could hide in one of the numerous priest's holes scattered around the labyrinthine house. There are hidden rooms below removable floors, hiding places behind bookshelves, secret spaces in the attic, and an inner room used as a chapel with cavities for secreting vestments and chalices.

At the core of the Hall is a medieval timber-framed hall, but most of the rambling house is Elizabethan, extended in the 1560s by the Pakington family.

Just to the west of Harvington is the village of **Stone** (2/3B), where all the houses are of brick. Beyond the church of St Mary is a wonderful walled garden (open in summer) in the grounds of Stone House. It is planted in cottage garden style, and many rare and tender plants flourish in the warm and sheltered microclimate provided by the brick walls.

South-east of Harvington, on the A448, is the large and attractive village of **Chaddesley Corbett** (2/3B). The church of St Cassian stands at the southern end. Its large tower gives it a predominantly 18th-century aspect: only the south door prepares visitors for the splendidly tall Norman arcade within. This is of two periods, for the rounded arches of the mid-12th century give way to late 12th-century pointed arches at the western end.

The chancel is Decorated and one of the best examples in the county, with a complete set of piscina, aumbry, sedilia and image niches, all with crocketed ogee arches. The brilliantly inventive tracery is better appreciated from the outside, since garish Victorian glass prevents a proper appreciation from within. Much better is the glass of the south aisle, filled with pinks, irises, crocuses and chrysanthemums (all in perversely simultaneous bloom).

The Norman font is one of the works of the Hereford School, exuberantly carved with interlace and dragons.

The active local history society has produced guides, available at the church, to the many interesting houses that line the long village street. Some of the best are close to the church, including the early Georgian Lychgate House with its oddly large keystones and pretty doorcase, the Old Schoolhouse of 1809 with its Gothic windows, and the Charity House, opposite the church, of 1812.

Hatfield *see* Pudlestone

Hereford (1/4E)

The flavour of the countryside permeates Hereford's streets. On Wednesdays the cattle market brings farmers and their wives from miles around to buy, sell and exchange news in the gentle accents of the county, mixed every now and again with the lilt of Welsh. Most wear well-worn corduroys and tweed, but here and there less traditional fashions point to young people who came in and collectively bought Herefordshire smallholdings in the 1960s and 1970s (when they were still cheap) and who are now accepted members of the community.

The covered market is piled high with local dairy produce, fruit and vegetables, so plentiful and at what to strangers must seem like the low prices of times past.

This rural flavour is all the more easily savoured now that traffic is barred from most of the centre. This encourages people to congregate around the Old House in the heart of the city and simply enjoy a chat. This house was once part of Butcher's Row; it is a splendid timber-framed building of 1612, now a museum full of Elizabethan and Jacobean furniture. To the right is the belltower that chimes the hours above the covered market. High Town stretches out beyond, lined with pastel-painted shops and recently planted trees.

Terminating the view is the prominent, slightly twisted spire of All Saints' church. This has one of the finest roofs in the county and a magnificent set of 14th-century stalls under richly traceried canopies.

Broad Street spreads southwards from the church towards the cathedral, past the Green Dragon Hotel with its colourful cast-iron balcony and dragon pediment, and the Gothic Public Library and City Museum and Art Gallery, which has stone monkeys scampering along the roof parapet.

Hereford's cathedral is not the kind that takes the breath away by soaring elegance; rather it is one whose accumulation of details slowly wins the affection. The Norman nave arcade is covered in chevron ornament, and the capitals nearest the tower crossing have the interlace carving characteristic of the Hereford School of masons.

The south transept has the most extensive Norman work; it dates from 1107–15, when the cathedral was built anew after the destruction of its predecessor during the sack of the town by the Welsh.

The next stage of rebuilding began in about 1220, when the east end of the cathedral was substantially enlarged. Compared to the Norman

work, the Early English style of the Lady Chapel seems almost too rich. Characteristically, all the lancet windows are deeply splayed and ornamented with clusters of shafts. Under the Lady Chapel is the Diocesan Treasury, which contains an outstanding early 13th-century Limoges enamel reliquary illustrating the martyrdom and funeral of St Thomas à Becket.

The outstanding feature of the north chancel aisle is the tiny chantry chapel, built for Bishop Stanbury (d. 1473) and an exquisite example of Perpendicular style, with a delicate fan vault.

Near by is the entrance to the cathedral's famous chained library, a collection of some 1500 manuscripts and books, tethered against theft to Jacobean bookcases. On the wall opposite the entrance is the absorbing *Mappa Mundi*.

In 1987 the future of the *Mappa Mundi* was put in question by a plan to sell it to raise funds for the maintenance of the cathedral fabric.

This map of the world has been in Hereford since 1290, when it was drawn by Richard of Haldingham, a prebend of the cathedral. The world depicted is scarcely recognizable: the map is drawn on theological, rather than geographical, principles, and provides a wonderful insight into the medieval mind. Jerusalem is at the centre and places named in the Old Testa-

Hereford Cathedral seen across the River Wye

ment – including the Garden of Eden – figure prominently.

From the cathedral southwards, the Bishop's Meadows spread down to the banks of the Wye, where some of the best views of the cathedral are to be had and where, early in May, crowds gather to watch the gruelling River Wye Raft Race. This three-day event begins upstream of Hereford at Hay-on-Wye and teams compete to be the first to reach Chepstow, 100 miles downstream. This is followed by the Hereford Regatta at the end of May, the climax to a month of festivities that includes the Hereford May Fair and the Herefordshire Music Festival. The Three Choirs Festival, which Hereford Cathedral shares with WORCESTER and Gloucester (*see* Glos.), takes place here in the city every third year.

During the rest of the year there is much to interest the visitor, for Hereford has no fewer than eight museums. In addition to the Old House Museum and the City Museum and Art Gallery in Broad Street, the Churchill Gardens Museum contains furniture, costume and paintings. Outside stands 'Roaring Meg', the huge cannon cast by the Parliamentarians for the storming of GOODRICH Castle.

The Coningsby Hospital, Widemarsh Street, is a delightful quadrangle of almshouses, founded in 1614, with a museum of relics of the Knights of St John of Jerusalem. The Herefordshire Regimental Museum is in Harold Street.

The excellent Cider Museum and King Offa Cider Brandy Distillery, off Whitecross Road, tells the story of cidermaking from the 17th century to the first mass production of the 1920s (*see* 'Cider making' p. 144).

At the Waterworks Museum, Broomy Hill, visitors can operate a variety of hand pumps and admire magnificent gleaming vintage steam engines.

Just as the A465 emerges from the south-western suburbs of Hereford into open country-side, the bulk of Belmont Abbey looms into view. It was founded in 1854 for the Benedictine order and still functions as a school and monastery.

The abbey church of St Michael is huge, as befits the former Cathedral of the Catholic Diocese of Newport and Menevia, now part of the Archdiocese of Cardiff. The church, built by Pugin & Pugin, is handsome, if a little restrained,

The 'Chained Library' in Hereford Cathedral

with Decorated tracery, lush carving to the capitals of the tower crossing and a painted nave ceiling.

Hinton on the Green *see* Childswickham

Hoarwithy (1/4F)
The church of St Catherine, on the bank of the River Wye, some 6 miles north-west of ROSS-ON-WYE, is a masterpiece, the brilliant work of a bold and confident architect. Fortunately, the Reverend William Poole was wealthy enough to transform the ugly brick building he found when he was appointed to the living in 1854. Poole employed his friend, J. P. Seddon, as architect and, for the next 30 years, craftsmen laboured to fulfil his designs.

Seddon made the best of the church's hillside position by building a noble Romanesque campanile which is visible for several miles around, while the rest is artfully hidden by trees. The church is approached by a steep flight of steps; all you see at this stage is a doorway formed by a tunnel of yew, inviting you to come and see, but giving away nothing of what lies beyond. Only at the top do you discover that the doorway leads to an open cloister running the length of the nave, truly Norman in style and spirit.

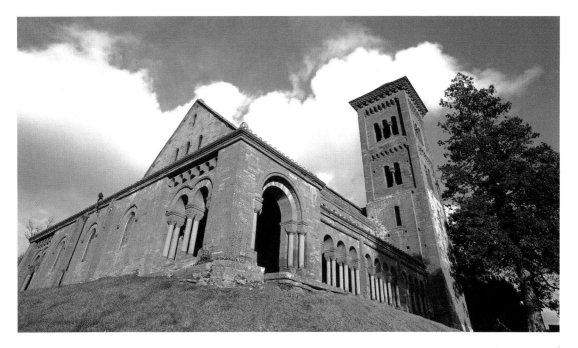

St Catherine's church, Hoarwithy

The interior of the church is a superb achievement. The altar is raised, theatrically, several feet above the nave under a series of domes supported by crisply carved cushion capitals. Sparing but effective use is made of semi-precious stones: lapis lazuli and chrysolite (tiger eye) inlay on the altar; green marble and porphyry for the pulpit. Christ hovers in glory above the altar in blue, red and gold mosaic. The floors are ornamented with acanthus leaf and guilloche – motifs found on Roman mosaics (*see* Cirencester, Glos.).

Only the Gothic choir stalls are a discordant element – accomplished in their own right, but stylistically at odds with the Byzantine splendour of the rest of the church (the fabric of which is, unfortunately, deteriorating).

From Hoarwithy an attractive walk leads past the shell of Caradoc Court, 16th-century and sadly damaged by fire in recent years, down to **Sellack** (1/4F) on the bank of the Wye. The church is dedicated to St Tysilio, an early Celtic saint, once Abbot of St Asaph's monastery. The graceful octagonal spire is 14th-century, with ribs running to the pinnacle and gabled lucarnes in four of its faces. Inside, the pews are arranged so that the tall Jacobean pulpit and tester is as much a focal point as the altar.

Emerging from the church, you are greeted by lovely views of the wooded hills and, immediately north, of the 1895-ft suspension bridge that has replaced a treacherous ford linking Sellack to King's Caple (*see* Brockhampton).

Just over a mile east, the church of St Mary at **Foy** (1/4F) has an exact copy of Sellack's east window, paid for under the terms of John Abrahall's will of 1640. There is a lovely and unusual 17th-century chancel screen which retains its original gates, decorated with angels.

Foy is linked to the hamlet of Hole-in-the-Wall on the opposite bank of the Wye by a suspension footbridge of 1876. The gently hilly countryside is popular with walkers, as is the river here with canoeists.

Holme Lacy *see* Mordiford

Holt *see* Ombersley

Honeybournes, The (2/6E)

About 5 miles east of EVESHAM, **Cow** and **Church Honeybourne** now form one village, but with two churches. Although less than ½ a mile apart, the churches once not only belonged to different abbeys; they were even in different counties. The B4085 (Ryknild Street, a Roman road) that passes through the middle of the village was formerly the boundary between Gloucestershire and Worcestershire.

Now only one church remains in use, for the Victorian church at Cow Honeybourne has been converted to dwellings. St Ecgwin's at Church

Honeybourne has a distinctive and appealing tower with massive buttresses and an octagonal 14th-century spire pierced by three tiers of lucarnes. The nave is very tall, and the porch is charmingly tiny and out of proportion with it. The interior of the church is pleasing for having a wholly untouched 13th-century chancel and a good Perpendicular roof supported on angel brackets.

The Domestic Fowl Trust in the village specializes in rare breeds of domestic and water fowl and is open all year round, except Fridays.

Pebworth (2/6E) is 2 miles to the north-east. Its church is an almost complete and untouched Perpendicular work surrounded by pleasing stone houses. The Jacobean oak pulpit is crisply carved with arches and arabesques.

Hope under Dinmore (1/4C)

St Mary's church and the school are cut off from the village by the busy A49, which links HEREFORD and LEOMINSTER, about 5 miles to the north of the village. Noise thus spoils enjoyment of the delightful position of the church under the green slope of Dinmore Hill. Inside is a lovely 13th-century font carved with the seated figures of Christ, the Evangelists and Saints John the Baptist, Peter and Paul.

Hampton Court, just under a mile east of the church, is not open to the public and its magnificence can only be savoured from the A417 where splendid wrought-iron gates afford a view to the 15th-century gatehouse. To the left is the chapel with an exceptionally fine roof and stained glass (one panel, depicting St Lawrence is on display in the Victoria and Albert Museum, London).

After flowing through the parkland surrounding Hampton Court, the River Lugg bends south to grace the village of **Bodenham** (1/4C), one of the most attractive in the region. The core of the old village, with handsome Georgian and timber-framed houses, lies close to the bridge, and the riverside setting is the best reason for visiting St Michael's church. Begun in the 13th century, it has much Decorated tracery and ballflower ornament; the spire, however, was never completed and remains as a truncated pyramid on the west tower.

Two miles north-east of the village, many-gabled Broadfield Court is, in parts, contemporary with the church and was once the property of the Knights Hospitallers. The vineyard in the grounds is open by appointment.

The Knights had their local headquarters at **Dinmore**. The Manor, which stands on the site of their preceptory, is open all year and can be reached by taking a minor road off the A49 2 miles south of Hope under Dinmore. This climbs through oak woods up the hillside, eventually reaching Dinmore Manor, its colourful garden sheltered by trees and so high up that nothing interrupts the eastward views to the MALVERNS.

The house side of the garden is enclosed by a Gothic cloister and music room, added in 1929–36, and some parts of the building stand on the visible foundations of original 12th-century walls. The Knights Hospitallers' chapel stands in the garden; it was given a tower and spire in the 14th century.

Queen's Wood Country Park adjoins the Dinmore estate. It consists of 170 acres of oak woodlands, designated a Site of Special Scientific Interest. There is also an arboretum planted with rare specimen trees. An information centre (with car park) by the A49 provides details of woodland trails.

How Caple *see* Brockhampton

Huddington (2/4D)

This is perhaps the best of a group of villages in the pleasing countryside just to the west of WORCESTER. What makes it outstanding is Huddington Court which, although private, can be viewed discreetly from the churchyard. It is a breathtakingly beautiful 16th-century building, timber-framed, with an elaborate chimney of rubbed brick, leaded oriel windows and a garden full of topiary pheasants.

The house passed by marriage to the Wintours, staunch Catholics who were involved in the Gunpowder Plot – said to have been hatched at the Court. Thomas and Robert Wintour were both executed in 1606, having confessed to being part of the conspiracy.

St James's church is now in immaculate condition, restored after several decades of neglect. It is entered through a fine 15th-century porch with cusped bargeboards. The nave arcade is handsome Early English work, and the chancel, rebuilt in 1585, retains all its contemporary glass and choir stalls.

Oddingley (2/4D) is 2½ miles north-west of Huddington and reached by narrow roads. Its church of St James is easily missed since it lies

Opposite: Huddington Court

well back from the road, hidden by a lime avenue. It was largely restored in 1851, but old bench ends have remained, one with a reading stand and hourglass holder. The church has a beautiful and complete set of stained glass of *c.* 1500 in the chancel. North of the church a field contains substantial and prominent remains of a moat and house platform.

Tibberton (2/4D) is 2 miles south of Oddingley. Its 1868 church of St Peter ad Vincula is of stone outside but polychrome red, yellow and black brick within, an interesting specimen of its type. It stands next to the large 17th-century timber-framed Rectory Farm and its weatherboarded great barn.

The road from Tibberton to **Crowle** (2/4D) crosses the railway linking Worcester and Birmingham. Crowle's church of St John the Baptist stands by a large farm, whose derelict and ivy-grown buildings include a barn and the former kitchens of Crowle Manor. The splendid 14th-century timber porch has a worn carving of the Annunciation in its gable, a coffered ceiling and figure corbels. The remarkable limestone lectern depicts a kneeling figure emerging from vine scroll. This much of it dates from *c.* 1200 and is influenced by early 11th-century Italian sculpture; but some of the carving is suspect, perhaps recent – or embellished when the piece was restored to the church in 1845, having lain in the churchyard for many years previously.

Huntington (1/1C)

The village is 4 miles south-west of KINGTON and right on the border with Wales, with everything that that position suggests; a prominent castle with remains of walling but much overgrown, and a church of the utmost simplicity, built in *c.* 1300. It is dedicated to St Thomas of Canterbury, and is fitted with massive, 3 in thick pews with trefoil-headed bench ends. The roof of golden oak was added in the 19th century, but is very much in the local tradition, with cusped windbraces. A more recent addition is the colourful 1950s stained glass of St Francis and the birds.

Inkberrow (2/5D)

This is another Worcestershire village that claims to be the original of England's most famous rural community, the Ambridge of *The Archers*, the BBC radio serial (*see also* Ashton under Hill, Bredon). This one is some 12 miles east of WORCESTER, along the A422. Right by the church is the rambling Old Bull Inn which not only shares the name of the pub in the serial, but often features in books on Ambridge. Inside there are photographs of the cast.

There are both brick and timber-framed houses around the village green. St Peter's church stands opposite the tithe barn and the

The Old Bull Inn at Inkberrow

red-brick Tudor-style Old Vicarage. From the outside it is one of the grandest churches in the region. The north aisle is Perpendicular with battlements and crocketed finials and the splendid north porch has big gargoyles. The inside is spacious, with a series of tall octagonal piers forming the nave arcade. Charles I visited the Vicarage in 1645 on his way to Naseby and left behind a book of maps, copies of which are displayed in the church.

Ipsley *see* Redditch

Kemerton *see* Bredon

Kempsey (2/3E)

The village is 4 miles south of WORCESTER and cut through by the A38. St Mary's is a large cruciform church with an exceptional Early English chancel of 1250–60. It has tall, stepped lancet windows shafted internally, sedilia with cusped arches and a trefoil-head piscina. The chancel side windows contain excellent 14th-century stained glass, and an 18th-century wall tablet reads:

> Underneath the corruptible parts of a vicar, one husband, two helpmeets, both wives and both Anns, a triplicity of persons in two twains but one flesh, are interred.

On the Worcester Road and elsewhere in the village there are some good timber-framed and Georgian houses.

Kentchurch (1/3F)

The parish is situated on the border with the Welsh county of Gwent, about 2½ miles southeast of EWYAS HAROLD. There is almost no village and St Mary's church of 1859 is mainly of interest for the figures from the Scudamore monument of 1616: John, his wife and their ten children, one in a cradle.

Kentchurch Court (open by appointment) was originally a Border castle and retains a mighty 14th-century tower and gateway. At some time between 1795 and 1807 John Nash was invited to rebuild the house. It is one of his early works, predating Regent's Park and Regent Street in London.

His remodelling very much followed the style of the buildings that were already standing, so that it now has the appearance of a castle made domestic by the insertion of sash windows. The very fine wood carving in the house is by Grinling Gibbons, originally made for the Scudamore's principal family seat at Holme Lacy (*see* Mordiford). The Scudamores have owned this house at Kentchurch continuously since the 14th century.

Kidderminster (2/3B)

This town on the River Stour has been weaving cloth since the 13th century; latterly it has been most famous for its carpets. John Broom set up the first broadloom for carpet weaving in 1735 and nearly went bankrupt trying to establish the industry. It did take off, however, and was essentially a cottage industry until the introduction of power looms in the mid-19th century.

It is from then that most of the town's buildings date, including the surviving carpet mills alongside the Staffordshire and Worcestershire Canal. Brintons Limited, in Exchange Street, is one of the oldest established firms and provides guided tours of the Axminster weaving department by appointment. The Art Gallery and Museum in Market Street is a good starting point for an understanding of the industry.

Kidderminster's most famous son was Sir Rowland Hill (1795–1879), inventor of the adhesive postage stamp who saw his plan for a penny postage adopted (Parliament had preferred a twopenny rate). A fine bronze statue of Hill stands outside the Town Hall. Another statue here is of Richard Baxter, the 17th-century Independent clergyman whose name is perpetuated in the Baxter Congregational Church, one of Kidderminster's many Nonconformist chapels.

St Mary's church is large and mostly Victorian and rather gloomy, but it contains worthwhile monuments.

Wolverley (2/3B) lies in the northern outskirts of Kidderminster yet is wholly unaffected by it, a settlement built on and around the sandstone cliffs carved out by the River Stour. In the centre of the village is the surprising Court House, formerly the Sebright School. The 1620 date stone refers to the school's foundation, not the building which is early 19th century and in a combination of styles. The colonnade is formed of three tall pointed Gothic arches; the flanking stair turrets are Tudor; and the windows have Perpendicular tracery.

Nearby cottages are also Gothic in style, but of the Victorian rather than Strawberry Hill variety. The Queen's Head pub stands beneath cliffs into which 'cave cottages' were cut in the 19th century.

The church of St John the Baptist stands above this cliff, approached from one direction by a steep path cut into the rock. It is a sturdy red-brick building of 1772. Galleries line three sides of the interior and there are many Georgian monuments, including a small semi-reclining female figure by John Flaxman.

Kingsford Country Park (2/3A) lies just under 2 miles to the north of Wolverley and is the most rewarding of the four parks in the north of the county. The geology is exposed at Vales Rock, a short walk from the car park and information centre, and shows various sandstone strata – ranging from pebbly conglomerate to almost pure sand. Caves occur naturally in the soft rock, but at Vales Rock they were enlarged to form dwellings. These remained occupied until the 1960s, when they were considered unsafe. Vandals have contributed to their deterioration, but there are plans to restore the caves and reopen them in due course.

Much of the park is now under forest – part commercial conifers, part naturally regenerated birch wood. The latter is especially rich in wildlife: jays and woodpeckers are common. Adders and lizards can also be seen on the heathland areas in summer.

Kilpeck (1/3E)

The tiny red sandstone church of St Mary and St David at this village about 9 miles south-west of HEREFORD is one of the highlights of a visit to the county, a building of such national importance that many substantial books have been devoted to its interpretation. On one level it can be enjoyed simply as a wholly unspoiled example of mid-12th-century Norman architecture, sumptuously decorated with carvings that have survived in pristine condition. At another level it helps to know a little of the reasons for the scholarly excitement.

Serious attempts to understand the disparate origins of the English Romanesque style – remarkable for its vestigial Viking and Saxon motifs – did not really begin until the 1930s. Quite a number of Victorian architectural historians in fact believed that 'proper' architecture began with the Gothic; Norman was dismissed as primitive and omitted from the textbooks.

In 1929 a 12th-century history of Wigmore Abbey was discovered in the University of Chicago Library. This manuscript contained the fascinating information that Oliver de Merlimont, Lord of Wigmore, made notes of what he saw as he travelled on pilgrimage to the shrine of St

Detail from the south doorway of Kilpeck church

James at Compostela in north-west Spain. On his return he used these as the basis for the new church he built at SHOBDON, completed around 1140.

Merlimont's church proved highly influential. Other wealthy patrons, who had made the same pilgrimage and returned impressed by what they had seen on the way, endowed churches to be built in similar style. Thus the mid-12th century was a great period of church building. Schools, or workshops, of masons could count on a constant supply of work. One such, working locally, is known as the Hereford School. There were others at important centres elsewhere. But only in this county, and in neighbouring Gloucestershire, has their work survived in substantial quantity: no fewer than 30 churches have fonts or tympana attributable to the Hereford School.

Kilpeck is the very best and most complete surviving example. The corbel table is a riot of carving, exhibiting all the features that offended the Victorians. Little of it seems specifically Christian; but to the medieval mind these carvings emphasized the chaos and sinfulness of the world which the church existed to challenge and overcome. Outside the church was the world of monsters and darkness; inside, all was peace and spirituality.

The figures in the corbel table personify the various sins: they were probably here to admonish rather than titillate. Lust is depicted twice, in the carving of the grotesque couple kissing and fondling each other; and in the monstrous figure with bulging eyes, flagrantly exhibiting her genitals.

The south doorway is a masterpiece of sculpture, the shafts carved with tail-biting dragons and huntsmen in long tunics. Their rope belts are knotted into an interlace pattern and the arch above the door is carved with beakheads. These all indicate that motifs introduced by the Anglo-Saxons and Vikings were still part of the English masons' repertoire in the 12th century.

After the wildness of the church exterior the inside comes as a complete contrast. The chancel arch is carved with saints whose faces express the serenity that the church offers to refugees from the dark world outside.

The graveyard at Kilpeck is worth exploring because it stands within a well-preserved Norman motte and bailey.

Much Dewchurch (1/3E) about 2½ miles east of Kilpeck, is a village now mostly of modern housing, but the church of St David is Norman, with a 13th-century tower. There are pieces from an interlace cross shaft in the porch.

Kimbolton (1/4B)

The rugged red sandstone church of St James stands on a hilltop overlooking LEOMINSTER, about 2 miles to the south-west. Its Norman tower is topped by a tall shingled broach spire. The fronts of the stalls in the chancel are made up of 16th-century linenfold panels with a decorative frieze of bows and foliage.

About 3 miles north-east along the A4112 is **Leysters** (1/4B). The church of St Andrew is well out of the village, peacefully apart and towered over by tall cedar trees. The surprise and the pleasure is the stunning roof, tier upon tier of cusped windbraces creating a dancing pattern across the ceiling. Only that in the nave is 14th-century; the chancel ceiling is a crude and painted Victorian imitation.

Two miles north-west, **Middleton on the Hill** (1/4B) is something of a misnomer: if anything, the church and village are in a hollow, but surrounded by gently rising ground. St Mary's

two Norman doorways both have elaborate zigzag mouldings and everything inside is Norman but plain and overcleaned, the walls scraped of all plaster. Opposite the church is Middleton Farm, built in 1692, with a little gazebo peeping above one corner of the garden wall.

King's Caple *see* Brockhampton

Kingsford Country Park *see* Kidderminster

Kingsland (1/3B)

The village, some 4 miles north-west of LEOMINSTER, has a long street of timber-framed houses, several of considerable charm and age. St Michael's church is full of surprises. The north porch hides a tiny chantry chapel built outside and up against the south wall. It is barely big enough to squeeze into, but contains a miniature altar and an empty coffin in a tomb recess.

The south doorway has a cusped 'Berkeley arch', so called because it appears at Berkeley Castle (*see* Glos.) and nowhere else except here and in Bristol. Its presence here suggests the mason had some experience of the others.

The Perpendicular arcade consists of slender octagonal pillars with a concave rebate, rising to a clerestory of circular windows enclosing sexfoils. The whole is highly distinctive and well set off by the walls that are, for once, plastered and not scraped, as in the case of most other churches in the county.

Even the Victorian work is good. G. F. Bodley's 1866 chancel has a prettily painted roof in colours and style that we now associate with Laura Ashley.

King's Pyon *see* Canon Pyon

Kington (*near* Worcester) *see* Dormston

Kington (1/1C)

About 14 miles west of LEOMINSTER and on the border with Powys, this is the only town of any consequence in the west of the county and it prospers on the custom of the local farming community. The buildings are mostly unadorned country versions of Regency or Victorian, with only here and there a bay window or fanlight adding a touch of urbanity. The narrow streets meet at the Market Hall, an 1885 building of liverish brick with a portrait medallion of Queen

Victoria in the pediment. An earlier predecessor stands alongside, an open hall with a bell turret and weathervane, next to the small museum of local history.

The grandest buildings are at the eastern end of the High Street, past a number of old-fashioned butchers' shops. The classical former Town Hall of 1845 is decorated with wreaths and Corinthian capitals, and the Oxford Arms Hotel has a pretty wooden balcony.

St Mary's church is on the western outskirts. Bracken-clad Bradnor Hill looms above it to the north, site of a border castle built in 1100 but now scarcely traceable. The land is owned by the National Trust and rises to 1284 ft, with a golf course on the summit that claims to be the highest in Europe.

A massive, once-detached, belltower stands beside the church. The base is slightly battered out so that it looks defensive, and no doubt it served as a refuge in times of trouble. The splendid Early English chancel has a row of six splayed lancet windows that form a nice regular rhythm but are compromised by garish glass. By the font, covered by a trapdoor, is a tank for baptism by total immersion.

Hergest Croft Garden near Kington

Hergest Court is a lovely (but private) 15th-century house 2 miles south-west of the town. It should not be confused with Hergest Croft, 1 mile east of Kington, whose famous gardens are open daily in summer. The woodland was planted in 1910 with rhododendrons that are now up to 30 ft tall. Closer to the Edwardian house, the walled gardens are full of interest throughout the year. Bulbs, primulas and colourful auriculas give way to herbaceous plants and old-fashioned roses, and by autumn the many maple and birch species are in full blaze.

The area around Kington is ideal – but testing – walking country. A good stretch of OFFA'S DYKE is found on Rushock Hill, north of the town, and, to the west, Hergest Ridge rises to nearly 1400 ft, providing extensive views.

Kinnersley *see* Eardisley

Knighton on Teme *see* Eastham

Kyre Park *see* Edwyn Ralph

Lea (3/3C)
Four miles south-east of ROSS-ON-WYE, on the busy A40 Gloucester road, Lea's church of St John the Baptist contains a rare treasure, a superb font bought for the church in 1907 and made up from pieces of early Italian sculpture. An endearing stone elephant, with leonine paws, forms the base and is dated stylistically to the late 11th century. Its saddle is decorated with inlay and two figures of saints. The bowl is late 12th century, carved with human and animal figures, standing on a knotted shaft. It is a surprising and beautiful object that adds a touch of exoticism to a church that is mostly Victorian restoration.

Two miles west, towards Ross-on-Wye, is the large village of **Weston under Penyard** (3/3C). It has Roman antecedents: the town of Ariconium is believed to have stood hereabouts in what was then an ore-smelting area.

St Lawrence's church contains several reminders that the Forest of Dean (*see* Glos.) is near by. The late Norman nave arcade has capitals carved with a muzzled bear and a hound, and uses Forest timber for the 14th-century scissor-braced roof.

As the name suggests, the village lies close to Penyard Hill, and stones from the 14th-century castle that once stood on its summit provided some of the building materials for the 18th-century Gothick Bollitree Castle near by.

Church Street, Ledbury

Ledbury (3/3B)

The main street of this handsome town stretches for almost a mile and is lined with an abundance of fine buildings. Many date from the 16th and 17th centuries, when cloth and leather working made many of the townspeople prosperous. Good examples are the Feathers Hotel, carved with Prince of Wales feathers, and the noble many-gabled Ledbury Park, of about 1600. The house on the corner of New Street, opposite, has a pronounced jetty that forms an arcade over the pavement (and sadly suffers frequent vehicle damage).

These buildings are all timber-framed, but when brick became the fashionable material in the 18th century several houses were refronted. These can be seen in Homend, the continuation of the High Street. No. 30 is a charming house with bay windows either side of a pedimented porch, and No. 36, Shell House, is so called for its lovely shellhood doorcase. Close by, Abbey House of about 1600, now a bakery, has a prominent porch with Venetian windows that thrusts forward across the pavement.

The centre of the town is dominated by the Barrett Browning Institute of 1892, a rather German-looking structure – incongruous in this setting – with a clocktower, raised in memory of Elizabeth Barrett Browning, whose family lived at nearby COLWALL. Alongside it are the almshouses of St Katherine's Hospital, founded in 1232 for 'wayfarers and the poor'. They were rebuilt in the 19th century, but the 14th-century chapel survives with a splendid timber roof.

The Market Hall on the opposite side of the street is one of the many in the county said to have been built by the architect-carpenter John Abel – although it shows none of his characteristic love of flamboyance (*see* Abbey Dore and Leominster). Indeed, it reserves its decorative herringbone timberwork for the sides that can be seen from the High Street. It is, nevertheless, an impressive structure, standing on chestnut pillars, completed in 1655, and the focus of the weekly market and the October Hop Fair.

Numerous alleyways run between the houses and shops lining Homend, vestiges of the street plan laid out in 1120 when Ledbury was granted its market charter. One of these, Church Lane, has survived almost entirely in its medieval form; the jettied houses that overhang the cobbled pathway make it irresistible to photographers. Two of its finest buildings are now museums; the Old Grammar School of 1500 and the 16th-century Butchers' Row, which originally stood on an island in the middle of the High Street before being resited here.

Church Lane leads to St Michael's church, as ornate outside as it is within and particularly well-endowed with monuments. The west front survives in Norman form with turrets either side of a central gable. The big, detached belltower stands by the splendid north chapel. Its ornate tracery and ballflower decoration is unmistakably the work of the masons who enlarged Leominster Priory in the early 14th century.

Inside, the nave is Perpendicular with an arcade of concave octagonal piers. Deeply splayed Norman clerestory windows survive in the chancel and the north chapel is studded with the same ballflower ornament that graces the outside.

About 3 miles south of Ledbury, off the A417, the gardens of Haffield House are occasionally open under the National Gardens Scheme. The house was built in 1818 in neo-Grecian style by Robert Smirke. The pride of the garden is the tall tulip tree; the latest addition is a quarry garden with waterfall and lily pond.

The Malverns

CHRISTOPHER CATLING

It cannot be long now before somebody sits down to write a history of that complex part of contemporary culture that we call 'conservationism'. When they do, the story of the Malverns will feature prominently. The Malverns Act of 1884 was one of the earliest pieces of legislation in Britain designed specifically to safeguard an area of outstanding beauty from destructive exploitation. Even so, the threat to the hills, especially from quarrying, only ceased as recently as 1977; and only in the last decade have the conflicting demands made upon the Malverns been reconciled successfully.

As early as 1820, local people were becoming concerned at the damage caused to the Malverns by tourism. The donkeys hired out to visitors to carry them to popular viewpoints, such as the Worcestershire Beacon, were blamed for overgrazing the slopes and eroding deep pathways, and litter was a growing nuisance.

The problem only increased during the middle decades of the 19th century as thousands of visitors came to Malvern, attracted by the supposed curative powers of the local waters. Fresh air and exercise were part of the regime prescribed by Malvern's many hydropathic institutions, with the consequence that the hills were becoming intolerably crowded. Moreover, houses and hotels were being built further and further up the slopes, thus threatening to destroy the very scenic beauty that attracted visitors to the area.

When the railway came to Malvern in 1859, putting the hills within reach of day trippers from the industrial Midlands, the problem of overexploitation became so acute that the *Malvern News* ran a leader calling for the formation of a management committee to put the hills in order. 'The commons,' it said, 'are in a wretched condition . . . ruts here, rubbish there, broken glass . . . blades of grass that should be green are begrimed with the shakings of some soot bag. Surely these commons might be made places of pleasant resort.'

The idea of a management comittee was not a new one. Several attempts to galvanize local concern into action had foundered because of the conflicting interests of the freeholders with ancient grazing rights, various private landowners, and the commercial lobby of hoteliers, shopkeepers and medical practitioners. Even so, there was a growing recognition that, unless something was done, the basis of Malvern's prosperity would be threatened.

In the 19th century, even more than today, governments were reluctant to legislate where rights of property were concerned. Nevertheless, the passage of the Commons Act in 1876, as well as acts to conserve specific areas of common from what would now be termed development, provided the people of Malvern with a model for their own bill, and a measure of encouragement that their objectives might meet with success.

The first draft of a bill to protect the hills was prepared in 1882, but the Malvern freeholders thought it placed too much emphasis on the recreational value of the hills at the expense of their grazing rights. Another determined opponent of any form of bill was Lady Foley, owner of the manor of Malvern, and one of the chief culprits in building on common land. As a result of her intervention the Parliamentary bill that was finally given the Royal assent in 1884 was much more limited in scope than had originally been intended.

Even so, it was a remarkable piece of legislation for its time, hailed by *The Times* as being of national importance. It created a body of 15 Conservators with the power to take action against anyone who encroached on, enclosed or abused the common land. In addition the Conservators were empowered to levy a local rate of a ½d in the pound to pay for path maintenance and planting. In effect, this Act created the structure under which the Malverns have been managed and preserved from that day to this.

The Act was, however, weak in one important respect: it excluded all those lands that were in private ownership, including sites that had only recently, and by means of dubious tactics, been enclosed. The consequence of this did not begin to emerge for some time, but in 1907 private landowners began to quarry the Malverns on a large scale, and the Conservators seemed powerless to stop it.

Historians have blamed one or two individuals for this desecration of the hills, but in truth the issue of quarrying was far from clear cut and threatened to divide the community. Malvern's heyday as a spa town was over; the local economy was in decline and commercial quarrying offered an important source of employment and prosperity. Demand for road stone increased dramatically

The Malvern Hills seen from Elgar's house at Birchwood where he wrote The Dream of Gerontius

with the growing popularity of the motor car (ironically, a very early British example was called the Malvernia and built at Malvern Link in the 1890s).

Despite the rate they levied, the Conservators' funds were far from sufficient. This remained the case even when a new Act of 1924 raised the rate to 3d in the pound to enable the Conservators to make compulsory purchases of the quarries. Eventually most of the usable stone had been exhausted and the last quarry finally closed in December 1977 – a historic day for the Conservators.

It is remarkable how little lasting damage quarrying has wrought upon the hills. They have yielded a vast quantity of stone without losing their distinctive outline. Quarrying has also contributed to our better – although by no means complete – understanding of the geology of the Malverns.

Dating the Malverns is difficult because the hardness of the rock makes drilling cores for analysis prohibitively expensive. The oldest rocks predate organic life, so there are no fossils to help with dating. Furthermore the complex mineralogy of the rocks admits of several different interpretations of their origin. As its name suggests, the

Warren House Volcanic series at the centre of the range contains minerals of volcanic origin, while the Malvernian rocks of the eastern slopes may have been formed by a combination of intense subterranean heat and pressure. Both are dated to the pre-Cambrian era – which makes them more than 600 million years old and therefore among the oldest rocks in England.

The hardness of these rocks accounts for the particular purity of Malvern water. Rainfall passing through the hills dissolves little by way of minerals and organic matter before issuing in numerous springs and wells. Since the 18th century, when the first analysis of the water was undertaken, it has been famous not for its mineral content but for the lack of it. Similarly, the distinctive shape of the Malverns is due to the exceptional durability of the rock; wind and rain, rivers and ice have made little impression, and most of the apparent valleys or gullies that separate the peaks were caused by faulting rather than erosion.

Geologists have never agreed on when the Malverns were thrust upwards to form such a dramatic contrast to the Severn plain. Two possible explanations are given of why the movement occurred; that the upthrust resulted from large-scale movements in the earth's lower crust; or from localised faulting which squeezed up the Malvern range while the surrounding terrain dropped.

Geologists do not regard these explanations as definitive, and so the Malverns remain one of the most intensively studied hill ranges in the country. Local field study centres cater for school and university students who constitute just one of the many groups of people who make use of the hills. For most of the visitors, however, this complex geology is only of passing interest – indeed the slopes of the hills, at a fairly consistent 26 degrees to the surrounding plain, give the Malverns a monolithic appearance of deceptive simplicity.

This gentle incline is easily negotiated by car; no one is allowed to drive to the peak of the Worcestershire Beacon any more, as Edward VII once did in his Daimler, but numerous car parks are provided by the Conservators close enough to the peaks for even the frailest to manage the short walk to any of the Malverns' many viewpoints.

Despite the occasional overcrowding that results from the Malverns' accessibility, it is still possible to find a tranquil spot where the only sounds are those of the lark and the bumble bee. Most visitors to the Malverns want no more than this: peace and repose, the opportunity to contemplate the noble views of the Severn plain to the east, the rolling hills and tapestry fields of Hereford to the west and the contoured terraces and ramparts of the Iron Age British Camp, as it is called, to the south.

Such views have inspired much poetry, most of it too banal to be memorable. One poet, however, captured the friendly mood of the Malverns as long ago as the 14th century. *Piers Plowman*, William Langland's satire on the indolence and corruption of the clergy, begins with his narrator seeking rest from his wanderings:

In a somer sesoun, whanne softe was the sonne,
I shope me in-to a shroud, as I a shep were;
In abite as an ermyte, unholy of werkis,
I went wyde in this world, wondris to here,
But on a May morwenyng on Malverne hilles
Me befel a ferly, of fairie me thoughte.
I was wery for-wandrit and wente me to reste
Undir a brood bank be a bourne side;
And as I lay and lenide and lokide on the watris,
I slomeride in a slepyng, it swighede so merye.

(In a summer season when soft was the sun,/I dressed me in a shepherd's smock/As though I a shepherd were,/In the habit of a hermit, though of no holy life,/I wandered about this world, wonders to see,/In a May morning on Malvern Hills/A strange thing befell me, a fairy vision methought;/I was weary of wandering and went me to rest/Under a broad bank by a stream,/And as I lay and leaned and looked upon the water,/I slumbered in a sleep, so pleasantly it sounded.)

Langland expresses very well the reason why the Malverns have such an appeal. They are gentle hills, perfect for the reluctant mountaineer who likes to feel up on top of the world, but doubts his abilities to tackle more challenging peaks; who derives comfort from knowing that there is sure to be a seat for the weary climber around the corner, donated by someone who has also loved these hills. Even the views, magnificent as they are, are gentle: comfortably Betjemanesque rather than ruggedly Wordsworthian.

To admit this is not to diminish their importance; on the contrary, the Malverns have become, to use the planner's jargon, 'a valuable recreational resource'. They attract casual walkers as well as veterans of the northern fells. Young guides, scouts and cadets receive their first taste of adventure on their slopes. Pilgrims mix with sponsored walkers and marathon trainees. Artists come to paint the views while hang-gliding enthusiasts float across the near horizon. How many of them know what a debt they owe to the Conservators who have safeguarded the hills for over a century? Enough, it is to be hoped, to ensure that any new threat to these ancient hills will be met with spirited and indignant resistance.

Leigh (2/2D)

This hamlet 4 miles west of WORCESTER is undergoing a slow transformation. The great tithe barn in the grounds of Leigh Court is being restored with a government grant, and will eventually be open to the public. It is a building of awe-inspiring grandeur and dimensions, 150 ft long, built entirely of cruck trusses under a tiled roof. It is tentatively dated to the early 14th century, although tests may yet prove it to be even older.

The buildings around it consist of a complete set of 18th- and 19th-century cartsheds, hop kilns and dairy, representing the activities of a typical farm 100 or more years ago. They could, in due course, form the core of an interesting museum of agricultural history; it would be a great pity if they ended up as 'executive' dwellings, as so often happens.

The key to St Eadburga's church is available at the Post Office during business hours. It is well worth obtaining since the very fine sculpture that was once on the exterior nave wall has been moved inside.

This is something of a mystery piece, once described as an 11th-century figure of Christ. Current opinion favours an early 13th-century date, on the basis of French parallels with the beautiful carving of the drapery, and it is evident that it is an effigy – of an unknown saint or ecclesiastical figure – from a tomb or coffin lid.

Part of the churchyard has been planted with flowering shrubs; at the east end it is being allowed to grow wild as it contains rare flora and fauna. From here it is possible to look down into the equally wild walled garden of Leigh Court. Fronting the house are two charming miniature gatehouses under big Dutch gables, both with sundials and both crumbling. Sensitive visitors will leave Leigh hoping that it may yet be possible for the good work that has begun with the barn to be continued, so that this very special assemblage of historic buildings can be rescued from neglect.

Leinthalls, The (1/3B)

These two hamlets stand at the foot of Gatley Hill, a mile or so east of WIGMORE in the north of the county. The church of St Mary Magdalene at **Leinthall Starkes** sits alone in the fields, guarded by yew trees that tower over the east and west ends. It is a simple Norman building with tiny windows and a lovely 14th-century roof of three tiers of windbraces. An ancient

boiler in the nave announces 'Slow but sure combustion' and a tortoise sits on the cast-iron lid.

At **Leinthall Earls** the church of St Andrew stands by a big quarry, but screened from it by huge and ancient sweet chestnut trees. It too is Norman with thick, outward-leaning walls under a collar-beam roof with windbraces, later strengthened by the addition of queen posts.

By the church a track leads to Gatley Park, a square brick Jacobean house in a lovely hillside position. The gardens are occasionally open under the National Gardens Scheme.

Leintwardine (1/3A)

The complex geology of this far north-western corner of the county is evident in the many different types and colours of stone used for the village houses. They range from yellow-green lias through variously coloured sandstones to an almost marble-like grey limestone. The village also shows evidence of having been planned, for two parallel main streets are linked by secondary streets and alleys at regular intervals to form a grid: a 12th-century layout, perhaps, rather than a legacy of the Roman settlement that underlies today's houses.

The church of St Mary Magdalene is in the centre of the village, a very large building whose Perpendicular panelled roof has numerous bosses at the rib intersections. The chancel stalls may have come from Wigmore Abbey at the Dissolution of the Monasteries and the misericords, although defaced, depict the Annunciation, Resurrection and a pair of wrestlers. From the church the streets lead down to a pretty stone bridge and riverside inn close to the confluence of the Teme and Clun.

Lenches, The (2/5E)

North of EVESHAM is an area of rich soils that support many market gardens, orchards and dairy farms. In this gentle working landscape, some of the best everyday architecture is seen in the farm buildings and estate houses put up by the Reverend W. K. W. Chafy, who lived at Rous Lench Court from 1876.

Chafy's home village was **Rous Lench** (2/5D), about 6 miles north of Evesham, where even the pillarbox received his attentions for it is housed in a gabled stone and half-timbered surround – a miniature version of his neo-Tudor houses surrounding the green.

St Peter's church is entered through a fine south doorway with fluted columns and a figure of Christ in Majesty above. He is seated in a vesica, one hand raised in blessing, the other holding a book. The flat drapery folds are finely delineated. The date is probably around 1140.

The interior, restored by the local architect F. Preedy, is a likeable but incoherent jumble of true Norman (the nave columns) and high Victorian neo-Romanesque (the skylit north apse and Italianate baldachino). To add to the muddle, the chancel has two very fine Elizabethan pulpits and 19th-century chairs and prie-dieux in the same style, but a neo-Gothic rood screen.

Rous Lench Court, home of the Rous family from 1382 until Chafy bought it in 1876, is a rambling picturesque timber-framed house with a remarkable topiary garden, and terraces littered with sculpture and architectural fragments. It is private, but something of its splendour is visible from the road, including the 16th-century west range, the 1840s additions and a forest of barley sugar-twist chimneys. Towering above it all is a machicolated tower, a close copy of the campanile of the Palazzo Vecchio in Florence. Chafy built it in honour of Richard Baxter (see also Kidderminster), the clergyman who wrote the *Saint's Everlasting Rest* at the Court in 1647.

A group of Chafy's buildings, now converted to holiday accommodation, can be seen at **Abbots** (or **Ab**) **Lench** (2/5D), where they take up one side of the triangular green. They are typical of his style, built of salmon-pink brick with round windows, or owl holes, in the gables. Doors, windows, and even the eaves, have rubbed brick bullnose mouldings.

The road continues south-east to **Church Lench** (2/5D), the biggest of the Lenches and high enough up to command views over the Vale of Evesham to the MALVERNS. All Saints has a three-stage tower with pinnacles and weather-vanes at each corner. The entrance has fragments of 15th-century stained glass set above the doorway.

Pink walls, a rose-coloured ceiling and an 1886 Christ in Majesty on the east nave wall, and a scarlet and gold chancel roof, greet the visitor to this church, which has a good deal of Victorian work. Pieces from a 16th-century cope are displayed by the pulpit, embroidered with saints on a golden background.

Atch Lench (2/5D), just south-east of Church Lench, has a group of Chafy buildings, near the brick Baptist church of 1825. There are further exceptional examples at Sheriff's Lench, just over a mile to the south-west, where all the cartsheds have blind arcading and repeated series of concentric semicircular arches.

Leominster (1/3C)

This is the principal town in the north-west of the county, and farmers and their families come from miles around to shop here. The town divides into two distinct parts: the Priory at the east end; the market place well to the west. The car park off the A44, Etnam Street, is a convenient midway point from which to begin exploring the town. Etnam Street itself is largely Georgian, including the Baptist chapel of 1771, but with some timber-framed buildings.

From here a footpath skirts Priory Park, following the line of the town's former defences. It then turns to approach the magnificent Grange Court, the most ornate timber-framed building in the county. Originally it served as the Market House and stood in the High Street before being re-erected on its present site, first as a private house, now as the offices of Leominster District Council. It was built in 1633 by John Abel (1577–1674), the brilliant architect-craftsman who received royal recognition with the honorary title 'King's Carpenter'.

The county has many buildings attributed to Abel, but this is one of very few that are documented as his work (see also Abbey Dore). He must have enjoyed himself immensely on this job; every carvable surface is covered in humorous caricatures and mythical beasts.

The path continues on to the south side of the Priory of St Peter and St Paul. For the earliest surviving fabric of Leominster Priory it is necessary to go to the west front, which has an imposing Hereford School portal of the mid-12th century. The carvings on the capitals include men reaping, birds, serpents and two lions. These may have been carved in the mistaken belief that Leominster – rendered in Latin as *Monasterium Leonis* – meant 'monastery of the lions'. In fact, the first part of the name is probably an English adaptation of an old Welsh word meaning 'streams', a reference to the many watercourses that almost entirely encircle the town. It is also said that the medieval Latin *leonis* meant 'of the marshes'. What the visitor needs to know is that the place is pronounced 'Lemster'.

Inside the Priory the impression is of three naves side by side. The northernmost was the original mid-12th-century monastic church; the southernmost is the parochial nave built in the 14th century; the middle one was rebuilt after a fire in 1699 and remodelled again by Sir George Gilbert Scott in 1872–9. The blaze destroyed most of the furnishings so that the church is now unusually – and pleasingly – uncluttered.

A late 15th-century chalice of great beauty is displayed in the safe in the Lady Chapel. Because of their great value, most churches with vessels of this age and quality keep them in bank vaults and it is rare to be able to see such a splendid piece at close quarters.

From west of the Priory, Church Street leads to the town and is lined with Georgian and Regency buildings. The rest of the town is of mixed quality as the Corn Square illustrates. Here some fine timber-framed buildings (the Three Horseshoes and the pharmacy of around 1400) are partnered by 19th-century buildings of white and yellow brick (Lloyd's Bank and the 1858 Corn Exchange), and by featureless 20th-century structures (the Job Centre).

From Corn Square, narrow alleys and streets preserve the medieval town plan and good buildings – like the delicatessen in Victoria Street, with its splendid Victorian shop front – stand out among a jumble of styles ranging from provincial and simplified Georgian to overblown Victorian. Even so, Leominster is an endearing town with a rural atmosphere that the completion of the ring road will enhance. Anyone interested in the region will find the maps, photographs and implements in the Leominster Folk Museum in Etnam Street a mine of information.

The parish of **Eyton** (1/3B) lies 2 miles north-west of Leominster on marshy land around the River Lugg. Eyton Court is a picturebook house with a timber-framed gable wing with studs close-set and an oriel window. Opposite, a 14th-century hall house, The Marsh, has recently been excellently restored: no intrusive modern windows have been added, and the original fabric has been touched as little as possible.

All Saints, Eyton, is a simple church with an outstanding rood screen. Its coved and coffered canopy is ornamented with bosses and an intricate frieze of vine leaves runs across the top.

Two miles north-east of Eyton is the hamlet of **Eye** (1/3B). Its name comes from an Old English word meaning island. The church of St Peter and St Paul is entered by a 14th-century timber porch of a type common enough in the region, but not always so well-preserved as here. The cusped bargeboards are ornately carved and pierced by quatrefoils. Inside it is the pulpit and some splendid monuments that capture the attention. The pulpit is carved with American Indians in blankets and feather head-dresses; its Jacobean style suggests that the date of 1681 was carved on it some time after it was made.

Eye Manor (private), next to the church, looks unexceptional from the outside, but contains very fine plaster ceilings. It dates from the late 17th century and was built for a Barbados sugar merchant.

Berrington Hall is a National Trust property just east of Eye, and 3 miles north of Leominster along the A49. It consists of a late 18th-century house designed by Henry Holland set in a park

Berrington Hall from the park (National Trust)

landscaped by the architect's father-in-law, Capability Brown. The exterior of the house is extremely simple – even a little dour – but the interior is a neo-classical masterpiece full of Adam-style ceilings of rare delicacy.

The client and owner was Thomas Harley, a local man (the family owned BRAMPTON BRYAN Castle) who made his wealth in the City of London. Building began in 1778 and was still in progress when Harley's daughter got married. That event is commemorated in the drawing room ceiling, the finest in the house. The plaster roundels are painted with deliciously sensual portraits of Venus and Cupid; delicate plaster-work, based on classical Roman motifs, spills across the ceiling and down the coving. Other ceilings of similar spirit lend the whole house an atmosphere of lightness and gaiety.

Airy spaciousness characterizes the staircase hall. It rises the full height of the house, lit from above by a glass dome, filled with statues in niches and pastel scagliola columns.

The house is unusual in the completeness of its family possessions and memorabilia, including a nursery stuffed with antique toys, beneath whose chaos a colourful carpet in the style of Kate Greenaway can just be glimpsed. The dairy has pastel ceramic wall tiles and a patterned stone floor.

The house is surrounded by open parkland planted with strategically placed chestnuts and clumps of trees to create an attractive and, in autumn, colourful vista.

Letton *see* Winforton

Leysters *see* Kimbolton

Lickey Hills (2/4B)

The hills form a green lung between BROMS-GROVE and Longbridge on the doorstep of the West Midlands. Suburban villas enjoying fine views had already engulfed the lower slopes before building was halted in the late 19th century, but the hilltops still feel wild. Beacon Hill has a castellated toposcope on its 987-ft summit; and although the views one way are of Birmingham, the other direction looks to the MALVERNS. The woods on the Lickey and Cofton Hills are marked out with nature trails and provide a sanctuary for birds and wildlife. The NORTH WORCESTERSHIRE PATH links this area with other country parks.

Alvechurch (2/5B) is the big village 2 miles south, substantially larger now than it was when it was the residence of the Bishops of Worcester. Fishponds and the moat that surrounded their house, pulled down in 1780, remain east of the village.

The tower of St Lawrence's church has the date 1676 carved into its clock face and a Norman door with reset heads of monsters, a bishop and a king; but these are the principal old parts. The rest is William Butterfield's work of 1859, of red and white brick within.

At **Wythall** (2/5B), some 4 miles north-east, is the extraordinary church of St Mary. This remains closed while the restoration appeal raises funds to repair the roof, but in fact the exterior tells all. Its chief feature is the huge tower in scarlet brick pierced through by tall Gothic arches. It dominates the view for miles around and was added in 1903. The ugly brick does not make it easy to like; in stone it might have more closely resembled the 13th-century church in Normandy that inspired it.

Limebrook Priory *see* Byton

Lingen *see* Byton

Linton *see* Ross-on-Wye

Little Comberton *see* Bredon

Little Hereford *see* Tenbury Wells

Little Malvern *see* Malverns, The

Littletons, The (2/5E)

The three villages, North, Middle and South Littleton, lie to the north-east of EVESHAM in marshy meadows close to the River Avon.

North Littleton and **Middle Littleton** (2/5E) are almost one village, linked by a winding lane that runs beside a stream lined with pollarded willows. The great tithe barn at Middle Littleton (National Trust) is still part of a working farm. An informative display in the porch recounts its history. According to documentary sources it was built by the Abbey of Evesham in the 14th century, but carbon dating suggests a date of around 1260 (many monastic chronicles were written long after the events described, so discrepancies are not altogether surprising). All but the two aisle end bays of the barn are cruck-built – i.e. the simplest form of timber framing is used – and this fits the 13th-century date. Other indicators of the early date are the clover-leaf finials of the roof ridge, an intriguing survival of Scandinavian ornamentation that may have come to England with the Viking settlers.

Opposite the tithe barn is the lovely mid-17th-century Manor House, and across the fields the church of St Nicholas. The pretty tower arch inside, carved with roses, was probably reset here by F. Preedy when he rebuilt the church in 1871. The bench ends and pulpit all have 15th-century traceried panels.

St Michael's church at **South Littleton** (2/5E) is almost a twin of its neighbour, with similar bench ends and a Norman font decorated with rope moulding. Opposite is a house called Hathaways, a very fine brick building with timber mullioned and transomed windows and leaded lights, with parts dating from the 16th to the 18th centuries. Its beauty is compromised, however, by the massive arcaded chimney stacks and lantern weathervane (dated 1721), which makes the whole composition top heavy.

Offenham (2/5E), the next village westwards, stands on the banks of the Avon, surrounded by acres of greenhouses. Like Middle Littleton, the church of Saints Mary and Milburga received Preedy's attentions in 1861, and has a similar tower arch with leaf carving in the spandrels.

North-east of Offenham the B4510 meets the river by the appropriately named Fish and Anchor pub: it is popular as a mooring point for leisure craft, and much frequented by anglers. To the east Cleeve Hill rises abruptly from the flat, cultivated river terrace. The road climbs this hill and runs along its edge to **Cleeve Prior**, a village where all the houses are of stone, not of timber as might be expected.

On one side of the main street is the King's Arms of 1542, with contemporary barn and pigeon holes, alongside the Old Cider Mill which has ancient agricultural implements displayed on its front wall. Opposite these a footpath runs up to St Andrew's church, completely hidden from the road by barns and farmhouses; 17th- and 18th-century headstones line the path – including one to Sara Charlett that claims, incredibly, that she died aged 309 in 1693.

The 14th-century tower is unusually ornate, decorated with image niches and traceried sounding holes. The church underwent a thoroughly Victorian restoration in 1863. It has a richly coloured window of 1902 in memory of Elizabeth Warner. A sunset pastoral scene, worthy of Samuel Palmer, illustrates the words 'fast falls the eventide' from her favourite hymn 'Abide with me'.

Little Witley *see* Witleys, The

Llandinabo *see* Michaelchurch

Llanrothal *see* Garway

Llanveynoe *see* Craswall

Llanwarne *see* Michaelchurch

Longdon *see* Upton upon Severn

Longtown *see* Clodock

Lower Broadheath (2/3D)

The village, 3 miles north-west of WORCESTER, was the birthplace of Sir Edward Elgar (1857–1934). The cottage called 'The Firs' in which he was born, the fourth of seven children, is now a museum (open most of the year) containing photographs, letters, scores and other memorabilia of the great man, perhaps this century's most popular English composer. The museum is

Elgar's birthplace at Lower Broadheath

the starting point for the Elgar trail, a signposted 42-mile circular route taking in the houses he lived in and the places associated with his music. Trail leaflets are available at local Tourist Information Centres.

Cotheridge is on the A44, and 2 miles south-west of Lower Broadheath. The church is found down a track to Cotheridge Court, once home to one of the branches of the powerful Berkeley family. The whole exterior of St Leonard's church has been whitewashed – not just recently but over several centuries, so that a build-up of lime rather obscures the detail of the timber-framed tower. This is a pity because the lower stage of the tower looks distinctly like the nave of the Saxon stave church at Greensted, Essex.

At Cotheridge, the construction is identical: of tongued and grooved oak planks slotted into a timber cill. Similar techniques are used in the roofs of 13th- and 14th-century churches further west in the county, but the church here is Norman and it could be that the tower is earlier and therefore of national importance. Inside is a fine mid-17th-century pedestal pulpit, box pews and an 18th-century altar rail.

Lower Brockhampton *see* Bromyard

Lugwardine (1/4D)
As you drive eastwards along the A438 from HEREFORD, the road crosses the River Lugg before entering the village by means of a bridge that has stood since the 14th century. The big church of St Peter was remodelled in 1871, with the result that its chronology is now difficult to read. The eastern ends of the aisles, however, seem to have been the transepts of a large 13th-century cruciform church, of which the chancel, with its pointed trefoil head lancets, has survived unchanged.

The attractive cottage north of the village, ornamented with blank arcading and pilasters, is the late 19th-century former office of Godwin's brickworks.

Before this, though, a minor road leads from the A438 past the 17th-century stone Hill End farmhouse to **Weston Beggard** (1/4D). The oasthouses of the farmyard next door come right up to the north wall of the church of St John the Baptist, and the churchyard has a tiny bronze sundial, dated 1649, engraved with a smiling sun and set in a cross base. Inside the simple mainly 13th-century church is a sumptuous gabled tomb recess, carved with foliage and figures.

The A438 continues through Bartestree,

where the huge Gothic convent of Our Lady of Charity and Refuge, founded in 1863, is an unmistakable landmark.

Lyonshall (1/2C)
The village lies 2 miles east of KINGTON, and although much of the church of St Michael is G. F. Bodley's work of 1872, it presents a timeworn appearance. Mosses and lichens have colonized the stone roof tiles and the Victorian porch is as ornate as any 14th-century work, with cusped bargeboards pierced by quatrefoils. Inside is a very simple Jacobean communion table and a headless 13th-century effigy of indeterminate sex.

Remains of the large 13th-century castle rise behind the church, and on the opposite hill is an especially prominent stretch of OFFA'S DYKE.

Madley (1/3E)
This big village about 6 miles west of HEREFORD has a church of considerable grandeur, dedicated to the Nativity of the Virgin. The fine early 13th-century tower is the first striking feature, with stepped lancets in the first stage and pairs of lancets in blank arcades above; the Victorian battlements are out of keeping. Inside, the nave rises tall and wide, terminating in a long polygonal apse flooded with light from the large Decorated windows. The central one is filled with 13th- and 14th-century stained glass.

In the north aisle a 17th-century parclose screen re-uses pieces of 15th-century traceried panels; its mighty balusters are crowned with pineapple finials. It was later used as a family pew and retains wooden hatpegs and velvet curtains. The Chilston chapel in the south aisle has more fine woodwork: a Spanish or Portuguese reredos flanked by big pillars covered in luscious vineleaf. At the rear of the church, the splendid tombchest of Richard Willison (d. 1575) is covered in Renaissance portraits.

The church of St Michael in the neighbouring parish of **Eaton Bishop** has a substantial quantity of very fine 14th-century glass.

Some 2½ miles west along the B4352 is St Mary's church at **Tyberton** (1/2E). This stands in the grounds of John Wood's Tyberton Court, now demolished. The church itself may predate Wood's involvement, but it has splendid panelling, which he did in fact design, lining the chancel.

This itself is something of a surprise, because from the outside the pink brick church, completed in 1720, looks square-ended. Only on entering do you discover that it is apsidal under a coffered half-dome. The furnishings are all 18th century and complete, including box pews and candlesticks in the form of Ionic pillars.

Madresfield *see* Newland

Malverns, The

The Malvern Hills, which stretch for about 9 miles north to south, are the setting for the three places that bear this name.

Today's visitors, arriving at **Great Malvern** (2/2E) by car, miss out on the pleasures that awaited 19th-century travellers who, spilling out of railway carriages in holiday mood, were greeted by the grandest of railway stations. This 1861 building, now restored to pristine condition after a fire, is a splendid work of cast-iron tracery and florid capitals painted in a wide range of colours.

It could not be a better mood setter for the pleasures to come, for Great Malvern is a living textbook of Victorian architectural styles. The predominant theme is Italianate, but with admixtures of neo-Tudor, Jacobean, Grecian, Gothic, Queen Anne and even Scottish Baronial.

Detail on cast-iron capital, Great Malvern station

The only regret is that you cannot get close enough to study them all in detail, for many are set well back along the Abbey, Priory, College and Wells Roads, half hidden by trees. The National Gardens Scheme offers the best opportunity for a nearer view. Gardens occasionally open include those of Barnard's Green House, once the home of Sir Charles Hastings, founder of the British Medical Association, and of the Abbey School, West Malvern.

Priory Park, below the Winter Gardens, preserves typical Victorian planting. Around miniature lakes that once served as monastic fishponds, formal beds are planted between trees chosen for their showy flowers, bark and foliage. They frame views that naturally draw the eye upwards to where the bare hillside forms a clean and uncluttered contrast to the built-up lower slopes.

These are views that inspired Sir Edward Elgar, the town's most famous long-term inhabitant. Many of his works were written for the Malvern Festival, and performed in the pastel-pink Winter Palace. This was also the venue for the first performances of plays by George Bernard Shaw and J. B. Priestley.

Above the Winter Palace is the oldest part of town, dominated by the stately Malvern Priory. From the outside it is the ornate Perpendicular tower and windows that strike most; inside, nothing dilutes the impact of the noble Norman nave, built around 1120, that blends, with surprising harmony, with the Perpendicular clerestory. This, and most of the windows, are filled with 15th-century stained glass of extraordinary comprehensiveness.

The chancel misericords are typically bawdy and humorous. Most of these seats were carved around 1350 but the unusually detailed cycle of the Labours of the Months belongs to the mid-15th century.

The tiles that once covered the chancel floor have been mounted on a screen behind the altar. Malvern tilemakers supplied many of the parish churches round about, as well as the Priory, from their huge repertoire of designs. Here alone are 95 different motifs.

The buildings on Belle Vue Terrace above the Priory were formerly all hydrotherapeutic institutions. The Tudor Hotel was once Doctor Gully's Water Cure Establishment, where the sexes were segregated for the good of their health and the regime included cold douches at 6 am, followed by a brisk walk up the hills to take the waters. This latter part of the cure is

one that many modern visitors are happy to take, climbing the steep steps to St Anne's Well, named after the patron saint of springs, or on up to the 1395 ft summit of the Worcestershire Beacon.

To do so is to follow in the footsteps of the great, from the 14th-century poet, William Langland, to Sir Edward Elgar who said his spirit would for ever haunt the hills; from Queen Victoria to Sir Edmund Hillary, who went from this small peak to conquer the highest of all. From the top the views stretch from the Brecon Beacons to the Clee Hills of Shropshire, from the Cotswolds to the Severn Estuary. It is, as John Evelyn recorded in his diary, 'one of the goodliest views in England'.

Malvern Wells (2/2E), where the medicinal springs were discovered in the 17th century, lies south of Great Malvern. St Peter's church was built in 1836; some of the stained glass is of this date, but there is also later work, including a William Morris window of 1885.

Little Malvern (2/2E). The Roman Catholic church of St Wulstan in Wells Road receives many visitors, for it is the burial place of Sir Edward Elgar and his wife Caroline. Further along the same road is 'Craiglea', the house that was Elgar's home from 1899 to 1904.

Few groups of buildings look so inviting or well-composed as the Priory here and Little Malvern Court, framed by the wooded slopes of the hills behind. The Priory – the church of St Giles – seems higher than it is long, for all that survives are the tall tower and short chancel. A fine 15th-century screen divides the chancel from the altar and beyond it are stalls with carved armrests, one illustrating a fierce human head wearing a beard net.

The hatchments in the chancel bear the arms of the Beringtons, who acquired the Priory at the Dissolution of the Monasteries and have lived there ever since in Little Malvern Court (open on certain days in summer). This stands on the site of the cloisters and incorporates the 14th-century Prior's Hall or refectory, complete with its original five-bay roof of two tiers of cusped windbraces.

The house was a refuge for recusant Catholic priests in the 17th century and contains concealed rooms in which they could hide. The Berington family has remained Catholic and has made a

Opposite: Little Malvern Priory framed by the wintry woodland slopes behind

fine collection of 18th- and 19th-century vestments, displayed in the house.

Mamble (2/1B)
The village lies about 7 miles south west of BEWDLEY, in hilly country surrounded by the vestiges of ancient forest. From the outside the church of St John the Baptist looks pristine, and therefore suspiciously over-restored, but within it is nearly all early 13th century. The nave has a good king-post roof and the bell turret is supported on massive scissor braces. In the east window is a superb 14th-century Crucifixion, richly coloured and expressive. The 16th-century Blount Chapel, burial place of the local family that lived at Sodington Hall, is now roofless, its ruinous brick walls covered in ivy.

Bayton (2/1B) is just over a mile to the north. As would be expected from a church that once stood in the now-diminished Wyre Forest, St Bartholomew's roof is generously timbered, with massive tie beams and two tiers of arching windbraces. The chancel arch is of timber, too, inserted in 1905 but ageless in character. The fine Norman font is carved with interlace and panels of stylized foliage.

Mansell Gamage *see* Staunton on Wye

Mansell Lacy (1/3D)
Some 6 miles north-west of HEREFORD the village stands on the edge of the Foxley estate, once the home of Sir Uvedale Price (1747-1829). His views on landscaping, published as *An Essay on the Picturesque* (1794), were enormously influential in their time and converted Sir Walter Scott, among others, to the concept of naturalistic planting. Much remains of Price's own extensive woodlands to the north and west of the village, once admired by Wordsworth and many other visitors.

The churchyard is a good point from which to view the varied architecture of the village. Opposite is a much photographed early 16th-century cottage, timber-framed in part but with a stone cross wing whose gable is pierced with numerous pigeon holes. In the opposite direction is a courtyard farm whose big timber-framed entrance gate is crowned by a pyramidal roof and weathervane. It looks as if it was transplanted here from Normandy.

St Michael's church has a feline head of Norman date above the south door. The fine 15th-century chancel roof is of the trussed rafter type with curving soffit ribs.

The village of **Norton Canon** (1/2D), about 3 miles north-west of Mansell Lacy, has the handsome church of St Nicholas. Of pink brick under a stone roof, it was rebuilt in 1716, with a sensitive re-use of the medieval windows. The interior is less pleasing, having undergone Victorianization in 1868, and again eight years later: all the arches have alternate bands of yellow and white stone. The view through the clear glass of the east window is of the Rectory on the hillside above. Jacobean panelling has survived, along with a reredos, communion rails and altar of the same date.

Marden (1/4D)

Some 4 miles north of HEREFORD, Marden's church of St Mary stands less than 20 ft from the fast-flowing Lugg, in a churchyard that is managed as a conservation area; bulletins in the porch tell visitors which wild flowers are in season. The big church is filled with light from the Decorated windows of the polygonal apse.

Just south of Marden the road skirts a prominent tree-covered hillock rising from the flood plain of the Lugg. On it is the Iron Age hillfort of Sutton Walls. Quarrying has now eaten away much of the interior. Many skeletons were discovered when it was excavated, some decapitated and many with wounds. This has been interpreted as evidence of a battle between the Belgic inhabitants and Roman invaders.

Sutton St Michael and **Sutton St Nicholas** (1/4D) lie below the hill to the south; one village now but once two parishes, each with diminutive churches. St Michael's is a simple Norman building with the remains of a wooden weather-cock in the porch, and two fonts, both gems. One is Norman and supported by four lions, the other is a lovely mid-17th-century urn carried by an angel.

St Nicholas's church is larger only by virtue of its tower. Inside is a pretty chancel screen with linenfold panels and a double-decker pulpit.

Martley (2/2C)

This village, 6 miles north-west of WORCESTER, is the starting point for a tour that takes in some of the most delightful countryside in the northern part of the county.

The church of St Peter is a delight. In the churchyard there are some nice Victorian benches with cast-iron animal armrests, and the exterior of the nave has Norman strip pilasters and ornate doors. Inside, the chancel is covered with unusually pristine 13th-century wall paint-ings, mostly of ashlar and rosettes, but the east wall has curtains framing mythical beasts. There are 15th-century paintings in the nave.

From Martley the B4204 drops to Ham Bridge over the Teme and then climbs steeply to **Clifton upon Teme** (2/2C), a misleading name since the village is 2 miles from the river. Attractive Georgian redbrick and older timber-framed houses surround the green, and the restored church of St Kenelm contains two monuments by Grinling Gibbons. Both are recognizably in his style, with pendant bunches of flowers below the inscriptions, but are carved in marble rather than wood, his usual medium.

From Clifton upon Teme, a minor road heads west out of the village and after a ½ mile a turning to the left is signposted 'Lower Sapey Church'. This track descends through a delight-ful valley that has not changed since Arthur Mee visited it in the 1930s and wrote lyrically of its beauty, and of the sadness of the forlorn church.

The ancient church still stands – but only just, for it has been disgracefully neglected. A service is held once a year, with straw bales serving as pews, but the roof is holed and each winter takes its toll. Already the Norman wall paintings that can just be discerned – a horse and rider on the north wall – are probably lost for ever. This is a charming place, by the side of an ancient farmhouse with pond and humble barns, but voices ought to be raised in protest at the negligence before it is too late.

The village of **Upper Sapey** (2/1C) is 2 miles to the north-west. Here St Michael's church is surrounded by a cluster of cottages and farm-yards. The cottage by the path to the church has a fine carved timber door, perhaps by the same carpenter, John Kitchen, who undertook a good deal of the woodwork for the church from around 1860. His contribution might easily be mistaken for much older work, for the panelling in the chancel, the pulpit and the benches are in the same rustic spirit as two genuinely 16th-century panels at the rear of the church, beside the splendid Norman tower arch.

From here a roller-coaster of a road (the B4203) passes north-eastwards through wood-lands to **Stanford on Teme** (2/2C) where St Mary's church stands on one of the many prominent hillocks of this undulating country-side. It was built in 1768 and the huge tower, as tall as the nave is long, gives the building a foreshortened appearance. Victorian restoration and awful stained glass have robbed the interior of its 18th-century elegance.

The redundant church at Michaelchurch

From these peaceful heights the road descends eastwards to Stanford Bridge, built in 1905 with pretty wrought-iron railings. The view is marred by a caravan site and hot dog stalls, for the bridge and its pub are a popular mooring point for leisure craft on the River Teme.

From here the road ascends to the farming village of **Stockton on Teme** (2/2C), a mile to the north, where barns and rook-filled trees surround St Andrew's church. This has a 14th-century south porch of massive timbers and cusped windbraces, a miniature version of the roof within. The complete and well-preserved chancel arch is carved with two charmingly inept versions of the Lamb of God and the Lion of St Mark. The excellent stained glass is based on that in the Accademia in Florence.

Mathon (2/2E)

The village enjoys a pretty position in the western foothills of the MALVERNS. Herring-bone masonry on both sides of the thick nave wall indicates a Norman date for the church of St John the Baptist and the 14th-century roof is a fine example of the local style, with its two tiers of windbraces.

Cradley (2/2E) is a mile to the north, a village of pleasing timber-framed cottages. St James's church is largely Sir George Gilbert Scott's design of 1868, but there is a length of Anglo-Saxon carved frieze in the tower wall. The parish hall in the churchyard is 15th century, timber-framed with a jettied upper storey, and was once the village Grammar School.

Michaelchurch (1/4F)

Five miles west of ROSS-ON-WYE, the tiny church of St Michael is parishless and maintained by the Redundant Churches Fund. It is a low building of the utmost simplicity, standing in a hollow by the pond. A Roman altar, now used as a holy water stoup in the north doorway, is inscribed with a dedication to the 'god of the crossroads'. The existence of this altar almost certainly points to a religious site of considerable antiquity.

The nave and chancel are continuous, divided only by a simple screen and filled with pews of indeterminate date. A kneeling angel and St Michael slaying a dragon decorate the bench ends.

Michaelchurch is one of the few English place names in this formerly Welsh-speaking part of the county. More typical of the region is **Llandinabo** (1/4F), about 2 miles to the north. Here village and church are both named after the Celtic Saint Dinabo, of whom little is known. The church is nothing like so ancient: a good late Victorian building, surrounded by a tidy farmyard of old stone barns, dovecot and a late 17th-century house.

The church has a remarkable early 16th-century screen with typically Tudor motifs: dolphins, mermaids, exotic fish, and figures hidden among cornstooks. It also incorporates a medallion carved with a grotesque face – an early example of a popular Jacobean style.

At **Llanwarne** (1/4F) the ancient church of St John the Baptist is now a roofless ruin standing in a well-tended churchyard. The new Christ Church was built in 1864 and is reached through wrought-iron gates, up steps and under the entrance arch of the fanciful tower. The font is a lovely 17th-century piece carved with swags and acanthus leaf, and the nave windows contain many Continental stained glass roundels.

Michaelchurch Escley (1/2E)

This tiny hamlet in the far south-west of the county is almost the sole settlement in the valley of the Escley Brook, which runs parallel to the ridge of the Black Mountains to the west. The north wall of St Michael's church is painted with a rare depiction of Christ surrounded by 30 or more tools, such as shears, rakes, axes, wheels, saws and scissors.

The subject has been interpreted as a warning to Sabbath breakers that they wound the body of Christ by their work. Equally, it has been attributed with an opposite meaning: that Christ blesses the humble workman.

Middle Littleton *see* Littletons, The

Middleton on the Hill *see* Kimbolton

Moccas (1/2D)

Not even Spain or France has a more perfect Romanesque village church than this Norman one. St Michael's has none of KILPECK'S sculpture, but is perfectly proportioned, with a series of descending roofs from nave to chancel to semi-conical apse. It is built entirely of local tufa, a delicate pink, spongy, but surprisingly hard and durable rock. It was formed – recently, in geological terms – from calcium carbonate deposited by lime-rich springs as they bubble out of the hillsides here, some 10 miles west of HEREFORD.

Inside, arches from nave to chancel and from chancel to apse form a perfect sequence. The windows contain only the architectural canopies from a 14th-century stained glass sequence of saints; the saints themselves have been lost to the iconoclasts' hammers.

The church stands in the peaceful grounds of Moccas Court (open on Thursdays in summer). The house was built in 1775 to Robert Adam's designs and, although externally plain, contains a sumptuous circular drawing room in Pompeian style and an elegant hall with curving staircase. Capability Brown was one of several garden designers who contributed to the landscaping. His style is evident in the deer park; the terraces that lead down to the River Wye have been attributed to Humphry Repton.

Blakemere (1/2D), to the south-east of Moccas is an attractive hamlet of red-brick Georgian farm buildings and older timber-framed cottages standing beneath tree-covered Blakemere Hill. St Leonard's church was rebuilt in 1877, but the pulpit is a striking piece composed of 17th-century panels and balusters, and the font is Norman, decorated with rope moulding.

To the east of Blakemere the road heads back to the flat river meadows and the village of **Preston on Wye** (1/2D). St Lawrence's church sits handsomely beside the red-brick Preston Court. The Court's owners have made a colourful garden in the former farmyard, with beds around an old cidermill and shrubs planted right up to the church gate: a lovely approach to the church, which contains massive rustic benches and a graceful Jacobean pulpit.

Monnington on Wye *see* Staunton on Wye

Mordiford (1/4E)

The best approach to this village is from HEREFORD, eastwards along the B4224. This road affords the best views of the broad meadows beside the Lugg, crossed by a 16th-century causeway, with a 14th-century bridge over the river. The church and handsome Georgian rectory stand side by side, closing off the prospect.

The surrounding landscape is watery and liable to flood, since the Frome and the Lugg meet just north of the village, and the Lugg flows into the Wye just to the south. Yet none of these has caused as much chaos as the tame-looking Pentaloe Brook, which flows through the heart of the village. A note in the porch of the Holy Rood church records that this swelled to 20 ft deep and 180 ft wide during a storm in 1811, sweeping away buildings and drowning four villagers.

The church has a Victorian arcade whose capitals are carved with hopflowers and berries.

Due north of the village is Sufton Court (open occasionally in summer), a Palladian house of Bath stone, designed by James Wyatt in the

1780s, that sits handsomely in Humphry Repton's open park. A short distance north is the house that preceeded it, Old Sufton, dating in part to the 15th century and home of the Herefords since the Norman Conquest.

On the opposite bank of the Wye to Mordiford is **Hampton Bishop** (1/4E), a village that is almost entirely encircled by the ancient embankment thrown up along the river as a protection against flooding. St Andrew's church is Norman (except for the timber-framed upper stage of the tower) and it contains a 15th-century stone reredos which, although damaged and missing the images that once filled its niches, is still a rare survival.

Due south of Hampton Bishop, in this gentle pastoral landscape of flat meadows rising to wooded hills, lies **Holme Lacy** (1/4E). This large estate belonged to Walter de Lacey until the 14th century, when it passed to the Scudamore family. The grand Palladian stone house, the building of which began in 1672, can just be seen from the road; but the Grinling Gibbons woodwork that once ornamented it has been scattered far and wide – some is now at KENTCHURCH, some in the Metropolitan Museum, New York. Near by, St. Cuthbert's church is full of theatrical monuments.

St Cuthbert's church was considerably remodelled at the same time as the house was being built and is oddly plain, with a plaster, tunnel-vaulted interior.

Dinedor Hill is a ridge that rises to 500 ft, about midway between Holme Lacy and Hereford. It has a large Iron Age hillfort on its summit, and is worth climbing for northward views of Hereford Cathedral.

Mortimer's Cross see Aymestrey

Much Cowarne see Ullingswick

Much Dewchurch see Kilpeck

Much Marcle (1/5E)
The combination of the church, the house called Hellens and Weston's ciderworks makes a visit to this village, some 4 miles south-west of LEDBURY, well worth while.

The path to the church passes the great Marcle yew, a tree whose age can only be guessed at; its hollow trunk is 30 ft in girth and contains benches able to seat eight people comfortably; yet still it flourishes, with branches spreading 70 ft across.

Its scale is worthy of St Bartholomew's church, a huge building with a long, tall 13th-century nave and a group of outstanding monuments. First among these is the strikingly beautiful and naturalistically carved figure of Blanche Grandison, née Mortimer (d. 1347).

By contrast the impressive painted wooden effigy of Walter de Helyon (also mid-14th century) is rustic work depicting a giant of a man, fully 6 ft 4 in from head to toe.

Finally, the Kyrle Chapel has two monuments, one a late 14th-century tomb of an unknown knight and his lady, the other that of Sir John Kyrle (d. 1650) and wife, a triumph of the mason's art.

On leaving the church it is worth walking all the way round to the north, where a tree-covered mound is all that remains of one of the Mortimers' castles.

The entrance to Hellens (open weekends and Wednesdays in summer for guided tours) is opposite the turning to the church. Named, perhaps, after the de Helyon family, this is a lovely manor house in mellow Tudor and Jacobean brick, full of original furnishings, tapestries, armour and family memorabilia. The charming terraced gardens, laid out with box hedges, contain an octagonal brick dovecot built in 1641.

H. Weston and Sons ciderworks is on the A449 Ledbury to ROSS-ON-WYE road. Products can be sampled at the shop and tours of the plant can be arranged (see also 'Cider making' pp. 144).

Munsley see Pixley

Naunton Beauchamp see Spetchley

Newland (2/2E)
This northern suburb of Great Malvern (see Malverns, The), on the A449 WORCESTER road, has a church that is remarkable for its 19th-century wall paintings. St Leonard's was built in 1864 to serve the Beauchamp Almshouses, endowed in 1863 under the will of the 3rd Earl Beauchamp. The almshouses themselves are built in an extraordinary mixture of styles: they include a large French Gothic gatehouse with a steep pavilion roof and a neo-Tudor accommodation range built around a quadrangle.

The nave and chancel walls are covered in frescos designed by T. Gambier-Perry. The scenes are drawn in red and green outline, very simple, like a child's picturebook, but powerful in their overall effect. The ceiling is painted in gorgeous colours and there is a fine set of chancel gates in wrought iron with gilded flowers.

One mile south-east, **Madresfield** (2/3E) is within sight of Great Malvern but reached down leafy lanes and distinctively rural in atmosphere. Madresfield Court, the home of the Lygon family, is generally accepted as the inspiration for Evelyn Waugh's *Brideshead Revisited* (1945). The gardens are open one day a year under the National Gardens Scheme and are well worth visiting, especially for the chapel, which is a treasure house of Arts and Crafts furnishings.

The parish church of St Mary was built in 1866 by F. Preedy. It has a number of remarkably reticent monuments to the Lygon family, simply recording names and dates. William Lygon, the 7th Earl Beauchamp (1872–1938), was the model for Lord Marchmain in *Brideshead Revisited*.

North Littleton *see* Littletons, The

North Worcestershire Path. This recently designated footpath is 30 miles in length, and for much of its route follows the county's northern boundary with the West Midlands and Staffordshire. It is not an arduous walk and passes mainly through largely agricultural landscapes, taking in the country parks of the LICKEY HILLS, WASELEY HILL, CLENT HILLS and KINGSFORD (*see* Kidderminster). There is a visitor centre at Waseley, and guides to the route are available at local Tourist Information Centres.

Norton *see* Harvington (near Evesham)

Norton Canon *see* Mansell Lacey

Oddingley *see* Huddington

Offa's Dyke Path
The history of this earthwork is recounted under Offa's Dyke Path (*see* Glos.). Unlike neighbouring Gloucestershire and Powys, Hereford and Worcester has few outstanding sections of King Offa's great earthwork; the best stretch is at LYONSHALL, and KINGTON has a good section just to the north-west. Nevertheless, the Path takes in some spectacular upland countryside, notably the knife-edge ridge of the Cat's Back, between Cusop and Longtown, where the views to either side are of the arcadian Ewyas and Olchon valleys.

Offenham *see* Littletons, The

Interior of St Martin's church, Holt

Ombersley (2/3C)
Four miles north of WORCESTER, this is a picturebook English village, especially when seen from the south over the cricket pitch looking towards the slender spire of the church rising above black-and-white gables.

It does not matter that St Andrew's church was built in 1825, it still looks the part, in Decorated style with flying buttresses from the tower to the spire adding poise and delicacy. In the very large churchyard are the remains of the old church, used as the Sandys family mausoleum. The interior of the new church features wooden galleries, box pews and a stove in high Victorian Gothic style in deference to its ecclesiastical setting.

Ombersley Court, to the west of the church, is the home of the Sandys family. This Georgian house is chiefly distinguished for its splendid interior.

Opposite the church are several substantial

red-brick estate houses with trefoil-headed windows in the gables. Dotted around them are early timber-framed cottages.

North-west of Ombersley, at Boreley, is Clack's Farm, open on occasional weekends. This is the setting for the popular 'Gardening Time' television programme.

At Sankyn's Green, 2 miles to the west, Eastgrove Cottage Garden is open most afternoons in summer. It has a collection of old-fashioned hardy plants growing in the grounds of a 17th-century timber-framed house.

Two miles west of Ombersley, at Holt Fleet, Telford's 1828 bridge carries the A4133 across the River Severn and, shortly after, a concreted farm track leads to St Martin's church, **Holt** (2/3C). The setting must once have been idyllic, just the church and the 14th-century castle opposite. Now sand and gravel pits ring the south-western horizon and a sea of vegetables, part of a market garden, laps up against the churchyard.

The Norman church, one of the most profusely decorated in the county, is always firmly padlocked and information about the key is simply not to be had. This rare obstructiveness serves to make us more thankful for the trusting majority who keep their churches open. Fortunately there is almost as much to see outside the church as within. The south door is carved with interlace, a fine dragon and a grimacing head. Windows are ornamented with chevrons and a string course of vine leaves run beneath them, continuing on the north side where the doorway is carved with a fox and a goose drinking from a barrel.

Two miles south of Ombersley the National Trust-owned Hawford dovecot, a 16th-century half-timbered building, is open daily in summer.

Orleton *see* Richard's Castle

Overbury *see* Bredon

Pebworth *see* Honeybournes, The

Pembridge (1/2C)
Some 6 miles west of LEOMINSTER on the A44, this small town – or large village, perhaps – is Hereford and Worcester's half-timbered counterpart, in terms of consistency, to the best of Gloucestershire's stone villages. All the houses are timber-framed, with not one ugly or out-of-place building to destroy the unity. They date from the 14th to the 19th centuries. Nearly all

The detached tower of St Mary's church, Pembridge

have brick nogging infill between the studs of their box frames, some gentle red to pink, others painted white.

A few, such as the New Inn, have gabled cross wings and projecting upper storeys. This pub forms a group around the Market Place, off the main road, with the early 16th-century Market House and the former Rectory, now a shop, whose bargeboards are carved with dragons, fruit and flowers.

St Mary's church continues the theme of fine timber architecture. The impressive detached 14th-century tower is akin in its structure to the stave churches of Norway and the bellhouses of Sweden. The first stage is an octagon of four long and four short sides, roofed in stone. It forms an ambulatory around the dramatic structure of scissor-braced timbers that support the upper bell stages.

The church itself is of cathedral-like proportions. It was begun in 1320, but not completed for 40 years as the Black Death intervened. Its noble arcade rises on octagonal piers, and the nave is lit by unusual clerestory windows, shaped like five-petalled flowers.

The 17th-century woodwork is among the best in the county: a talbot, or hunting dog, attacks a dragon on the reading desk, and the pulpit is carved with wyverns, sphinxes and ornate foliage. The communion rails consist of a delicate sequence of flat, pierced balusters.

North of the village, Bridge Street runs down to the River Arrow where footpaths lead westwards along its peaceful banks to the Rowe Ditch, an ancient earthwork of uncertain date. It is possibly an 8th-century predecessor to OFFA'S DYKE, which can be seen 4 miles further west at LYONSHALL.

Pembridge Castle *see* Garway

Pencombe *see* Ullingswick

Pensax *see* Rock

Peopleton (2/4D)

This village between WORCESTER and PERSHORE is typical of the south-east of the county, where the population growth since the Second World War has been so rapid that new housing smothers the traditional core of church, manor, rectory and timber-framed cottages.

St Nicholas's church is Perpendicular, with an early 19th-century brick tower encasing the older timber belfry. Parts of a 15th-century wagon roof and a contemporary oak door to the vestry survive. The original rood beam, now by the tower arch, is elaborately carved with foliage on one side, but bare on the other face, which would have been up against the chancel wall.

Stoulton (2/4E), just over 2 miles to the west, is another village that has grown rapidly, with developments including recent conversions of redundant farm buildings. You can understand the need for new housing without liking the form it takes – especially here, where garishly coloured tile and brick, and ginger-coloured doors and window frames predominate, instead of more natural, softer colours.

St Edmund's church is far enough away from all this to be enjoyable. It is essentially Norman, with flat pilaster buttresses and two projecting doorways ornamented with blank arcading. The 14th-century nave roof is beautiful, with arched braces and cusped struts forming a quatrefoil pattern in the apex of the trusses.

Pershore (2/4E)

This town some 8 miles south-east of WORCESTER cries out for a bypass to relieve its handsome streets of the heavy burden of traffic. Fortunately, the Abbey is well away from the High Street in its own peaceful green precinct.

What remains of Pershore Abbey since the Dissolution of the Monasteries is largely the buttressed chancel and weighty tower. It all looks massive, but it is one of the great achievements of medieval architects that, no matter how solid their works look from the outside, the interiors are often surprisingly light, airy and spacious. The Abbey surprises us in just this way. On entering, the eye is immediately drawn upwards to the lantern tower, such a feat of gravity-defying architecture that you wonder how the building stands up. It is 14th-century work and so like the interior of Salisbury Cathedral's tower that both have been tentatively attributed to the same architect.

Next you notice the arches and lierne vaults of the chancel, above the exuberant ripples of the many-shafted arcade piers. What at first appears to be the work of one period in fact dates from two. The arcade and clerestory were built before 1239; the vault was reconstructed after a great fire in 1288, yet blends perfectly with the earlier work.

Besides these immediately striking features there is the Norman work in the south transept to be discovered. This dates from an earlier building, probably begun in 1090, which was also partly destroyed by fire. Contemporary with it is the Norman font, carved with apostles, but much weathered from its long use as a garden ornament.

The former parish church of St Andrew lies to the east of the Abbey, a Norman building enlarged in the 15th century and now used as a parish hall.

The town's best houses are at the junction of Broad Street (once the Market Square), Bridge Street and High Street. The ashlar-fronted Three Tuns Hotel has a delicate Regency ironwork veranda that would not look out of place in Cheltenham. In both directions on either side, the road is lined with brick houses, many with Venetian or bay windows, pedimented doorcases and fanlights.

Bridge Street leads south to the River Avon and the largely 14th-century bridge, whose central arch was blown up by Royalists in 1644, alongside the modern one. Over the bridge is the Pershore College of Horticulture, whose ornamental gardens, arboretum and high-tech glass-houses are occasionally open in summer.

Opposite the College, a minor road leads off the A44 to **Wick** (2/4E). Wick Manor is a brilliantly deceptive building of the 1920s that looks authentically ancient. It draws all its motifs from local architecture; multiple gables are jettied out over oriel windows with leaded lights to form everybody's dream of a perfect house.

Opposite, St Bartholomew's church looks wholly Victorian but is completely Norman within, except for a 15th-century wagon roof and Jacobean communion rail.

Birlingham (2/4E) lies about 2 miles south-south-west of Pershore. The village church of St James, surrounded by a stone wall topped with coping stones, looks older than its date of 1871. Built of limestone under a Cotswold tile roof, it has weathered to a lovely golden, lichen-covered pile. Inside, the arches are made of contrasting bands of sandstone and limestone.

Defford (2/4E) is a mile to the west, across the A4101, the next village west. St James's church has a timber-framed bellturret, and a dormer window in the nave roof lights the simple Georgian musician's gallery. The little elongated female head, re-used as the keystone to the south door, is Norman.

A mile to the north-west, the church of St Peter at **Besford** (2/4E) is unusual for being built almost entirely of timber. The nave is 14th century with wooden traceried windows and queen-post roof; the belltower and spire were added in 1880 by William Hopkins.

Besford Court, north of the village, is now a school and can just be seen from the road. Part of it is a fine early 16th-century timber-framed building with a gateway and oriel window. Much of the rest is inspired neo-Tudor work of 1912 by Randall Wells.

Peterchurch (1/2E)
This village some 10 miles west of HEREFORD styles itself the capital of the Golden Valley and is a good base for walking – either along the old railway track that follows the River Dore, or up on the surrounding hills and commons.

Despite a new spire of fibreglass on its 13th- to 14th-century tower, St Peter's church is largely an exceptionally unspoiled Norman building of great size. A noble series of arches, diminishing in height and width from west to east, leads the eye to the Saxon altar in the domed, apsidal sanctuary. All the windows are deeply splayed, their sills cut in a series of steps, and even the south door still hangs on its original Norman hinges.

Just north-west of the church is a bridge over the Dore and the beginning of a footpath that follows its course for 1½ miles south-eastwards to **Turnaston** (1/2E). The river was diverted in places in the 19th century when the Golden Valley railway from Pontrilas to Hay-on-Wye was built; the original river bed can be seen at various points along the route.

St Mary Magdalene, at Turnaston, is a pretty church with a wagon roof and several interesting monuments.

Vowchurch (1/2E) is just to the east, across the Dore; St Bartholomew's church stands by a pretty bridge over the river. Its queen-post roof has such a profusion of heavy timbers that the walls were inadequate to carry the weight without the assistance of wooden pillars of tree-trunk dimensions. The rustic screen, dated 1613, is carved with the figures of Adam and Eve below the Forbidden Fruit: pears here rather than the more traditional apple.

Pinvin see Throckmorton

Pirton (2/3E)
This is the northernmost of a group of villages in the flat meadowlands to the east of the MALVERNS that are watered by the River Severn to their west and the River Avon to the east. Pilgrims heading for Tewkesbury (*see* Glos.) must have passed this way, for Pirton's church of St Peter contains a replica mould (the original is in the Ashmolean Museum, Oxford), believed to be for casting ampullae. These slim, flat-sided tin vessels were sold as souvenirs to pilgrims, who would fill them with holy water. The 13th-century mould is of stone and incised with the Crucifixion, the Virgin and St John.

The church also has an interesting 14th-century tower, timber framed with side wings and massive crucks. The rest of it is Norman; unusually, both doors have survived with their original 12th-century ironwork. The figure of St Peter, patron of the church, has been set in traditional manner upside down at the apex of the chancel arch.

The church of St Mary Magdalene at **Croome** is a mile to the south. The key is obtained from Corner House, at the corner of the Pirton to Severn Stoke road. The church was open until thieves struck twice in successive years, stealing the exquisite 18th-century wooden font, 17th-

Monument to the Earls of Coventry in the church at Croome d'Abitot

century oak chairs and even the stone figures from the Coventry monuments.

Despite these thefts, the church remains a great delight, one of a very small number whose interior and furnishings were designed by Robert Adam. The exterior, attributed to Lancelot (Capability) Brown, is rather forbidding, so Adam's delicate plasterwork inside comes as a complete surprise. Its elegance is somewhat compromised by the clutter of family monuments, placed here by the 6th Earl of Coventry after the church was completed in 1763; the tombs themselves, however, are remarkable. The earliest has been attributed to the workshop, if not the hand, of Nicholas Stone. Thieves have desecrated it by stealing the figures of Justice and Virtue that flanked Thomas, 1st Lord Coventry (d. 1639), who was Lord Keeper of the Great Seal. Grinling Gibbons carved the effigy of the 4th Lord Coventry (d. 1687), with attendant figures.

Lancelot Brown and Robert Adam were also responsible, respectively, for the exterior and interiors of Croome Court, begun in 1751. There is a perfect view of the house, with the Malverns beyond, from the churchyard. The future of the house and estate is uncertain and many of Adam's most gracious plaster ceilings were stripped out after the Second World War, some to end up in the Metropolitan Museum in New York.

Government grants, however, have been used to maintain some of Adam's lovely classical garden buildings, including the temple-like Panorama Tower of 1766 that stands on Knight's Hill, clearly visible from the road from Croome to Severn Stoke.

The church of St Nicholas at **Earl's Croome** (2/3E), about 2 miles south of Croome, has a neo-Norman tower but the rest is genuinely Norman, including the 12th-century plank door and ironwork. The delightful chancel arch frames the splayed east window containing a colourful 1864 stained glass Crucifixion. The shafts have the same chevron ornament as the north and south doorways, and the imposts are carved with oak leaf and a rampant lion.

Pixley (1/5E)
Recorded in the Domesday Book as *Picheslei*.

There is nothing here now except a farm on the A4172, 3 miles west of LEDBURY, and the little church of St Andrew, whose 14th-century roof is a forest of long pegs, fixing the arched braces to the tie and collar beams. The chancel screen is of massive plain timbers and visitors are forced to bow piously on passing under as the central arch is so low. Pretty glass in the east windows depicts two Pre-Raphaelite angels in rich green velvet cloaks.

Less than a mile south, just off the same A4172 – a dead-straight, originally Roman road – is **Aylton** (1/5E). Again, the church is tiny, with scarcely any churchyard, flanked by an 18th-century farmhouse, pond and ancient barns, in a poor state of repair. The oak chancel screen is assembled from 15th-century woodwork totally without respect for symmetry or pattern, a strange work that must be a constant distraction for parishioners at prayer.

At **Munsley** (1/5D), 2 miles to the north of Pixley, there is another diminutive and isolated church. It looks Victorian externally, but has a nice plain Norman round-headed chancel arch and deeply splayed windows. An odd stone in the nave wall is covered in a barely legible inscription. The letters E, O and Y are just decipherable. The last letter is a rendering of the Old English letter *thorn*, standing for the 'th' sound. The letter continued in use well into the 18th century, so the verdict on whether or not the stone is Saxon, as claimed, must remain open.

Powick *see* Worcester

Pudleston (1/4C)
Although over-restored, St Peter's church is worth seeking out for the sake of the delightful countryside east of LEOMINSTER. Getting there, along any of the winding lanes, some gated, is more than half the pleasure; especially if your taste is for unspoiled countryside, meadows cut by streams, full of grazing sheep and cows, gently undulating wooded hills, and the occasional distant view.

The church fits naturally into this landscape, for the lichens and mosses on its sandstone roof tiles lend colour and an appearance of great age. The tower, indeed, could be Saxon with its characteristic long and short-work quoins. Much of the rest dates from rebuildings of 1813 and 1851, with glass by A. W. N. Pugin, not his most inspired work. However, the Victorian Gothic woodwork in the chancel is very splendid.

Immediately south of the church is the castellated gatehouse of Pudlestone Court, and a little further on the house itself can be seen, an eccentric Gothic building of 1846 surrounded by terraced gardens above Stretford Brook.

St Leonard's church at **Hatfield** (1/4E), 2 miles further east, is endearing for its simplicity. A monolithic tufa tympanum, carved with a lozenge pattern, is surrounded by Norman herringbone masonry up to the eaves. The tub font is just a hollowed-out boulder and the chancel arch a simple unadorned arc.

Queenhill *see* Upton upon Severn

Redditch (2/5C)
This is a large, relatively new town. Despite its size it retains a rural atmosphere by virtue of the many hawthorn hedges and trees that once enclosed fields and now – having, very sensibly, been kept – screen new housing estates from view. Old Redditch was, and remains, a centre for the manufacture of fish hooks and needles. The National Needle Museum, situated off the A441, 2 miles south-west of Beoley (*see below*), is housed in an 18th-century mill on the River Arrow. It reveals, through models and exhibits, the many varieties and uses of these humble pieces of pointed steel.

Beoley (2/5C) The church of St Leonard here is found halfway up a steep hill north of Redditch, invisible from the road and surrounded by trees, directly opposite the prominent Norman motte known as The Mount. It is a pleasant, well-kept church with a Perpendicular sandstone tower, fine tombstones east of the porch and an unusual half-timbered clerestory window.

Four steps lead up to the chancel and the two impressive Renaissance monuments to William Sheldon (d. 1570) and his son Ralph (d. 1613). Both are very fine examples of lifelike portraiture in painted stone.

The Sheldons founded the English tapestry weaving industry. William hired Flemish weavers to teach English craftsmen their skills; one of his principal workshops was at Bordesley, now a suburb of Redditch, just 2 miles west of here. Surviving examples of their highly prized work can be seen in the Victoria and Albert Museum, London.

The church of St Peter at **Ipsley**, in the south-eastern suburbs of Redditch, contains good alabaster reliefs of Nicholas Huband (d. 1553) and Sir John Huband (d. 1583). The Hubands owned Ipsley Court next door. This is now a handsome courtyard office development for the Law Society which incorporates some of the surviving 17th-century buildings. The church and Ipsley Court stand on a hill above the River Arrow, now dammed to provide an ornamental lake surrounded by a public park.

Ribbesford *see* Bewdley

Richards Castle (1/3B)

St Bartholomew's church stands below the castle on a hill on the Shropshire border. Richard FitzScrob was a Norman who arrived in 11th-century England before the Conquest and built the castle, and founded a settlement that never grew beyond a scattering of cottages around the bailey. It was to be abandoned in favour of the village in the valley below, but later parishioners could still count on the shelter of the big detached bell tower in the churchyard, built about 1300, if they needed a stronghold. In the 14th century the church was considerably enlarged by the addition of an ornate aisle and transept, built to serve as a chantry chapel for the Knights Hospitallers.

In 1743 the church was heightened to its present great size. The parishioners must have continued to trek up the hill in sufficient numbers to fill the church, since its stone-flagged nave was furnished with box pews, a semicircular musicians' gallery, and a completely enclosed family pew for the Salweys, lords of the manor.

Since then, the numbers have fallen away and now the church is redundant, recently restored, and well worth visiting for the lonely splendour and the sense of forgotten history all around.

By contrast, **Orleton** (1/3B), 2 miles south, is a prosperous village with much recent housing that makes it no longer quite the pretty village described by previous visitors like Arthur Mee, writing before the Second World War. Even so, several outstanding and untouched timber-framed houses have survived west of the church. St George's church is crowned by an outstanding king- and queen-post roof and contains an excellent Hereford School Norman font. Nine of the Twelve Apostles are carved under arches in a style that gives the whole piece a Byzantine appearance.

Ripple *see* Strensham

Rochford *see* Tenbury Wells

Rock (2/2B)

In the hills about 4 miles south-west of BEWDLEY, St Peter's is an impressive and very accomplished Norman village church, the best of a group in the northern part of the county that all have elaborate doorways set in a projecting portal. There are three orders of columns and six concentric arches to the porch, each carved with a different ornamental motif, one being a much simplified form of beak head stylized to the point that the beaks are little more than flat darts. The nave and chancel, moreover, have flat buttresses, a string course and much eroded corbel table.

Inside, the tall nave arcade is Perpendicular with characteristic octagonal piers and flat arches, but the chancel arch is again Norman and so richly decorated that scholars have detected the same hand at work here as at SHOBDON – that of one of the founding masons of the Hereford School.

Two miles south at **Pensax** (2/2C), the church of St James hides away at the end of a long footpath. Trees grow so close up to its walls that only the porch and tower are visible until the last moment. Expecting something relatively humble, the visitor is surprised by its grandeur: convincingly Perpendicular in style, it was in fact built in 1832. Recent repairs to the fine roof have been sensitively carried out.

Romsley *see* Clent

Ross-on-Wye (3/2C)

The approach from Bridstow (*see below*) on the opposite bank of the Wye is the most beautiful. Visitors park on the bridge to admire the view of the town rising from the flat river meadows, with the tall spire of St Peter's church soaring above the houses that cling to the sides of the sandstone cliffs. Since the 18th century this view has attracted tourists. In the 19th century they used to arrive by river steamer from Chepstow or Monmouth. The Royal Hotel, built in the 1830s, was part of an ambitious plan not only to accommodate them but to become itself an enhancement to the skyline. At the same time, the western approach was convincingly 'medievalized' by the addition of mock Gothic town walls with arrow slits and a round tower.

Perhaps none of this would have happened were it not for the philanthropy of John Kyrle (1637–1734), known as the Man of Ross for his generous benefactions. He donated the Prospect cliff-top gardens to the town, and, in dedicating them to public enjoyment, effectively prevented

The Market Hall in the square at Ross-on-Wye

building along the riverside, so preserving the famous prospect.

Kyrle did much more than this, however, giving freely from a legacy he had inherited. His money provided the town with a water supply, and repaired the church spire. The narrow streets of Ross above the Market Place are lined with handsome red-brick and timber houses – again built with money loaned by Kyrle, who insisted only on being consulted on the design.

Alexander Pope considered Kyrle a paragon and in 'Of the Use of Riches' (1733) praised his spending on practical projects for the public benefit, rather than on vainglorious fountains and waterfalls.

St Mary's church, which includes 13th- and 14th-century, as well as Perpendicular work, contains an unusual and fitting memorial to Kyrle. In the spot where he used to pray in the north aisle, two creepers, planted in troughs, grow up the walls and window tracery. Originally two elms grew here, said to have sprung up spontaneously at the death of the man who so loved trees.

The east window has a complete set of 15th-century stained glass, moved here from the residence of the Bishops of Hereford at Stretton Sugwas. A plague cross in the churchyard marks the common grave of the 315 victims of the epidemic that struck Ross-on-Wye in 1637.

Bridstow (3/2C). The village stands on the opposite bank of the river to Ross-on-Wye. Immediately north-east of the bridge, and south of the busy A49, is the ruinous, ivy-hung Wilton Castle, originally built around 1300 by the de Greys, now standing in the grounds of a hotel. The church of St Bridget has a Perpendicular tower, Norman and Early English features inside, and much 1862 work outside.

The village of **Upton Bishop** (3/3C) is 3 miles north of Ross-on-Wye. The chief reason for visiting the church of St John the Baptist is the sculpture on the outside wall of the chancel, placed here during Sir George Gilbert Scott's 1862 restorations. It consists of a near-complete Roman tombstone, missing the inscription but showing the head and shoulders of a man with raised hand in a niche. It resembles late Roman Christian funerary sculpture and so could be 5th century in date.

A mile south, on the other side of the M50, is the church of St Mary at **Linton** (3/3C). The nave arcade has big columns of tufa on which the later arch does not sit comfortably. The Perpendicular tower is an ambitious structure with a lierne vault. A few enjoyable tombstones are found on the north side of the churchyard – 18th-century and carved with cherubs.

Rous Lench *see* Lenches, The

Rowlstone *see* Ewyas Harold

Severn, Wye and Teme

WILSON STEPHENS

Three rivers frame the Three Counties scene and dictate the routes of travellers. The Severn is famed 'worldwide, the Wye nationwide; history has paused at their banks. The Teme is the essence of Worcestershire.

All three flow from the Powys mountains. Their common origin keeps alive the long-receded presence of Wales, a past wildness still just perceptible behind the settled Englishness of farms and villages, and the assured grandeur of mansions and churches. They set the tone for the way of life. Habits and values have changed little in their valleys. The best of the past survives sturdily. The rivers have maintained local privacies and kept identities separate.

The Severn enters north Worcestershire from Shropshire at Upper Arley. It is a wide and peaceful river there. Its 180 miles make it Britain's longest. Cargo boats navigated it for half its length during the centuries when it was the chief route into and out of England's heartland. Its breadth made long stretches of it unbridgeable until the Industrial Revolution. Even now, despite our ability to change the face of Nature, it still channels east–west roadborne traffic to relatively few crossing points.

Those first Worcestershire miles tell why. The weight of water from countless mountain tributaries gave the Severn the power to cut across the grain of the country in primeval times. Only where high ground on either side narrowed it into a gorge could bridges be built. Where it flowed wide, unconstrained, and liable to flood, ferries were needed.

Bewdley, just south of the Shropshire border, has grown up in one of the gorges, the little town hanging steeply above its bridge. In winter flood, brown with topsoil swept down from upstream, and bearing an overload of wrecked farm gates and uprooted trees, the Severn is an awesome sight. In summer she provides a place of pleasure.

She? We moderns think of rivers as masculine: Father Thames for instance. But this was not always so. The Romans thought Severn feminine. To them she was Sabrina, the name of the guardian goddess of the great vale that, in present terms, stretches from the Black Country to Wales. The question that confronted armies and colonizers alike still confronts the motorist. Where do we get across?

Geography and human need combined to space the Severn bridges ten miles or so apart. Next below Bewdley is Stourport, where cabin cruisers now tie up instead of the barges that loaded and offloaded there in pre-railway times. Above the confluence the Stour provided a water route to the craftsmen's villages that grew together and became Birmingham.

A modern bridge further south at Holt provides a third road westward above Worcester. That city has two bridges, one old, one new, but the widening river has no other crossing point until Upton upon Severn, the customary ten miles further down, a gracious place that seems to have been designed to persuade bridge users to break their journey here.

Then comes a great leap across the M50 downstream of Ripple, where the motorway bridge, although modern, nevertheless has its symbolism. The haste and pressures it represents are hoisted up and away from the lanes and villages, the woods and orchards where the life of the countryside goes quietly on. The nearest thing to a metropolis that anybody needs hereabouts is ancient Tewkesbury, where Shakespeare's Avon joins the Severn. The bridge and wharf here have been economic power centres since time immemorial.

Tewkesbury was the downstream limit for bridges while the map of England was taking shape. Below it the Severn was thought too big to be bridgeable until some adventurers put the second minor road across it, from Apperley to Tirley. Other visionaries decided that Gloucester could not for ever remain cut off from Hereford and the highway bridge was built outside the city near the hamlet of Over.

Until our own time that was enough. The Severn south of Gloucester has outgrown the name of river. The gulls wailing round the cathedral towers are the first voices of the sea. Southward the country flattens on the eastern bank and a maritime countryside opens out beside the sandbanks, mudflats and the tide-scoured channels where cargo ships come and go and salmon trappers ply their secretive craft.

Here begins the Severn Sea, as the locals prefer to know it. Here too, defiantly representing our dying century, is the last bridge of all. The Severn Bridge, hugely elevated and storm-rocked, is the road artery of South Wales; whether temporary or permanent, only time will tell.

The Severn Bridge, from the west

With hundreds of feet between wheels and water, Severnside is scarcely a reality to those who cross by this bridge. The full flavour is far away, in the rural intimacy of the middle reaches, where the Three Counties' nine bridges draw travellers to themselves and have given lasting seclusion to the miles between.

Up and down the river away from the bridges, Severnside is a land of roads to nowhere, most of them made to serve the ferry points of bygone times. Big flat craft, looking clumsy yet worked with great skill, shuttled ceaselessly across. They could carry the squire in his dogcart, a four-horsed wagon, a flock of sheep, schoolchildren, the parson on his rounds, or a single old woman with a basket of eggs on her way to market. They were great, relaxing equalizers.

The small worlds of local villages became even smaller when motor transport brought bridges within reach of all and put the ferries out of business. But the old outlook, the social ease and openness, survives, far from the madding crowd. Still self-contained, they are still friendly, too, to visitors who do not cause nuisance.

In full maturity, England's longest river flows through a lush landscape. Severnside is rich land for corn, beef or dairy; and Sabrina is a friendly goddess, even at her worst. When the river bursts its banks and spreads miles wide across the fields,

cathedral, have often been under water just when they were needed.

Severnside is best seen in summer, except by fishermen who are impervious to weather. In sunshine months the river is bright with pleasure boats. Each bend opens up a new vista for those aboard, each old-time port a chance for exploration. The bankside miles between have their picnic spots, their freedom, and their peace and quiet for those who choose with care, anywhere above Gloucester. Below, the scene changes.

The tide flows past Sharpness, still an active port for timber boats and seasonally for more exotic trades, to the broad reach of Framilode. This is where to observe the famous Severn bore that at certain times sweeps upstream from the sea – a great wave produced by the conflicting pressures of spring tides against descending landwater. But already the river is becoming an elusive presence, distant instead of intimate as the view radically alters.

The Cotswolds, majestic in the background of Gloucester's silvery stonework, fall behind. On the opposite bank the Forest of Dean looms darkly. Lost between them, the Severn seems to have put to sea already, leaving behind a wide, open estuary sacred to the wind and little lonely villages. The sound effects confirm it. No more the voices of rooks and wood pigeons; instead the cries of sandpiper, plover and redshank thread the wind. This is wild goose country – Slimbridge, Sir Peter Scott's bastion of the northern hemisphere's waterfowl populations.

But it is hardly time-out country for family parties and individual enthusiams. For that we must return upstream. For fishermen and their families the Severn has a special attraction, but calls for a warning. Big rivers must never be trusted; even where they seem innocent there can be deep holes, cross-currents and undertows. Except where river bathing is clearly organised, with safety precautions, to swim or paddle in it is to ask for trouble.

Practically every species of British freshwater fish can be caught in the Severn, nearly all of them in the Three Counties reaches. So big a water makes local knowledge – more than can be given here – essential.

The best of middle Severn angling is for coarse fish. Associations, clubs and hotels hold rights on much of it. Nearly all allow permits to visitors, as do many farmers. The Severn–Trent Water

Authority Fisheries Division, Meadow Lane, Nottingham (0602 865007), gives advice and issues rod licences.

From tidal water upstream roach, chub, bream, dace, and perch are well distributed wherever the water suits the species; carp and tench are only occasional, in backwaters. Severn pike are often heavyweights, but barbel are the river's pride, bigger and better than ever in recent years. These powerful, athletic fish lie wherever deep currents are strongest and the river bed cleanest. Bridge piers channel the flow and produce this effect – those at Bewdley are greatly favoured.

Most Severn salmon are caught in Wales. But they have to get there somehow, and the prospects are good for anglers who know their resting and taking places *en route*. Diglis Weir at Worcester is one such (a special permit is required); there are others near Bewdley. Trout and grayling fishing begins to be good there, too. Big river tactics are best for trout, with emphasis on spinning.

Everything happens at Tewkesbury. Salmon lie there before running the weir, and for fishermen seeking something new, twaite have a brief season in early summer. This herringlike shad breeds nowhere else in Britain.

Below Tewkesbury the elver catch is not only sport but business. Elvers are young eels that hatch in the Sargasso Sea and are carried by the Gulf Stream to the European rivers where they grow. They enter the Severn in multi-millions, and are netted wherever the current carries them close to the bank. Elver-pie feasts (not forgetting the beer) are traditional in south Gloucestershire. Commercial netting in the tideway produces mass catches shipped in tanks from Sharpness docks to Holland and Germany. The annual take of elvers has been enormous over many centuries, yet the population of adult eels within the Severn watershed remains enormous too.

Lampreys still thrive in the main river and tributaries wherever water of the right depth and cleanliness flows over the right bed at the right speed. But these pernickety creatures are difficult to catch in quantity. They live by bloodsucking other fish, and when not feeding anchor themselves to stones.

Towards the sea, beyond that last great bridge, a rocky beach interrupts the miles of sands and mudflats, insignificant except in name. It is called the English Stones. It bears an English label because the opposite bank is looked on as Welsh – anywhere west of Chepstow, where the Wye joins the Severn Estuary. So meet the two rivers that characterize the east and west of the Three Counties.

The Severn near Arlingham, south of Gloucester

Shorter, less exploited, but still a formulator of human history, the Wye has more contrasts than links with the Severn although they rise only two miles apart. The Wye outgrows its turbulent youth in Wales before crossing into Herefordshire at Hay-on-Wye, behaving thereafter in the bland manner that Welsh folk sometimes regard as typically English. Where the Severn's flow suggests in musical terms a march, the Wye has a *largo* progress – expansive, serene, grand. The place names on its banks bear witness.

The opposition of Celt and Anglo-Saxon repeatedly recurs. Villages duplicate, with the river between, one for each nation – Welsh Bicknor and English Bicknor for example. The odour of sanctity from a once-almighty Church pervades both banks, and even the fishing rights: Eaton Bishop, Canon Pyon (to distinguish it from King Pyon, Church versus State yet again). Brampton Abbotts, and that shrine for salmon fishers the Dean and Chapter Pool, mirrored repeatedly by others similar, are the legacy from centuries of well-entrenched clerics unashamed of leading the good life.

Except for its last miles, where its gorge divides Gloucestershire from Monmouthshire, and visitors converge on Tintern Abbey, St Briavels, Brockweir, and the finale of Offa's Dyke, all the Wye's English course is in Herefordshire. This is England's least-changed county. Ways of life essentially unaltered by the two world wars, although now much enriched and immensely eased, are the basis of the peace that typifies it.

This was not always so. The Wye itself, and the mere name Hereford, express what went before. Even less than the Severn, this was not a river

Wintour's Leap from the 'Eagle's Nest' viewpoint on the Wyndcliff Walk near Chepstow

where men thought of bridges in the pioneering days a thousand years ago. Had they been built, the wrong people might have crossed them. Better to leave things in a state of nature, so the old-time settlers thought. Let those who wished to cross get wet; that at least discouraged casual visitors from Wales, even if it did not always stop them. For non-casuals, stronger measures existed.

Hereford, like the similarly named Herford in Germany, probably meant a place where the river could be crossed by defending Anglo-Saxon forces (*Heer*, meaning army, survives in modern German). The 'army ford' now designates the cathedral city for all the world, but for locals a score of other Herefords exist as villages, hamlets, farms and field names, reminding where bygone soldiers passed to death or glory on what was the more bloodstained of England's land frontiers.

When life settled, and civilization enabled the Wye to be crossed dry-shod, prosperity spread. A hundred Herefordshire acres can make a family fortune from the white-faced cattle that now graze around the world. The economic background affects visitors to the river, and the fishing rights.

Stock raising has implications for security and public safety. The Wye fishing rights are divided between private owners and associations or clubs. In either case they are valuable assets costing more to maintain than more casual waters. Nevertheless permits or memberships are sometimes available.

The Wye is taken seriously by anglers of all kinds. Throughout its length it is England's greatest salmon fishery. It is also outstanding for coarse fishing, especially around Ross-on-Wye, and for trout and grayling higher up. Most of its salmon anglers are incomers from across the

The River Wye near Fownhope

country and from abroad; its coarse fishers commute in hundreds from Birmingham. All soon learn that the Wye also has moods and hidden dangers, which every newcomer should heed.

Above Hereford, the bed often consists of football-sized boulders, rounded by centuries of abrasion. They look innocent, but they can roll beneath the weight of a wading man, with perilous consequences; the whole river bed seems to move like an ever-deepening escalator. Safety depends on sense, experience, and skill with an iron-shod wading staff to give anchorage.

Below Hereford the pace slows, the pools deepen, and much fishing is done from moored punts. Here the great angler Robert Pashley fished the Kerne and Goodrich waters, achieving

his lifetime's record: a self-estimated 11,000 rod-caught salmon.

Between the two big rivers flows another, by comparison almost a secret stream. Bred in the same Welsh hills, the Teme comes into Hereford-shire at Leintwardine, digressing briefly into Shropshire. It then returns to the Three Counties to become the figurative life blood of Worcester-shire, scenically underrated, but well representing England as we hope she will remain.

The Teme has left no great mark on history. Men in a hurry are little conscious of the winding valley, for miles open and bright with orchard blossoms in the spring, in places deep-cut and secret. This river is a cult as much as a waterway, a magnet for some widely differing people.

High up at Leintwardine the keynote comes from the calls of curlew, dipper, ring ouzel. These wide open stretches draw fly-fishers, especially connoisseurs of grayling, those fish of very pure water only, the colder the better; here they have both.

River alterations below Worcester have freed the salmon spawning route and the Teme has the king of fish back after years of near extinction. At Tenbury Wells and the next ten miles downstream hopes are highest.

Tenbury is the Teme's unofficial capital, where all its interests meet. Boat people, anglers, walkers, naturalists, huntsmen in winter, car rally folk in summer, all make this small spa their headquarters. Downstream the river snakes between the uplands of the Clifton Hills, where steep gradients and sandy tracks, as at Shelsley Walsh, are challenges to sporting motorists.

Thereafter the river falls under the spell of Worcestershire: quiet, well-groomed, prosperous and above all natural, the essence of what the English see as home.

One drawn more than most to this calm landscape was Sir Edward Elgar, the composer. That embodiment of Englishness distilled Worcestershire into his music as he walked the banks of the Teme.

It is not far from Knightwick Bridge to Worcester city, but there is plenty of Teme still for those who do their exploring with thorough-ness and tact. Through picnic country past Broadwas, Leigh and Bransford, and across the meadows where Cromwell's Roundheads defeated Charles II in 1651, the Teme flows on like a minor Wye. The attractions are on a smaller scale but the hazards just as great. All kinds of fish can be caught there, from salmon on a fly to minnows in a jam pot. But this river, too, can be a fickle friend to those who are having most fun. Best be safe.

The River Teme: (above) fish can just be seen in this stretch near Shelsey Beauchamp; (opposite) the river near Eastham

Rushock *see* Elmbridge

St Margarets *see* Abbey Dore

St Michael *see* Tenbury Wells

St Weonards (1/3F)
This village lies some 7 miles west of ROSS-ON-WYE, in delightfully hilly country. Both village and church are named after a little-known Celtic saint who is depicted in stained glass holding an axe, suggesting that he was a woodcutter.

Some 16th-century German glass, in the aisles and depicting St Peter walking on the water, was bought in HEREFORD market in 1952. There is also a small Flemish frieze of Abraham about to sacrifice Isaac (with a woodman's axe). Other treasures that make this church interesting include a lovely brass Empire candelabrum, Jacobean box pews, screen and pulpit.

The church stands on a prominent mound, proud of all the surrounding countryside and visible for miles around. Close to it is a small tump, which local people once believed covered the golden coffin of St Weonard. It was excavated in 1865 and revealed two Bronze Age cremation burials.

Salwarpe *see* Droitwich

Sedgeberrow *see* Childswickham

Sellack *see* Hoarwithy

Severn Valley Railway *see* Upper Arley

Shelseys, The (2/2C)
These twin villages stand either side of the River Teme, about 3 miles north-west of MARTLEY. The church of All Saints at **Shelsey Beauchamp** is spectacularly sited above the river valley. It was rebuilt in the Early English style in 1846. We can only wonder why the architect chose red sandstone for the church, soft and liable to erosion, when hard limestone was locally abundant in the region. (This is now quarried commercially.)

The Normans knew better, for they used the pale pink tufa or 'travertine' from nearby Southstone Rock to build the church of St Andrew at **Shelsey Walsh**. This material, one of the youngest rocks, has a hole-filled, spongy, soft appearance, but is in fact very durable.

The little church stands on the steep wooded slopes of the Teme valley, overlooking a cluster

St Andrew's church, Shelsey Walsh

of timber-framed cottages. On most days the valley is peaceful, the only sounds those of birds and farmyard animals; but occasionally the roar of tortured engines is heard on the hill climb above the village.

St Andrew's has possibly the finest Perpendicular chancel screen in the county. It is richly carved with vines and leaf tendrils, while its arcades are filled with delicate tracery and its dado with linenfold panels. The chantry chapel, later used as the Squire's pew, is surrounded by a parclose screen with the same lovely carving Above this, the roof is equally extraordinary, the apex of the truss being filled with panels cut through by foiled circles. Painted stars cover the ceiling boards.

Shobdon (1/2B)
A visit to Shobdon, about 6 miles west-north-west of LEOMINSTER, is rewarded by the remains of one of the most important Norman churches in England and its successor, an extraordinary Gothick confection. Both are in the grounds of Shobdon Court, but there is public access to the churches.

The dull exterior of St John the Evangelist

Bateman around 1752. A visit to his friend Horace Walpole's house at Strawberry Hill infected him with enthusiasm for the Gothick (the earlier intention had been to build a chinoiserie church, which would have seemed even more exotic).

An endearing feature is the fireplace in the Bateman family pew that takes up the whole south transept.

The Norman font from the earlier church is carved with four bold lions. The porch contains a series of drawings executed in 1852; these are well worth studying, since they show what the original church looked like before its sculptures in soft sandstone were virtually destroyed by subsequent exposure to the elements. What remains of these sculptures can be seen at the end of a steep avenue, half a mile long, where they were assembled and built into Shobdon Arches, an 'eye-catcher' north of the Court. Just recognizable now are Christ in Majesty in a mandorla, some Zodiac symbols, interlace and dragon heads – sufficient to show that this is sculpture of extraordinary accomplishment and greatly superior to run-of-the-mill Norman work.

We know that the sculpture was commissioned by Oliver de Merlimont in the mid-12th century for the new church he built on return from a pilgrimage to Compostela. It is not known whether he employed Continental craftsmen, but the local masons quickly learned to produce what he wanted and developed the distinctive style characteristic of the Hereford School. The best-preserved example of their work, with strong resemblances to the Shobdon sculpture, can be seen at KILPECK.

Snodhill Castle *see* Dorstone

Sollers Hope *see* Woolhope

South Littleton *see* Littletons, The

Spetchley (2/3D)
Three miles east of WORCESTER, the gardens of Spetchley Park (open daily in summer, except Saturday) are as much a delight to the interested

St John the Evangelist's church, Shobdon

amateur gardener as to the dedicated plantsman. They were laid out in the late 19th century by Rose Berkeley with the help of her sister, the great gardener Ellen Willmott.

The 30 acres of formal garden are themselves but an entrée to the splendid park laid out in the mid-17th century, where herds of red and fallow deer graze beneath the great cedars planted by the diarist John Evelyn, a friend of the Berkeley family. The house (not open) is a dignified Bath stone structure with an Ionic portico, built around 1811.

All Saints' church is outside the grounds, high up on an embankment below the cast-iron bridge that links the two halves of the park. The outstanding south chapel was built in 1614, re-using 13th-century windows, as the Berkeley mausoleum.

About 2 miles south-east of Spetchley is **White Ladies Aston** (2/4D), so named because of the colour of the habits of the Cistercian nuns who owned the manor. The tall bell turret and spire look incongruously modern since the weatherboarding was renewed, but the massive timbers inside betray their true antiquity.

Naunton Beauchamp (2/4D), 2 miles south,

is a compact village of timber-framed houses, the substantial former homes of prosperous yeoman farmers. A huge cedar tree dwarfs the Perpendicular tower of St Bartholomew's church; the rest was rebuilt in 1897 but contains much good 16th-century woodwork.

Stanford Bishop see Acton Beauchamp

Stanford on Teme see Martley

Staunton on Wye (1/2D)

This orchard village is 10 miles west-north-west of HEREFORD. Its church of St Mary contains an extraordinary set of carvings dating from the latter years of Henry VIII's reign – the 1530s or 1540s. They consist of six portrait medallions, subsequently set in Jacobean panelling here, in the style that is peculiar to the English Renaissance. The women have exaggeratedly flat brows and pointed noses, the men braggart beards; all have headgear of astonishing extravagance. They are wholly secular in spirit and so may have originally been made for one of the big local houses.

The churchyard overlooks acres of apple orchards with the silvery gleam of the Wye just visible. Down in among them, the church of St Mary at **Monnington on Wye** (1/2D), a mile to the south, takes some finding. A grassy track leads off the road to follow a brook and only after a quarter of a mile does the little church come into view. It is worth the effort, for nothing inside has changed since it was built in 1679. The most recent innovation, itself of some antiquity, consists of the oil lamps that still light the church.

A large and colourful coat of arms of Charles II indicates the date of the handsome benches, pulpit and lectern that fill the nave. The font is dated precisely, 1680, along with the initials VMT, for Uvedall and Mary Tomkins, former inhabitants of Monnington Court, who paid for the rebuilding and furnishings.

The hamlet of **Mansell Gamage** (1/2D) is on the opposite side of the A438 Hereford road, at the entrance to the Garnons estate. The house of 1860 stands in fine grounds landscaped by Humphry Repton. It is well worth visiting for the gardens (open under the National Gardens Scheme), especially in spring when the surrounding orchards have begun to burst into riotous bloom.

Stockton on Teme see Martley

Stoke Bliss (2/1C)

This village in a landscape of gentle hills is some 5 miles north of BROMYARD. Its relative remoteness did not, in this case, save the church from rebuilding in 1854; but it looks very fine from a distance, with a sweeping roof from high ridge to low aisle walls. The restorers kept the 1635 lectern and 1631 pulpit, carved with dragons and fantastic figures. Pretty oil lamps on the bench ends have been converted to electricity.

Stoke Edith see Dormington

Stoke Lacy see Lillingswick

Stoke Prior (2/4C)

The industrialized stretch of countryside between BROMSGROVE and DROITWICH has acquired the status of a historical landscape. It is cut through by the WORCESTER, and Birmingham Canal, dating from the great canal-building era of the 18th century, with its multitude of locks, still busy with leisure craft. Stoke Prior itself is a monument to the philanthropy of John Corbett, the man who did so much to make Droitwich a popular spa in the 19th century. His saltworks, south of the village where the Worcester to Birmingham Railway meets the canal, were a model factory designed to provide congenial working conditions for his employees. The factory was begun in 1828 following the discovery of substantial rock salt deposits.

Corbett built many of the cottages in the village, and the school dated 1871 bears his crest, the east window of St Michael's church commemorates the abolition of female labour from his factories in 1860. Surprisingly, the church itself escaped improvement; it might be thought a prime candidate for Victorian aggrandisement, but Corbett's beneficence was, mercifully, secular. Thus it has survived as a substantially Norman church with a sturdy tower, built at the time in the early 13th century when round arches were just giving way to the pointed lancets of the Early English.

North of the village is the excellent **Avoncroft Museum**, a remarkable collection of historic buildings rescued from demolition and re-erected on a 15-acre site beside the A38 Bromsgrove bypass. Recent additions include an 18th-century tollhouse from Malvern, and the New Guesten Hall from Worcester with its magnificent 14th-century roof. An audio-visual presentation explains the many buildings on the site, from a three-seater earth closet to a postwar prefab.

onish, wanting nothing to do with 'Brindley's stinking ditch', as they called it, the Staffordshire and Worcestershire Canal was cut to join the Severn some 3 miles south of that town. Almost nothing existed here until the canal came in 1771, so the town of Stourport is wholly a late 18th-century creation, built around the wharfs at the meeting point of the canal and the Rivers Severn and Stour.

Today, the canal is still a source of prosperity and employment, for The Basin is full of leisure craft, and yards are kept busy repairing old narrow boats. The riverside west of the 1870 Severn bridge has been laid out as a public park. The streets leading up from the river east of this bridge contain some of the oldest and most attractive buildings.

The 18th- and 19th-century inhabitants of Stourport were not snobbish enough to want to distance themselves from the source of their income, and so we find in Bridge Street and York Street brick town houses intermixed with warehouses, a diverse and interesting prospect. Only New Street is wholly domestic, lined with Georgian terraces and a diversity of doorcases and fanlights.

The High Street is somewhat meaner; built for commerce, not for show, most of the shops and houses that line it are low and unadorned. St Michael's church was originally of brick, built in 1782, but was swept away for a more ambitious building designed by Sir George Gilbert Scott in 1875. Work did not begin until 1881, by which time Scott was dead and his son, John Oldrid Scott, supervised the building. In the end, neither the chancel nor the tower were built, so the church consists just of a lofty six-bay nave.

On the opposite bank of the River Severn is **Areley Kings** (2/3B). Its church of St Bartholomew is at the northern extremity of the village, overlooking Stourport, but with a rural feel. The Norman font is inscribed with the name of Layamon, the author of one of the first epics written in the English vernacular, who was a priest here in the late 12th century. In his poem 'Brut' he describes the promontory on which this church sits and the sudden drop north of the churchyard which reveals the River Severn in the fields below.

it was furnished as a library using oak from the former village windmill.

Strensham (4/2B)

This place is known to regular users of the M5 as the site of a motorway service area. How many of those who stop at this symbol of the modern motor age realize that a delightful church lies just across the fields, to the north. St Philip and St James is isolated in fields and, although not interesting as a building, contains a complete set of oak furnishings of various dates. The nave is filled by early 16th-century pews, linenfold panelling and wooden hat pegs. The enclosed family pew is Jacobean and the double-decker pulpit 18th-century.

The west gallery, carried on pillars from the former chancel screen, is fronted by a set of 23 painted saints under tracery arches, dated to the end of the 15th century. Thus far the church gives the impression of having remained almost

18th-century stable and granary, Avoncroft Museum

untouched since the Reformation and is therefore a rare treasure on that ground alone. However, a further surprise awaits in the chancel, for it contains brasses galore. By the 17th century brasses were out to be replaced by alabaster effigies, which are also well represented here.

There is yet more to discover: a Norman font, 15th-century encaustic tiles, 17th-century hatchments and 18th-century painted boards all add to a church that is outstanding and undemonstrative in the typical English way. It has survived, although the village has gone. Visitors who arrive at Strensham in the evening can shut their ears to the motorway noise and from the churchyard enjoy dramatic sunsets above the sweep of the MALVERNS.

At neighbouring Upper Strensham, west of the motorway, there are the Russell Almshouses. Lower Strensham has the 18th century Moat Farmhouse.

Two miles west of Strensham, still within sight of the M5, is another outstanding church in the village of **Ripple** (4/1B). St Mary's is a noble building, nearly all of the late 12th century, with transepts marking the transition from Norman to Early English and then a rebuilt late 13th-century chancel, well lit by the big Decorated windows.

The 15th-century stalls are remarkable, for the misericords have survived untouched and every one is carved with a lively narrative scene, full of detail – better, even, than the more famous seats in Malvern Priory or HEREFORD Cathedral. There are 16 in all, representing the Twelve Labours of the Months, plus Day, Night, Sun and Rain. The carving is so crisp that we can even pick out such details as mittens on the figure by the fireside in December, or seed being scattered broadcast in March.

Stretton Grandison *see* Fromes, The

Stretton Sugwas *see* Burghill

Suckley (2/2D)

In the gently hilly country around BROMYARD, north-west of the MALVERNS, there are few villages of any size, but many fine manors and farmhouses. One such is the White House, 1 mile north of Suckley, a lovely Queen Anne building. As its name suggests, this has had its original brick whitewashed. The village church, of St John the Baptist, is a domineering building of 1878 but with richly decorated capitals to the chancel arch, carved with ferns and birds.

The lane to Alfrick runs south through cuttings in the red sandstone, meets and then follows the Leigh Brook through a very pretty wooded valley. It turns sharply north at Tundridge Farm, a house worth stopping to admire. The earliest part of the farmhouse is boldly studded with timbers and the original mullioned and transomed windows have survived, projecting out from the walls under tiled dripmoulds.

Next, the lane crosses the brook at Mousehole Bridge before climbing the hill to **Alfrick** (2/2D). Here, St Mary Magdalene church has everything scaled down to doll's house dimensions, from the diminutive tower and spire to the tiny chancel and low entrance door. Did it give Lewis Carroll ideas? His brother was curate here and Carroll used to stay with him in the Rectory. The nave walls of the church are only just tall enough to admit windows, and these contain many panels of 16th- and 17th-century glass from the Netherlands.

Just north west of the village, the Knapp and Papermill Nature Reserve consists of 60 acres of varied woodland, marsh, stream and meadows. Nature trail guides are available from the Warden's house.

Sutton St Michael and Sutton St Nicholas
see Marden

Tardebigge (2/4C)

Traffic thunders along the A448, linking BROMSGROVE and REDDITCH, that splits this village in two. To the east is the village centre; to the west the graceful church of St Bartholomew stands alone, its slender elongated spire visible to everyone who travels this road. To say that it is well worth halting for is an understatement, for it is a gem of 18th-century architecture.

It is believed that a church has stood here from the earliest times. But when the tower of the old church collapsed in 1775, it was decided to build anew. The architect was Francis Hiorne, from WORCESTER, and outstandingly talented, as can be seen from this and his church at Tetbury (*see* Glos.), which he worked on simultaneously.

The portico and tower are admirable, rising by stages to a baroque bell chamber with columns and urn finials, then sweep up to the needlepoint tip of the spire. The inside is light, airy and dramatic, with the apse (added in 1879) forming a theatrical punctuation to the long nave.

Flanking the chancel arch are two wall monuments. One shows Lady Mary Cookes (d. 1693) and her husband, affectionately embracing.

story is linked to the equally apocryphal story that Sir Thomas killed his butler in a drunken rage, said to explain the hand grasping a red dagger in the family crest.

Many of the splendid furnishings are the work of local men and women who, along the lines of Arts and Crafts movements elsewhere, were encouraged to keep crafts alive under the patronage of Robert George, Earl of Plymouth. He himself designed the reredos and the upper part of the Ascension window.

Below the church is one of the most interesting sections of the Worcester and Birmingham Canal: a flight of nearly 40 locks raises the cut by 300 ft over a 3-mile stretch.

Tarrington *see* Dormington

Tenbury Wells (1/4B)

This town on the Shropshire border, some 9 miles north-east of LEOMINSTER, might have been very different if the discovery of a mineral spring in 1839 had led to anything. Bath houses were built in 1862 by the Kyre Brook, at the south end of Teme Street, in an attempt to emulate the MALVERNS and DROITWICH. These buildings, halfway between a gaudy Victorian greenhouse and Gothic folly, are now boarded up.

Tenbury is all the better for its failure to develop as a spa for it is now a town that belongs very much to the local farmers. They come into town to buy essential supplies, so the streets are full of friendly talk and greetings.

The northern approach to Tenbury crosses the Teme, a good fishing river, over a medieval bridge decorated with Victorian ironwork. Along Teme Street, the main street of the town, an extraordinary number of Victorian and Edwardian shop fronts has survived. Some are classical with dentil cornices and Corinthian columns; others are of no particular style, but carved and painted with emblems of the countryside, oak leaves, corn stooks and foliage.

At the south end of the town the road twists east, past the decorative Jacobean Royal Oak and into the Market Square. Here, the 1811 Market House stands exactly as built, an oval of brick with Gothic windows and fitted with ranks

flood damage, for the Teme flows round the western edge of the churchyard and occasionally changes from gentle stream to unruly torrent.

Fortunately the Norman tower was saved, together with the 13th-century chancel with its Easter sepulchre. Among fragments of masonry in the north aisle is the shaft of a cross carved with crisp interlace. Its Northumbrian style dates it to the late 9th century.

Along the south-western exit from the town the road comes upon a wide stretch of common and, at the end of it, a building that looks like a French cathedral. This is the church and college of **St Michael** (1/4B) built in 1856 by the Rev. Sir Frederick Gore Ouseley, priest and baronet, composer and student of ancient music, who founded the school, convinced that English church music was in the doldrums. Henry Woodyer designed the steep-roofed church and its wooden cloister; the excellent stained glass is the work of John Hardman.

To reach **Rochford** (1/5B), it is best to take the B4204 east from Tenbury then, after a quarter of a mile, the unclassified road that leads off it and follows the River Teme for 2 miles. The hamlet consists of little more than a farm, and through its yard a path leads to St Michael's church, sitting right on the bank of the Teme beside a motte and bailey, built to defend a now defunct river crossing. The church is a wholly Norman building with a projecting north portico carved with a Tree of Life tympanum.

The stained glass in the east window, in memory of Sarah Clarke (d. 1863), is by William Morris, an early example of his work, and shows angels playing musical instruments and a Nativity. Surprisingly, it is outshone by the 1951 glass in the south nave window, of a fiery and colourful Archangel Gabriel. The church also possesses a pretty chamber organ of German origin, made around 1810, with a walnut case, surmounted by a double-headed eagle.

Little Hereford (1/4B). About 3 miles west of Tenbury Wells, and miles from its bigger namesake, this hamlet has a most handsome church – wholly unadorned but in its massing and materials near to perfection. The tower is of pink sandstone under a tiled pyramidal roof and adjoins the steep-pitched roof of the barn-like nave. Tall lancet windows and the tower arches date St Mary Magdalene to the 13th century, but its stately simplicity is timeless.

Thornbury see Edwyn Ralph

Throckmorton (2/4E)

The village, 3 miles north-east of PERSHORE, was abandoned not only by the villagers but also by the squire; for the Throckmortons moved to Coughton, over the border in Warwickshire. What the visitor sees now is the lonely church surrounded by ridge and furrow, the bumps and hollows of the deserted village and the moat that once surrounded the manor.

The simple church therefore received little attention from the 13th century until the 19th, when the village began to grow again and some restoration work was carried out, in the same style as the earlier work.

The road to **Pinvin** (2/4E) skirts the disused Second World War airfield. St Nicholas's church is ingloriously surrounded by cabbage fields; the reason for visiting it is the 13th-century wall paintings under glass in the nave, simple outline drawings with little colour or modelling. The Nativity and the Crucifixion are the best preserved.

Tibberton see Huddington

Turnaston see Peterchurch

Tyberton see Madley

Ullingswick (1/4C)

About 5 miles south-west of BROMYARD, the little church here stands in a remote position and contains two gems: in the east window a lovely 15th-century Virgin and Child; and in the nave an unusual monument to John Hill (d. 1591). He lies in an ermine-trimmed gown, but the family might not have been as wealthy as this would suggest: the monument is merely a painting on stone, a much cheaper alternative to a sculptured effigy. As well as his wife, daughter and two sons kneeling around him are two pathetic bundles in shrouds, the children who died in infancy.

At **Pencombe** (1/4C), 2 miles north, the church of St John is a neo-Norman riot of zigzag used in profusion and without a care for correct precedent. The tower, however, is good and stately and the apsidal chancel has a boss carved with a dragon.

Attractions in the immediate neighbourhood include the famous Herb Gardens at **Stoke Lacy** (1/5D), open all year, and Symonds Cider and English Wine Company (tours by arrangement) in the same village; see also 'Cider making', p. 144.

The church of St Mary at **Much Cowarne** (1/5D), south of Stoke Lacy, is a grand building for a now sparsely populated parish, and it must have been even more splendid before the spire was demolished. Numerous buttresses of different dates against the tower represent repeated efforts to shore it up before the final solution of removing the spire was decided upon. The north aisle came down, too, although the arcade can still be seen in the nave wall; but the south aisle survives, a lofty and elegant 14th-century work.

Upper Arley (2/2A)

There are two ways of reaching this delightful hamlet on the River Severn, just south of the Shropshire border and some 4 miles north-west of KIDDERMINSTER. One is by road, but if you choose the scenic route through the WYRE FOREST from the west, you have to park and cross to the main part of the village by footbridge; the road stops abruptly and without warning at the water's edge.

Alternatively, you can take the **Severn Valley Railway** and enjoy one of the most scenic train journeys in the country, chugging up the river bank to the accompanying sounds of a puffing steam engine. The railway runs through most of the summer, providing several services a day in both directions between Kidderminster and Bridgnorth, stopping at BEWDLEY, Upper Arley, Highley and Hampton Loade.

Upper Arley is the line's most attractive station, familiar perhaps from its frequent use by television and film companies as a location with a Victorian or Edwardian atmosphere.

A lane descends to the Severn where, until the footbridge was built in 1971, a ferry carried passengers over to the east bank powered only by the force of the current. On the other side a steep lane climbs past the Valentia Inn to St Peter's church, standing in the wooded grounds of Arley House.

A romantic neo-Norman castle used to tower above it, but was demolished in 1962.

From the village you can walk on either bank of the Severn for miles in both directions. One day, no doubt, it will be designated a Severn Valley Long Distance Footpath, but for now its tranquil wooded banks are frequented only by a few walkers and anglers.

Upper Sapey *see* Martley

Upton Bishop *see* Ross-on-Wye

Upton upon Severn (4/1A)

This former market town about 10 miles south of WORCESTER seems now to be devoted to serving the visitors who arrive by the coachload for a walk along the river or, in bad weather, to sit the afternoon out in one of the tea rooms or hotel restaurants. The old quay, alongside the cast-iron bridge built in 1939, is the starting point for Severn River cruises, and the former warehouses are now chandlers' shops supplying the needs of the boat owners who moor in the marina on the north side of the river.

The old church by the bridge is the best place to start for an understanding of the town. All that survives is the handsome tower of 1769, with its distinctive copper-covered cupola that has earned it the nickname 'pepper pot'. It now serves as a heritage centre, full of details of Civil War battles and photographic reminders of the town's heyday as a port – when Severn trows would dock with timber and coal from the Forest of Dean (*see* Glos.), and salt, cider, pottery and brick from the north of the county.

Maps also show clearly that Upton was a planned town, with two parallel north–south

Upton upon Severn

streets linked by a network of alleys crammed with houses. From these it can be seen that the backs of many houses are medieval and timber-framed, despite their handsome stucco and red-brick fronts, with their bay and Venetian windows. Not all were given a new Georgian façade, however: the Anchor Inn of 1601 is still a rambling, higgledy-piggledy timber building.

The new church of St Peter and St Paul was built on the western outskirts of the town as it began to spread in the 19th century. It was begun in 1878, in Decorated style, to the design of Sir Arthur Blomfield. A large, craggy building of rusticated stone, it contains some monuments from the old church.

Victorian church builders were especially active in the villages south of Upton. At **Queenhill** (4/1B) St Nicholas's church stands in the grounds of Bredon School. Sir George Gilbert Scott had a hand in the restoration of 1855. Despite the off-putting exterior, the inside is pleasing. A 15th-century carved oak screen has survived, and there is a fragment of 14th-century glass in the nave.

Sir Edward Elgar is said to have conceived the idea for his great oratorio *The Apostles* while sitting in the porch. The view is less inspiring today as the M5 motorway has interrupted the prospect.

St Mary's church at **Longdon** (4/1B), just over a mile to the west of Queenhill, is built in the elegant domestic, rather than ecclesiastical, style of the late 18th century, with round-headed and Venetian windows, and a dome from which hangs a lovely spidery brass chandelier, dated 1789. The fine inlaid pulpit and tester are of the same era.

At **Hanley Castle** (4/1A), about 1 mile north of Upton, the castle survives only as an earthwork reached by the footpath south of the church. It was briefly the seat of the Earls of Gloucester and Warwick in the 13th century, the date of some of the earliest parts of the church. Nowadays, however, the predominant flavour is 17th-century, the date of the handsome brickwork of the tower, north chapel and chancel.

The setting is pleasing, for around the church is a row of almshouses built in about 1600 and the original timber-framed Grammar School founded in 1544, now somewhat hidden by 1868 brick extensions. The tiny village green is overshadowed by a huge cedar tree and lined by good timber-framed buildings, notably the Three Kings public house with its herringbone-patterned gables.

Vowchurch *see* Peterchurch

Walford (3/2C)
The church of St Michael and All Angels, 2 miles south of ROSS-ON-WYE, is approached through an avenue of lime trees planted in 1918, one for each parishioner who died in the First World War. Until 1842 the county boundary passed through the church, so that worshippers had to walk from Herefordshire (the nave) to Gloucestershire (the chancel) to receive communion. The nave is essentially 13th-century work, with round piers and capitals carved simply with apples, pellets, stiff leaf, and a trumpet scallop.

Hill Court is to the north-west of the church, a monumental William and Mary mansion approached through impressive wrought-iron gates and up a long tree-lined avenue. The grounds (open daily) are run as a garden centre where visitors can see plants growing before making their selection. A recent addition is the water garden and gazebo, from which there are unrivalled views south-west to GOODRICH Castle.

Warndon *see* Worcester

Waseley Country Park (2/4B)
This is one of the four nature reserves linked by the NORTH WORCESTERSHIRE PATH, set aside for the children of the West Midlands to experience a little of the countryside. From the top of Windmill Hill there are views of adjoining parks in the chain: Lickey Hills 2 miles to the southeast and Clent Hills to the north-west. The land is still farmed and wild flowers thrive in the woodlands and on the margins of small ponds.

Welsh Bicknor *see* Goodrich

Welsh Newton *see* Garway

Weobley (1/3C)
Of all the black-and-white villages of the county, Weobley, 6 miles south-west of LEOMINSTER, is the best. It is not at all showy and does not court the attention of tourists. Rather is it a place for the working farmer, who can still buy the necessities of life, rather than souvenirs, in the village shop. And once it was a borough, returning two Members of Parliament. It is also a village for the connoisseur of vernacular architecture who is as excited by the construction techniques used in cottages as by their beauty.

Thus the Unicorn Inn immediately stands out as an odd specimen in the western counties, a house with an inset, coved central bay, flanked by jettied wings, all under the same roof. The style is common to the Kentish and Sussex Weald, but very unusual elsewhere.

More typical of the county is the 14th-century hall and cross wing of the Red Lion, and the even earlier cruck-framed building alongside. The village store is also worth a close look: under coved eaves it has its original timber mullioned windows, and a door in the upper storey suggesting that the roof space was used for storage. The narrow green up the middle of Broad Street marks the site of a row of back-to-back cottages lost, unfortunately, to fire earlier this century.

Broad Street leads north to the church of St Peter and St Paul, an impressive building with a soaring sandstone 14th-century spire. Flying buttresses clasp the tower, which stands at an inexplicably odd angle to the rest of the church, leading by means of an off-axis arch to the north aisle. The raising of the aisle roofs has effectively blocked the clerestory windows so the interior is surprisingly gloomy, but even so nobody could miss the splendid lifesize effigy of Colonel

View to Weobley

John Birch (d. 1691), the town's benefactor and former MP.

At the opposite end of the village from the church, Hereford Street leads to the deep ditches and high motte of the 13th-century castle, past more exceptional houses, including The Throne of *c.* 1600 and the Old Grammar School, Jacobean with ornate bargeboards to the porch.

Weston Beggard *see* Lugwardine

Weston under Penyard *see* Lea

Whitbourne (2/2D)
By the River Teme, 4 miles north-east of BROMYARD, the church of St John the Baptist forms a good group with the Georgian Rectory and the rambling Court. The medieval lychgate, with its stone-tiled roof, was well restored in 1911 at the same time as other improvements were being made to the church to compensate for heavy-handed Victorian restoration. In particular, the 1912 painted marble and mosaic reredos depicting the Nativity does much to mitigate the harshness of the scraped walls.

Whitchurch (3/2D)
The village below Symonds Yat rock (*see* Glos.) offers a variety of incongruous attractions. There is a big funfair and leisure centre; a World of Butterflies and a Bird Park; the Jubilee Maze and Royal Garden, both planted in 1977 for the Queen's Jubilee; and, in summer, river cruises along the Wye Valley. Then, too, there is the church of St Dubricius, largely rebuilt in 1860, in a fine position on the river bank; and south of Whitchurch the excellent Rural Heritage Museum. This consists of a large collection of farm machinery, not just horse-drawn wagons, but also vintage tractors, traction engines and hundreds of household items that were the commonplace tools of domestic life until the 1950s.

For anyone unable to undertake the whole WYE VALLEY WALK, the 3-mile stretch south of Whitchurch is one of the most varied and dramatic along the route. It follows the river in a loop around the Little and Great Doward hills, limestone outcrops with a rich flora and several caves. One, called Arthur's Cave, was excavated in the 19th century with dynamite. Palaeolithic remains were nevertheless found among the debris. There is a 26-acre Iron Age hillfort on top of Little Doward: tradition has it that this was the site of Caratacus' last stand against the invading Romans in AD 51.

White Ladies Aston *see* Spetchley

Whitney-on-Wye *see* Winforton

Wichenford (2/2C)

In the watermeadows some 5 miles north-west of WORCESTER, little remains of the village but for the church and Wichenford Court. St Lawrence has a handsome broach spire, Victorian like most of the church. Inside, the Washbourne monuments of wood are so badly painted and carved that they are worth seeing, if only as a reminder of how good, in contrast, most 17th-century memorial sculpture really is.

The charming late-17th-century red-brick Wichenford Court is surrounded by farm buildings of equal age. The timber-framed dovecot belongs to the National Trust and is open daily throughout summer; the Court gardens are open occasionally under the National Gardens Scheme.

Wick *see* Pershore

Dovecot at Wichenford (National Trust)

Wickhamford (2/5E)

Anyone who has read *Ancestral Voices* (1975), James Lees-Milnes' entertaining biographical work, will instantly recognize the village, about 3 miles south-east of EVESHAM, from his descriptions. At the northern end of the village is the rambling stone and half-timbered manor of his childhood, the little bridge over the Badsey Brook in which he used to play, and the golden ashlar church of St John the Baptist in the orchard next to the house.

In his original *Shell Guide to Worcestershire* (1964), James Lees-Milne described the church as 'one of the best in Worcestershire'. That is still true, and it is partly so because his father, G. C. Lees-Milne, restored it with sympathy and conservatism in 1949.

The interior is welcoming and full of the warm patina of woodcarving of diverse dates and sources: 17th-century figures adorn the tall three-decker pulpit, and there are Flemish panels on the nearby pew. Some box pews have Elizabethan linenfold carving and the west gallery has three beautiful Jacobean panels from a London church.

Of the wall painting of the Virgin and Child, little survives except the outline, but the coat of arms above the chancel is clearer – and of

The area around Wigmore in the far north-west of the county has great beauty and interest. The beauty derives from tier upon tier of hills, rising east and west of the village; the interest from the geology of those hills and the sheer number of earthworks, from Iron Age enclosures to medieval castles, that stand upon them.

The geology of the Wigmore incline is so rich that the Forestry Commission has laid out a trail with leaflets to explain the rocks that can be seen in the exposures along the route. The gently uplifted strata reveal most of the rocks that underlie the county, from the oldest yellow-green Downton stone to the younger fossil-rich carboniferous limestones.

Few castles are more prominent, dramatic or complete than that high up on the hill above Wigmore. It was founded by William the Conqueror's close ally, William FitzOsbern, created Earl of Hereford and charged with securing the border with Wales. Wigmore Castle

The ruins of Wigmore Castle

went out to battle at Mortimer's Cross and on to be crowned Edward IV. The castle remained inhabited until the 17th century and the Civil War. Only since then has it become ruinous and overgrown. Even so, there is enough to indicate its former size and appearance, and the views from the hilltop are unsurpassed.

FitzOsbern created the village of Wigmore under the protective eye of his castle. The main street has a timeless appearance; remove the cars and a 16th- or 17th-century inhabitant would have little difficulty in recognizing the scene.

It is a stiff climb from the village up to St James's church with its 15th-century porch ornamented with carved roses. Inside, more steps lead up into the aisle and only then is the great size of the church fully revealed. The aisle is a 14th-century addition to the Norman nave. Many of the benches have traceried panels and poppyheads; the Elizabethan pulpit stands on a wineglass pedestal.

Wigmore Abbey is 2 miles to the north in the flat, sheep-grazed meadows of Wigmore Moor.

It is a private house, but the former abbot's lodging and gatehouse can be seen from the road. It was founded in 1179 by Hugh Mortimer for the Augustinians.

East of the Abbey the road follows the winding River Teme through a steep-sided valley to **Downton on the Rock** (1/3A). Old St Giles's church, in the village, is now ruinous. Its successor, New St Giles's, was built in 1861 and the chief reason for visiting it is for a distant glimpse of Downton Castle (not open to the public), in whose grounds it stands.

The castle was designed by Richard Payne Knight, who inherited the house and a fortune from his ironmaster grandfather. He rebuilt it between 1772 and 1778 as a fortified mansion with classical interiors. Of equal interest is the picturesque landscaping of the grounds and their buildings, which include an artificial cave and mock-Roman bath houses. The setting of the castle was already so much in line with Payne's liking for wild vistas that he was able to achieve his vision of perfection with minimal new planting.

Wilden *see* Hartlebury

Winforton (1/1D)

Although it straddles the A438 HEREFORD to Hay-on-Wye road, the village is an unspoiled cluster of timber-framed houses and farms, including the Jacobean Winforton Court, decorated with a series of concentric lozenges.

The upper part of St Michael's church tower is also timber-framed; the space between the studs is filled with planks, not plaster, to give the appearance of solid wood. The lovely roofs have never been painted or stained so they glow golden brown and the Victorian chancel arch is of the same rich oak. The Jacobean pulpit is dated 1613, and the communion rails date from 1701.

Three miles east of Winforton, at **Letton** (1/2D), all that remains is the timber-framed Court and the church of St John the Baptist. This is almost completely Norman down to the spiky hinges of the door. The fine early 18th-century pulpit and tester came from a Bristol church.

Two miles west of Winforton, the original church at **Whitney-on-Wye** (1/1D) was washed away in the great flood of 1735. Its successor, St Peter and St Paul, stands 100 yds from the river on a rising bank. Some of the pews and panelling from the wreck of the old church were rescued

and installed in the new one, completed in 1740, with a pretty west gallery and communion rails of the same date. The reredos, dated 1629 and with purely secular motifs, came from Whitney Court.

On the hill above the churchyard is a wooden footbridge over the Hereford, Hay and Brecon Railway (opened 1864), whose course makes a delightful walk though the surrounding woods.

One and a half miles further west is the picturesque Rhydpence Inn, a timber-framed and jettied 16th-century building on the border with Wales. Its old name was the Cattle Inn and drovers would refresh themselves here while their herds could drink from the river.

The road to **Brilley** (1/1D) leaves the flat Wye meadows behind and climbs steeply northwards through stone-banked lanes and broadleafed woodland. Suddenly the woods give way to bare sheep-grazed hillside. The parishioners of the hillside hamlet used to cast grave slabs in iron because of the erosive force of the weather here. Two of these weighty 17th-century tombstones are under the tower of St Mary's church alongside a pair of wrought-iron candelabra, decorated with ivy leaf. A dramatic roof covers the nave and eastern end, coved to form a baldachino over the chancel.

One and half miles north-east of Brilley is the isolated farmhouse of **Cwmmau**, owned by the National Trust and surrounded by bracken and gorse-covered heath. The house stands a little lower, in a sheltered hollow, with fine panoramic views of the ridges that unfold in sequence to the Black Mountain. The Jacobean stone and timber-framed building is home to the tenant farmer, but open on Bank Holiday weekends (not Christmas or New Year) and at other times by appointment.

Witleys, The

The church of St Michael at **Little Witley** (2/2C) some 6 miles north-west of WORCESTER, was rebuilt in 1867 and would only be of passing interest but for the carvings executed by the rector's wife, Mrs Sale, an accomplished and witty sculptress. The chancel arch capitals are bold and spirited, covered with feeding birds, with one on its nest and almost invisible among the foliage.

A mile to the north-west, a turning off the A443 leads to the ruins of Witley Court (English

The ruins of Witley Court (English Heritage) and the fine Baroque church of St Michael

Heritage, open daily) an awesome monument to vainglorious ambition. Until fire struck in 1935 it was one of the grandest mansions in Europe. The original Jacobean manor was enlarged by the 1st Lord Foley in the early 18th century but its current appearance owes much to the 1st Lord Dudley, an industrialist, who acquired it in 1838.

In its heyday crowned heads of Europe danced and dined within its splendid walls. The orangery was filled with exotic flowers and the Poseidon fountain, then the largest sculpture in Europe, could throw a jet of water 100 ft into the air.

Now the roofs, windows, plasterwork and sumptuous furnishings have gone. Rook-haunted bare walls remain, and rough meadows where once topiary hedges and knot gardens filled the prospect from the windows of the Royal Suite.

The building was saved by local men and women who launched a successful campaign, in 1967, to stop further robbery and vandalism and restore the sumptuous church of St Michael. This started out as a simple brick building, erected in the early 18th century to replace the old parish church. In 1747 the 2nd Lord Foley bought the contents of the chapel at Canons, in Edgware, up for auction. Included were paintings by the Venetian artist, Antonio Bellucci.

Foley also took casts of the stucco work at Canons. He employed Giovanni Bagutti, one of the leading *stuccatori* of his day, to use these casts to re-create the gilded plasterwork, but here *papier mâché* was the medium. By 1756 the work was completed and immediately hailed as the finest Baroque church in England. Later, in the mid-19th century, the Dudleys completed the metamorphosis by replacing the simple furnishings with a huge pulpit and pews in the same high Baroque style.

Recently restoration work has brought the church back to its full glory. The best time to see its brilliantly fresh, rich interior is by night, at one of the occasional musical recitals, when artificial light softens the bright gold, and shadows throw the plasterwork into relief. It is easy then, for a brief while, to imagine yourself in another world and time.

The pot-holed road north of the court eventually reaches **Great Witley** village (2/2C), created when the Dudleys persuaded their tenants to move to the edge of the estate so that their houses would not interrupt the prospect. From here the A443 climbs steeply, skirting the edge

of another great house, Abberley Hall. Its large Italianate clock tower is visible for miles around and was built in 1883 as a memorial.

The village of **Abberley** (2/2C) lies in a very fine situation, completely surrounded by hills formed by outcrops of ancient and hard pre-Cambrian metamorphosed shale. This is quarried for roadstone at Shavers End, a mile east, but nothing of that is visible from the village. Instead it looks across glorious hills in which Owen Glendower (Owain Glyndwr) and Henry IV fought frequent skirmishes.

St Mary's is an unusually noble Victorian church in Early English style with marble columns and capitals. It contains a Saxon tomb cover from the old church of St Michael, now in ruins. This is one of the places claimed to have been the site of the meeting between St Augustine and the Welsh Bishops, convened to settle, among other things, a common date for the celebration of Easter. Opposite the church is the red-brick Manor House, a fine late 17th-century building with Dutch gables.

Many gardens in the village are open in summer under the National Gardens Scheme.

The road east to **Astley** (2/2C) skirts Abberley Hill, then drops to cross the Dick Brook before climbing to the hillside hamlet. St Peter's church is Norman, of pink sandstone. Half-round pilasters divide the nave exterior into bays separating lengths of the corbel table into groups of three, each carved with human or animal heads, above round-headed windows. The south door is a polychromatic arch of yellow and red sandstone above white limestone shafts. Such inventiveness and grandeur may be explained by the presence of a Priory here, founded in 1102, of which the only surviving evidence is the Prior's Well, south of the church.

Inside, a fine collar truss ceiling rises above the Norman arcades and the north chapel contains a cluster of good monuments.

Woolhope (1/5E)

The village is 7 miles east-south-east of HEREFORD and sits in the middle of Woolhope Dome, a roughly circular outcrop of ancient Silurian limestone, some 12 miles in circumference, left standing proud by the erosion of the softer overlying sandstone. Many of the village houses are built of this whitish-yellow rock.

St George's church contains 13th- and 14th-century coffin lids: one a lifesize figure with hands crossed under a canopy, the other a strange figure of a woman in cloak and tunic,

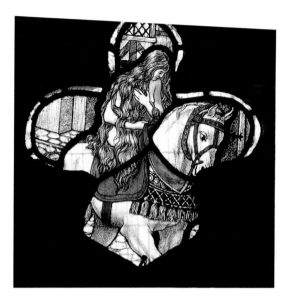

Stained glass depicting Lady Godiva, Woolhope church

wearing a flat hat held on by a big chin strap, holding a candle and surrounded, so it appears, by mystical symbols.

The village is surrounded by fine walking country. A mile east is 'The Wonder', site of a landslip in 1575 when the water-eroded hillside slumped into the hamlet of Kynaston below. To the west is Haugh Wood, laid out with Forest Trails by the Forestry Commission. The unclassified road through the middle of the wood is lined by vestigial ancient forest maintained by the National Trust.

On the southern edge of the wood is a memorial to the bare-knuckle prize fighter, Tom Spring (1795–1851). Below is his native village, **Fownhope** (1/4E), to which he retired as landlord of the Green Man Inn, under his real name of Tom Winter. This pub is the centre of the Oak Apple Day celebrations held every May to commemorate the return of Charles II to London at the Restoration.

St Mary's church has a splendid central Norman tower and, inside, a very good example of Norman Hereford School sculpture: a tympanum carved with Christ seated in the Virgin's lap, both their hands raised in blessing.

Sollers Hope (1/5E) is 2 miles south-east of Fownhope. It consists of little more than a remote, early 16th-century timber-framed farmhouse with lovely decorated chimney stacks, and

Worcester (2/3D)

Prince Charles, in his Mansion House speech of 1987, shocked the sensibilities of the profession by stating that architects had done more harm to London than the Luftwaffe. He was only echoing what many have said before him: from John Betjeman – poetically – on Slough, to Nikolaus Pevsner – angrily – on the postwar rebuilding of the 'once great city of Plymouth'.

The sad truth is that they were not picking isolated instances. Worcester is just one of many towns whose essential character has been destroyed by insensitive development. Worse still, the destruction continues, not in the heart of Worcester, but in the surrounding countryside, with ever bigger hypermarkets and sprawling housing estates.

What, then, remains? Worcester's fine cathedral, the backdrop to England's most beautiful County Cricket ground, a handsome Guildhall, the riverside and a handful of other notable buildings, nuggets of gold among the concrete and heavily congested roads.

It is best to begin at the cathedral, since it reflects so much of the city's early history. The crypt is the earliest surviving building in Worcester, a relic of the cathedral begun in 1084 by St Wulstan, the only English bishop not to be replaced by a Norman after the Conquest. His church was by no means the first. The crypt is built of masonry from St Oswald's Benedictine priory, founded in AD 961; and a church must have existed as early as AD 680 when the first Bishop of Worcester was enthroned.

The crypt, with its forest of stone columns supporting a simple 14th-century vault, is the largest in England and originally had an ambulatory forming a one-way system to control the flow of hundreds of pilgrims to the shrine of St Oswald, then at the east end.

The eastern staircase leads to the Early English part of the cathedral, built by Bishop Blois. It must have seemed that building work would never finish, for the central tower had collapsed in 1175 and fire had destroyed much of the cathedral in 1203. The cathedral had only just been rededicated after these disasters when Blois began pulling it down again and rebuilding in the latest Gothic style.

Work began at the east end with the Lady

Worcester County Cricket Ground with the cathedral beyond: a famous summer scene

Chapel, which has characteristic pointed arches and clusters of Purbeck marble columns. The aisles and transepts came next, all ornamented by a running blank arcade of trefoil-headed arches, each with a carving in the spandril.

Next to be rebuilt was the nave, begun under Bishop Cobham early in the 14th century, in the Decorated style. The north side was nearly complete when the Black Death struck, decimating the city's population and interrupting the work. The south side was completed later in less elaborate form.

All this work was made possible by the revenue from pilgrims and by Royal patronage. King John asked to be buried in the choir and his tomb, before the High Altar, is a masterpiece of medieval sculpture, showing the King flanked by Bishops Oswald and Wulstan. To the right is the elegant lierne-vaulted chantry of Prince Arthur, Henry VIII's elder brother.

The choir stalls are high Gothic, designed by Sir George Gilbert Scott. They incorporate the misericords from the original stalls of 1379, an excellent group of scenes from scripture and fable, all rich in the detail of everyday life.

A stroll around the quiet cloisters reveals more accomplished carving, especially in the bosses of the south cloister. Off this is the 14th-century refectory that contains a lifesize Christ in Majesty of 1220–30. Even in its mutilated state it is obviously the work of a master carver. The north range leads to the Chapter House, a round building with a central column. Built around 1120 it is, with the crypt, the most complete example of Norman architecture to have survived here.

The cloister leads out to College Green, lined with the buildings of the cathedral school, and thence, beneath the great 14th-century Edgar Tower, to Severn Street. This was once lined with the houses of salmon fishermen, but it was aggrandized in the 18th century and shares with Edgar Street a number of fine Georgian houses with oriel and Venetian windows.

On the right is the Dyson Perrins Museum, containing a comprehensive collection of Worcester Royal Porcelain, from the earliest products of 1751 to the present day. The adjoining Royal Worcester Spode works are so popular that it is advisable to book tours well in advance.

Severn Street leads down to the river and Diglis Basin, a reminder that Worcester was once at the hub of the inland waterways network, the meeting point of the River Severn and you negotiate the busy main road and try to ignore the utilitarian Giffard Hotel that stands opposite the cathedral before entering the pedestrianized High Street where Elgar's statue stands at the head.

It is therefore a surprise to find, among the modern shops, the dramatic Guildhall of 1721–3, adorned with the statues of Charles I and II and Queen Anne, a pediment filled with a flurry of war trophies, and Justice on the parapet flanked by the Four Seasons. It is hard to believe that this handsome Baroque building, which contains an Assembly Hall with decorations of 1791, was threatened with demolition. Only public outcry saved it, unlike the medieval houses that once surrounded it.

The token handful of 15th- and 16th-century timber-framed buildings that have been spared are in Cornmarket, New Street and Friar Street. They include Ye Olde King Charles House in which the young Prince Charles, later Charles II, hid before escaping to France after his defeat at the Battle of Worcester in 1651. Another is The Greyfriars, built around 1480 on the site of a Franciscan friary and now owned by the National Trust.

Further down is the Tudor House Museum of domestic utensils and agricultural implements, and, at the end of Friar Street, the Commandery. This pleasing group of canalside buildings began as the Hospital of St Wulstan, founded in the 11th century. It was rebuilt around 1500 and of that period the splendid hammerbeam roof of the Great Hall and wall paintings of saints have survived.

Later, as the home of the Wylde family, Prince Charles used the house as his base during the Battle of Worcester, hence its current name. From the Commandery, College Street leads back to the cathedral, then Deansway follows the main road past the Old Palace, formerly the town house of the Bishops of Worcester, and the Deanery of 1730. Further on is the Elgar School of Music and the Countess of Huntingdon's Chapel, one of the most splendid Nonconformist chapels in the country, now converted to use as a concert hall.

Near by is the spire, all that remains, of St Andrew's church, nicknamed the 'Glover's Needle' because it soars 245 ft from a base only

The Greyfriars, Worcester, one of the finest timber-framed buildings in the county (National Trust)

20 ft wide to a mere 6¾ in at the apex. Here, too, is the church of All Saints, completed around 1742, with a splendid Georgian interior of Tuscan columns.

It stands close to the river and the Severn Bridge, built in 1780 and widened in 1931, with a balustraded parapet. It is worth crossing to the west bank, and the County Cricket ground, for the classical view of the west end and tower of the cathedral rising magnificently above the leafy green slope of the river bank.

Worcester Country Park is a recently designated reserve consisting of 125 acres of ancient woodland east of the city. The Countryside Centre, off the A422 by County Hall, provides an introduction to the park which is remarkable for its 600 year-old oaks, wild service trees and fungi – and also for the fact that it has survived at all, well within the city boundary.

At **Warndon** the forlorn church of St Nicholas and its companion, the early 17th-century red-brick Warndon Farm, stand in need of repair on the eastern outskirts of Worcester. Perhaps when the new housing development under way in the adjoining fields is completed there will be enough of a parish again for the church to be brought into full use and repaired to reveal its underlying beauty.

Wormsley *see* Burghill

Wribbenhall *see* Bewdley

Wychavon Way
The Queen's Silver Jubilee in 1977 was marked by the establishment of this footpath that links Holt (*see* Ombersley) on the River Severn with Winchcombe (*see* Glos.). It passes through gentle, undemanding countryside and provides the opportunity to see many hamlets and houses from viewpoints that the motorist would miss. Trail guides are available from local Tourist Information Centres.

Wye Valley Walk
The whole Wye Valley is designated, with justice, an Area of Outstanding Natural Beauty and the river itself, one of the few in southern Britain to be relatively free of pollution, is a Site of Special Scientific Interest. Now, to add to the flurry of titles, the paths that walkers have frequented since the 18th century have been designated officially as the Wye Valley Walk. It follows only the last 51 miles of the river's convoluted course from HEREFORD to its confluence with the Severn at Chepstow. Maps are available from Tourist Information Centres.

The walk falls into two distinct parts. The first 17 miles, from Bishop's Meadows below Hereford to the meadows outside Ross-on-Wye, pass through gentle countryside. From Ross south, a distance of 34 miles, the going gets tougher, sometimes involving the negotiation of rocky riverside terrain, but sometimes following the track of the former Wye-side railway.

Wyre Forest (2/2B)
Lying to the west of KIDDERMINSTER, the forest consists of well over 6000 acres of ancient and, in places, impenetrable woodland, home to herds of long-coated deer and much wildlife. Permanent settlements within the forest are of relatively recent date. Places like **Far Forest** grew out of assarts, or clearings in the woods, where squatters would live illegally, fighting shy of contact with outsiders and ready at any moment to abandon their makeshift huts for the protection of the forest.

Their trades were based on the materials that grew around them in abundance: basket weaving, broom making, and the manufacture of whisks used for drawing the pile out of the carpets made at Kidderminster. Charcoal burning and iron smelting, as well as felling timber for shipbuilding, were important industries, but also a threat to the forest which is now a tenth of its former size.

Today any timber that is felled is renewed and areas of woodland have been set aside to grow naturally. Many rare plants, some unique to the Forest, can be found in the oak woods and along the hedgerows. A visitor centre at Callow Hill, off the main road west of BEWDLEY, is the best starting point for the numerous waymarked Forest Trails.

Wythall *see* Lickey Hills

Yarpole *see* Croft Castle

Key to Maps

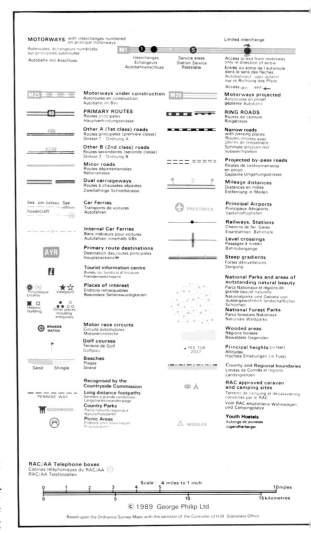

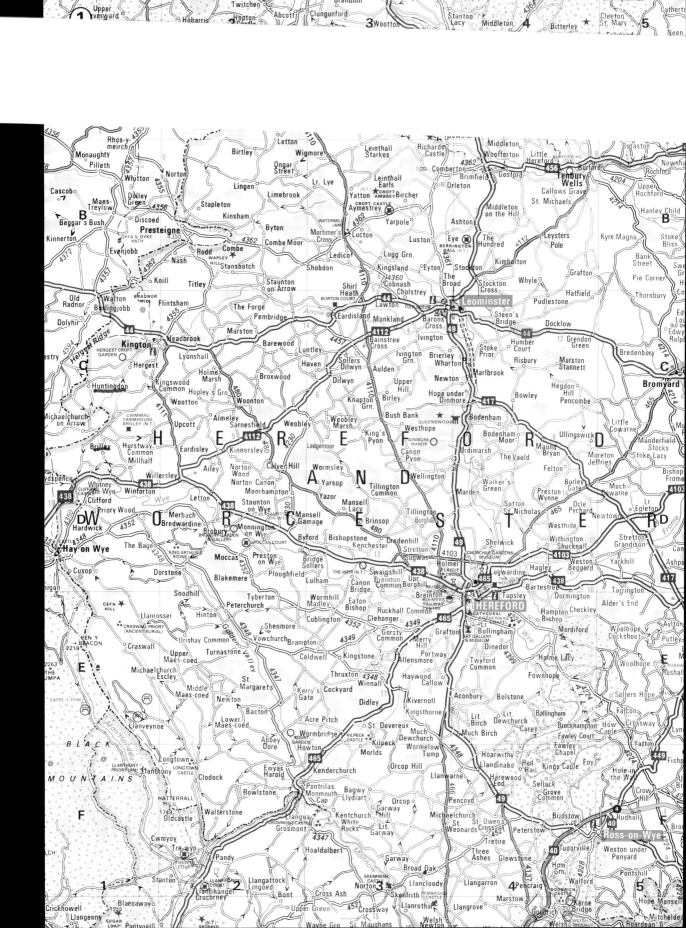

WORCESTER

GLOUCESTER

Great Malvern
West Malvern
Ledbury
Newent
GLOUCESTER
Ross-on-Wye
Monmouth
Cinderford
Coleford
Lydney
Sharpness
Frampton on Severn
Dursley
Wotton-under-Edge
Chepstow
Caldicot

Mansell
Marden
Preston Wynne
Ocle Pychard
Lr. Egleton
Norbridge
Mathon
Guarlford
Rhy
Cublington
Clehonger
Grafton
Bullingham
Mordiford
Woolhope
Cockshoot
Putley
Ayitton
Little Marcle
Eastnor
Hollybush
Castlemorton
Birts Street
Rye Street
Birtsmorton
Sledge Grn.
Coldwell
Kingstone
Merry Hill
Haywood
Portway
Allensmore
Callow
Dinedor
Twyford Common
Fownhope
Holme Lacy
Woolhope
Rushall
Preston
Much Marcle
Camer's Grn.
Brownis End
Pendock
Swinley
Eldersfield
Corse Lawn
Thruxton
Kingstone
Didley
Aconbury
Bolstone
Ballingham
Sollers Hope
Falcon
Crossway
Lyne Down
Dymock
Ryton
Redmarley D'Abitot
Playley Grn.
Kerry's Gate
Cockyard
Kivernoll
Lit. Birch
Lit. Dewchurch
How Caple
Yatton
Kempley
Fishpool
Poolhill
Brand Green
Staunton
Snig's End
Wormbridge
St. Devereux
Much Birch
Casey
Crossway
Kings Caple
Foy
Upton Bishop
Gorsley
Kilcot
Newent
Malswick
Highleadon
Hasfield
Ashleworth
Howton
Kilpeck
Morlds
Orcop Hill
Llandinabo
Red Rail
Harewood End
Sellack
Grove Common
Hole-in-the-Wall
Crow Hill
Linton
Gorsley
Clifford's Mesne
Tibberton
Highnam Grn.
Maisemore
Kenderchurch
Bagwy Llydiart
Garway Hill
Michaelchurch
St. Weonards
St. Owen's Cross
Peterstow
Bridstow
Weston under Penyard
Aston Ingham
Aston Crews
May Hill
Glasshouse Hill
Huntley
Bulley
Highnam
Pontrilas
Monmouth Cap
Orcop
Garway
Kentchurch
White Rocks
Lit. Garway
Tretire
Three Ashes
Glewstone
Hom Grn.
Tudorville
Ross-on-Wye
Pontshill
Hope Mansell
Lea
Mitcheldean
Longhope
Birdwood
Churcham
Northwood Grn.
Oakle Street
GLOUCESTER
Hoaldalbert
Garway
Broad Oak
Llancloudy
Llangarron
Pencraig
Marstow
Walford
Ruardean
Drybrook
Blaisdon
Minsterworth
Cross Ash
Norton
Skenfrith
Llanrothal
Llangrove
Goodrich
Kerne Bridge
Welsh Bicknor
Ruardean Woodside
Nailbridge
Flaxley
Eltor
Westbury-on-Severn
Elmore Back
Elmore
Hempsted
Wayne Grn.
St. Maughans
Newcastle
Welsh Newton
Whitchurch
Gt. Doward
Ganarew
English Bicknor
Upr. Lydbrook
Brierley
Cinderford
Littledean
Boxbush
Longney
Hardwicke
Llanfaenor
Maypole
Llangattock-Vibon-Avel
Onen
Buckholt
Rockfield
Dixton
Symonds Yat
Edge End
Mile End
Ruspidge
Upr. Soudley
Newnham
Rodley
Llanvihangel-Ystern-Llewern
Wernrheolydd
Penrhos
Monmouth
Wyesham
Over Monnow
Wonastow
Staunton
Christchurch
Berry Hill
Arlingham
Upr. Framilode
Moreton Valence
Whitminster
Tregare
Pen-yr-heol
Dingestow
Mitchel Troy
Mitcheltroy Common
Penallt
Coleford
Broadwell
Lane End
Tufthorn
Forest of Dean
Dean Heritage Museum
Saul
Raglan
Pen-y-clawdd
Caer Llan
Newland
Pen-twyn
Newmills
Clearwell
Milkwall
Ellwood
Parkend
Ayleford
Awre
Frampton on Severn
Nupend
Randwick
Raglan
Twyn-y-Sheriff
Kingcoed
Llangoven
Whitebrook
Clearwell Castle
Trow Green
Yorkley
Whitecroft
Blakeney
Stonehouse
Llandenny
Trelleck
Llandogo
St. Briavels
Bream
Breams Eaves
Purton
Cambridge
Eastington
Leonard Stanley
Frocester
Woodchester
Gwernesney
Llangwm-isaf
Llanishen
Parkhouse
Hewelsfield
Lydney
Newerne
Sharpness
Halmore
Slimbridge
Gossington
Coaley
Nympsfield
Llangwm
New Inn
Tintern Parva
Brockweir
Netherend
Woolaston
Alvington
Aylburton
Wanswell Green
Breadstone
Lower Cam
Wolvesnewton
Devauden
Chapel Hill
Tidenham Chase
Berkeley
Berkeley Castle
Ham
Stinchcombe
Dursley
Uley
Llantrisant
Gaerllwyd
Newchurch
Stroat
Wibdon
Bevington
Woodford
Nibley
North Nibley
Kingswood
Earlswood
Utton Common
St. Arvans
Boughspring
Sheperdine
Upr. Hill
Hill
Stone
Michaelwood Services
Woodmancote
Pen-y-cae-mawr
Woodcroft
Tutshill
Tidenham
Sheperdine
Rockhampton
Falfield
Charfield
Tortworth
Newark Park
Wotton-under-Edge
Boxwell
Ventwood
Llanvair Discoed
Mynydd-bach
Mounton
Sedbury
Oldbury upon S.
Whitfield
Kingswood
Charfield
Tresham
Penhow
Shirenewton
Chepstow
Beachley
Littleton upon Severn
Morton
Thornbury
Milbury Heath
Cromhall
Churchend
Alderley
Crick
Mathern
Aust Services
Oldbury on the Hill
Caerwent
Runston Chapel A.M.
Severn Road Bridge Toll
Aust
Elberton
Alveston
Tytherington
Wickwar
Hillsley
Didmarton
Llanfihangel Rogiet
Portskewett
Severn Rail Tunnel
Northwick
Olveston
Ingst
Ruddgeway
Rangeworthy
Yate
Hawkesbury
Hawkesbury Upton
Magor
Undy
Rogiet
Sudbrook
Redwick
Tockington
Itchington
Llandevenny

M50
M4
M5
M48

Index

Numbers in italics refer to illustrations